ENERGY HEDGING IN ASIA

Energy Hedging in Asia: Market Structure and Trading Opportunities

PETER C. FUSARO AND
TOM JAMES

palgrave
macmillan

First published in 2005 by
PALGRAVE MACMILLAN
Houndmills, Basingstoke, Hampshire RG21 6XS and
175 Fifth Avenue, New York, N.Y. 10010
Companies and representatives throughout the world.

PALGRAVE MACMILLAN is the global academic imprint of the Palgrave Macmillan division of St. Martin's Press, LLC and of Palgrave Macmillan Ltd. Macmillan® is a registered trademark in the United States, United Kingdom and other countries. Palgrave is a registered trademark in the European Union and other countries.

ISBN-13: 978–1–4039–3468–0
ISBN-10: 1–4039–3468–1

This book is printed on paper suitable for recycling and made from fully managed and sustained forest sources.

A catalogue record for this book is available from the British Library.

A catalog record for this book is available from the Library of Congress.

10 9 8 7 6 5 4 3 2 1
14 13 12 11 10 09 08 07 06 05

Printed and bound in Great Britain by
Antony Rowe Ltd, Chippenham and Eastbourne

Contents

List of Tables and Figures

TABLES

FIGURES

Preface

Asia is the second largest oil importing region in the world, second only to the United States of America and since the world's two most populous nations are located in Asia (China and India) it may not take much time before Asia becomes the largest oil importing region in the world.

Risk avoidance rather than risk management has been the operative word in Asian oil markets. That is about to change due to the twin engines of deregulation and privatization driving competition. The business-as-usual approach no longer works as a sharp increase in oil dependence adds more price uncertainty and undoubtedly more future price volatility. The annualized volatility of oil, which ranges from 40–50% per year, is almost the highest of any commodity. Timing is everything. Now is the time for using energy risk management tools. Deregulation and globalization of energy markets are bringing with it the need for active management of market risks. The markets are becoming more price-sensitive with the rapid dissemination of price and market information. The need to use these financial tools exists.

In 2004, we could see that this continued rapid rise in demand from Asia, finally brought an imbalance to the supply/demand of the global oil market. Global demand had finally outpaced the speed at which new oil reserves could be found and exploited, resulting in the highest prices of crude oil seen in the world since the oil crisis of the 1970s. The very crisis that spawned the birth of oil futures markets around the world allowed oil consumers to hedge (insure) themselves against high prices from another price crisis.

High prices of crude oil are good for oil producers, but Asia is a huge net importer of oil, the very life blood of economies and as a result unhedged countries can experience sharp drops in GDP growth and inflation, and energy dependent industries can face big bills or even face financial difficulty if they can not pass costs on to their customers.

Headlines like these became every day news in 2004, "Price Rise To Fuel India Inflation, Fiscal Gap," "Global Oil Price Surge May Cost China Dearly," "Japan Keeps Its Cool Despite High Crude Prices," and "High Oil Prices Damp S. Korea's Economic Recovery."

By 2005, Japan, South Korea, China, India, Taiwan, Thailand, and Singapore will all be importing oil at over 1 million bbl/d each. While some Atlantic Basin crude oil from West Africa and the North Sea may supply some of the older, less flexible Asian refineries that have an appetite for those sweet crudes, the key issue is the growing Asia Pacific dependency on Middle Eastern sources of crude.

This increased dependency on oil foretells an era of continued price volatility and the growing need for more risk management instruments to be developed and utilized in the Asian markets. China already turned into a net oil importer during 1993 and its needs continue to grow. And Indonesia, an OPEC member and current oil exporter, seems to be slipping to the position of an importer of oil recently.

With about half of world oil growth projected to continue to be in the Asia Pacific region, rising product demand and tightening fuel quality standards driven by rising environmental awareness, the need for managing energy price risk seems poised for explosive growth over the next several years. However, it has taken an inordinately long time to get started in the region compared to the North American and European experiences, particularly because of the more protectionist Asian economies.

As Asian energy markets continue to be liberalized and open up to free market economy mechanics, the burden of protecting economies and industry to high prices of energy and also volatile energy prices is increasingly falling upon the oil consuming industries.

Whether it is due to their size, the globalization of their products, or the nature of the close relationship of the raw materials and finished products, the energy markets are unique among the traded commodity markets. It is almost unthinkable to conduct a major energy transaction today without also taking a position in a corresponding derivatives market, either exchange-traded or over-the-counter.

This book offers a comprehensive guide to the principles and tools of energy risk management. In 1978, energy market traditionalists at first likened using the futures derivatives market to speculating. Considering the volatility of energy pricing and the array of financial instruments that can be used from almost any market point of view to mitigate that volatility, it must be asked of those who do not hedge and manage their risk whether they are not in fact the true speculators. This book demystifies today's world of Risk Management and effectively explains to the reader the tried and tested price mitigation tools and strategies available in the market, new developments, and what the future may hold in the Asian energy hedging market.

Foreword

In the late 70's when a large conference met to consider the need for a petroleum exchange in London the Buying Director of a major world food group was invited to address the audience on his experience of managing price risk in cocoa and coffee using the existing futures markets of New York and London. To the embarrassment of those who had invited him the major oil companies in the audience treated him with scant respect. "Oil is the business of multi-nationals and governments" – not as implied the corner shop market place of cocoa and coffee. There must have been some wry smiles around the "AAA" food group's board table as they watched the demise of Enron and others who failed to hedge prudently. Today, the management of Price Risks in Energy is at the heart of the business of many producers and consumers in Europe and North America. Recent commercial success stories such as low-cost airlines would not have worked with their modest original capital base without cost efficient means of managing their major variable cost – jet fuel. A review of financial problems of Power Generators would closely correlate with whether or not they hedged.

Prudent bankers in today's competitive financial markets are lending at margins with no cushion for bad debts, so, any long term project financing or medium term trade financing requires the removal of as many risks as possible. Integration of hedging into financial structures makes good projects cheaper to finance and marginal projects possible.

Whilst these hedging markets are fairly mature and well understood in Europe and North America, the Asian markets have still a long way to go in meeting the needs of their industry in smoothing financial performance and attracting the investment capital needed to fuel Asia's impressive levels of economic growth.

We live in the period of a second industrial revolution with the transfer of major portions of global manufacturing capacity into Asia. With this comes an inevitable surge in the demand for all forms of energy. Most Asian markets now operate at around world prices for energy and therefore with a high level of volatility.

For the Asian economic growth story to continue there is a need for a fast track learning process in the prudent use of modern risk management techniques in energy – whether the user is a producer or consumer.

The Asian market is more diverse than Europe or North America. Distances are greater and there are fewer pipelines with a greater need for sea freight and longer delivery times. Each of these elements contributes to higher risk not only the price risk of the underlying commodities but also the associated financing costs and freight prices.

In this book you will find fact, flavour, and formulae. Each are key elements in running a successful hedging strategy but they must be integrated into the management ethos of the firm. Therefore, this is a book not just to be read in the trading departments, but, also in the boardroom; in the finance department and by shareholders in the enterprise.

Whilst the media make much of derivatives scandals and corporate collapses, there are thousands of success stories for every disaster. Failure to hedge is to run risks and sooner or later these risks will come to bite. To hedge is to prosper.

Roy Leighton
U.K. Chairman, CALYON Bank
Chairman, Futures & Options Association, UK

CHAPTER 1

Megatrends of the Asia Pacific Energy Trading

In a survey conducted in March 2004 by the International Swaps Derivatives Association (ISDA) (www.isda.org), 100 of respondents agreed with the following statement: *Derivatives help companies manage financial risk more effectively*.

The survey was conducted amongst finance professors at the top 50 business schools worldwide with the aim of exploring perceptions of derivatives, as well as their impact on the global financial system (see Appendix 1 to Chapter 11 – Executive Summary of ISDA report). The comments from respondents emphasized the key benefits provided by the use of derivatives. The most commonly cited one was the ability of companies to use derivatives to customize their risk profile and to assume only those risks that add value. Participants noted that by serving as effective risk management tools, derivatives enable companies to concentrate on their business operations. Respondents to the survey also agreed that derivatives will continue to grow in use and application. This book aims to arm companies with an up to date perspective of "Energy Hedging in Asia."

The Asia Pacific region overall is experiencing rapid economic growth which is fueling greater requirements for crude oil and refined products supply. The largest consumer in the region, China, is currently the world's third largest oil consumer, behind the United States and Japan. It is expected to surpass Japan soon, and could reach a consumption level of some 10.9 million bbl/d by 2025, with net imports of 7.5 million bbl/d, in order to support its domestic growth, giving it a major role in the world oil market. This growth in demand is driving rapidly increasing supply chain complexity as new trading patterns develop. Growth in the region, and in China specifically, is leading to the development of new supply markets in both the Middle East and Russia and in new infrastructure construction from point of supply to the refinery and beyond. Since most shipments are undertaken by water, the new infrastructure includes tankers, terminals, storage facilities, refineries, and overland distribution systems.

While trading remains largely based on term, Over-the-Counter (OTC), contracts without a standard regional marker for price transparency, it is this supply chain complexity that will drive costs and risk in the medium term, both in China and the Asia Pacific region generally. The risks and costs involved are becoming too great to rely on the in-house developed or spreadsheet-based energy trading, transaction and risk management systems in use today by many of the region's major energy companies.

THE MARKET DRIVERS OF ENERGY TRADING

While energy trading and the use of energy risk management tools have been slow to evolve in Asian energy trading, that present state of affairs is beginning to change across the board in the energy complex. Driven by energy market deregulation, globalization, and privatization trends in many countries, risk is becoming pervasive. As many Asian countries move toward open markets, competitive forces are coalescing and that will lead to much more active energy risk management. It can be argued that risk is endemic in market economies which means that risk management techniques are becoming essential to the survival of Asian corporations. It also means that active energy risk management will become a fiduciary responsibility of Asian energy companies.

Short-term physical oil trading has always existed in most Asian countries, but the energy complex is now broadening to include gas, power, petrochemical, coal, and weather risk management. Lurking on the horizon is emissions trading to reduce plant emissions and reduce greenhouse gas emissions. Asia is now primed to embrace the active use of energy derivatives, much more sophisticated trading techniques and financial engineering. Borrowing heavily from the institutional memory of well-developed New York and London capital markets, energy trading and risk management are on an upward trajectory in Asia, fueled by growing oil and gas dependencies and the need for more electric power. Similarly, credit risk management is an area of exponential growth in Asia, as the need to manage counterparty risk actively is highlighted in the wake of the demise of Enron and many US and European trading companies.

The deregulation of the electric power industry brings these risks into a particularly sharp focus. While paper market trading for oil and gas has grown on both established futures exchanges and the OTC forward markets for the past decade, electricity paper trading is still in its infancy.

Electricity deregulation has driven the commoditization process, and there is convergence of both gas and electricity that has accelerated much more on the physical side of the market than on the financial trading of power. In fact, the relationship of natural gas marketers and electric power marketers can not be understated. However, power marketing is a more demanding market as it is a next-hour, next-day, next-week, and next-month business. Power marketers and traders provide greater efficiency by buying and selling power and transmissions capacity. Electric power is a 168-hour, seven-days-a-week market with prices that change hourly, half-hourly or quarter-hourly. It is the most volatile commodity ever created with price volatility of over 1000% in some cases. The transition in the market from monopoly to competitive markets has fundamentally changed how utilities and others buy and sell electricity. It is now the beginning of the transition to competitive markets and trading in Asia Pacific.

We have worked with energy companies in Asia Pacific energy markets as advisers, brokers, traders and bankers for more than a decade. Our experience in this culturally rich and varied area of the world leads us to believe that the time is right for a rapid acceleration in energy trading and risk management throughout the region and that Asia is ripe for fundamental change in its trading and risk profile. This book is our attempt to harness our collective knowledge and to assist the market to assume a leading role in the world energy derivatives market. We hope that this book produces more energy trading and risk management that will benefit both Asian producers and consumers by smoothing price volatility and reducing costs.

The book lays out the fundamental evolution of Asian energy trading. Chapter 2 gives an elementary overview of energy risk management terms and applications for the energy complex. Chapter 3 focuses on the role of energy futures exchanges as well as providing context for OTC trading. In Chapter 8, we shall explain the dynamics of the Japanese energy market and its own unique characteristics. Chapter 5 makes an assessment of the South Korean energy trading market and examines the new Asian economic powerhouse called China. We will then assess developments in the actively traded Southeast Asian energy markets as well as the emerging South Asian energy trading markets in Chapter 9.

The following chapters will focus on the newest developments in the Asian energy trading markets. Chapter 7 deals with LNG hedging and project finance implications. We assess the state of the electronic energy trading markets in Chapter 10 and provide an overview of the need for energy risk management software solutions to provide for the execution of successful hedging strategies. Chapter 12 goes into some detail on why International Accounting Standard (IAS) 39 the financial standard for hedge accounting, is important and how it is applied to energy trading. Chapter 5 discusses hedging approached using derivatives including jet fuel hedging which has always been a viable paper market in Asia (in fact the first ever reported OTC swap in energy between a bank and an end user of energy, is understood to have been conducted in Asia between an Airline in Hong Kong and a Western investment bank as early as 1988). The new emerging markets of environmental financial products for greenhouse gas trading and renewable energy trading is explained in our chapter on Green Trading in Chapter 13. Finally, the authors provide an overview of the next wave of Asian energy trading and risk management in Chapter 14.

CHAPTER 2

The ABCs of Energy Hedging

OIL TRADING

Crude oil and petroleum products are traded globally 24 hours a day, every business day in both the physical and paper markets. With the daily physical consumption of oil of almost 80 million barrels and annual trade valued at over $1 trillion, the growth in paper energy trading seems assured, with new financial products evolving to meet the needs of producers, refiners, marketers, and consumers. Paper trading for oil has grown on established futures exchanges to almost 400 million bbl/d with much greater growth on the OTC markets. Moreover, because major oil companies must now buy and trade on the spot markets to meet more of their supply needs that were previously met by their own production, their active involvement in paper trading has increased over time. These changes, coupled with periods of supply-tightness and higher prices since late 1998 and the current oversupply and lower prices, have led to greater oil price volatility, and show that energy price risk management must be increasingly managed by a wide variety of existing and emerging financial instruments for the longer term.

Because of the great price volatility endured by the energy business during the past decade, the industry adopted short-term hedging tools, such as forward and futures contracts, as well as the use of longer-dated instruments including price swaps and OTC options to manage price risk. (Swaps and OTC options are also used to manage short-term price risk). Changes in management thinking have made it unacceptable in today's volatile price environment to remain unhedged and acceptable to use the financial tools available to manage price risk. This sea change is becoming paramount in Asia today. These financial tools can not only be used as a means to hedge price risk but are beginning to be employed to manage corporate assets more effectively for the longer term. Thus, energy companies can utilize their corporate assets and extract their present value rather than simply wait for earnings through future oil production and retail sales.

Because risk management tools are now more widely accepted and available as a means to reduce financial risk in the commodities markets, their application in the oil markets has accelerated over the past 20 years. They provide a degree of certainty for oil producers, refiners, airlines, shipping companies, and manufacturers who use them. The off-exchange OTC instruments allow custom tailoring of agreements to meet the needs of the user while the financial intermediary (oil companies, banks or insurance companies) assumes the risk. Moreover, these agreements arrange fixed price deals for the energy producer or consumer for periods ranging from one month to 10 years forward. These advantages over the shorter-term futures contracts demonstrate that price swaps and OTC options are not only complementary to futures in meeting different needs for their users, but also have become competitive and superior to exchange-traded contracts because of their flexibility and customization attributes. In effect, in many oil markets, the OTC markets set prices not futures contracts.

The application of technologies of the financial markets to the energy markets in a wide variety of strategies has made it necessary to think of oil as money: in other words, a fungible commodity. Oil has been stripped of its physical delivery and has become the province of financial specialists, oil traders, and oil companies who can now assist the industry to tap into their corporate assets more efficiently. The selective use of financial instruments ranging from forwards, futures, and options to price swaps and oil-linked debentures can not only aid in managing price risk, but also protect cash flow, meet operational needs, finance prospective projects, and service debt obligations for producers, refiners, marketers, and end users. These parties now face economic, political, and environmental uncertainties that impact on how they conduct business under present market conditions and in the future. The use of currency trading tools and techniques indicate that oil has become a substitute for money due to its fungibility as a global commodity.

OTC oil trading is not conducted on regulated, established financial exchanges such as New York Mercantile Exchange (NYMEX), International Petroleum Exchange (IPE), or Tokyo Commodities Exchange (Tocom); yet it is a market that is monitored but not regulated by government agencies. OTC markets can also be cleared on existing energy futures exchanges. As the energy industry continues to reintegrate vertically once again with new supply arrangements between producing and consuming countries, the uses of financial instruments of the off-exchange markets and regulated exchanges provide both financial price risk management and the access to the tremendous capital needs of the energy industry. Conservatively estimated at $2 to 3 trillion notionally for all price deals, the OTC energy swaps and options markets are dwarfed by the $120 trillion global interest rate and currency swaps markets.

The maturation of the energy swaps and OTC options market has brought to the fore the fundamental concerns of credit risk and contractual performance. Credit risk concerns the ability of swaps counterparties to perform for the length of the transaction. It has become a leading market issue due to the Enron financial debacle and is continuing to resonate in energy markets. Credit risk has always been a significant factor in all swaps markets, as the pressure to preserve capital and reduce risk are preeminent factors among many market makers. It is now of rising importance due to the fact that the energy industry companies have less creditworthiness.

The proprietary and somewhat secretive nature of the price swaps and OTC options off-exchange markets makes it very difficult for public disclosure of individual transactions. Some of these financial transactions are an "off balance sheet" item (again highlighted by Enron), and thus there is no ability to investigate the outstanding commitments of the financial intermediaries. Today, we are seeing the proliferation of energy risk management services, primarily offered by banks, serving as principals and the growth of swaps brokerage services for crude oil, gas, petroleum products, electric power, weather and emissions. After transactions are undertaken, the matching transaction of the counterparty is often unknown by other market participants. In fact, banks should be the clear beneficiaries of the Enron disaster since they have stronger balance sheet than many energy companies.

The OTC oil markets exist in Asia primarily because financial futures for energy have failed on the Singapore Exchange and are quite illiquid on the Tocom, and customized OTC financial instruments can be developed more rapidly to meet changing market conditions. However, both markets count on the financial performance of their participants to honor their commitments.

OTC energy derivatives create both new opportunities and challenges for companies with price exposure. OTC trading practices have therefore been a matter for study by boards of directors and senior management of energy companies. If defined at the highest level of policy and decision making within an energy company, the policies set forth can prevent trading disasters which still occur noticeably in energy markets. Some very basic guidelines in the establishment of a risk management portfolio came from the Group of Thirty report on "Derivatives, Practices and Principles" released in July 1993. Their recommendations for the OTC markets included the following: that derivatives should be valued at the market (marked to market), market risks should be quantified, credit risks assessed, and management information systems that are sophisticated enough to measure, manage and report risks should be established.

All derivatives trading disasters have been due to the breakdown of controls, inadequate systems, management failure, and human error. Rogue traders exist because of the lack of internal controls to ensure that the risks of OTC transactions are appropriately managed. Since the OTC market place is comprised of bilateral, privately negotiated trades, which are conducted in a manner that exempts them from most regulatory requirements up to the present time, extra vigilance is in order so that breakdowns in trading do not occur.

THE ABC OF ENERGY DERIVATIVES

- Swaps usually settle as calendar monthly, against the average of the daily commodity price in that period. For example, January will cover the pricing period January 1 to January 31.
- Quarterly and annual structures are possible, but even these settle out every month. For example, in a quarterly contract, one third will be settled out each month during the pricing period.
- Energy futures contracts tend to have expiry/termination dates during the month they are named. So January IPE Brent will expire three days prior to January 15. It is important to make sure that the futures contract chosen will give price coverage for the required time window.
- In swaps pricing against oil markets, there are half-month contracts, for example, 1–14 of the month , and 15 through to the last trading day of the month, but not as liquid and usually only available for relatively prompt dates.
- Natural gas is typically traded in spot markets, calendar month contracts in the future, and winter/summer month trade as packages.
- Coal markets typically are traded as calendar monthly contracts both in OTC and futures (where available).
- Power markets around the world trade in off-peak, peak and monthly forwards, and weekly periods, and spot markets (like day ahead) are generally traded in 30-minute blocks, so 48 contracts are accommodated in one 24-hour day. Weekends tend to trade at different prices as opposed to weekdays.
- Payment due dates tend to differ, so for petroleum products in Asia payment due date on OTC derivatives tend to be between 10 and 14 business days after the last settlement date of the contract (This is always specified in the contract confirmation).
- Cash flow risk should be predicted and planned for, when hedging so that provisions can be made for it. This kind of risk can be created when the timing of payables/receivables on physical energy buying/selling and derivatives hedges do not match up.

FAS 133

FAS 133 (Financial Accounting Standards) was implemented on January 1, 2001, and comprise the new rules for hedge accounting in the US. It seems evident that these standards will be adopted globally in the future. There are numerous reasons why the Financial Accounting Standards Board (FASB) came up with these new accounting rules for derivatives. However, foremost is the fact that over the last ten years a large number of derivative instruments fled the global futures exchanges for the OTC derivatives markets, which added significantly to the already existing lack of transparency in these markets. There is a general consensus that the development of derivatives has outpaced the development of standards to account for them. The general practice for dealing with trading or market-making positions is to mark them to market, valuations being included in the bottom line of the firm. It has been harder to pinpoint how to account for derivatives that have been used to hedge (hedging inventory in the commodity markets, import/export transactions in the foreign exchange markets, etc.). Without clear accounting standards for derivatives, practitioners have been left to interpret and extend standards to cover hedging derivatives as best as they can. As a result, derivatives have, in general, been treated as items off the balance sheet.

Since there has been a tremendous growth of derivatives instruments and not enough transparency in the market place, there were a number of large failures during the 1990s (Metallgeselschaft, Orange County, Barings, and now Enron), for which derivative instruments got the blame. Over the last few years, two accounting organizations responsible for defining consistent standards for financial statements have developed standards to address some of the issues specific to the reporting of derivatives. The US-based FASB came out with the FAS 133, effective from the beginning of 2001. The London-based International Accounting Standards Committee (IASC) issued International Accounting Standards (IAS) 39, effective June 1, 2001. The new standards are designed to address the rules surrounding mark-to-market, or the fair value accounting approach. Both organizations agreed that trading books should be marked to market. It seems evident that FAS 133 will now become the global accounting standard for hedge accounting for energy derivatives trading.

PRICE SWAP

A price swap is an agreement between two parties to buy or sell a commodity for a given price, quantity, and time period with no physical commodity being exchanged. For oil trading, it can be either short-term, one to three months, or long-term, six months to fifteen years forward in duration. Because no physical delivery is present, it is best to think of swaps as an exchange of cash flows, one at a fixed rate and the other at a floating rate. The contracting parties agree to pay each other the difference between an agreed-upon fixed price and an average floating market price. These payments are made during predetermined time periods in the future such as monthly, quarterly or semi-annually using an agreed-upon price index. The swaps provider or market maker, either an oil or gas trading company, or financial institution, can either match both ends (fixed and floating) of the transaction or assume the price risk itself. Swaps do not involve upfront cash premiums but are settled in cash against an agreed price index. Cash settlement allows energy producers and consumers to buy and sell the physical commodity, oil or gas, with their appropriate buyers and sellers and yet receive price protection.

The reason one enters into a swap contract is that there are different price expectations between two parties where one party agrees to pay the other the difference between an agreed-upon price and an average market price during predetermined future dates. It should be remembered that no transfer of a physical commodity takes place. In effect, by separating pricing from supply, two markets are created, one for the physical commodity and the other for its price.

Oil price swaps are tailor-made hedging vehicles that allow the participant to fix the price of oil and ensure the participant's financial position against future adverse price movements. There are no standardized energy risk management swaps as each agreement is customized to meet the needs of the participants. Swaps are indexed against a benchmark and are settled in cash, unlike some energy futures contracts. Price swaps indices can be set regularly on a monthly, quarterly, semi-annual, or annual basis. Oil price swaps agreements can fix the price of oil for up to ten to fifteen years in advance, although most are set for less than one year forward particularly in the light of the demise of Enron and many other energy merchant companies. Other contracts can have tenures of one, three, or five years forward. Another way of looking at swaps conceptually is to view them as a series of forward contracts that are wrapped into one contractual agreement. Price swaps agreements can also include an agreement to manage credit risk within the transaction. This is an area where banking expertise can be effectively applied. In fact, money center banks can offer these structured derivative products as a transaction that is linked to the company's financing in such a way that the market value of the company's assets and the market value of this financing can be positively correlated so that there is a reduction in the asset/liability mismatch. What this means is that the cost of financing can be lowered by bundling its borrowing with a commodity swap transaction; in effect, creating a commodity-linked security that is not dependent on commodity price swings.

Firms writing swaps hedge their risk by taking the long position in short-term delivery with their contract appreciating as the contract nears expiry or by taking the opposite position. The underwriters can run matched books using futures markets to balance their portfolio by transferring excess risk to the futures market (Books are the record of all outstanding positions in the futures and OTC markets). They can also run unbalanced trading books when it is opportune for them; however, this is primarily used by oil companies active in using derivative instruments, because they possess the physical product and feel that they are knowledgeable about those markets. Unbalanced books can also be run by those banks that have enough liquidity to do so. Swaps agreements can be customized to meet the internal cash flow requirements of energy producers and consumers; they are a form of price insurance, for the middlemen assume most of the risk and are responsible for managing their own books.

These financial arrangements are extremely discreet transactions because of the competitive nature of the oil markets and the need to protect the client's position in the physical as well as the futures markets. The swaps market is by nature a very private business with few deals made public partly because of the lower liquidity of the secondary markets, although the entry of swaps brokers have brought better price transparency to these markets by providing more competitive bid/ask price quotes. The electronic media, such as Reuters, Platts, and Bloomberg now provide swaps quotes on their terminal screens.

Price swaps offer both short-term and longer-term solutions to energy price risk and market volatility. They can be very effective in dealing with basis risk which is the differential between the physical commodity and the futures price. Basis risk can vary widely in the oil markets and even more so in the natural gas markets, and therefore, requires active management by the swaps underwriter to protect price exposure.

Price swaps can be considered somewhat complementary to futures, as they allow hedging activity to go beyond the six to nine months of viable liquidity in the futures markets. Some brokers actually consider them "longer-dated" futures contracts. While futures only cover a small number of products, swaps and OTC options offer an almost infinite variety of customized arrangements for different products and time periods. For example, besides exchange-traded oil contracts, swaps can be made for naphtha, jet fuel, non-exchange-traded crude oils such as Dubai and Tapis, and fuel oil. They work similarly to futures contracts in that the transactions have the same goals but can be used for longer-term periods. Shorter-dated swaps for one to three months forward are actively written as well as longer-dated swaps from six months to as far ahead as 10 to 12 years forward for oil and 30 years for natural gas. Because longer-term instruments involve more complicated price movements and can be hedged against a wider variety of contracts than futures, their transaction costs can be higher, although replication of deals and more competition has brought costs down during the past deal. Swaps fill the void in futures contracts where liquidity after six months forward becomes problematic although the futures contracts are listed for several years forward.

Caps and floors

Caps and floors are energy risk management strategies that are similar to swaps but offer price protection in a different manner. For one thing, an upfront cash premia must be paid when using caps and floors. Second, the benefits from a change in prices are unlimited as consumers benefit from falling prices and producers benefit from rising prices. Caps and floors are complementary trading strategies. A cap sets a maximum or ceiling price and is used by energy consumers that desire full price protection from rising energy prices and no loss of benefits if prices were to fall. Airlines would be a natural user of caps because of the volatility of jet fuel. A floor creates a minimum or bottom price level, and is used by energy producers that desire full price protection from falling energy prices. There is no loss of profit participation on the upside if energy prices were to rise. Oil producers are natural users of price floors. Oil refiners would be obvious users of price caps for crude acquisition.

Why use energy swaps?

An energy producer which is constantly selling crude oil into the open market is exposing its revenue stream to the volatility of the market. The company's risk can be neutralized by converting the variable price (market price) that it receives from the market from sales into a fixed price. The swap is then set up in which the company receives fixed price payments and pays variable price payments. Conceptually, that is a very simple swap for an oil or gas producer. On the other hand, an energy consumer is concerned about rising energy prices and takes the other side of the swap in order to pay the fixed price and receive the variable price.

The swap agreement for the producer eliminates price fluctuations for what the company receives in the market and provides income stability. This agreement is obviously valuable for an energy producer because of fluctuating energy prices. The income stream is now ensured and risk reduced through the swap. While it can be argued that some upside appreciation is given away, the downside risk is also protected. Turning to the consuming side, the energy consumer can insulate itself from the risks of energy price fluctuations in the market by taking the opposite side of the swaps transaction.

Of course, the natural match between the commodity producer's and consumer's hedging needs could mean that each party simply enters into a series of forward transactions without the intermediary of a bank or energy company middle man. However, the commodity risk exposures of both the producer and consumer do not exactly match and intermediaries add value by standing in between counter parties and assuming the price risk.

DIFFERENT TYPES OF SWAPS USERS: OIL PRODUCERS

Since most energy swaps transactions were originally written for crude oil, it would be helpful to discuss briefly some of the different types that are used, before discussing other petroleum product and natural gas swaps. Swaps and options, like futures, can be used to hedge crude oil production and product prices, carry inventory costs, and finance projects. Oil price swaps protect the value of oil in the ground and allow producers to hedge long-term price risk for their assets. Oil producer swaps are simply transactions that use these tools to sell production at market prices. Producers receive a fixed payment based on the contracted price with the third party. The transaction is made for an agreed upon period of time. Banks can also arrange oil producer swaps to pay down debt and tie in interest rate and currency risk as well. Oil price swaps are particularly good instruments for exploration and production companies. These companies need to incorporate a price floor in their development loans in order to mitigate their repayment risk by assuring that cash flow requirements are met. In effect, the swap instrument maximizes the borrowing capacity by ensuring that future cash flow will meet loan payback by providing downside price protection.

During the past few years, the most popular swaps products have been fuel oil swaps, gas oil swaps, and crack spread options (also called refiner margin swaps). Fuel oil is a very difficult product to hedge due to its underlying illiquidity in the physical market as evidenced by seven contract failures. Swaps deals have been written for three to six months and up to four years for fuel oil. Gas oil is very popular in both Rotterdam and Singapore as it represents the middle distillate cut of the barrel. Options on crack spreads allow refiners to lock in the differential between crude and refined products which gives the refiner additional flexibility in hedging his price risk (the crack spread is a popular hedge on the futures market as well).

Refiner price protection programs

Refiners are natural price risk users, because they continually need to satisfy their crude oil requirements in markets where prices constantly fluctuate. For refiners, the value of the barrel of crude input determines the price of the products produced and sold. While their price risk exposure is short-term, running from crude acquisition to product sales (about a 60-day horizon), refiners use swaps to fix crude acquisition costs and lock in their margin to sell products at an agreed price. Refiners also wish to eliminate price risk on their inventory and usually use futures to protect the price of products in storage. Since refiners actively use spreads to hedge refinery production and crude input costs, applying price swaps on spread trading can be quite complicated. Basically, the concept is to fix crude acquisition costs, which are variable in price, in order to lock in future profits for the products produced. In this way, refining margins are locked in through a swaps arrangement. The financial intermediary takes positions on guaranteed differentials between crude oil and its refined products in these agreements.

Refiner margin swaps are also called "crack spread" swaps because of the ability to use the NYMEX 3-2-1 futures contracts to hedge the transaction and to employ these futures contracts as a liquid and transparent benchmark. The crack spread refers to the refining of crude oil to produce refined products. On the NYMEX futures market, it is the relationship between the WTI crude contract and the gasoline and heating oil contracts, and its use as a proxy for refining margins. European refiner margin swaps use the IPE Brent crude oil and gas oil contracts as an acceptable surrogate for a European gasoline contract. Far Eastern refiners use surrogates in the physical markets based on Platts Oilgram or Petroleum Argus price quotes for products, or an agreed upon crude oil benchmark such as Dubai or Tapis crudes.

Refiner margin swaps became very popular during the past decade. The duration of these deals can be as short as six months and as long as four years. Fuel specifications for reformulated gasoline and the inability to hedge the new US gasoline specification on the NYMEX have made these deals more viable since they can be customized. It is only recently that NYMEX gasoline contracts have regained their lost liquidity of the mid-1990s. (It should be remembered that commodity futures contracts must be changed over time to reflect changes in the physical underlying market. This has been harder due to the many fuel changes and specifications of the US EPA fuel reformulation program).

Other swaps transactions include the airline, shipping, and natural gas industries. The airlines and the shipping industry use price swaps primarily to fix their product acquisition costs, but more innovative airlines use price swaps and options to assist in financing aircraft purchases. Large manufacturers can use swaps to fix the cost of their large fuel requirements.

Market making: oil companies and banks

Swaps agreements should be viewed as long-dated futures transactions that derive their liquidity through middlemen who act as market makers.

These middlemen match party and counterparty, or run unbalanced books, offset some of their risk on futures exchanges and generally assume the risk of these transactions. In effect, they create a market where none previously existed, for besides exchange-traded products, they are able to trade products not listed on exchanges. While no trading vehicle completely eliminates financial risk, swaps and long-term options are better tools to manage price risk than futures, because they can be individually customized for the end-user, basis risk can be avoided.

Financial intermediaries in a swaps arrangement allow both the buyer and seller of the commodity protection on the downside while curbing some upside gain. However, the middlemen assume the price risk and, in some cases, the credit risk as well, and they can also assume basis risk for the physical commodity. Basis risk is confusing to players active in the physical markets, but generally it is the price relationship between the physical commodity in the cash market and its futures price.

Principal providers involved in the OTC markets that write swaps, options and other synthetic instruments are oil trading companies, banks, and some natural gas companies. Each has a specific orientation to the energy markets. The oil trading entities such as British Petroleum, TotalfinaElf, J Aron, Texaco and Shell, to name a few, not only assume price risk for crude oil and petroleum products but are also active in the physical market for these commodities through another transaction. Oil traders are capable of assuming basis risk for diverse locations because of their activity in the physical markets, an extremely vulnerable area of some banks which prefer to lay off price risks using third parties. Oil companies can, therefore, take the physical risks.

While oil companies are involved in the OTC markets and act as market makers, a larger part of the longer-term commodity swaps business is becoming the preserve of large banks specializing in this business. Banks have the ability to assume credit risk as well as price risk. Larger banks are able to build on their presence in project finance and futures trading to form commodity-index type units that are able to structure longer-term deals and manage the longer-term strategic risks of their clients. As these larger banks take positions on their own books, these units are able to create a market in swaps as part of other bank underwriting and are able to offset swaps through paper hedging using the underlying commodity as its offset. In effect, the financial institution offers energy and financial brokering. This type of swaps transaction is also used in other commodities transactions such as metals. Those banks that cannot assume price risk lay it off using financial instruments through market makers and by not taking the counterparty risk themselves. They are becoming subordinate in swaps underwriting. These banks need to replicate these deals many times in order to create the volumes necessary to provide reasonable profits, since their intermediary function makes it difficult to achieve profit levels of the primary market makers.

Banks are involved in interest rate and foreign exchange risk management, and sometimes these factors are built into these deals. The longer term risk then is more fully hedged. The bank syndicates the deal to other international banks. Banks active in the off-exchange instruments include JP Morgan Chase, Bank Tokyo Mitsubishi, BNP Paribas, Deutsche Bank, Bank of America, and Citibank to name a few.

Swaps brokers

The introduction of brokerage firms into the energy swaps markets since the early 1990s signal the maturing of these markets. The role of the broker is to offer financial instruments to parties with differing views. In effect, they broker information between both sides of a transaction. Brokers bring a more definable marketplace and pricing system to the market as prices become more visible. Swaps brokers serve the Singapore oil markets primarily.

In Asia Pacific, the rise of brokers has facilitated paper trading, because prior to fuel oil futures trading in 1989, derivatives oil brokers did not exist. Now there are at least seven active brokers in Singapore which signifies the health of that market. Brokers have boosted the naphtha, gasoline, gas oil, and Tapis crude oil swaps business in Singapore and even now they are proactively sponsoring the development of Petrochemical and Freight Rate derivatives markets (See Chapter 6 for more details).

Jet fuel swaps: the airlines (end-users)

According to an IATA report (International Air Transport Association) presented in early 2003, every additional cent per gallon that is added to the price off Jet Fuel, costs the airlines an additional US$600 million per year. Anything affecting operating costs in such a way is a key concern. This combined with the unpredictability of jet fuel costs has made airlines active users of both futures and price swaps as ways to fix jet fuel costs. Jet fuel swaps can be specifically tailored to quantities, dates, and fuel type used by an airline even though no futures markets exist for that fuel. In this way, airlines are able to determine their operating costs based on more predictable, fixed jet fuel costs. The market has become so active that swaps brokers have appeared in Europe, Asia, and the United States to offer their services. Moreover, jet fuel costs are a large and volatile component of an airline's operating costs and can vary from 15 to 30% of operating costs depending on jet fuel prices. This incentive to contain jet fuel price escalation was an additional impetus for the airlines industry to use financial instruments.

Charter airlines, involved in a highly cyclical business, were the first players in significant numbers to actively become involved in longer-dated swaps (12 to 18 months), because they needed to lock in ticket prices for the next year. Some European charter airlines have hedged 100% of their fuel requirements. Advance bookings expose airlines to significant jet fuel repricing risks, and these risk management tools allow airlines to fix costs and predict their operating margins more accurately. In practice, airlines sometimes use short-term hedging strategies such as price caps and forwards as well as longer-dated instruments such as swaps for most hedging over six months. Jet fuel buyers prefer not to pay upfront premiums and use less expensive short-term strategies although swaps prices have continued to drop and become more competitive as the market has matured. Swaps can, however, also be used for seasonal periods of heavy fuel USAge, such as for three to six months during the summer peak demand periods.

The airlines have also passed their price risk back to their suppliers. Many jet fuel swaps are now bundled in the physical contract for jet fuel with many deals written one year forward. These deals are competitively bid between suppliers.

Some banks, acting as middlemen, have been able to manage not only fuel price risks but also interest rate and currency swings by bundling these into a jet swaps package. Because of the multinational nature of the airline industry, overseas currency fluctuations impact directly on the bottom line and can add to operating risks. Some airlines have been particularly clever in realizing that their perpetual debt arising out of financing needs for new equipment make them active in many multinational markets. Therefore, these airlines are active in different capital markets in order to attract capital at the most favorable terms to meet financing needs. High interest rate costs are a key component of airline expenses. Currency options are used to hedge against aircraft purchases, and financing transactions use floated or fixed debt obligations that can be converted in swaps agreements. Because it is important to protect profit margins when purchasing equipment in foreign currencies, options and swaps can be built into these transactions in order to lower the price of purchasing aircraft.

Most airline carriers use either oil companies, oil traders, or commercial banks, primarily because they are "massively short [of] jet fuel" as described by one swaps trader. Airlines in Europe do not own storage. Their limited access to stored supplies of jet fuel make all airlines throughout the world extremely vulnerable to price volatility in the oil markets.

The swaps dealers involved in jet fuel swaps hedge in cash, futures, and forwards to underwrite their jet fuel deals. Because jet fuel prices do not track an established futures contract, many jet fuel swap deals are built around other futures contracts or Platts Oilgram price quotes in the various active physical markets throughout the world. Although many airlines do not want to assume basis risk (the difference between cash and futures prices), some airlines actually use a combination of futures and physical buying. These airlines use strike price deals through brokers in the futures market and formula price purchasing from refiners in the physical market to manage their risk. These risk management strategies develop tighter price correlations between crude oil and jet fuel price. In practice, it involves converting paper crude and heating oil contracts in the NYMEX into physical jet fuel delivery to the airlines. In effect, these airlines use a more sophisticated hedging instrument to reduce the substantial basis risk inherent in the jet fuel markets. Most airlines either do not want to assume basis risk, or establish and run their own futures trading operations. These airlines enter into third party swaps agreements to manage their price risk.

The jet fuel swaps market remains very competitive. Airline fuel purchasers choose the best deal by getting three or four price quotes from providers. Often, jet fuel purchases go to the major market makers who are willing to assume both price and counterparty risk. These market makers have the expertise of doing back-to-back deals or running an unbalanced book. Risk exposure to the swaps maker's book is limited by futures, options, and other financial tools, including average price options and participation hedges which are built into the deal to offset risk. Jet swaps deals are often done in rapid succession in a short period of time, that is, something of a "cluster phenomenon" as described by one swaps dealer. In effect, windows of opportunity arise followed by relatively slack periods.

Price hedging in the shipping industry (end-users)

The shipping industry has a need similar to the airlines industry which is to fix their fuel costs. Fuel price swaps and options are used to fix bunker and diesel fuel costs for shipping transportation up to two years or more as well as to fix freight rate for tanker charterers. Typically, about 40% of a shipowner's costs are fuel-related, and therefore, control of bunker fuel costs is a crucial part of the business. Because of the difficulty in hedging fuel costs on the futures markets by using the mostly illiquid fuel oil futures contracts when available, which trade in extremely thin markets, most shipping companies do not use fuel oil futures to control their bunker costs. Some use crude oil futures to manage their risk. Some develop a bunker fuel hedge with market makers who use crude oil to base the hedge. The shipping industry has been slow to adapt to using risk management tools for hedging its bunker requirements or hedging its freight rates.

The utilities (end-users)

Relating to the oil side rather than the power side of the equation, electric utilities must constantly purchase fuel oil to meet their fuel inputs. In recent years, they have been active purchasers of price swaps based on fixed price deals fuel oil swaps for either their summer or winter peak seasons. PTT of Thailand has been one of the more active fuel oil swaps players, and even has a Singapore representative office to monitor the market.

THE MAJOR MARKET PLAYERS IN SINGAPORE

The major market players in oil trading are very diversified. At the present time the major oil traders include: Caltex, J Aron (Goldman Sachs), Morgan Stanley, Bank of America, Mitsubishi Securities International (formerly Tokyo Mitsubishi Corp), Mitsui. Glencore, Hin Leong, Vitol, Deutsche Bank, Calyon (formerly known as Credit Lyonnais Rouse Derivatives), Societe General, BP, Shell, Unipec, China Oil, CNPC, SK Energy, Samsung, Sinochem, and Emirates National Oil Company (Enoc). These oil traders make markets in all petroleum products and crude oil except for Enoc which specializes only in naphtha, middle distillates, and jet kero, and Calyon which focuses on jetkero, gas oil, and fuel oil. The remaining oil trading players are the state-owned companies in Southeast Asia including Petronas, PTT, Pertamina, Petron, and SPC.

Major brokers in the Singapore market include Intercapital (ICAP), Traditional Financial Services (TFS), Tullett and Tokyo, Prebon, Radix, Ginga Petroleum, and Amerex Petroleum. ICAP and TFS are strong in brokering middle distillates. Tulletts and Prebon broker both crude and products. Radix brokers gasoline and distillates. Ginga Petroleum is mainly brokers for naphtha and some freight rate swaps for tankers. Amerex focuses on crude oil.

ASIAN OIL TRADING

The Asia Pacific markets are net crude oil and petroleum product imports, primarily from the Middle East. The region also sources crude and products from West Africa, Alaska, and the North Sea. These increased arbitrage opportunities have significantly increased the need to use risk management tools to hedge growing price exposures over different time horizons. Thus, the market drivers of increased physical oil trading activity, shifting trade patterns, and fuel specification changes due to environmental imperatives are all pushing the region's oil producers and consumers to manage price risk more proactively.

One glaring problem in Asian oil markets has been the lack of liquid price benchmarks, particularly for crude oil. The role of a price benchmark is useful as it provides price transparency, reference, discovery, and facilitates risk management through price certainty. Successful and liquid benchmarks provide market efficiency by lowering costs and increasing price information. They also allow risk shifting (not elimination) with more players participating in the markets. Benchmarks provide a mechanism to separate price from supply. In more mature markets, arbitrage opportunities are more complex and price spreads narrow over time. Asian oil markets, however, remain relatively immature paper markets at the present time due to the lack of trading volume and a lack of active participation of Asian oil producers and consumers; however, this is starting to change.

Regarding crude oil trading, Asia has never had a liquid marker crude. The two relatively liquid Asian crude oil swaps markers for the past decade have been Malaysian Tapis and the United Arab Emirates' Dubai crude oils. Tapis and Dubai production is significantly less than Brent blend and is declining. Nevertheless, they have been the most visible Asian crude oil price indicators, but are prone to periodic supply problems or pricing patterns that are sometimes detached from other price markers.

Paper Tapis trades in 50,000 to 100,000 barrel lots, and enables traders to lock in price spreads typically in Tapis/Brent swaps trading. The paper players in Tapis include Morgan Stanley, Vitol, Koch, and Elf Trading. The Tapis swaps are priced at Tapis APPI (Asian Petroleum Price Index) related prices and book out against the APPI average. The Malaysian Malacca refinery has hampered liquidity in Tapis as it uses the crude for the refinery.

The APPI has been used for many years as the standard for crude oil pricing in Asia. This index was launched in January 1986. It is a biweekly panel assessment by industry players, and is used intensively in Asian crude term contracts by oil producers. Twenty-one Asian crudes including Tapis, Australian, Chinese, and Indonesian crudes are assessed in this index. The APPI is administered by SeaPac Services Ltd in Hong Kong. However, the APPI index is not used for pricing OTC paper deals.

Dubai is traded in 50,000-barrel increments which are called the partial Dubai contract. It has been a major Middle East pricing indicator since most Persian Gulf oil producers do not want to disclose their spot prices and prefer to price their crude at their official selling price. Unfortunately, Dubai production is continuing to decline so its viability as price market remains in doubt. Dubai production has declined from 420,000 bbl/d in 1991 to 170,000 bbl/d in 1999. Japanese refiners have been active in locking in Dubai swaps for their crude acquisition costs. Dubai is being replaced by Omani crudes. Incidentally, Dubai has already been tried as an Asian futures contract on the IPE and SIMEX when they launched a contract, unfortunately during the Gulf War. The contract failed to gain any liquidity.

STANDARD TERMS AND CONDITIONS (ISDA)

The primary documentation used in the energy OTC markets have been developed by the ISDA. ISDA is the global trade association representing leading participants in the privately negotiated derivatives industry, a business which includes interest rate, currency, commodity, credit and equity swaps, as well as related products such as caps, collars, floors, and swaptions. ISDA was chartered in 1985, and today numbers over 550 member institutions from 41 countries on six continents. These members include most of the world's major institutions who deal in and are leading end-users of privately negotiated derivatives, as well as being associated service providers and consultants.

Since its inception, the ISDA has pioneered efforts to identify and reduce the sources of risk in the derivatives and risk management business. Among its most notable accomplishments has been the development of the ISDA Master Agreement. The ISDA Master Agreement, the authoritative contract widely used by industry participants, represents a milestone achievement because it has established international contractual standards governing privately negotiated derivatives transactions that reduce legal uncertainty and allow for reduction of credit risk through netting of contractual obligations. As the business has developed and grown, ISDA expanded and updated the Master Agreement and its supporting documents, a process that continues today.

Ensuring the enforceability of the netting provisions of the ISDA Master Agreement has been, and remains, a key initiative, because of its importance in reducing the credit risk arising from the business. The association's work in this area has resulted in a series of laws being passed in various countries that ensure legal certainty in those nations. Since its original request for opinions from the G-10 countries in 1987 that only addressed the enforceability of certain provisions of the 1987 Master Agreement, ISDA has expanded the number of countries solicited to thirty six. The scope of the opinions now includes the enforceability of the termination, bilateral close-out netting and multibranch netting provisions of the 1987 and 1992 Master Agreements. ISDA continues to expand its efforts related to the enforceability of netting provisions in emerging markets jurisdictions, working with the relevant legislative and regulatory representatives. Today, ISDA documentation remains the standard for the energy industry, and is used in most trading agreements.

The pricing of petroleum products in Asia

Table 2.1 shows the average daily volume for the Singapore swaps markets for 20 trading days per month on the average.

If we include open-naphtha in the above total which trades 17,550,000 barrels per month, then we arrive at a total monthly turnover in the Singapore swaps market of approximately 275,000,000 barrels. In 1997–98, the Singapore swaps market was estimated to be from 150,000,000 to 200,000,000 barrels per month. Its present rate represents a steady

Table 2.1 Monthly Singapore paper market volumes (bbls)

Gas oil	64,350,000
Kero	42,900,000
Fuel oil	63,232,000
Dubai/Tapis	80,000,000
Naphtha	6,500,000
Open Spec	17,550,000
Total	274,532,000

Source: Global Change Associates Inc, 2004

upward trend, but is still significantly smaller than the European swaps markets.

The Asia Pacific market will grow incrementally over the next decade due to rising oil dependency, rising consumption, price volatility, and the rapid growth of the Internet in the region. The active swaps brokers community in Singapore adds to market liquidity be developing two-way markets for buyers and sellers of oil.

Another significant difference between Asia and Europe is that OTC contracts are for a shorter time duration than those in the European markets. Asian markets are also more oriented toward plain vanilla swaps rather than more exotic financial instruments and structures, and a shorter trading horizon.

Moreover, since security of supply in Asia still is of primary concern over price considerations, the OTC paper markets have evolved much more slowly than in Europe or the United States. Nevertheless, the OTC oil derivatives markets are providing paper markets with trading liquidity and price discovery without viable futures contracts or a price discovery mechanism. The change from a physically oriented market to a financial market will continue to be a slow process. Longer-term swaps deals will be very rare if they occur at all.

The major problem that occurred from time to time, and more so in the Singapore swaps markets have been physical squeezes on gas oil and fuel oil. They have failed in these attempts to squeeze the market. By and large, the Singapore market functions quite well as there are a limited number of counterparties so traders just will not trade with companies that do not make a good faith effort to perform.

PLATTS ASSESSMENT METHODOLOGIES IN ASIA

Platts dominates oil market pricing and it quotes daily price assessments for a number of products. If the quality or grades assessed change, Platts informs subscribers in advance through the various wires, faxes, printed products, and electronic systems. Platts price specialists focus on price discovery and follow prices in all main trading markets. In markets where there is continuous trading activity, Platts price specialists cover those markets continuously as well, with the editorial responsibilities transferred across the globe. In Asia, Platts energy reporters in Singapore, Tokyo, Sydney, and Hong Kong track down prices starting at 9:00 am Singapore time. The Platts methodology reflects the activity of the market players and takes into account industry practices in each reporting region. FOB Singapore assessments reflect trading activity up to 5:30 pm Singapore time.

Industry practices include quality specifications, typical volumes, loading timing, and location. The Platts assessment reflects the standard grade and therefore market participants can determine more efficiently what the quality differentials should be versus the benchmark grades. Platts also assesses paper values for two months forward. The typical trading volumes also vary greatly and the prices for the parcels vary depending on the volume. For the gas oil assessments, Platts focuses on volumes for a minimum of 150,000 barrels, for jet fuel 100,000 barrels, for fuel oil 20,000 metric tonnes, gasoline 50,000 barrels and naphtha C+F Japan 25,000 metric tonnes. The price assessments for Singapore reflect pricing for products loading 15–30 days from the date of publication. For instance, on July 16, Platts assessments reflect the product market 15–30 days forward, namely July 31–August 15.

The timing specification is important due to variability in pricing in the various windows, particularly when a market is steeply in contango or backwardation. It is not uncommon in times of tight supply for the backwardation to be over $2.00/month or roughly 6 cents per day. This means that cargoes loading one week apart can vary in price by close to 30 cents/bbl, or even more, depending on the steepness of the forward price curve. Thus it is extremely important to follow pricing windows very methodically. In a contango market, the excess of prompt barrels causes the front end to be significantly cheaper than forward barrels, while in backwardation the tightness causes the front barrels to be much higher.

Singapore product price assessments take into account the prevailing trading practices in the Asian region. Most companies tend to cover their requirements far in advance with sellers also selling forward. As a result, most of the liquidity is centered on this time period for physical transactions (only up to two months forward). By not taking the first two weeks into consideration, transactions reflecting distressed prices are excluded.

The locations used on the Asian assessment are Singapore, the Arab Gulf, South Korea, and Japan on a FOB basis, China, Japan, and Australia on a C+F basis. Spot transactions in the region are typically done at a differential versus the Mean Of Platts Singapore (MOPS). The main benchmarks are FOB Singapore and bids/offers FOB from any terminal or refinery are accepted as a basis for pricing.

All Asia-Pacific/Arab Gulf product cargo assessments are assessed up until 17:30 (09:30 GMT) Singapore standard time. Transactions and bids/offers after 17:30 Singapore time deadline will not be taken into account. All Singapore assessments are FOB and are assessed 15–30 days from date of publication. Assessments reflect merchantable grades. All product prices are quoted in US dollars. All FOB Singapore product assessments, with the exception of fuel oil and MTBE are quoted on a dollars per barrel basis. FOB Singapore fuel oil and MTBE are quoted on a dollars per metric tonne basis.

The FOB Singapore premium/discount assessment takes into account physical cargo activities 15–30 days from date of publication. Both the Singapore gas oil paper market and the jet paper assessment reflects a minimum of 50,000 barrels paper transactions. Assessments for paper are for one and two months forward and are quoted on a full calendar basis. As an example, during the month of February, Platts would quote paper for March and April. Both paper gas oil and jet kerosene are non-deliverable contracts.

In conclusion, Platts price assessments will reflect the closing levels, and the three main factors in price determination are: fixed price, premiums, and paper/swaps.

- *Fixed price:* The ultimate question in the mind of an end user, a producer, refiner, trader, or broker is price, which in turn determines expense, refining margin, profit, or loss. The spot market trades actively on a FOB Singapore basis on a fixed price basis. Activity has been commoditized and most players now can focus fully on prices as the qualities, volumes, and loading procedures have become more standardized each year.
- *Premiums:* Many transactions are carried out in relation to a standard commodity. In this case a differential, also known as premium in the Asian markets, is generated. Premiums will arise if the quality, volumes, or loading times differ from the benchmark. In addition, the floating transactions (variable prices) are done in relation to the assessments. Premiums will usually rise in those times when the market is backwardated and the steeper the curve the greater the premium. In a contango situation, premiums will have a tendency to turn into discounts.
- *Paper/Swaps:* Paper/swaps are another major determinant in price. Swaps trade freely in an OTC market and can trade at any time. Paper markets are very reactive and provide players with an instant feedback of market conditions. Swaps react to arbitrage conditions or movements in overseas market as well as local conditions. Paper hedges allow users to lock in price because swaps players can transform floating prices to fixed or fixed to floating.

FEOP PRICING: AN ALTERNATIVE TO PLATTS FOR PETROLEUM PRODUCTS

The Far East Oil Price (FEOP) Index was developed by Oil Trade Associates, an oil consulting firm, and Reuters in Singapore. The index is a calculated average of daily price levels of benchmark physical oil products and crudes in the Far East based on assessments submitted by the panelists. It offers an accurate and independent contract pricing mechanism for the physical Asian oil markets as the oil trade generates price discovery for its financial products not oil price reporters. It is a direct competitor to Platts. FEOP's strength has been in jet fuel FOB Singapore, gas oil FOB Singapore, HSFO FOB Singapore, and the Indonesian LSWR (Low Sulfur Waxy Resid) FOB Singapore. It is used by airlines such as JAL, ANA, Singapore Airlines, and Malaysia airlines, but has never been firmly established enough to displace Platts in either the physical or paper markets. Platts still remains the dominant pricing services for paper trading in Asia at the present time.

Annualized price volatility

The following tables show the price volatility for the products markets for Singapore. As can be seen over the past few years annualized price volatility has increased and remained very high. Normal price volatility would be in the 20–40% range for these petroleum products (see Table 2.2).

Price trends and convergence for petroleum products

Since paper market prices track the underlying physical market, the slowdown in the world economy has dampened oil demand. In effect, it has not lessened price volatility as the market is under price pressure to go down.

Asian oil products swaps

Swaps in the Far East have become the main hedging mechanism where there are no futures exchanges for a particular product or crude. Reportedly

Table 2.2 Annualized price volatility for Singapore market (*Cargo Lots*)

Product	2000 (%)	2001 (%)
Gas oil (Cargo)	174	149
HSFO 180 CST	181	144
HSFO CST	172	145

Source: Credit Agricole IndoSuez Group

up to 70–80% of the total volume of trade in Singapore now centers on swaps particularly for the petroleum products markets rather than the crude markets. Most product swaps trade two to six weeks forward and are priced over a five day average using Platts mean FOB Singapore (also referred to as MOPS, that is Mean Of Platts Singapore). Asian product swaps trading still remains short-term due to the orientation of Asian refiners toward security supply issues over price risk management. The depth of the European product swaps market is a reflection of the confidence of European refiners and traders with market performance and the corporate need to manage price risk and so it trades much longer term.

Naphtha swap traders price off the Platts FOB Singapore naphtha quotation and the C+F Japan physical quotation. C+F Japan swaps trade 45–75 days forward. Gasoline/naphtha spreads are traded using the differential between the two Platts FOB Singapore quotations.

Jet and gas oil trade on a monthly, quarterly, and calendar year basis. Time spreads are popular such as third quarter 2001 against first quarter 2002. Jet/Gas oil swap spreads trade is based on the differential between the two products.

Both 380 and 180 CST fuel oil trade on a monthly, quarterly, and calendar year basis. In the past, swap trade could be offset by the SIMEX fuel contract, but that contract is now illiquid. The fuel oil market is the most long-term Asian products market.

Interrelationship with the physical market

The OTC swaps markets in Singapore closely tracks the physical markets – so much so that Platts, which started as a physical price reporting service, dominates the price reporting of the majority of OTC oil swaps business. In effect, Platts prices became an integral part of the swaps markets as a means for determining paper market prices. Its franchise in the OTC price swaps market seems secure for the present time although competitive services have tried to move toward more electronic media for index construction such as FEOP.

Because of this close relationship with the physical market price reporting, the Platts prices can be manipulated by clever traders who can raise or lower their bids and offers. While Platts denies that this actually occurs since their methodology is oriented toward a "deals done" approach, the reality is that price reporters are human beings and frankly not as sophisticated as savvy oil traders. Moreover, they are getting younger in age and more inexperienced. As the age of Internet oil trading approaches, it seems only a matter of time until Platts is displaced by Internet exchanges such as ICE and electronic indexes created by the energy trade.

Change in players

The Singapore trading market went through a contraction in activity following the Asian financial crisis in 1997, but has been rebuilding since that time. The latest development is the establishment of a Bank of America and Standard Charter Bank trading teams in Singapore focused on oil market derivatives trading. Several other banks such as Maguire Bank are eyeing entry into the market. There has also been the entrance of more financial institutions in energy trading (this is occurring in the New York and London markets because of the demise of Enron) and the banks are willing to take on more financial risk and typically have stronger balance sheets than energy traders and energy companies.

In oil markets, over time, companies go up and go down in volumes, prominence, and market power. The human factor is that the same traders usually remain in the market and switch companies. They remain as significant factors in the market due to the strength of personal business relationships in the Asia oil markets.

Another new development in the Singapore market is that of Omani crude oil swaps. This change should impact the Dubai swaps market, and is already seeing a lot of trading volume out of London. Omani crude will probably overtake Dubai by the end of this year as the leading Middle East swaps marker. The reason for this change is that Dubai production continues to decline and its viability as a price marker is waning.

Change in contract or fuel specifications

The one clear advantage of OTC energy derivatives over exchange-traded products is that they are not standardized contracts. Standardized futures contracts must be approved by regulatory authorities as well as any changes to these energy futures contracts. This leads to delays in responding to market changes. This was true of the switch from leaded to unleaded gasoline on the NYMEX in the 1980s (in fact, there were two gasoline contracts trading which split liquidity) and has been true of the NYMEX reformulated gasoline contract of the 1990s. This is not the fault of the exchanges, but it is a fact that futures contracts must be modified over time to reflect changes in the underlying physical market. The OTC market does not have this problem. OTC contracts can be modified relatively easily to accommodate physical market changes, and as many deals are customized, these changes are made immediately. The only proviso is that both counterparties to the deal agree to its contract specifications. They usually do so and this is really not a big issue on the OTC markets, although it is a very large issue on the NYMEX and IPE because of the inflexibility of their product contract specifications.

GENERAL MARKET TRENDS

Aside from electronic trading, which will be discussed later in this section, the major issue on the horizon for the OTC energy markets is the question of the degree of future regulation of these markets. At the present time, they are not regulated in Rotterdam or in Singapore. However, regulation is surely on the way. This change will most likely start in the United States, but will spread globally. Fundamentally, it is being driven by the Enron financial meltdown and the advent of electronic trading. Enron is calling into question more issues regarding accountability and financial disclosure. The electronic platforms for energy commodities call into question the role of floor-based trading regulatory regimes in the age of the Internet. This issue will have worldwide implications for energy trading as the electronic platforms continue to gain liquidity. Regulation of OTC Internet trading, therefore, will require global government solutions that is, agreement between many government regulatory agencies to work together on financial disclosure and performance issues. It is a complex task.

Marking to market (FAS 133)

The enforcement of the new accounting rules for derivatives by the FASB is forcing risk managers, traders, and sales people to ask the following questions: (1) what derivative instruments should they choose for their hedging practices? (2) Which instruments should they trade? (3) Should they choose more "plain vanilla" type instruments, which would eventually facilitate the process to qualify for hedge accounting? Along with these, they have to consider a number of other related issues which were not part of their concerns before the introduction of FAS 133.

Without clear accounting standards for derivatives, practitioners have been left to interpret and extend standards to cover hedging derivatives as best as they can. As a result, derivatives have, in general, been treated as items off the balance sheet. These new accounting rules include an entirely new model for accounting for derivative hedges. It does away with deferral and synthetic accounting by making all derivatives instruments appear on the balance sheet at "fair value." In addition, it requires companies to maintain hedge program accountability by posting any hedge ineffectiveness in current income. It is important to mention that FAS 133 focuses on hedge tools and not on the type of risk that has been hedged. FAS 133 now allows revenues from derivatives-hedged transactions to be identified and to be more transparent on financial statements. In other words: income from derivative hedges posted into the OCI account is recycled into recognized income to coincide with the recognition of the hedged asset. If the transaction fails to qualify for hedge accounting treatment, the overall change in fair value is posted directly to earnings.

Fair value accounting is used for fair value hedges which are derivatives that are used to hedge transactions that are marked-to-market – for example, trading assets. The accounting treatment of the hedge follows the accounting treatment of the asset. Both are marked-to-market and both cash flows are recognized in current earnings and recorded through the earning cycle right away. Since both the asset/liability position and the hedge are marked-to-market, the effectiveness of the hedge is directly reflected in earnings of the current period. The accounting for the derivative is the same as that for speculative applications, but in this case, due to the risk being hedged in the underlying, the hedged exposures must also be marked-to-market; after which the results must be posted to current income. Ideally, the hedge will be a perfect hedge whereby the gains and losses will offset the losses/gains on the underlying exposure, so there will not be any impact to earnings.

Positions will be represented on the balance sheet with more transparency than was previously required. This clears the way for further developments in reporting derivatives and risk. Many derivative markets may not be liquid (for example, the power market), and these standards do not address the method to value these assets fairly. It is to be expected that FASB will make some adjustments in order to facilitate the implementation of these new accounting rules as they evolve and that FAS 133 standards for hedge accounting will be applied throughout the world as the accepted accounting standard.

Enron's fallout on energy trading

The impact of Enron's demise will be the movement to more government oversight of the energy derivatives market by regulators involved not only in market surveillance but also in reporting requirements. The upshot is more financial disclosure of derivatives positions by both energy companies and major banks. Some market makers are now touting that there will be flight to quality in using their energy risk management services. They are probably right.

The final impact will be more financial scrutiny of the counterparties involved in energy derivatives trading particularly regarding their ability to perform. Senior management at energy companies will be asking many questions regarding credit risk and length of contracts. There will be a reluctance to go very long (over one year) in energy markets for fear of financial performance risk. The good news is that this change may lead to a healthier energy derivatives market with more marked-to-market accounting disclosing financial positions, superior software technology applications to measure and manage risk, and more sanguine trading strategies (not trading for the sake of trading). There may also be a flight to quality with the better energy risk management companies demonstrating their superior financial accountability.

It has been 26 years since the first oil futures contract traded on NYMEX, and we are still just beginning to trade energy globally. Commodity contracts can trade six to twenty times their physical volume on futures exchange. Oil only trades three to four times its physical volume if we include both NYMEX and the IPE, so it still has long way to grow in trading volumes. Many companies still do not hedge their price risk and are reluctant to change, despite the unprecedented price volatility of energy markets during the past three years. It is not going to get any easier to ignore price volatility and do nothing. Internet trading will add more price volatility to the equation. One only has to look at the NASDAQ and New York Stock Exchanges over the past few years to see the increased price volatility in equity trading due to electronic day traders. Why should the energy complex be any different? The Internet has no large barriers to entry – it just requires a personal computer and a trading account. The good news is that energy risk management is now considered a fiduciary responsibility at many energy companies, and that energy risk management tools exist to manage those risks. This trade will mostly be OTC-based as the futures exchanges can not adapt fast enough to the rate of change in technology.

Electric power trading

The transition in the market from monopoly to competitive markets has fundamentally changed how utilities and others buy and sell electricity. While paper market trading for oil and gas has grown on both established futures exchanges and the OTC forward markets over the past decade, electricity paper trading is still in its infancy. Electricity deregulation has driven the commoditization process, and there is convergence of both gas and electricity that has accelerated much more on the physical side of the market than the financial trading of power. In fact, the relationship of natural gas marketers and electric power marketers can not be understated. However, power marketing is a more demanding market as it is a next-hour, next-day, next-week, and next-month business. Power marketers and traders provide greater efficiency by buying and selling power and transmissions capacity. Electric power is a 168-hour, seven-day-a-week market that changes prices hourly, half-hourly or quarter-hourly. It is the most volatile commodity ever created with price volatility of over 1000% in some cases.

Hedging electricity price risk

Historically, electric utilities entered into long-term wholesale sales contracts to municipal, cooperative, and investor-owned utilities. Under these power contracts, utilities committed to price the power needed for that contract period and often rolled over or extended the contract term. The movement from these long-term contracts to more spot market purchasing also occurred in oil and gas markets during the past 20 years. This change brings with it price risk and the need to manage that price risk with financial tools such as futures and forward contracts, and OTC price swaps and options. It is part of the commoditization process. In 1992, electricity trading began in Nord Pool, and in late 1993 OTC financial instruments for power entered the US market without an established futures contract, price discovery mechanism, or liquid cash market precisely because of the need to manage price risk. Electricity trading is also different from oil and gas as that trading has been much more short-term oriented. A long-term deal in electric power is beyond one year.

Characteristics of electric power

When investigating the electric power markets, it is helpful to define the terminology which is confusing to the layman. The electric power industry is complex and involves peak and off-peak demand periods. Generally, peak power is from 6 am to 10 pm, and off-peak the remainder of the day when demand is lower. The other consideration that needs to be defined is that of firm and non-firm power (interruptible). Only in the electric and gas industries can customers be curtailed from their access to these commodities due to demand and system constraints. Turning to generation, the system that generates power uses many fuels to produce the commodity. These include oil, gas, coal, hydropower, renewables, and nuclear. Coal continues to be the predominant fuel in Asia Pacific electric power generation mix accounting for over 50% followed by natural gas with 30% and 10% apiece for oil and nuclear power. After the generation of electricity, the power is transmitted through a grid system where the laws of physics take over. Power travels in loop flow directions and can have line losses of over 20%. Therefore, the economic dispatch of power is of primary concern in competitive markets. The system usually has many transmission bottlenecks. Demand is rising each year due to increased economic activity as well as electricity use by the Internet (an unforeseen factor).

These factors make the trading of power more complex as well. Trading desks are a mix of skill sets with knowledge of how the system works as well as the trading expertise of how to buy and sell power.

Electricity futures

There have been many electricity futures contracts throughout the world that have not worked. One reason is that the futures exchanges, in their quest for standardization, have tried to force the industry to use monthly contracts to manage price risk in hourly, daily, weekly and monthly markets. While monthly futures contracts for oil and gas have worked quite well, in electricity they have created a market mismatch. In effect, financial markets in electricity futures have not become relevant on regulated futures exchanges. The only successful electricity futures contracts have been on the simple Nord Pool market which works well due to its fuel mix and small size. Thus, while electricity proves to be the most volatile priced commodity ever created, there are few liquid financial instruments to manage that risk.

The truth is that electricity price volatility is too great to manage effectively by monthly futures contracts. It is not how the electricity markets actually work. Normally oil and gas futures exhibit 30% and 50% annualized price volatility (and sometimes higher). Electric power is substantially different. Because electric power is priced in half-hour or hourly increments (or less), it is a very volatile commodity. Power is sold forward in hourly, daily, weekly and monthly markets. This is unique in the energy industry. It also can not be stored; in effect, it is a real-time commodity.

Electric power can go from $25 per megawatt hour (how it is sold) to $10,000 per megawatt hour. According to all statistical models, this type of event would happen one time in 10,000. Electricity is just different. It can not be stored. It has various fuel inputs to be produced (oil, gas, and coal). Moreover, while the oil and gas industries adopted price risk management tools to manage their high price volatility, electric utilities have been unable to assume the unprecedented price risks of power markets. No one has been able to do this to a substantial degree. Consequently, almost all electric power deals remain physical supply deals not financial hedging transaction. Thus, electric power is a very unique commodity, and has not been conducive to the use of standardized futures contracts.

The lesson of Enron is that physical assets are needed to make money in power trading and that is why financial institutions are now holding on to physical electric power generation assets. These are backed up by trading physical generation assets that is, the so-called "asset optimization" strategy. Capital is needed to back up these trades. Financial performance is king, as strong counterparty relationships are needed. In effect, the derivatives market for power has basically evaporated. The Enron debacle has become a financial wake up to regulators, exchanges, and traders to the need to scrutinize credit and counterparties in energy trading more carefully. More market transparency and financial disclosure will also occur due to the price pressure in the equity markets.

Moreover, the electricity market needs viable electricity trading benchmark to trade off for deal making. Unfortunately, the financial price spikes in 1998, 1999, and 2000 have effectively forced out many counterparties for a potential electricity deal. You can't have one-way markets. The failure of financial futures contracts for electricity has compounded the problem. The need for price discovery creates offsetting benchmarks for longer-dated deals. The fact that there is no viable price index for longer-term deals versus the daily market price swings, which are substantial, has created an almost purely physical market for electricity trading. The financial market is still-born. Thus, hardly any trades are settled against an index today and what has occurred is a series of one-off transactions and bilateral trade. Hopefully, the electricity derivatives market may reestablish itself in coming years.

The physical nature of the energy network has bred more price volatility in deregulating markets. Physical plant outages, weather, and capacity constraints add more uncertainty to the system. Financial hedging has generally not worked. The problem is that indexes are used for physical power trading but not financial settlement. The crux of the problem is that there is no upside price protection, especially for longer-date power contracts settled on an index. In other words, no one company wants to take the market risk of price spikes that are thousands of percentage increases. It has bankrupted companies and led to less liquidity. It is estimated that after the 1998 power spike in the MidWest, 45 power marketers exited the market. The failure of electricity futures contracts have made hedging problematic.

Price volatility

Electricity prices are volatile. The following graph demonstrates that annualized price volatility is incredibly high compared to oil and gas which historically generated 25% and 40% annualized price volatility. In effect, it has made managing this amount of price risk almost impossible. It should be noted that these are the annualized number, if you look closely at the graph, the price can spike into over 1000% price movements.

Electric power prices are continuing to rise, due to the fact that new generation equipment is not rate-based (see Figure 2.1). Many in the industry privately concede that eventually a market clearing price of $40 per megawatt hour will be the end result of deregulation, which is higher than today.

Power price spikes and credit issues

As deregulated markets behave differently to regulated cost of service markets, they can experience severe price spikes. Weather is the major variable in power. The problem is that free markets allow prices to rise to whatever the market will bear. This is a normal function of markets.

What was abnormal in the first incident was the poor creditworthiness of the power marketer. This incident caused tremendous attention to be paid to the performance of counterparties in financial arrangement. It had

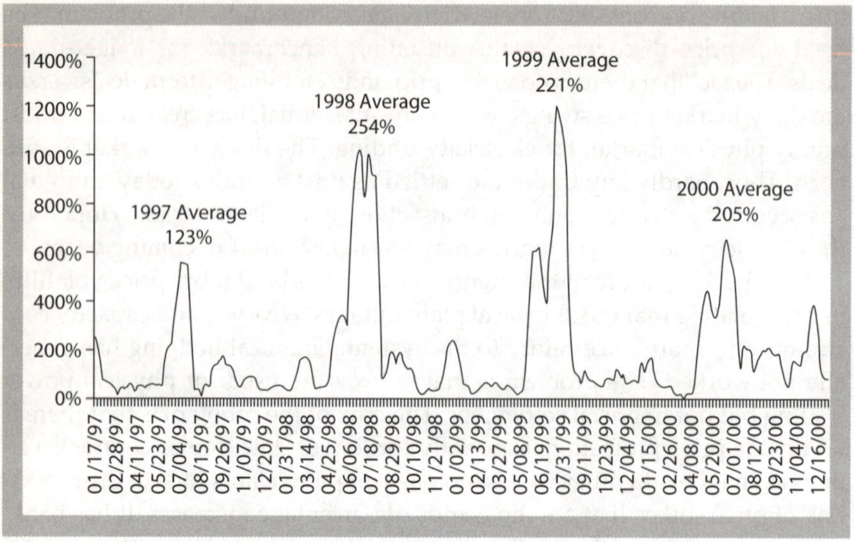

Figure 2.1 Electricity price volatility
Source: Industry sources

the effect of driving away market liquidity for derivatives trading. The second event that has just about destroyed the derivatives market is the Enron financial failure. Creditworthiness in the energy complex has always been worse than in many other industries. Because of this fact, many energy companies are very careful about who they will enter into bilateral agreements with. Counterparties are very worried about performance. There is no quick-fix solution to this problem. But since electronic trading for power is still just beginning, it is not a heavy user of electricity derivatives. The financial futures exchanges have the advantage of their substantial clearing operation for trading but as we have noted do not have viable electricity futures contracts.

Commodity market development

Normally, the development of spot markets gives rise to forward contracts that lead to futures and then OTC trading. However, in electric power, we are still stuck in the movement from spot markets to forward supply contracts. Futures have totally failed, and OTC derivatives trading is for very short-term duration.

Electricity reliability is a growing issue of concern in many parts of the United States. There have been an increased number of major utility disruptions due to a lack of generation capacity or as a result of equipment failures. There is also the increased need for electricity reliability of the growing Internet-related electricity consumption as well as information technology which is particularly sensitive to power disruptions. The reduction in utility reserve margin in several regions of the country are adding to system fragility. Price spikes are often the result of these unforeseen events.

IPPs or merchant power producers

The trend in recent years is for non-utilities to build new capacity. In recent years, over three-quarters of new capacity was added by non-utilities. Energy merchants act as intermediaries that physically move power along the grid for wholesale producers and consumers of energy. These merchant power producers sell their capacity on wholesale electricity markets, and in effect, function as traders. They have no obligation to serve native load, and can turn off equipment if market conditions warrant it. Merchant power players offer both physical power delivery and financial intermediation such as fixed price deals. They bear the price risk that now exists in the electric power industry and have trading desks, as they act as market makers in the delivery of power and gas. Much of this capacity is gas-fired leading to problems of gas supply delivered to new plants. In effect, gas production is not meeting rising demand.

Energy merchants trade around physical assets. In today's power markets, longer-dated deals are more risky unless they are tied to actual production from physical power generation. The majority of transactions still remain short-term. The problem is that long-dated contracts in illiquid markets have more risk; therefore, energy merchants favor portfolios of shorter duration.

The present day electricity trading markets are still oriented toward the physical delivery of the commodity, not the financial risk management of that commodity. The fundamental weaknesses in the electricity commodity markets will not go away soon. Some of these weaknesses are transmission bottlenecks, sensitivity to weather-related demand surges, the regional nature of the electricity markets, NIMBY (Not In My Back Yard) resistance to siting in urban areas, incomplete deregulation and growing demand. Power is moved (and will eventually be traded) in regional markets in much of the world.

Electricity as a commodity has unique factors that make it hard to trade. One is its lack of storage capability. The inability to store the commodity leads to price spikes when demand outstrips supply. The lack of viable price risk management tools has severe impacts on those end-users that are short of capacity. The markets will continue to be volatile with little willingness on the part of market makers to take the price risk of markets that can spike as high as $10,000 per megawatt hour. This price volatility is not easily managed, no matter how sophisticated the financial modeling has been. Forward price curve development today has been predicated on financial modeling; in effect, mark to model to create forward prices.

The complexity of the electric power markets makes electricity risk management more difficult than in oil and gas. Some of these obstacles to commoditization involve the physical qualities of electricity in that it can't be stored, and its transmission is on system-constrained networks. In recent years, there has been continued increasing load versus less capacity additions and there is a need to alleviate transmission bottlenecks through new capacity additions to make the transmission system more reliable. On the financial side, electricity continues to exhibit unprecedented and almost unpredictable price volatility due to its physical characteristics. Added to this equation are the complexity of fuel inputs to manufacture the commodity and vast influence of weather on its demand. Because of these factors, electricity has become a physically traded commodity that has evolved into a robust and functioning market.

Its commodity price risk has hardly evolved at all since 1993. The market has devolved into a short-term hourly, day-ahead and weekly market in most of the world. Long-term deals are too risky to credit issues and financial performance by counterparties. The long-term market is still stuck in one-off deals that create no liquidity. Markets don't like complexity; it is the replication of trading that creates standardized contracts and trading liquidity. Regulating an immature market will take away none of these financial problems. It will probably move the process backward to fuel adjustment clauses at electric utilities where fuel costs were passed through to consumers that is, a passive hedge. It will also create a disincentive to merchant power producers, who now are building over three quarters of new capacity additions. Market-based rates in recent years have been one of the incentive for additions to generation capacity. The movement to day-ahead and hourly trading is helpful as these indexes are used to price power in the physical markets. The emergence of the Intercontinental Exchange, with its many market makers, may provide viability for the paper trading of electricity power. The major finding is that electric power has not evolved like oil and gas trading which are now mature, liquid fungible commodities. Electric power is not. The market needs to be monitored more stringently by regulatory agencies and more voluntary financial disclosure must be forthcoming as requested by these agencies in order to become more transparent. Disincentives do not create markets.

The Asian power markets that need to be watched are Japan and Korea, which will both begin trading in April 2005. Their market maturation may be quite slow due to the lack of many competitors in each electric power market.

In conclusion, anyone who thinks the number of energy derivatives can be counted on the fingers of two hands should think again. Table 2.3 highlight some of the more liquid energy derivatives that are actively traded in Asia. It's a non-exhaustive listing since many more OTC contracts are created on almost a weekly basis.

Table 2.3 Actively traded energy derivatives

	Derivative contract	Unit measurement	Pricing link	Common usage
1	WTI 1st line swap	USD/bbl	NYMEX linked pricing	Global crude
2	WTI bullet swap	USD/bbl	NYMEX linked pricing	Global crude
3	Brent 1st line swap	USD/bbl	IPE Linked pricing	Global crude
4	Brent bullet swap	USD/bbl	IPE Linked pricing	Global crude
5	Dubai 1st line swap	USD/bbl	PLATTS linked pricing	Asia crude imports
6	Tapis 1st line swap	USD/bbl	http://www.gvsi.com/press_releases/pr-APPIfinal.htm	Asia crude imports
7	WTI bullet/Brent bullet	USD/bbl	NYMEX linked pricing	Crude export arbitrage between Europe/West Africa and USA
8	WTI 1st line/Brent 1st line swap	USD/bbl	NYMEX linked pricing	Crude export arbitrage between Europe/West Africa and USA
9	Brent 1st line/Dubai 1st line swap	USD/bbl	IPE Linked pricing	Hedging West African Crudes routed to Asia
10	Dated/Brent 1st line swap	USD/bbl	PLATTS/IPE	Hedging basis risk between dated Brent and IPE Brent futures
11	Tapis 1st line/Brent 1st line swap	USD/bbl	APPI/PLATTS	Locking in Tapis versus Brent level – moving price exposure to Brent a more liquid contract
12	Tapis 1st line/Dubai 1st line swap	USD/bbl	APPI/PLATTS	Locking in Economics of Tapis crude use versus Dubai related crudes
13	0.5% Sulphur Singapore Gas Oil swap	USD/bbl	PLATTS	Hedging Asian gas oil prices
14	IPE Gas oil 1st line swap	USD/mt	IPE Linked pricing	Whole month average of IPE gas oil front line – hedging trading European gas oil

Continued

Table 2.3 Continued

	Derivative contract	Unit measurement	Pricing link	Common usage
15	0.5% Sing/Dubai 1st line swap	USD/bbl	PLATTS/PLATTS	Hedging refinery margin in middle distillates using Dubai related crudes
16	0.05% Singapore Gas oil Platts Swaps	USD/bbl	PLATTS	Hedging low sulphur gas oil in Asia (market developing)
17	0.5 Singapore Gas oil /GO 1st line swap	USD/mt	PLATTS/IPE GAS OIL FUTURES	Transfer or lock in spread risk between Singapore gas oil and IPE gas oil futures
18	180cst Sing Fuel Oil swap	USD/mt	PLATTS	Hedge Asia fuel oil markets
19	3.5% MED FOB Cargo/3.5% Rdam Barges swap	USD/mt	PLATTS	Hedge 3.5% Mediterranean free on board (fob) versus Rotterdam market
20	180cst Singapore Fuel Oil Caroges/ 3.5% Rotterdam Fuel Barges swap	USD/mt	PLATTS	Lock in/transfer price risk from Singapore fuel oil to 3.5% European market
21	180cst Singapore Fuel Oil /Dubai Crude 1st line swap	USD/bbl	PLATTS	Hedge/trade Asian refinery margin for fuel oil
22	Singapore Jet Kerosene swap	USD/bbl	PLATTS	Hedge Asian jet fuel/kero prices
23	Singapore Regrade swap (The spread between Jet Kerosene and Gas oil)	USD/bbl	PLATTS	Hedge price spread between gas oil and jet fuel
24	Naphtha Singapore FOB Cargo swap	USD/bbl	PLATTS	Hedge naphtha across Asia pacific region including Japan
25	Naphtha Singapore FOB Cargo/ Dubai 1st line	USD/bbl	PLATTS/PLATTS	Hedge refinery margin between naphtha and Dubai related crudes
26	Naphtha NWE CIF Cargo/ Brent 1st line swap	USD/bbl	PLATTS/IPE BRENT FUTURES	Hedge refinery margin between naphtha and Brent related crudes
27	LPG Swaps Europe – Propane swaps against BP index	Europe		Liquid petroleum gas hedge for Middle East & Asia region

28	LPG Mid East/North Africa/Asia – Saudi CP Pricing used as Index for OTC Swaps	Mid East	SAUDI CP	Liquid petroleum gas hedge for Middle East & Asia region
29	JCC Crude Basket Swaps (JAPAN)	USD/bbl or Yen/Kl	JCC	Hedging long term (5 to 10 year forward) LNG exposures
Oil Futures Relevant to Asia				
30	IPE Brent Crude Futures www.ipe.uk.com	USD/Barrel		
31	IPE Gas oil Futures www.ipe.uk.com	USD/Barrel		
32	NYMEX West Texas Intermediate crude oil futures www.nymex.com	USD/Barrel		
33	TOCOM Tokyo Middle East Crude Oil Futures www.tocom.or.jp	Yen		
34	TOCOM Kerosene Futures domestic market Japan www.tocom.or.jp	Yen		
35	TOCOM Gasoline Futures domestic market Japan www.tocom.or.jp	Yen		
36	Singapore Exchange (SGX) MECO Middle East Crude Oil Futures contract www.sgx.com	USD/Barrel		
37	Shanghai Fuel Oil Futures contract	Yuan/MT	10 MT per contract, fuel Oil, 180CST, 3.5% sulphur	
FREIGHT SWAPS (www.ginga.com.sg and www.imarex.com)				
38	Singapore to Japan freight swaps – up to at least 1 year forward		Platts and other reference	Hedge freight exposure on import routes to Asia

Continued

Table 2.3 Continued

	Derivative contract	Unit measurement	Pricing link	Common usage
39	Arab Gulf to Japan LR1 – over 1 year forward traded in swaps		Platts and other reference	Hedge freight exposure on import routes to Asia
40	Arab Gulf to Japan VLCC – over 1 year forward traded in swaps		Platts and other reference	Hedge freight exposure on import routes to Asia
	Petrochemical swaps			
41	Ethylene Europe	USD/MT	ICIS LOR Pricing	
42	Ethylene Singapore (www.ginga.com.sg)	USD/MT	www.icislor.com	
43	Benzene	USD/MT	also swaps priced	
44	Xylene	USD/MT	against the Platts prices also available www.platts.com	

CHAPTER 3

Energy Futures Exchanges and OTC Trading

Energy trading began after the end of the Official Selling Price (OSP) programs by the major oil companies and OPEC nations after the 1973 Oil Embargo and coincided with the development of a spot market for crude oil and petroleum products. In 1978, the changing structure of the physical spot market for oil brought about the development and launch of a successful oil futures contract for home heating oil on the 132-year-old NYMEX which was tied to physical delivery of the oil in New York Harbor. Successive oil futures contract and the development of an active and viable OTC market for forward oil trading in the 1980s brought significant structural changes to the global oil industry. Oil had become a commodity. In effect, price transparency accelerated both the physical and financial trading of crude oil and petroleum products on an international scale.

Asia, however, has been a nascent and emerging oil futures and OTC market. Its exchanges have been slow to react to the changes underway in the physical oil world in Asia. Asia is driving world oil markets today but its energy risk management infrastructure barely exists compared to New York and London. Therefore, this chapter examines both New York's NYMEX and London's IPE as well as the smaller Asian oil futures exchanges. The NYMEX and IPE are the two most successful energy futures exchanges in the world. Their characteristics and functions will be discussed in this chapter.

Futures exchanges guarantee financial performance. Futures and options contract performance are supported by strong financial systems that are backed by the exchange's clearing members. Some of these members include oil companies such as BP, ChevronTexaco, Totalfinaelf, Statoil, ExxonMobil, and others. Other members are financial institutions such as Morgan Stanley, BNP Paribas, Goldman Sachs's J Aron trading arm, UBS, Deutsche Bank, JP Morgan Chase, ABN Amro, and Clarion Bank (merger of Credit Lyonnais and IndoSuez) to name a few. The performance of both NYMEX and IPE are not only backed by the financial performance of its members but protected by the financial standards and surveillance procedures regulated by the federal governments of the United States and United Kingdom respectively. Financial law is well developed in this area. This is lacking in Asia at the present time and is just starting to develop.

Futures exchanges have some common elements. The first is they offer standardized contracts for certain volumes of the commodity. In oil markets, they are for 1000 barrels of oil for NYMEX's West Texas Intermediate (WTI) crude oil and IPE Brent crude oil, and for 42,000 gallons for No. 2 heating oil and gasoline that are traded on the NYMEX. The IPE gas oil contract is traded in lots of 100 metric tonnes relating to the characteristics of the physical market. Futures contracts have the option of physical delivery of the commodity at the contract expiration date. Deliveries of most futures contracts represent only a very small share of the trading volume, less than 1% in the case of energy. Energy futures contracts should be looked at as a financial hedge and not a contract for physical supply of the commodity.

Futures contracts are firm commitments to make or accept delivery of a specified quantity and quality of a commodity during a specific month in the futures at an agreed upon price for delivery of the underlying commodity. The buyer of the commodity energy contract agrees to take delivery of the underlying commodity and is known as the short. Prices of the physical and cash markets converge at contract expiry which occurs once a month.

Most market participants choose to buy or sell their physical oil or gas supplies through their existing supply channels and use futures and options to manage their price risk. A futures contract does not have to have a physical delivery component and can be entirely "cash settled" although most energy futures contracts still rely heavily on physical delivery mechanisms. This is changing though due to the growth of electronic trading which is being used more as a financial hedge. While a small number of oil futures contracts goes for physical delivery, most oil traders offset their futures positions before the contract matures at expiry. This means that the buyer will sell his futures contract and the seller will buy back the contract. The difference between the initial purchase or sale price and the price of the offsetting transactions represent the profit or loss of the transaction.

Futures contacts are traded in very visible competitive market that have open auctions (called open outcry) which offer price discovery. In oil trading, futures prices are quoted for products with precise specifications delivered to a specified point during a specified time period. Both the NYMEX and IPE offer an anonymous auction where information is disseminated widely and instantaneously through electronic media. Future prices often serve as world reference prices for actual transaction of physical oil traded.

The oil futures markets were set up to enable traders to offset some of their risk by taking hedging positions or taking the opposite futures position than the physical position in the oil markets. The simplest explanation of these futures positions would be for a trader to buy a physical cargo of crude oil and then sell the futures contracts to protect against a fall in prices before the cargo is resold in the physical market.

Oil futures markets have become fully integrated with the rest of the world oil markets although many oil producers still do not participate in futures markets. Oil futures prices determine physical world oil market prices today rather than OPEC.

NYMEX

NYMEX is the world's largest physical commodity futures exchange and the preeminent trading forum for energy and precious metals. Transactions executed on NYMEX avoid the risk of counterparty default because the Exchange clearinghouse acts as the counterparty to every trade. Trading is conducted through two divisions, the NYMEX Division, home to the energy, platinum, and palladium markets; and the COMEX Division, on which all other metals trade. NYMEX pioneered the development of energy futures and options contracts 26 years ago as a means of bringing price transparency and risk management to this vital market. NYMEX trades energy futures contracts including crude oil, natural gas, electric power, coal, propane, home heating oil, and gasoline.

Crude oil is the world's most actively traded commodity, and the NYMEX Division's light, sweet crude oil futures contract is the world's most liquid forum for crude oil trading, as well as the world's largest-volume futures contract trading on a physical commodity. Because of its excellent liquidity and price transparency, the contract is used as a principal international pricing benchmark. Additional risk management and trading opportunities are offered through options on the futures contract, calendar spread options, crack spread options on the pricing differential of heating oil futures, and crude oil futures and gasoline futures and crude oil futures, and average price options.

The contract trades in units of 1000 bbls, and the delivery point is Cushing, Oklahoma, which is also accessible to the international spot markets via pipelines. The contract provides for delivery of several grades of domestic and internationally traded foreign crudes, and serves the diverse needs of the physical market.

NYMEX launched its highly successful natural gas futures contact in April 1990. Natural gas accounts for almost a quarter of US energy consumption, and the NYMEX Division's natural gas futures contract is widely used as a national benchmark price. The futures contract trades in units of 10,000 million British thermal units (mBtu). The price is based on delivery at the Henry Hub in Louisiana, the nexus of 16 intra- and interstate natural gas pipeline systems that draw supplies from the region's prolific gas deposits. The pipelines serve markets throughout the US East Coast, the Gulf Coast, the Midwest, and up to the Canadian border. An options contract and calendar spread options contracts provide additional risk management opportunities. The spread between natural gas futures and electricity futures – the spark spread – can be used to manage price risk in the power markets.

Because of the volatility of natural gas prices, a vigorous basis market has developed in the pricing relationships between Henry Hub and other important natural gas market centers in the continental United States and Canada. NYMEX makes available for trading a series of basis swap futures contracts that are quoted as price differentials between approximately 30 natural gas pricing points and Henry Hub. The basis contracts trade in units of 2500 mBtu on the NYMEX ClearPort^{sm} trading platform. Transactions can also be consummated off-Exchange and submitted to the Exchange for clearing via the NYMEX ClearPort clearing website as an exchange of futures for physicals or exchange of futures for swaps transaction

Heating oil, also known as No. 2 fuel oil, accounts for about 25% of the yield of a barrel of crude, the second largest "cut" after gasoline. The heating oil futures contract trades in units of 42,000 gallons (1000 bbls) and is based on delivery in New York harbor, the principal cash market trading center. Options on futures, calendar spread options contracts, crack spread options contracts, and average price options contracts give market participants even greater flexibility in managing price risk. The heating oil futures contract is also used to hedge diesel fuel and jet fuel, both of which trade in the cash market at an often stable premium to New York harbor heating oil futures.

Gasoline is the largest single volume refined product sold in the United States and accounts for over 40% of national oil consumption. It is a highly diverse market, with hundreds of wholesale distributors and thousands of retail outlets, often making it subject to intense competition and price volatility. The New York harbor gasoline futures contract trades in units of 42,000 gallons (1000 bbls). It is based on delivery at petroleum products terminals in the harbor, the major East Coast trading center for imports and domestic shipments from refineries in the New York harbor area or from the Gulf Coast refining centers.

The competitive electricity market has developed through structural changes in the power industry that have evolved in recent years, resulting in opportunities, price volatility, and market risk. The PJM Interconnection, LLC, administers the largest electricity market in the world serving more than 25 million customers in Delaware, Maryland, New Jersey, Ohio,

Pennsylvania, Virginia, West Virginia, and Washington, DC The power companies within PJM operate approximately 700 generating units, representing more than 70,000 mW of capacity, fueled with natural gas, oil, coal, nuclear, and hydro power. This generating and distribution network is also tied to the power grids of the Midwest, New York State, and other areas in the mid-Atlantic states. Electricity lends itself to futures trading. It meets the three broad criteria needed for successful futures markets: prices are volatile; there is a large, diverse universe of buyers and sellers; and the physical product is fungible. The NYMEX clearinghouse provides a system of guarantees that mitigates counterparty credit risk.

NYMEX provides a financially settled (not physically delivered) monthly futures contract for on-peak electricity transactions based on the daily floating price for each peak day of the month at the PJM western hub. The PJM western hub consists of 111 delivery points, primarily on the Pennsylvania Electric Co. and the Potomac Electric Co. utility transmission systems. Additional risk management and trading opportunities are offered through options on the PJM monthly futures contract.

Propane is a by-product of natural gas processing and oil refining. US demand is approximately one-third that of heating oil. Propane is used in diverse markets: residential cooking, crop-drying in agriculture, space heating in homes and industry, and as a feedstock for the production of vital petrochemicals. Natural gas utilities often store propane for use during periods of peak demand. The propane futures contract trades in units of 42,000 gallons (1000 bbls). It provides an effective pricing and risk management tool for the gas liquids sector of the energy industry. The contract is a natural complement to the NYMEX Division crude oil, heating oil, gasoline, and natural gas futures contracts.

Coal is the principal fuel for generating electricity in the United States, accounting for approximately 55% of total electricity output. The United States has more high-quality coal than any other country, with nearly 30% of the world's bituminous and anthracite coal reserves. The United States is one of the largest coal producers in world and US exports make up a significant share of the world export market. The coal futures contract trades in units of 1550 tons. It is available for trading nearly around the clock on the NYMEX ClearPort trading platform, and off-Exchange transactions can be submitted for clearing through the NYMEX ClearPort clearing website. The coal futures contract can provide both the coal mining and electric power industries with a range of risk management strategies.

NYMEX also clears OTC trades for market participants who wish to avoid counterparty credit risk by using standardized contracts for natural gas, crude oil, refined products, and electricity. By clearing OTC energy contracts through ClearPort, NYMEX provides guaranteed financial performance. In effect, these contracts become quasi-futures contract since they are cleared on the exchange.

The Exchange also lists e-miNY energy futures^{sm}, fractional light, sweet crude oil, and natural gas futures contracts that offer smaller investors and traders the opportunity for an efficient means of participating in energy markets. The contracts trade via the Chicago Mercantile Exchange's GLOBEX® electronic trading system and clear through the NYMEX clearinghouse.

The close of the open outcry session on the trading floor does not postpone the potential for risk in the energy and metals markets until the next morning. NYMEX ACCESS® allows participants to protect themselves from that exposure as the energy futures markets are available for trading for another 17 hours through the internet-based NYMEX ACCESS electronic trading system. With NYMEX ACCESS, the exchange is open virtually around the clock. The system operates via the Internet, so traders can log on from any internet-enabled computer almost anywhere in the world.

NYMEX ACCESS trading opens at 3:15 pm New York Time, Mondays through Thursdays and runs as late as 9:30 am the next morning, depending on the contract. Sunday evening sessions open at 7 pm NYMEX ACCESS trades are executed on the basis of price and time with total anonymity and absolute fairness. The first order in at the best price is the first executed. NYMEX ACCESS offers enhanced views of the market at any given time, and gives traders unparalleled flexibility in executing trading strategies.

Today, NYMEX is actively interested in growing its energy futures business in Asia for oil and gas trading. It is developing relationships with both the Singapore Exchange and Tocom to clear oil and gas products in Asia.

IPE/ICE

The London-based International Petroleum Exchange (IPE) was acquired by the Intercontinental Exchange (ICE) in June 2001. The IPE was founded by a group of energy and futures companies in 1980. The IPE trades crude oil, gas oil, and natural gas futures contracts.

The first futures contract, for gas oil, was launched the following year. In June 1988, the IPE successfully launched Brent crude oil futures. Volumes rapidly took off, and the exchange has experienced incremental growth, year-on-year for almost its entire history. New trading instruments such as swaps, futures, and options have grown up. Since its inception crude oil futures and latterly options have been traded in pits on the market floor using the open outcry system. As business volumes have grown the IPE has moved location several times to accommodate new pits and increasing number of traders.

In 1997 the IPE began trading its first non-oil contract with the launch of the IPE natural gas futures. These contracts were launched on the IPE's Electronic Trading Platform (IPE ETS). This platform has been further enhanced since its first launch and now also provides the medium for parallel trading of oil contracts. IPE gas oil options equip IPE market participants with the tools to carry out a range of sophisticated and highly efficient price risk management strategies, with the security and transparency of a regulated trading exchange. On the back of its success with futures contracts the IPE launched the gas oil options contracts in July 1987. The contract is based on the underlying futures and if exercised will result in a corresponding futures position and is for American style exercise, allowing the buyer to exercise an option any time up to, and including the expiry day.

The IPE launched a natural gas futures contract in January 1997. It is used primarily to manage price risk in the underlying physical natural gas market and to effect physical delivery into the UK gas grid. The contract also allows users to separate/reference the price element within a long-term physical gas contract. The natural gas contract results in physical delivery only if position(s) are not closed out prior to expiry. Physical delivery takes place within the UK natural gas grid at the National Balancing Point (NBP). Delivery must be made equally throughout the delivery period and equivalent to the number of lots open at the time of expiry.

IPE crude oil and gas oil futures and options contracts and IPE natural gas futures contracts are traded electronically on the ICE platform using either WebICE the ICE's proprietary Internet based trading front end, or Independent Software Vendors (ISVs). WebICE is a fully functional browser-based front-end to the ICE electronic trading platform, it provides instant access to the IPE markets through a web browser using industry standard data security and encryption technology.

IPE has recently become more active in Asia once again. It is known that electronic trading growth on the ICE has come from Asia. It will be interesting to see how both exchanges gain momentum in the vast Asia Pacific energy region. Since the energy commodities are the most volatile of all commodities and Asia is the growth region for oil and gas consumption, it seems likely that Internet trading will grow exponentially both on- and off-exchange in the region.

SHANGHAI FUTURES EXCHANGE

The last time a futures contract operated in China was when The Shanghai Futures Exchange (SHFE) ran a fuel oil futures contract from 1993 until 1995, when it was finally delisted as part of a drive by the Chinese government against extreme financial market speculation.

However, the last time an internationally utilized liquid fuel oil futures contract was traded in Asia was the SIMEX Fuel Oil Futures contract which actively traded from 1989 to around 1992. This contract was eventually delisted. There seemed little support from the energy industry to the futures contract that competed with an increasing and dynamic Singapore Platts pricing related OTC Swaps market.

That was until August 25, 2004, when the SHFE was launched. China's fledging fuel oil futures market appears to have taken off and looks like it will offer traders selling fuel oil in one of the fastest growing economies in the world, an opportunity to hedge. I think it is fair to expect in 2005/2006 an OTC market to develop indexed against this futures contract. Adding further liquidity to the futures contract as OTC market makers re-hedge their positions in to the Shanghai futures market. One criticism of the Shanghai futures contracts is its small contract size (in terms of tonnage per futures contract), and this may spark the development of an OTC market which meets the contract specification and currency needs of the international trading community. It merits close attention.

A combination of soaring crude oil prices and complex regulations governing specifications and physical delivery arrangements have proved a barrier to most traders involved in the fuel oil physical market.

As the contracts' quality standards are stricter than the active OTC Platts-related 180 cst fuel oil swaps, in terms of density, carbon residue, and other specifications, the amount of fuel oil available for physical delivery is limited and this puts a strain on the strength of the underlying contract.

Exchange officials were unavailable to give formal comment on the question of specifications, delivery, or volumes. Sources close to the exchange argue that the regulations are necessary and correct. They say the top priority for the exchange is not the trading volume, but the steady and healthy development of the futures market. At the time of writing this book, China's largest crude importer, said some companies want to wait till January 2005 to see if there is any problem in physical delivery before plunging into the market. In the meantime, majority of international and Chinese traders are continuing to use the Singapore paper market as their major hedging tool.

When fuel oil futures were launched, the fuel oil front month contract was five-months forward, compared with one-month for other futures contracts, as the Shanghai Exchange hoped to give the market plenty of time to get familiar with the new tool. This is probably a key reason why physical traders had been reluctant to trade the January 2005 contract, which was the front month contact as of August 2004. The Shanghai fuel oil futures market still needs more liquidity, which in turn should increase its price correlation and reliability with real local physical market fundamentals. It is too early to promote it as a key hedging instrument, but also too early to write it off as another failed oil futures contract in Asia.

I think this judgment can only be made at the end of 2005 at the earliest. Risk Managers selecting appropriate derivative markets should monitor open interest, trading volume and price correlation with local fuel oil markets on an ongoing basis and start using this contract when price correlation with local markets is within the IAS 39 derivative accounting requirements that is, more than 75% correlation.

Another problem facing futures trading in China is that foreign companies are banned from the market. It is not clear just when that might change – officials at the Shanghai Exchange were unable to comment on the question – but a source close to the Exchange said no specific timetable is being considered yet.

Thriving domestic futures market expected

Some players are using the Singapore paper market to hedge against the risk in spot market trading. But this hedging tool is far from perfect thanks to foreign exchange risk and price inconsistency between the Singapore market and the domestic Chinese market. Out of all the trading volume in the Singapore paper fuel oil market, nearly a third is associated with Chinese companies thanks to the continuously increasing demand from China. Even so, China allows only a few designated state-owned oil companies to enter the Singapore physical and paper market. These include Sinochem Corp., Unipec, China National United Oil Corp., or Chinaoil, a unit of PetroChina Co.

Physical players are keen to been able to use a thriving domestic futures market, but many traders and brokers feel it will take more time before the Shanghai exchange can claim success.

Limits on participation

There are relatively few players in the new market. Of the 225 members of SHFE, only 11 members are associated with fuel oil production or consumption, while the bulk are futures brokers (As of November 2004). Foreigners are barred from trading, unlike China's stock markets, which were opened to foreign investors in 2003 via the Qualified Foreign Institutional Investors scheme.

But equally, or more important, is the fact that many domestic institutional investors are not free to trade. Under current laws, futures funds are prohibited and futures brokers are not allowed to trade for their own account, and this lack of market makers has seriously hindered the SHFE's efforts to kick off liquidity. As seen in Western markets on the IPE and the NYMEX, speculators like these contribute large percentages of the daily turnover and help create liquid two-way markets.

Due to such restrictions, retail investors dominate. In China, nearly 80% investors in its futures markets are retail investors, quite unlike what happens in more developed financial markets. Not the basis for a strong commercial hedging tool!

Maybe things will change in time, and there are positive signs that the Department of Futures Supervision of China Securities Regulatory

Commission, the watchdog for futures markets, is examining whether and how foreign institutions might enter domestic futures trade. Only then could we see a swaps market based off the Shanghai Futures Markets contract develop for foreign traders with prices in dollars.

APPENDIX: STANDARD CONTRACT OF FUEL OIL OF SHFE AS OF DECEMBER 2004

Underlined product	Fuel oil
Trading unit	10 tonnes/lot
Quotation unit	Yuan (RMB)/tonne
Tick size	1 Yuan/tonne
Daily price limit	(±5% of the settlement price of the previous business day
Contract months	Jan. to Dec. (Except the Spring Festival)
Trading hours	9:00–11:30am and 1:30–3:00pm
Last trading day	The last trading day of the month before the spot month
Delivery period	Five consecutive business days after the last trading day
Delivery grades	Fuel oil, 180CST or higher standard (refer to the Attachment for detailed quality requirement)
Delivery sites	Designated by the Exchange
Minimum margins	8% of the contract value
Transaction fee	No more than 0.2% of the trading value (including reserve for risks)
Delivery method	Physical delivery
Symbol	FU
Listing exchange	Shanghai Futures Exchange

The attachment of SHFE standard contracts of fuel oil

1. Delivery unit The delivery unit of Fuel Oil prescribed in the standard contract is 10 lots (100 tonnes). And the delivery quantity shall be integral times of delivery unit.

2. Prescription of quality Quality standard of fuel oil of SHFE

Physical and chemical properties	Limit	Test method
Density (15°C, kg/l)	Maximum 0.985	ASTM D1298
Kinematic viscocity (50°C, CST)	Maximum 180	ASTM D445
Ash on weight Basis (m/m, %)	Maximum 0.10	ASTM D482
Couradson carbon residue (m/m, %)	Maximum 14	ASTM D189
Pour point (°C)	Maximum 24	ASTM D97
Water by distillation volume (V/V, %)	Maximum 0.5	ASTM D95
Flash point (°C)	Maximum 66	ASTM D93
Sulfur (m/m, %)	Maximum 3.5	ASTM D4294/D1552
Total existent sediment (m/m, %)	Maximum 0.10	ASTM D4870
Vanadium (PPM)	Maximum 150	ICP

3. The designated oil depots Designated and announced by the Exchange separately.

For more details and latest information please refer to the website of the Shanghai Futures Exchange – www.shfe.com.cn

OTC MARKETS WILL CONVERGE WITH ON-EXCHANGE FUTURES IN ASIA

In Asia the OTC market growth is only limited by trader's creativity and credit risk limits! If you are trading OTC, traditionally you take the credit risk of the other company, the other counterparty, you have traded with.

We have already experienced in America since early 2004, and now in Europe since October 2004, the NYMEX exchange (www.nymex.com) enabling the convergence of the OTC markets, such as Platts' (www.platts.com) related Swaps markets with the on-exchange and cleared futures contracts. Its platform is called "ClearPort" ((TM) NYMEX exchange).

It is just a matter of time before the new clearing platforms for OTC contracts come to the Asian energy markets, easing entry to the markets for new participants in the OTC derivatives markets, doing away with years of ISDA negotiations, and doing away with big credit line headaches, and bids above the offers and offers below the bids, just to attract people to take that extra direct counterparty credit risk with their company.

In the film "Field of Dreams" the central character builds a baseball field in his farm and attracts famous players to play a match, with the catch-phrase "build it and they will come." A similar phenomenon is occurring in the OTC energy derivatives markets. The futures exchanges have started to build common clearing and margining platforms for OTC commodity derivatives to compliment their existing on-exchange futures contracts, and the global trading community is now actively responding. This new clearing platform is creating a revolution in the fund management industry and the commodity markets are at the top of the funds' agenda. This is a positive sign for any company looking to hedge in energy derivatives. Hedge funds and speculators add liquidity. It is fair to say that generally speaking this extra money flow in the energy derivatives markets around the world could equal increased price volatility, but remember speculators don't make price trends, they follow and look out for trends. "The trend is your friend," as the old oil market motto goes.

Convergence is the key to the continued growth of the markets. The removal of the Credit Risk equation. This convergence was made possible by the fact that the energy had by the late 1990s standardized key contract terms of around 80% of OTC trades, making them ideally suited to the electronic trading medium and in turn a clearing platform alongside futures contracts.

Indeed the only significant difference between the standardized OTC contracts and the futures contracts was clearing and the mitigation of counterpart credit risk, which had been available to on-exchange futures contracts for several decades. But it was not until the well-publicized implosion of Enron in December 2001, and its impact on credit risk perceptions, that the clearing issue gained more prominence.

Enron also had another positive consequence for fund activities, and also for NYMEX. The success of Enron's electronic OTC trading platform – EnronOnline – identified the opportunity for a bilateral electronic platform providing OTC clearing. This led to the development of NYMEX ClearPort, which provides the opportunity to trade OTC swaps on literally hundreds of energy contracts globally with other counterparts. The main benefit of NYMEX ClearPort is its OTC clearing, which provides a key and major benefit for funds as it not only reduces regulatory and reporting risks, it also provides the funds with an end of day cleared position. As such these OTC contracts are in effect "quasi-futures" contracts with the risk managed and marked-to-market by NYMEX. This in turn provides investors with transparency and security, and regulated traders can trade these contracts as they become "futures" contracts, while funds can get prime brokers (who often provide key credit liquidity and leverage) to clear all their futures contracts in one single netted account. The OTC energy derivatives market has been opened for business. No longer is it the private trading ground of banks with large balance sheets and credit ratings!

There is a further revolution in commodity trading as a result of NYMEX ClearPort (www.nymex.com) and that is the reduction and simplification of documentation. To trade a number of OTC derivatives would normally require individual Master Agreements for each trading counterpart, and schedules to these agreements for each derivative product. This process can often take six months or more to set up (for each counterpart) and counterparts would not even get that far in discussions unless they could accept each other's balance sheet and credit worthiness. With NYMEX ClearPort there is no need for multiple-documentation as NYMEX acts as the central counterpart to all trades on ClearPort, opening up hundreds of OTC commodity products to new market participants.

NYMEX guarantees reduced legal costs, speed of entry to new market participants, reduced overall hedging costs through better access to more market makers that is more bids/offers as counterparts, and no need to be worried about credit.

Specific information on terms and conditions of this facility can be obtained from your Futures Clearing Merchant (FCM).

TOCOM – TOKYO COMMODITY EXCHANGE

The Tokyo Commodity Exchange (TOCOM) was formed on November 1, 1984, through the integration of the Tokyo Textile Exchange, the Tokyo Rubber Exchange, and the Tokyo Gold Exchange, in order to establish a comprehensive commodity exchange in Japan. Thanks to the continued support and cooperation of the exchange's membership and others concerned, and with careful guidance from the competent authorities, TOCOM has achieved significant progress over the past two decades. In 2004 it celebrated its twentieth anniversary and is considered the largest futures exchange in Japan, and world's second largest commodity futures exchange.

TOCOM lists 10 commodities: crude oil, gasoline, kerosene, gas oil, gold, silver, platinum, palladium, aluminum, and rubber futures contracts. The 2003 annual trading volume exceeded 87 million contracts, setting a new record for the sixth consecutive year.

The change and development of the past two decades have made a significant mark on the history of TOCOM, and of commodity futures industry in Japan. In the course of these 20 years, TOCOM has succeeded in listing gasoline, kerosene, and crude oil, among other contracts, on the back of deregulation in the oil sector. The oil market today occupies a key position among TOCOM's mainstay markets, alongside precious metals.

In June 2003, TOCOM also became the first commodity exchange in Japan to establish an in-house clearinghouse, which further enhanced its market reliability and attractiveness to professional foreign investors and traders looking for hedging instruments.

On November 4, 2003, The IPE, Europe's leading energy futures and options exchange, and The TOCOM, Asia's leading commodity futures market announced that they have entered into a Memorandum of Understanding (MOU).

Under the terms of the MOU, both parties will cooperate with a view to helping the other party to:

- Make available trading in financial instruments traded on each exchange via computer terminals in the country of the other party;
- Secure the appropriate regulatory approvals from the UK and Japanese authorities;
- Explore mechanisms which will enhance the liquidity, efficiency, and integrity of each market; and
- Discuss areas of cooperation, including new business opportunities or developments when they arise.

Then on July 13, 2004, The NYMEX, Inc., and the TOCOM announced that energy and metals futures contracts would become available for NYMEX ACCESS, internet-based trading in Japan on July 20, 2004.

When the oil contracts such as Gasoline were first launched in Tokyo, trading houses such as Mitsui, Marubeni, Sumitomo etc. were nowhere to be seen, trading volume was concentrated in the hands of small retail investors/traders. However times have changed and TOCOM's futures contracts have proven that oil futures can exist in Asia, (at least where a dynamic existing OTC market does not exist) since the demise of the Singapore Fuel Oil Futures contract *c.* 1993.

An established market that clearly serves the needs of the market will be difficult to replace with another new market place/mechanism that just serves nice to have ideals of some market participants.

This has been the downfall of failed futures contracts in energy across Asia for the past decade. TOCOM though has understood this, and now international traders and Japanese Shoga Shosha's are participating in the oil futures markets of Tokyo. See the website for contract specifications (www.tocom.org.uk) and remember that these futures are in Yen, but that an OTC market in US$/Barrel equivalent or Metric Tonne swaps is available from many bank market makers.

CHAPTER 4

Setting up Your Energy Derivatives Policy

If you buy or sell energy, at some point you will be at risk, so it makes sense to hedge. We are not talking about the kind of hedging that defends against volatility, because the single biggest fact of energy markets is that prices fluctuate wildly, and unexpectedly, particularly since the deregulation of markets. In order to monitor the effectiveness of energy derivatives properly and also to control their use within your organization it is important to set up a clear energy derivatives policy. Company shareholders are usually very demanding: on the one hand, they don't want companies to hedge away any of their upside profit potential, and on the other, they hate to see too much downside potential loss exposure. An energy consumer that implements a bad hedging strategy may end up paying high fixed prices for energy while its competitors pay lower spot prices. So how does a company choose the correct hedging strategy?

It is not easy. There are a huge number of options to consider, such as forward contracts with suppliers and derivative instruments to hedge price risk fluctuations. Options, swaps, collars, futures, and forwards are all techniques that must be investigated. To choose the right strategy, an energy consumer must carefully assess its current and potential risks.

Before designing and implementing a risk management program, senior management must perform a comprehensive review, or risk assessment, to determine all of the energy price risks facing the company. The risk assessment examines the company's operations and should determine how much of a particular energy risk a company either consumes or produces. The end result of the assessment is a report that clearly states the entire set of energy price risk exposures the company faces by energy type, location, volume, and price reference index. Using historical volatility data, the management can calculate a dollar amount that is at risk each year for the company. Many financial institutions like banks that are involved in energy price risk management can do a lot of this assessment/analysis work for end-users and producers. Once the assessment is complete, senior management and the board of directors can begin the process of establishing the firm's risk management policies and procedures.

In addition to the review of energy price risk exposures, the following important questions can help a company to collect key information that can assist in the creation of its policy for the use and application of energy derivatives.

1 What is your organization? A consumer, a producer, or a trader?
2 What products does the organization have price risk in?
   - Products
   - Fixed or floating price risks
3 Is your organization's aim hedging or trading? Which of these are you trying to do?
   - Mitigate a disaster risk scenario
   - Protect budgeted levels
   - Control overall price risk
   - Trade risk as speculator
4 Will you let traders speculate or only hedge?
5 What is your total volume of energy to hedge or how much do you wish to trade?
6 As a hedger, how much do you want or need to hedge?
   - When hedging look for upto 50% of exposure for general day-to-day hedging requirements.
   - Any hedging over 50% of consumption or production volume is speculative and should only be considered as rare case pre-emptive measures ahead of a "disaster scenario." This could be during protracted periods of extreme high prices (as a consumer) or extreme low prices as a producer of energy. Or it could be as opportunistic hedging when historically high profitability can be ensured by locking in low prices as a consumer or high returns as a producer.
      - One exception to this guideline is when as a consumer you have 100% of sales/income fixed (e.g. charter airline which has pre-sold all seats on flights and is exposed to the floating price of jet fuel).
      - Another example is if you are a trader buying a feedstock for your own refinery system, or you are buying power or gas for your company and you need to fix this cost so that other departments in

the organization can cost delivery of finished goods or products for customers.

- Normally end-users will hedge around 20–30% of volumes around budget levels up to 18-months forward, leaving an additional 20–30% (up to 50% total) for opportunistic hedging if levels come below budget levels.
- Also end-users should generally look to have another policy for hedging in times of extreme price moves, allowing the energy procurement department or the dedicated risk management departments to act quickly to protect the firm against extreme price moves that might be seen in times of war etc. For example, if you were an electricity consumer in the United States when power costs spiked to US$10,000 per mWh, you would have wanted to protect yourself before that happened perhaps by up to 100%. Or as an airline, as tension increased, you would have wanted to protect yourself ahead of the Gulf tension in the Iraq/Kuwait confrontation.

Answering all these previous questions will help an organization then look at the next step of putting together a risk management policy.

7 What types of derivatives should be used?

- Futures
- Options
  - OTC? On exchange ?
  - Can traders only buy options, or will they be allowed to sell options as well? (This can incur open exposures for companies if not as part of a larger structure. Also in some derivative disasters, the sale of options has been used to generate cash flow to cover up losses elsewhere in a portfolio.)
- Swaps

8 What tenures/how far forward can the organization utilize these derivatives?

- Normally, an organization should state in its risk management policy (as a hedger) or derivatives usage document (as a speculator) which derivative types can be used, in which markets they can be used and also how far forward each type of derivative contract (futures, options, swaps) can be utilized in each market (e.g. Singapore gas oil, Dubai crude, Brent, fuel oil Rotterdam).

9 Which derivatives markets to utilize

- *For hedgers:* this decision will be based on how well the available energy derivative markets correlate in terms of price (and also causation relationship) with the underlying energy markets that are to be hedged and in which the organization has price risk exposure.

Then, once a list of possible energy derivatives that match requirements is selected, an organization must then review this list with the contract liquidity in mind (checking with brokers on the average daily volume, normal bid/offer spread gap, number of active counterparts etc.). If liquidity is bad then an organization may have to consider a proxy hedge.

- *A proxy hedge example:* IPE Brent futures to hedge Middle East crude exposure. IPE Brent is not a Middle East crude contract, but it has high liquidity and has some price correlation relationship with Middle East crudes. This might be instead of using the OTC Dubai or Oman swaps which are much more closely linked with Middle East crude but price transparency and overall liquidity may not be good enough for some organizations.
- *For traders/speculators:* this decision will be based upon liquidity of the energy derivatives markets (volume and number of counterparts trading the market) and also the level of price transparency that exists. For a trader/speculator the lack of price transparency can be an attraction, whereas for a hedger, price transparency is more important than liquidity. Liquidity is more important for a trader since he/she will normally wish to trade out/close out a position ahead of its expiry/settlement. An organization hedging will normally let derivatives contracts run their full term through to expiry as it is hedging an underlying energy price risk. So, for a hedger, the ability to trade out/close out a derivatives position may be less of a concern. The price linkage between the derivative and the energy price risk being hedged may be more important to the hedger than the liquidity of the market.

10 How are operations departments going to manage these derivative positions?

- Will the organization require new IT infrastructure to process and manage these derivative positions?
- Does the organization have the relevant skill sets or will training be required prior to the start of this activity?
- How will these derivative positions be valued?
  - Valued against third party forward curve assessment for example, Platts Forward Curve or broker quotes/dealer quotes?
- How often will these derivative positions be valued?
  - Daily, weekly, monthly, quarterly?
- If a trader/speculator what position limits will we set?
  - Volumetric limits?
  - Notional value (NV) limits ?
  - Will the limits be set by tenure and product?
  - Which traders can trade what products and which types of derivatives can they trade?

- Who will be responsible for monitoring these positions and reporting any break in the organization's policy for derivatives usage?
- What reports will be produced to assist risk monitoring/performance function?
    - Open position reports
    - Market value reports
    - Profit + loss reports
    - Hedge effectiveness reports (correlation analysis between the derivatives used for hedging and the underlying energy risk being hedged)
- How often will these reports be produced?
- Who has to see these reports and sign them off as read?
- Prior to any activity starting, the organization must assess the operational risk of this new business, as well as credit risk, market risks, legal risks, tax risks etc. Who will be responsible for ensuring that there are ongoing regular reviews of these risks?

This is certainly not an exhaustive list but all of these questions can assist an organization's management to start looking at policy decisions and to put together a short paper on what they propose to let their risk managers and traders do. Accounts departments can also get a good idea of what type of accounting for derivatives will have to be handled, either as hedges or speculative trades (see Chapter 12 on Derivatives Wedge Accounting).

All the information from this short paper and feedback on it from the relevant line managers in the organization, should then be put together for presentation to the Board of Directors/Board of Management who should create a general policy and reporting structure for the organization. Line managers should then take this general policy and with reference to the Board's decision, fine-tune a more detailed risk management derivative usage guidebook for traders, operations, and managers. This operational document should be submitted again for approval by the Board of Directors.

CHAPTER 5

Energy Hedging with Derivatives – Applications

WHAT IS HEDGING?

Once the board has authorized and established policies and procedures for the risk management program, senior management must execute the strategy; in other words, they must start using energy derivatives to hedge. As touched upon in previous chapters, hedging is the process in which an organization with energy price risk takes a position in a derivative instrument (swaps, options, futures) that gives an equal and opposite financial exposure to the underlying physical position to protect against major adverse price changes. The volumetric price exposure of the derivatives hedging instrument should be equal and opposite to the price exposure of the physical energy commodity that the organization wishes to reduce its price risk exposure in. It is important for Board of Directors to take hedging very seriously. A prime example of how serious it can be *if you don't* let your company *hedge* are some legal cases where courts have found that directors have had a legal duty to mitigate commodity-linked price risk exposure. An early example of this was in 1992 in the United States, shareholders of a grain cooperative claimed that the directors breached their fiduciary duty by failing to protect the cooperative's profits through hedging in the futures market (Brane *v.* Roth, 590 N.E.2d 587 (Ind. CT. App. 1992)). The Indiana state court agreed and awarded the shareholders compensation!

In order to assist companies with ideas, here are some worked examples of energy derivatives applied in hedging strategies. These strategies can be

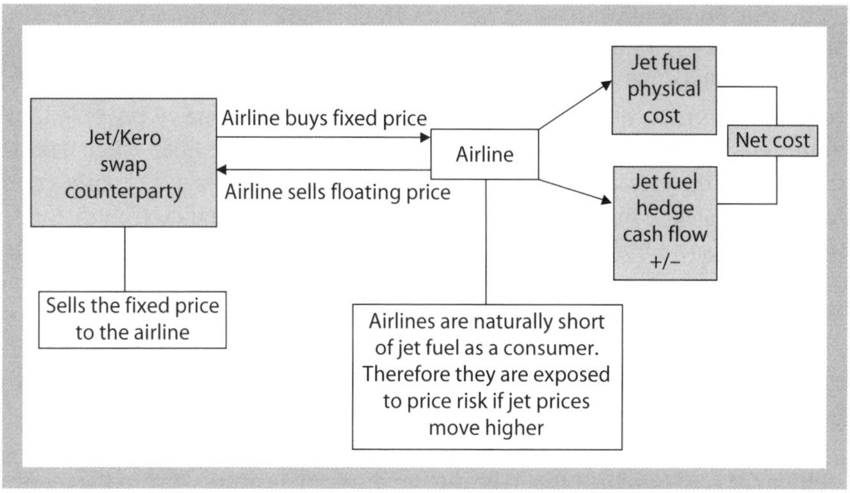

Figure 5.1 Fixed price swap hedge by an airline

applied across airlines, shipping companies, in fact anyone consuming energy, oil, gas, coal etc. All that is required is to replace the example given with a different pricing reference index of your choice.

Example 5.1: Fixed price swap hedge by an airline

In Example 5.1, an airline buys a fixed price swap from a bank or trader against its jet fuel price exposure (see Figure 5.1). It trades this swap under its ISDA Master agreement with its counterpart. In the majority of cases, airlines will hedge into the next financial accounting year, so from 1 month up to around 18 months forward. Hedging volumes vary from airline to airline but in general at least 20–30% of volumes are hedged ahead of the start of the next financial year around the annual budgeted price, with additional volumes of 10–20% of total annual requirements locked in as opportunistic or protective hedges whenever prices drop below the annual jet fuel purchasing budget price target. In "disaster" scenarios airlines hedge prices for up to 100% of short-term requirements (short term – present day to, say, around 3 months forward). This can happen in a Gulf War situation which would prompt oil prices to move higher on tension in Middle East.

Long-term large hedging of 100% of volumes is only seen in the market by charter airlines which have fixed income through forward seat sales to holiday companies. This means they have no way to increase prices later to accommodate higher jet fuel prices and therefore need to protect their usually thin and fixed profitability by fully hedging the price of forward jet fuel requirements.

In the above example, an airline buys US$25 fixed price swap for 50,000 barrels per month, against Singapore MOPS as the pricing reference (Mean of Platts Singapore www.platts.com) for the calendar year 2003. In ISDA contract terminology, the airline is the "fixed price payer." Total volume is 50,000 bbls x 12 months = 600,000 bbls. Remember when asking for quotes from traders directly or via brokers the quote is normally good for 50,000 bbls per month for products quoted in barrels or 5000 metric tonne (mt) per month for products quoted in barrels (unless otherwise specified).

In oil swaps there is a financial settlement every month (unlike financial markets where interest rates usually have a settlement at the end of the swaps whole pricing period; e.g., three month interest rate swap would have a settlement at the end of the third month). Taking this into consideration the cash flow of this 12-month hedge would look simple to Example 5.1, Figure 5.2.

As this is an Asian based swap (Mean of Platts Singapore) the cash settlement is normally going to be due on the tenth business day of the month preceding the month already priced out (e.g. for January 2003 the last pricing day would be Friday January 31, 2003). Payment for the cash settlement would be due on February 14, 2003 (subject to any banking holidays).

Example 5.2: Collar structure for end-user hedging

This is more flexible because airlines normally want protection against a disaster scenario increase in jet prices. Using the swaps market means they

Calendar 2003	A	B	C	Monthly settlement
	Volume	Fixed price	"MOPS"	(C – B) × A
Jan.-03	50,000	25	24.0	– 50,000
Feb.-03	50,000	25	25.0	0
Mar.-03	50,000	25	26.0	50,000
Apr.-03	50,000	25	26.5	75,000
May.-03	50,000	25	27.0	100,000
Jun.-03	50,000	25	27.0	100,000
Jul.-03	50,000	25	25.0	0
Aug.-03	50,000	25	23.0	– 100,000
Sep.-03	50,000	25	22.0	– 150,000
Oct.-03	50,000	25	24.0	– 50,000
Nov.-03	50,000	25	26.0	50,000
Dec.-03	50,000	25	28.0	150,000
Total vol.	600,000 Barrels			175,000

Figure 5.2 50,000 barrels per month of jet kero

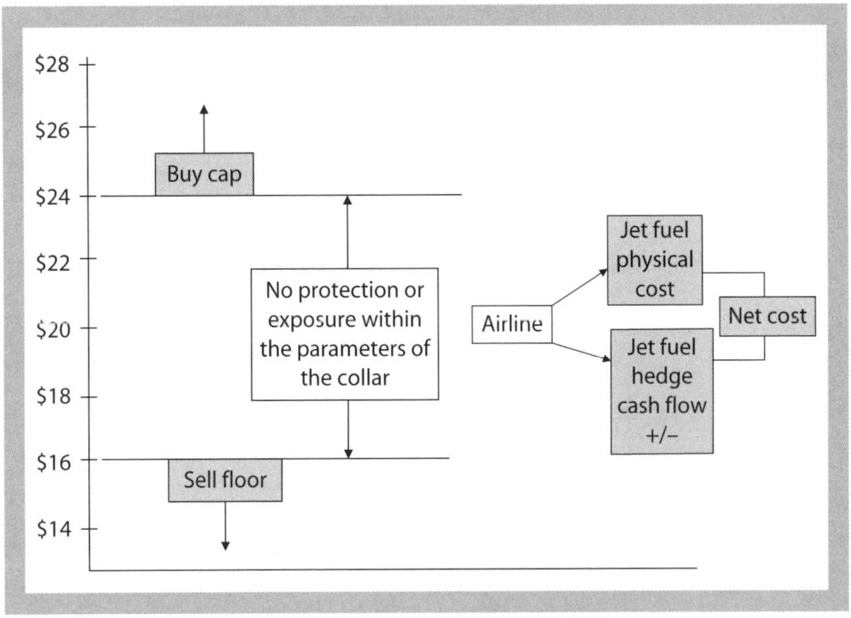

Figure 5.3 Collar hedge structure

must lock in their minimum net price receivable at the current perceived swap value (e.g. US$25 in Example 5.1). However, using a collar structure as shown in Figure 5.3 the airline can still protect itself from a worrying price increase, but can keep its minimum net price receivable locked in at a lower rate than the current swap price.

Using a collar structure you can tailor the protection point to suit your jet fuel budget level. It is created by buying a cap and selling a floor option. The purchase of the cap protects you against jet fuel prices rising above the strike of the cap, which in the example is US$24. The sale of the floor reduces the cost of the premium in the purchase of the cap (which can be sizeable given the usual twelve-month or more tenures in airline hedging programs).

A popular approach by end-users is to create a zero cost collar by selling enough floor options and receiving enough premium from these sales to compensate for the cost of the cap purchase.

The US$24 collar gives you 100% upside protection on any month that the average price of the market moves above US$24. The sale of the floor locks in the minimum net price you will receive on your jet fuel but at a lower level than the swap price you would have received at the same execution time point at this collar.

By playing with the level of the cap and the floor and also the volumes of the cap and/or floor it is possible to create a zero cost collar where the purchase of the cap is 100% subsidized by the sale of the floor (see Figure 5.4).

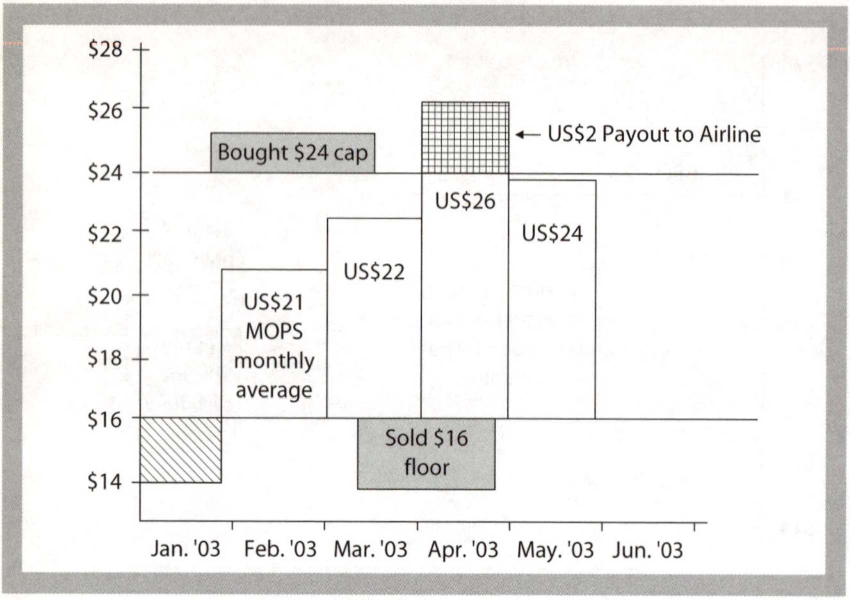

Figure 5.4 Zero-cost collar

Calendar 2003	A	Collar Floor	CAP	C	Monthly settlement	
	Volume	Strike	Strike	"MOPS"		
Jan.-03	50,000	16	24	14	–100,000	
Feb.-03	50,000	16	24	21	0	
Mar.-03	50,000	16	24	22	0	
Apr.-03	50,000	16	24	26	100,000	
May.-03	50,000	16	24	24	0	
				Paid/Received	0	Jan.–Mar.

Figure 5.5 Cash flow for collar hedge structure

Below is an example of cash flow for the Collar Hedge Structure using prices illustrated above, using 50,000 bbls per month as the contract volume (Figure 5.5).

Example 5.3: Electricity producer risk profile

In Example 5.3, a power producer (utility) has a more complex risk than an airline which is only worried about jet fuel price risk (and maybe forex risk). A power producer (except nuclear) may have up to four different types of fuel for power production: coal, fuel oil, gas oil, and natural gas, as

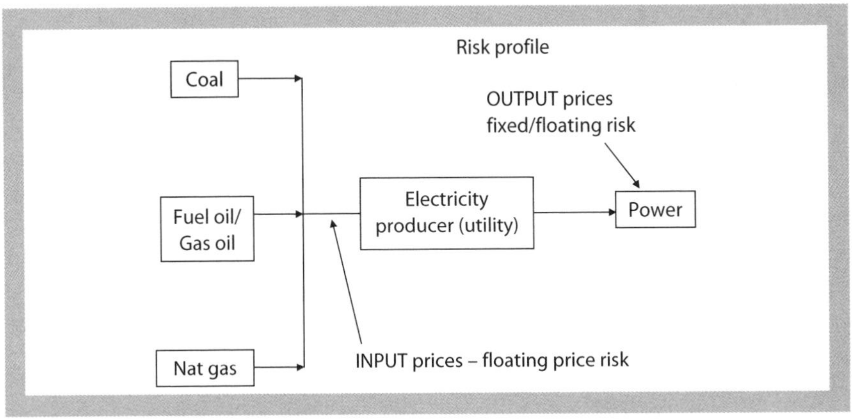

Figure 5.6 Electricity producer risk profile

shown in Figure 5.6. Because of this a power producer will have to observe movements in the spark spread, which is the term used to describe the gross margin (excludes cost of power company operation) between the cost of the chosen fuel for power production and the resale price of the forward electricity/power produced. A utility can control some of its price risk or profit margin risk (depending on the type of power stations it operates) by switching fuels if, for instance, gas oil looks more cost effective than fuel oil or vice versa. It will depend on the type of facility it operates. A coal power station would not switch over to oil-based products, nor would it switch from coal to natural gas and vice versa. On the rare occasions when utilities are very close to a refinery, they may sometimes utilize naphtha for power production. In normal circumstances though, naphtha is not a cost effective fuel and either coal, or fuel oil/gas oil, or natural gas is utilized.

In America there are coal futures on NYMEX and swaps and good liquidity in the NYMEX natural gas futures and there is also the OTC derivatives market. The OTC power market in the United States is very well developed so there are no issues there. Also for heating oil (gas oil) and fuel oil the OTC markets are very well developed and on the East Coast of the United States there is the possibility of using heating oil futures, although the majority of utilities will trade the natural gas versus the electricity spark spread. In Europe, utilities have a well-developed oil petroleum product swaps markets to utilize for hedging purposes and the IPE futures market also offers gas oil futures which may offer some protection. On the natural gas side, UK utilities can hedge in the IPE natural gas futures, and there is also a well-developed natural gas NBP (natural balance point) UK gas swaps markets (trading *c.* mid-2002, approximately six times the volume of IPE NBP UK Nat. Gas futures). Spark spreads are available from OTC traders as well, allowing the trading of the profit margin between natural gas piped in from the European North Sea and UK NETA forward power markets. In Continental Europe utilities and traders are able to utilize electricity futures markets.

SPARK SPREADS

When a spark spread order is given it is usually quoted as a spread price in Currency/mWh (the currency of the country or region per mega watt hour). A preferred power price will be given and negotiation will develop from there via brokers or directly with another principal. Obviously, natural gas is not traded normally in mWh and so the natural gas price has to be converted into an electricity equivalent. For example, in the United Kingdom, spark spread market a conversion rate of 49.1349% is used (representing 100,000 therms/60 mWs). Once a preferred fixed price on the power is confirmed, the gas price is then calculated in pence/therm corrected to 3 decimal places:

$$\text{Gas price in p/therm} = \frac{(\text{Power Price} - \text{Spread}) \times 24 \times 100 \times \text{Volume of power}}{\text{Volume of gas}}$$

$$= \frac{(\text{Power Price} - \text{Spread}) \times 24 \times 100 \times 60}{100{,}000}$$

Example 5.4: Metal producer risk profile

As shown in Figure 5.7, the metal producer can lock in the spread between using swaps or options between the energy markets utilized and the finished metal. Some banks can offer structures that give metal producers power prices/energy prices for their operation in a price related to the finished metal they produce. This is achieved by locking in the spread by

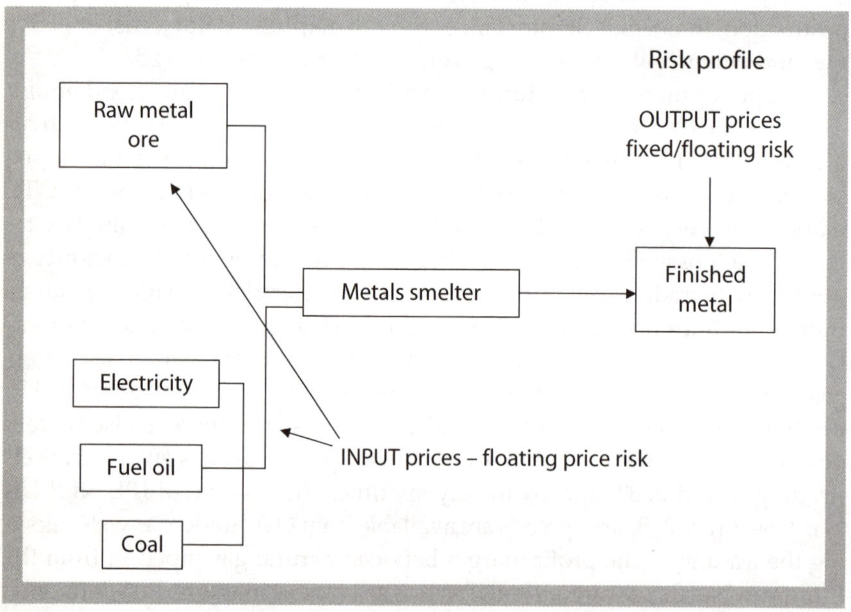

Figure 5.7 Metal producer risk profile

selling forward metal derivatives and buying forward energy derivatives. The smelter is exposed to energy prices going up which is protected by the long (purchased) energy derivatives. The smelter's profit margin is protected by the short (the sale) of metal derivatives.

Example 5.5: Crude oil hedge from Middle East to Asia

Typically, for crude oil cargoes you would be given a three- or five-day pricing window. Take an example of a cargo of 500,000 barrels which is destined for Singapore December 1–5, 2002. Using January 2003 futures you can sell 500 contracts of the SGX Middle East Crude oil futures (equivalent of 500,000 bbls of crude). A trader might typically sell these contracts 100,000 bbls per day on from December 1 to 5, as your crude cargo was pricing out against the Mean of Mcgraw Hill Platt's physical market assessment price (see the following box).

500,000 barrels pricing out over 5 days, i.e. 100,000 barrels per day
MECO futures contract 1000 barrels per contract; so 100 contracts per day must be sold to lock in a hedge

		December barrels	Contracts
Selling	1	100,000	100
Selling	2		100
Selling	3		100
Selling	4		100
Selling	5		100 so by close of business December 5 you are long (bought) 500,000 barrels of physical and also now short (sold) 500,000 barrels or 500 contracts of MECO futures
	6		
		Journey Time	
	16		
	17		
	18		
	19	December 21 – As a user of the crude oil you may have storage facilities and use the oil slowly over another 10 days time period in which case every day you buy back 50 lots or 50,000 barrels of hedge as you consume the oil	
	20		
Buying	21	50,000	50
Buying	22	50,000	50
Buying	23	50,000	50
Buying	24	50,000	50
Buying	25	50,000	50
Buying	26	50,000	50
Buying	27	50,000	50
Buying	28	50,000	50
Buying	29	50,000	50
Buying	30	50,000	50

So the Asian refiner buys Oman crude oil swaps. In this example the refiner wants to protect its January crude physical requirements from a price increase.

- October 1
- Buys January Oman Swaps @ US$27.00 fixed price (floating against Platts mean average of the whole month of January)
- December 10
- The refiner purchases its crude oil @ US$28.50
- Sells same volume Oman swaps (month of January) @ US$28.50
- Profit on hedge (fixed purchase versus sale) @ US$1.50 per bbl

  The effective netted buying price is = Hedge + physical purchase price
  = US$28.50 − US$1.50 hedge profit
  = US$27.00

Now imagine that in this scenario the refinery has put the crude oil into storage after the long journey from West Africa/Middle East to Singapore for refining. The refinery in this example is consuming 50,000 bbls a day and so during the course of 10 days (10 × 50,000 = 500,000 bbls) the trader will wish to remove, or close out the futures or swaps hedge against the physical crude oil; otherwise the crude oil will be consumed, leaving the trader with a naked derivatives position, that is, no physical commodity, so that overnight it would turn into a speculative trade.

Example 5.6: Hedge cashflow for a crude oil import hedge

Here we take the example of where a refinery which is naturally short crude, since a refinery must consume crude oil, and can't be switched on or off. In fact, most refineries have to run at a minimum of 60% capacity otherwise they have to be shut down, and that plus restarting a refinery is an extremely expensive and dangerous process. The risk profile here, is that the refiner is exposed to crude oil prices moving higher and threatening its profit margin on refining crude oil in to petroleum products.

		Bought Fixed Cash	Sold Fixed Futures
	1st to 5th	26	26.35
		Sold cash	Bought Futures
	21st to 30th	25	25.35
Gross Profit (loss)		−1	1
	Net position	0	

Example 5.7: Crude oil producer hedge

A simple crude oil producer hedge would be as follows. A crude producer is naturally long crude because it has crude in the ground, so it is exposed to prices going down. It therefore needs to create a short position in a derivatives hedge structure.

For this example, the producer sells its crude oil on a Brent crude oil related price basis, so its price exposure is in terms of Brent crude oil. The producer has seen crude prices reach a high level due to some Middle East political tension and related concerns, so it is too expensive to buy some put options (floor) on their own. One possibility is to do the following:

- Sell Brent related futures, for example, IPE Brent futures in London
  - A good idea if the producer wishes to remain anonymous and not scare the market that they are selling
- Sell Brent related OTC swaps with other oil companies and banks
  - Maybe more flexible but given this is a key producer hedging they might not wish to reveal their intentions directly to other traders in the OTC market place.

Using IPE Brent futures, we can illustrate this as

- December 5
- Sells January IPE Brent futures @ US$29.50 per bbl
- January 15
- Sells physical crude @ US$30.50 per bbl
- Buys back same volume of futures @ US$31.00 per bbl
- Futures loss @ US$1.00 per bbl

Effective netted crude sale price = Hedge + physical sale price
= US$30.50 + US$1.00 loss
= US$29.50 per barrel

Example 5.8: Crude producer hedge using floors with a knock-out

The other alternative which can be applied not only to a crude oil producer but to any energy producer situation is using floors (puts) with a knock out option. In this scenario, the producer had found that because the oil price had been moving higher, and they thought that prices would continue to move higher, they did not wish to sell futures or swaps and lock in the

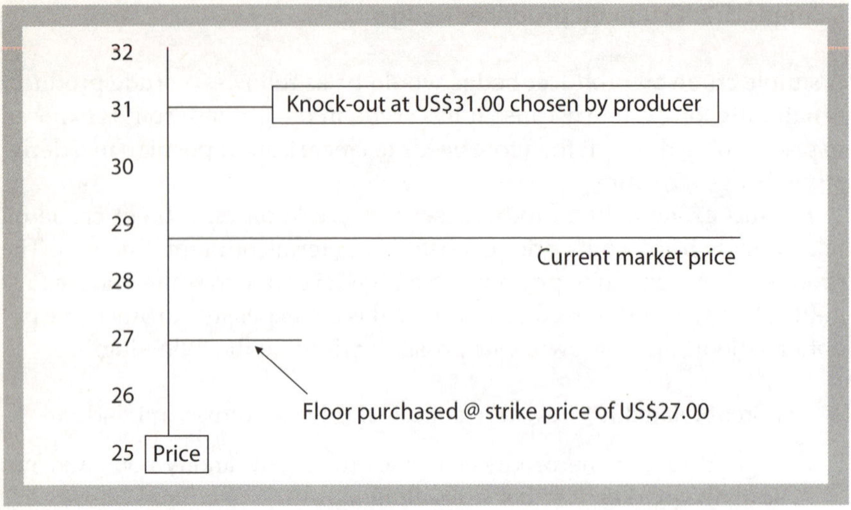

Figure 5.8 Knock-out optionality

price, creating some potential loss of opportunity if prices continued to rise (as shown by the previous example with a loss on the hedge).

A more appetizing solution is to buy floors (puts). In this scenario we will say that the cost of buying a floor is too expensive, so the producer could look at introducing a knock-out into the floor (put) structure in order to try to reduce the overall cost of the option. In a hedging scenario whatever the type of energy product being produced, you would look to buy an "out of the money" floor (put) and request a knock out above the market.

In this scenario the trader or market maker has given the producer a cheaper floor option to protect against prices going down, because the producer has given the seller some optionality. This optionality is the knock-out (Figure 5.8). What the producer has said to the seller of the floor, is that if the market goes up to US$31.00 during the lifetime of the option, the option is automatically cancelled. So the seller of the option has the added chance, the added potential of receiving premium for a long-term option, which may actually be cancelled before it reaches maturity or expiry date. This lets the seller of the option off-the- hook without any more exposure to the producer.

A rebate structure can also sometimes be negotiated. In this instance, if the option were cancelled, the producer who is hedging, might receive back some percentage of the original premium he had paid out for the option.

Example 5.9: Refinery margin hedge when margin positive on some products and negative on others

In this example, a refinery has good margins on jet kero and gas oil but fuel oil margins are negative (Fuel oil makes up to 25% of the output of some

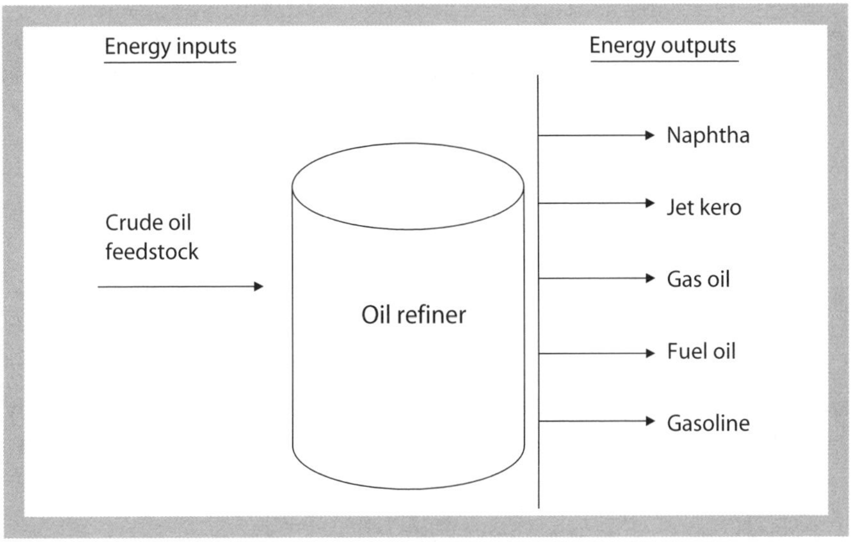

Figure 5.9 Refinery margin hedge

older refineries, although newer ones tend to reprocess a lot of fuel oil and a modern refinery may only produce an estimated 10% fuel oil). This refinery is using crude oil from the Middle East, pricing against the average of Platts Oman crude oil (see Figure 5.9). To hedge the crude oil imports for the refinery the traders will sell OTC crude oil swaps pricing against Platt's Oman average.

- So the refinery buys 2,000,000 bbl of Middle East crude priced against Oman on January 1–5. Since not all of the petroleum product output is being hedged, the first thing to do is to add up the volume of the products (convert into barrels where necessary) and make sure that only this amount of crude is hedged.

  For example, see the following box

		Crude Oil Import Feedstock			Petroleum Product Production Hedge		
					Sold Swaps Jet kero	Sold Swaps Gas oil	FUEL OIL CRACK OPTION BOUGHT FLOOR @ US$110 per MT (using 6.7 conversion from MT to barrels)
		Physical	Hedge Short	Volume			
January	1st	25	24.95	125,000	50,000	75,000	0
	2nd	24.89	24.84	125,000	50,000	75,000	0
	3rd	24.86	24.81	125,000	50,000	75,000	0
	4th	24.5	24.45	125,000	50,000	75,000	0
	5th	24.65	24.6	500,000	50,000	75,000	375,000
TOTAL	**6th**	**24.78**	**24.73**	**1,000,000**			

- Using the figures above, we are hedging 1,000,000 bbls of product, so we also need to lock in 1,000,000 bbls of the crude. So every day for 5 days during the pricing window January 1–5, the traders will sell 125,000 bbls of Platts Oman related swaps except for the last day which is 500,000 since the crack option on the fuel oil is placed in the option market all in one go. By day six, the trader will have a cargo of physical on the water on its way to the refinery and a paper hedge of 1,000,000 bbls notional quantity protecting the value of the crude.
- At the same time as hedging the crude oil cargoes, the trader starts hedging the future production of the refinery from this crude oil that is on its way to the refinery.
- For jet fuel and gas oil, the margin is looking healthy, so the trader may just sell the forward swaps to lock in the value of the jet fuel and gas oil. He makes sure that he sells swaps which cover the time period that the refinery will be producing petroleum products from the crude on the water on its way to the refinery. For example, if someone bought West African crude and shipped it to Japan for refining, it could take four weeks to get there. So, if you were hedging the crude oil you would want to make sure that the derivatives contract would not expire before the products could be produced from the crude. Also it might mean that the products would not actually be sold from the refinery for several months after the crude was purchased.

The issue in this scenario is that the fuel oil has a negative refining margin. They cannot shut the refinery down, so they need to protect against this margin getting still worse. However if they were to sell the swaps markets in fuel oil it would lock in the price 100% and if the refinery margin improved they would not be able to benefit from that improvement. However, the refinery in this scenario decides to utilize a crack option. As discussed in earlier chapters, you can buy (or even sell) crack options on refinery margins (the same thing in the power industry would be considered spark spread options – the spread between input energy like natural gas, gas oil, fuel oil, or coal and the output of electricity in mWhours). So, the refinery could buy a floor (put) option against the margin getting worse. The benefit of the option is that if the refinery margin improved, the refinery could benefit from 100% of the improvement (after the margin has improved enough to cover the cost of the option for the hedge). To reduce the cost of the crack option strategy, the refiner could ask market makers, banks, and traders to quote a zero-cost collar crack option structure. In this case the refiner would still buy a floor (put) on the crack margin against fuel oil, but would also sell some caps (calls) on the crack margin against fuel oil to generate some cash premium and subsidise or totally net out the cost of the floor crack option. In doing this the refiner would put a limit on the amount of improvement of the crack margin it can benefit from, but at least the cap can be placed higher than the current swap level. So the refiner would still have more chance to benefit from improvement than if it merely sold the fuel oil swaps at current market.

CHAPTER 6

Options in Hedging Applications

Energy "options" go one step further than an OTC fixed-for-floating swap contract. They can be compared to insurance policies, because there is a premium to pay but if the market moves against you there is no requirement to pay any more money. In the same way, the purchaser of an energy option is buying the right to claim price protection (or benefit as a trader) from the seller of the option if the price of the chosen energy market rises above the price specified in the contract (called the "strike price").

An option is exactly what the name implies: when traders buy oil options, they buy the right, but not the obligation, to purchase a certain amount of an energy market (oil, gas, power, coal) at a certain price at a certain future date. That means that the user can set a maximum price it would like to pay for the energy in March, for example, and then buy an option at that price. If somebody sells the buyer that option, they have promised to supply a particular amount of energy, in March, at that particular price. The majority of derivative options are never linked to physical delivery of energy, but merely give the user the benefit from the exposure to the cash flow of an equivalent position in the underlying energy.

The advantages of derivative option structures over and above a plain vanilla OTC swap contract hedge structure are as follows:

- Initial outlay of cash in many cases is restricted to the premium paid, which in the case of zero-cost collars (buy cap, sell floor, or sell cap, buy floor, depending on the underlying energy price exposure, but the two options' premium cost/revenue offset one another to create zero cost). This structure is very common among end-users with a short energy price risk (they are exposed to energy prices moving higher) so they need to buy caps (calls) and sell floors (puts) in order to create zero cost protection against prices moving higher.

- There is less opportunity cost than a swap or futures strategy, because option strategies can enable the user to protect against adverse price risk movements, but at the same time still benefit from beneficial price movements in the underlying physical energy market.
- Another advantage of option strategies (which we discuss in this chapter) is that traders who are unsure about the outright price direction of an underlying asset can take a position on volatility rather than market price.

TERMINOLOGY USED IN ASIAN OTC OPTION MARKETS

- *American option:* An option which can be exercised on any business day up to and including the expiry date. More expensive than European options.
- *Asian option:* The main option found in the OTC energy markets are Asian-style options. They are called path-dependent, because their final value is dependent on the path of the underlying energy market (e.g. in a December option, the option will eventually price out against the average price of the energy market the option is based on, over the whole month of December just like a whole month averaging swap). Basically, the profit from an Asian option depends on the price history of the underlying commodity that is being used as the price reference, over all or part of the life of the option. The advantage of the option is that if you bought the option when the market has moved against the option position (in terms of price movement) the only cost or loss of opportunity was the cost (or premium) of the option. However, with a swap position you would be locked in and have potentially unlimited "opportunity cost," if the market moved against the derivative position. These are normally cheaper than American-style or European-style options.
- *At-the-money (ATM):* Option whose exercise price is the same as the market price of the underlying energy.
- *European Option:* An option which can be exercised on the expiry date only. Cheaper than American options.
- *Fair value:* The combination of intrinsic value and time value, as calculated by an option pricing model.
- *In-the-money (ITM):* A call is said to be "in-the-money" when the value of the underlying energy futures or swap price is higher than the option's strike price. A put is "in-the-money" when its strike price is higher than the value of the underlying energy futures or swap price.

- *Intrinsic value:* The difference between the strike price and the current market rate.
- *Out-of-the-money (OTM):* A call is "out-of-the-money" when the value of the underlying energy futures or swap price is less than the option strike price. A put is "out-of-the-money" when its strike price is less than the value of the underlying energy futures or swap price.
- *Premium:* The price or cost of the option.
- *Strike price:* The entry price into the underlying participation level.
- *Time value:* The difference between the option premium and the intrinsic value, including time until expiry, volatility, and cost of carry (interest %).
- *Value date:* Date when the underlying is settled or delivered.

Types of options

In futures markets

- Calls: the right but not the obligation to buy the underlying futures contract at the strike price.
- Puts: the right but not the obligation to sell the underlying futures contract at the strike price.

In swaps markets

- Caps: OTC name for what structurally gives users the same protection and/or exposure to market price movement as calls in the futures market.
- Floors: OTC name for what structurally gives users the same protection and/or exposure to market price movement as puts in the futures market.

OTC option strategies for hedging energy price risk

Some simple option strategies for hedging against market price movements can be summarized as follows: If you have a "short" energy price exposure it means you are exposed to prices going higher; you may be a shipping company who has to buy fuel oil as bunkers for its shipping fleet. If you have a "long" energy price exposure it means you are exposed if prices of the fuel oil you are producing goes down; that is, you might be a refinery producing the fuel oil and you are "long" the physical fuel oil.

To hedge a "short" energy exposure with options	To hedge a "long" energy exposure with options
Buy call or cap	Sell call or cap
Sell put or cap	Buy put or cap
Buy call spread	Sell call spread
Sell put spread	Buy put spread

Table 6.1 Summary of exposures – options vs swaps/futures

Position	Risk	Reward
Long call	Limited to premium	Unlimited
Long put	Limited to premium	Almost unlimited*
Short (written)cap/floor (call/put)	Unlimited (if option position is not hedged)	Cash premium received
Long (purchased)	Almost unlimited*	Unlimited
Underlying swap/future		
Short (sold) underlying swap/future	Unlimited	Almost unlimited*

Note: * Since asset value and or derivatives a contract value cannot fall below 0

Financial exposure and/or protection received when using options compared to swaps/futures contracts can be summarized as in Table 6.1.

The flexibility of options really starts to become clear when we look at combinations of the above strategies of buying some calls/caps selling some puts/floors at different tenures, different strike prices, and for differing volumes. The variety of combination structures that can be created using options is as endless; the possibilities are only limited by our own creativity and the complexity of the exposure that needs to be protected against (or in the case of an investor/trader, an exposure that they wish to become exposed to). However, there are some quite regularly applied structures in the energy derivatives markets which can be discussed here as a base for traders/hedgers to work from.

Option strategies

Figure 6.1 illustrates how the value of caps in the OTC market (and calls in futures market), and floors in the OTC market (puts in the futures market) move compared to the overall value of the energy commodity they are valued against.

To recap:

- Buying caps/calls: A buyer of a cap (call) is protected for a fixed premium on the market price becoming stronger.
- Buying floors/puts: A buyer of a floor (put) is protected for a fixed premium on the market price becoming weaker.

Figure 6.2 illustrates the movement of price while selling caps/floors.

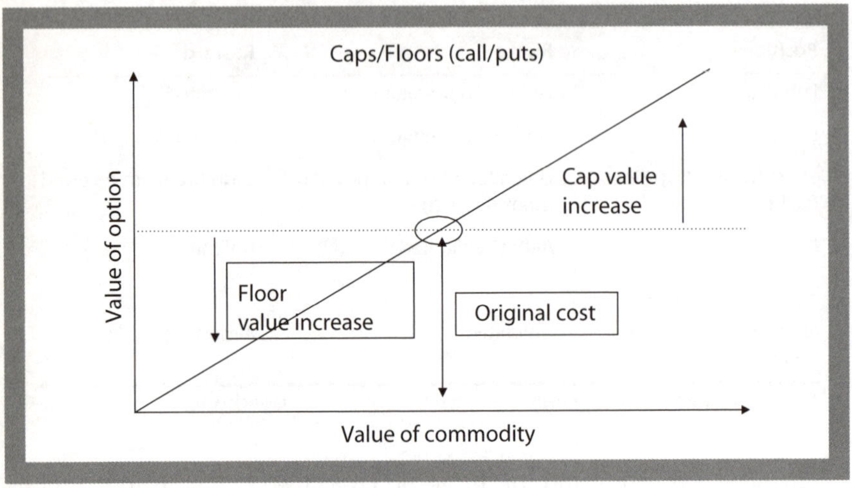

Figure 6.1 Value of caps/floors

Source: Corex Trading Limited, London, www.corextrading.com

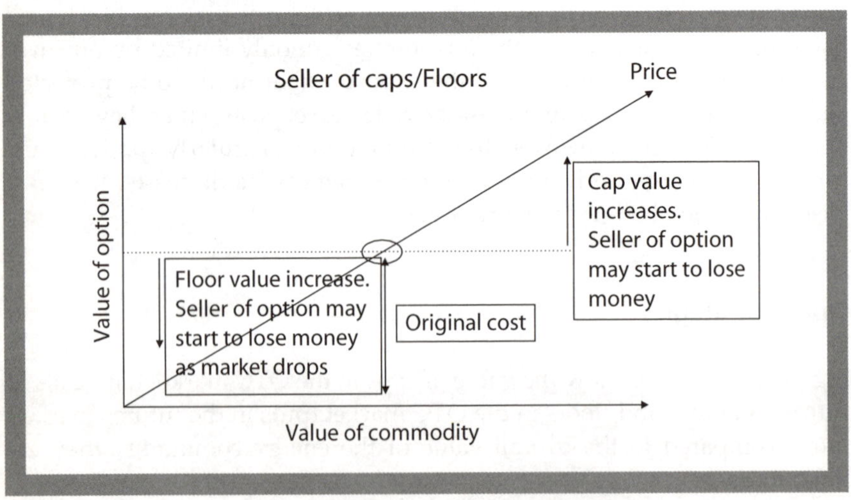

Figure 6.2 Seller of caps/floors

To recap:

- Selling caps/calls:
  - A seller of a cap (call) receives a fixed premium for selling the option.
  - Cash is received for selling the option (premium), this is what becomes useful in finance deals with derivatives.
  - There is exposure if the average market price during the life of the option goes above the fixed cap price/strike price.

- Selling floors/puts
  - A seller of a floor (put) receives a fixed premium for selling the option.
  - Cash is received for selling the option (premium), this is what becomes useful in finance deals with derivatives.
  - There is exposure if the average market price during the life of the option goes below the fixed floor price/strike price.

Where you have a short underlying physical position, the strategies to be adopted in hedging with options are tabulated in Table 6.2.

Table 6.2 To hedge short energy positions with options

	Anticipations	Characteristics
Short call	Implied volatility down	Limited profit, unlimited loss, limited protection, cash credit, risk profile at expiration equivalent to a short put.
Long put	Implied volatility up	Unlimited profit, limited loss, unlimited protection,important cost, risk profile at expiration equivalent to a long call.
Short call spread, or bull spread	Implied volatility direction depends on the strikes: Sell call and buy call with higher strike If a rise in implied volatility is expected: buy ATM call/sell ITM call equal volume If a fall in implied volatility is expected: buy OTM call/ sell ATM call with equal volume	Unlimited profit, unlimited loss, limited protection, low cost, risk profile at expiration equivalent to a long semi-futures.
Long put spread, or bear spread	Implied volatility direction depends on the strikes: Sell put and buy put with higher strike If a rise in implied volatility is expected: buy ATM put/sell OTM put equal volumes on both options If a fall in implied volatility is expected: buy ITM put/sell ATM put equal volume again	Unlimited profit, unlimited loss, limited protection, low cost, risk profile at expiration equivalent to a long semi-futures.

In long underlying positions the strategies to be adopted in hedging with options are tabulated in Table 6.3.

OTC OPTIONS AND POPULAR STRUCTURES

The option products that are most frequently used in the oil market are caps, floors, and collars and the most commonly traded OTC options are Asian options. These do not exercise into any other contract, they just cash-settle against the underlying price reference (unlike futures options which end up expiring into a futures contract which must be traded out of). The next most popular kind of option is a swaption which can be American-style or European-style. This exercises into a swaps contract buy or sell at the strike price selected.

Asian options

- The profit from an Asian option depends on the price history of the underlying commodity that is being used as the price reference, over all or part of the life of the option.
- It is sometimes referred to in the financial markets as a "path- dependent option."
- It is Cheaper than European options.
- We cannot use Black–Scholes formula for pricing options because this is an average price option; an average of prices are not log normally distributed.
- The alternative is the Monte Carlo approach (see Chapter 7 for more details). Note: Monte Carlo simulation of geometric Brownian motion and test empirical distribution of the average for log normality using a Smirnov–Kolmogorov test = Monte Carlo Ok for volatility below 40% in the market with averaging period up to one year long.

The collars structure is very popular with hedgers in the energy market. In particular, end-user consumers of energy often use the "zero cost collar" as it offers cheap insurance with no up front cost. It is made by simultaneously buying a cap and selling a floor and has no upfront cost. The option strategy pays the buyer of the collar (i.e. the buyer of the cap, the seller of the floor) if the market rises. However, if the market falls below the floor, the exposure is open. An oil consumer who buys a collar gets protection from adverse upward movement but pays nothing for it. But the oil consumer does not necessarily give away all of the benefit of lower prices.

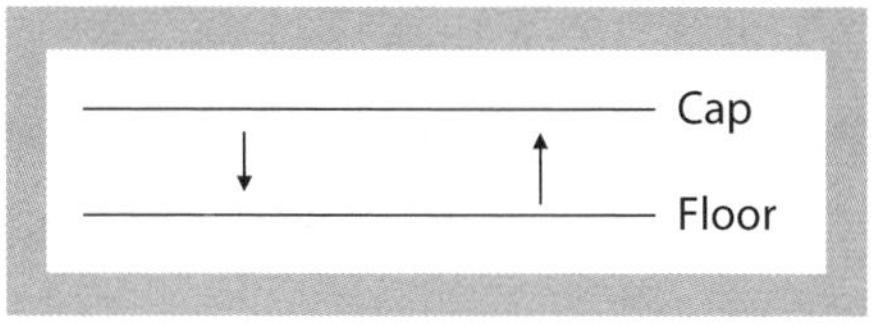

Table 6.3 To hedge long underlying position with options

	Anticipations	**Characteristics**
Short call	Implied volatility down	Limited profit, unlimited loss, limited protection, cash credit, risk profile at expiration equivalent to a short put.
Long put	Implied volatility up	Unlimited profit, limited loss, unlimited protection, important cost, risk profile at expiration equivalent to a long call.
Short semi-futures	Implied volatility direction depends on the strikes: Buy put and sell call with a higher strike If a rise in implied volatility is expected: sell OTM call/buy ATM put, equal volumes If a fall in implied volatility is expected: sell ATM call/buy OTM put, equal volumes	Limited profit, limited loss, unlimited protection, low cost, risk profile at expiration equivalent to a long fence or a bull spread.
Short call spread, or bull spread	Implied volatility direction depends on the strikes: Sell call and buy call with higher strike If a rise in implied volatility is expected: buy ATM call/sell ITM call equal volumes If a fall in implied volatility is expected: buy OTM call/sell ATM call, equal volumes	Unlimited profit, unlimited loss, limited protection, low cost, risk profile at expiration equivalent to a long semi-futures.
Long put spread, or bear spread	Implied volatility direction depends on the strikes: Sell put and buy put with higher strike If a rise in implied volatility is expected: buy ATM put/sell OTM put, equal volumes If a fall in implied volatility is expected: buy ITM put/sell ATM put, equal volumes	Unlimited profit, unlimited loss limited protection, low cost, risk profile at expiration equivalent to a long semi-futures.

		Out	In
Price	Up	Up-and-out	Up-and-in
	Down	Down-and-out	Down-and-in

Figure 6.3 Barrier options – caps/floors, knock in/knock out

Barrier options

Barrier options were invented to reduce the initial cost of hedging with buying of options. The barrier option either comes to life (is knocked-in) or is extinguished (knocked out) under certain conditions. In practice the event which activates or kills the option is defined in terms of a price level (barrier).

The barrier option may be combined with a rebate: for knock-out options, the rebate is paid when the option is cancelled as a compensation to the holder. A typical example of a barrier option is the "up-and-out floor" (put). A few of these combinations are shown in Figure 6.3. All the combinations illustrated above linked to a cap or floor are available in the OTC market.

Up-and-out floor (put)

This is typically purchased by energy producers who want to hedge their natural long position in the markets. An "up-and-out floor" (put) may be an attractive alternative to the normal floor/put option, as it is less expensive and provides the same price protection if prices move down from current futures/swap quoted levels. However, if prices move upwards, the increase in the underlying commodity's price reduces the need for downside risk protection at the original strike price. If the price moves up sufficiently to cross the selected "barrier" price, the "knock-out," then the option is cancelled or extinguished: it is "knocked-out." The hedger may then consider re-entering the market with a new hedge by buying another floor but at a higher strike price.

The up-and-out barrier is less expensive that a standard Asian, European, or American option because the underlying price may fall below the strike price after initially rising, hitting the barrier and cancelling the option.

Crack and spread options

Some banks and traders or market makers will even quote options on differentials such as the refinery margin – crude versus products. This is particularly useful when having to deal with negative system margins. When running a refinery an organization cannot choose to stop producing some petroleum product. Refinery engineers may be able to reduce the production of a loss-making product, but in the end you will still have to protect against the negative margin becoming worse. A crack option offers protection against the margin becoming worse, but at the same time allows an organization to benefit from an improvement in the margin. Compared to using swaps or futures to lock in the negative margin, you will not be able to appreciate from an improvement in the margin. This applies to petrochemical margins and power production margins such as spark spread options.

It is even possible to create a zero-cost collar spark spread option, or refinery option, where you can sell the margin option at one level and buy protection against the margin at another, getting protection from the margin going below the floor price margin option and locking in the margin at the strike price sold on the cap margin option.

Other spread or arbitrage options seen in the market from time to time include crude versus crude, the complete refinery margin options, and individual cracks between crudes and petroleum products such as gasoil, jet fuel, and fuel oil. There are also spark spread options, that is, natural gas versus power prices, or gasoil or fuel oil versus power prices.

Delayed start date options

As well as the knock-in and knock-out option into the caps and floors used for trading or for managing price risk, it is now also possible to obtain a delayed start date from traders and market makers. One example of the application for this can be found in Chapter 5 on hedging examples/scenarios. If an organization were trying to hedge the production of a new refinery, oil field, petrochemical plant, or utility power station, it is quite possible that it would have an approximate start date for production or completion, but between now and that date some delay may occur. The nightmare scenario for hedgers or risk managers is to be stuck with a hedge but the asset/energy to be hedged not turning up or being ready. Immediately that hedge becomes a speculative position for accounting purposes and is an unwanted, unprotected risk in its own right. This could certainly undermine a company's cash flow forecasts.

So, to reduce this risk it is possible (at a price) to obtain delayed start dates built into option structures and sometimes the optionality of this start date delay can be embedded into a swaps hedge structure as well. It usually means that at a certain date, perhaps three months before the derivatives hedge start date kicks in, the user of the hedge can nominate on a particular day or any day up to a certain cut off point, to delay the start of the hedge to another date. The delayed start date would normally be fixed, it would be possible to delay the hedge to another specified date or delay it by X number of days.

OPTIONS TRADING – VOLATILITY TRADING

Options can be used to trade the market price; in other words, they can be used to benefit from movements in the underlying swaps or futures market. But, for investment trading purposes, options can also be used to benefit from the market going nowhere!

At the beginning of this chapter we talked about two types of volatility, one of which was implied volatility. This is an important component in the cost or value of an option. By using special combinations of calls and puts or caps and floors for OTC markets, it is possible to make a trade based on whether as a trader you think volatility will increase or decrease. This is done by what is known as volatility trading and involves setting up a delta neutral portfolio (delta neutral = market price neutral).

Volatility strategies

A trader who wants to take advantage of the underlying volatility of the market increasing or decreasing can use the following option strategies:

- *Straddles:* Sell call (cap) and sell put (floor) at the same strike price in the same market. It is important to appreciate that although a short straddle is delta neutral (+/− balanced), it is not gamma neutral.
- *Strangles:* These are essentially the same as straddles except that a trader will use out-of-the money options. They also use different "strike" prices.

If a trader thinks the volume is going down he would normally short (sell) these options, while if he thinks the volume is going up, he would go long (buy) them.

If your view = volatility is going to increase,

- Buy (long) a straddle or strangle;
  - Long straddle involves buying purchasing the put (floor) and the call (cap) at the same strike price.
- Short (sell) butterfly strategy;

If your view = volatility is going to decrease,

- Short (sell) straddle or strangle;
  - Short straddle involves selling (writing) the put (floor) and the call (cap) at the same strike price.
- Long (buy) butterfly strategy;

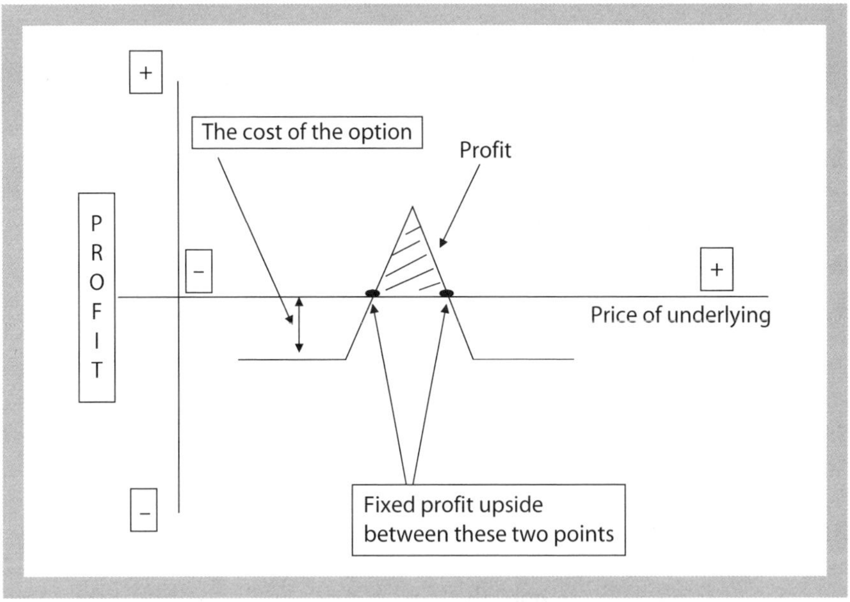

Figure 6.4 Butterfly strategy

Butterfly strategy

The only issue with using straddles and strangles is the potentially unlimited loss on the strategy. This can be managed but it must be actively hedged and monitored. However, because of this risk concern we should consider other trading strategies which have less up front risk.

The butterfly is an option strategy that has both limited risk and restricted profit potential. It is created by using four strike prices. The strategy may be set up using caps or floor options (see Figure 6.4).

Short/long butterfly

- It allows the trading of volatility.
- It has an advantage over a straddle and even less risk than a strangle because the structure creates a fixed cap on maximum loss. This is already built into the strategy, so active position management requirements are reduced.

Long (buy) butterfly

- Option premiums are paid.
- It offers limited risk.
- This is used when the view is that volatility is going to decrease.

Strike	Buy 1 × call	Sell 2 × call	Buy 1 × call
	US$20	US$22	US$24

Short (sell) butterfly

- It receives more premium than premia paid out.
- There is limited risk.
- It is used when the view is that volatility is going to increase.

Strike	Sell 1 × call	Buy 2 × call	Sell 1 × call
	US$20	US$22	US$24

Ratio backspreads

It is also possible to trade both the market price and volatility at the same time by using special options structures called ratio backspreads. A backspread is a delta neutral spread which is achieved by buying options with smaller deltas and selling options with large deltas. It will also consist of more long (bought) options than short (sold) options with all options expiring at the same time.

- *Ratio call backspread* consists of buying calls at a higher strike price than the strike price of call options sold.
- *Ratio put backspread* consists of buying puts (floors) at a lower strike price than the strike price of the puts (floors) sold.

Typically a trader will execute a backspread for some positive cash-flow, (i.e. some credit premium in their favor) since the amount of option premium received for the sold options is greater than the premium paid for the options bought in the strategy.

In a call (cap) backspread strategy (which is a directionally bullish strategy) if the energy market price collapses, then all the options in the strategy will most probably expire with zero value. In a put (floor) backspread strategy (which is a directionally bearish strategy) if the energy market price rises by an extreme measure, then all the options in the strategy will most probably expire with zero value. A trader would choose the type of backspread, either a cap or floor, which directionally reflected his or her price direction expectations.

Call backspread option strategy: In a call backspread, the profit potential is unlimited if the market price of the underlying energy market moves higher. The key to a backspread is that some price movement will happen during the lifetime of the option strategy. If the market price does not really move much, any backspread strategy is more than likely to end up being a losing strategy (see Figure 6.5). If we take the example of strike prices in a crude oil call backspread option strategy it might look something like this.

Long 600 December US$25 strike calls @ 24 cents
Short 200 December US$20 strike calls @ 78 cents

Long 400 March US$27 strike calls @ 23 cents
Short 200 March US$22.50 strike calls @ 51 cents

Put backspread option strategy: In a put backspread strategy the profit potential is unlimited if the market price falls. Again it should be noted that if the market price does not really move much any backspread strategy is more than likely to lose (see Figure.6.6). If we take the example of strike prices in a crude oil put backspread option strategy it might look something like this. To summarize, we can recapitulate options trade against market implied volatility as given in Table 6.4.

Long 600 December US$20 strike puts @ 20 cents
Short 200 December US$25 strike puts @ 120 cents

Long 400 March US$22.50 strike puts @ 150 cents
Short 200 March US$25.00 strike puts @ 249 cents

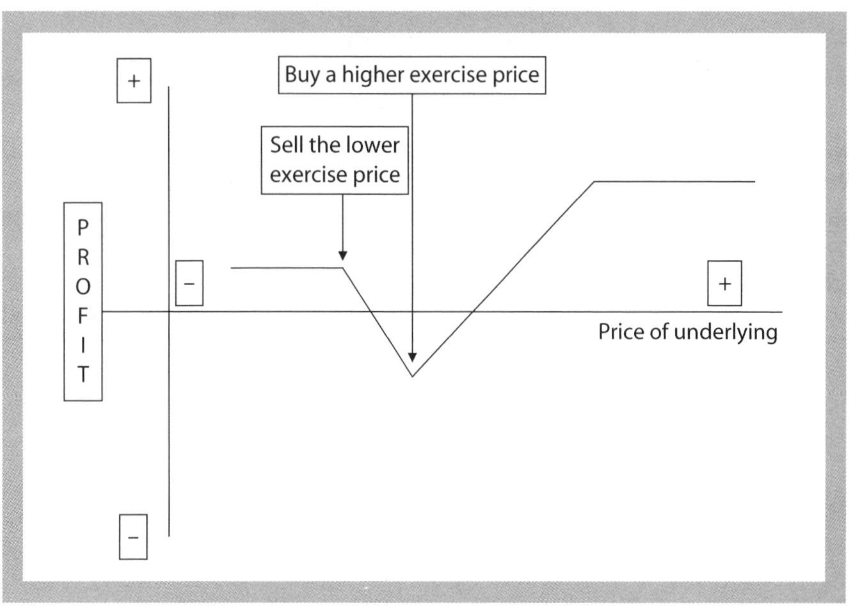

Figure 6.5 Call backspread option strategy

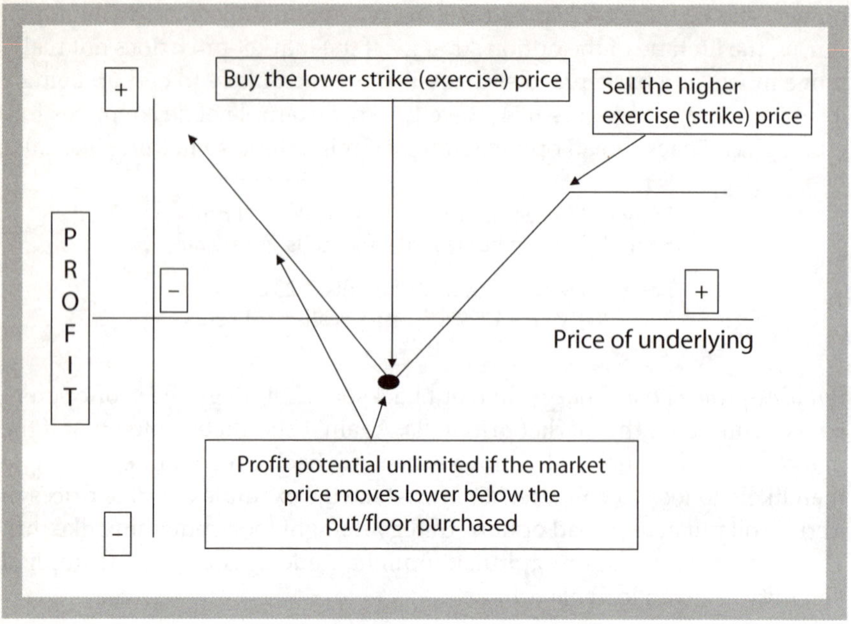

Figure 6.6 Put/floor backspread option strategy

Table 6.4 Options trade against market implied volatility

	Result of a large mkt price swing in the underlying swaps or futures contract	Increase in implied volatility	Decrease in implied volatility	Time value effect
Ratio call backspread	beneficial	beneficial	not beneficial	not beneficial
Ratio put backspread	beneficial	beneficial	not beneficial	not beneficial
Long straddle	beneficial	beneficial	not beneficial	not beneficial
Short straddle	not beneficial	not beneficial	beneficial	beneficial
Long strangle	beneficial	beneficial	not beneficial	not beneficial
Short strangle	not beneficial	not beneficial	beneficial	beneficial
Long Butterfly	not beneficial	not beneficial	beneficial	beneficial
Short Butterfly	beneficial	beneficial	not beneficial	not beneficial

CHAPTER 7

LNG Hedging

After several decades of relative inactivity, liquefied natural gas (LNG) imports are again in the forefront of US energy policy. As US access to world natural gas supplies requires a major expansion on LNG-terminal-import capacity and development of the newer offshore regasification technologies, the impacts on the Asian LNG markets are quite apparent. The largest energy consumer in the world is entering the world gas markets in a big way. This will impact supply, demand and pricing for future LNG suppliers and consumers in Asia. The United States will increase gas supplies quickly through imports of liquefied natural gas and will fast-track the development and construction of LNG receiving terminals, including the exemption of LNG terminals from the "open access" requirements of Federal Energy Requirements Commission (FERC).

In Asia however, the gas shares of total primary energy supply has to date been lower in than in Europe and North America: more than 20% in Europe and North America and less than 10% in Asia. Some Asian countries, however, do have high gas shares, notably Indonesia, Malaysia, and Brunei. In addition to catering for domestic use, these countries have exported LNG to Japan, Korea, and Chinese Taipei over the past 30 years.

But international pipeline gas trade is still at the preliminary stage in the region. There are still only a few international pipelines, including those projected to be built and Asia is clearly different from Europe and North America in this regard. And now additional Asian countries such as the Philippines, Vietnam, and Myanmar are promoting gas production and use. Gas will play an increasingly important role in the region in the next century!

The emergence of global business for natural gas has brought fundamental and rapid change to the natural gas business. As Northeast Asia (Japan, South Korea, and Taiwan) is the primary recipient of most LNG production and with the entrance of China as an LNG consumer in the future, the global LNG market is being transformed into a Pacific Basin and Atlantic Basin trading markets. This change has not been lost on Asian LNG consumers or producers.

Last year the US Department of Energy's Energy Information Administration (EIA) described in a comprehensive report on "U.S. LNG Markets and Uses" that LNG is expected to play an increasingly important role in the natural gas industry and energy markets in the next several years. Interest in LNG imports has been rekindled by higher US natural gas prices in recent years and technological advances that have lowered costs for liquefaction and regasifying, shipping, and storing LNG.

LNG has the advantage of allowing long-distance transportation of the liquid by ship across oceans to markets such as the United States and local distribution by trucks onshore. The ability to store LNG allows for its use to meet peak demand needs and in certain "niche markets" such as propane replacement and in vehicles. LNG generally is stored as a liquid in cryogenic tanks and then is regasified for further movement to consumers by pumping the liquid through heated pipes.

A critical factor in spurring the increased trade in LNG is the view held by many analysts that demand for electricity is on the rise. The emergence of natural gas as LNG as a global commodity is driven by the rise in electricity demand, which itself is driven by economic growth. In effect, natural gas has become the "fuel of choice" for electric power generation due to its comparatively benign environmental impacts as compared to oil and coal. In the United States alone, use of natural gas for electric power production has risen nearly 40% since 1990, and 90% of new generating capacity is fueled by gas.

However, growth in US gas consumption is small when compared to large developing countries. For example, growth in US electricity demand is only about two-thirds of the growth rate of the overall economy, whereas China's electricity consumption now is triple 1990 levels, and its electricity demand is currently increasing at an extraordinary 17% per year. Asia represents the rising demand for natural gas as well as the United States.

Another significant compelling cause of the increased focus on LNG is the general rise in US natural gas prices in this decade. During the winter of 2000–01, natural gas prices on the domestic spot market climbed above US$10 per thousand cubic feet (Mcf). Average wellhead prices in 2003 were well above US$4.00 per Mcf, despite sporadic price dips. A good rule of thumb to make LNG projects go forward is that the delivered cost of the gas should be in the US$3.25–3.50 range. Since the United States now represents a $4.00–$5.00 gas market, the highest in the world, these higher prices are driving many LNG projects forward in the United States and Mexico as well. These projects have direct impacts on the Asia Pacific LNG markets.

On the question of cost and price, the LNG value chain represents substantial cost and risk to the energy industry. Substantial savings have been achieved for both liquefaction and shipbuilding. Tankers today cost \$150 million rather than \$250 million as before. More importantly, the life spans of LNG tankers have been extended as many tankers have come off their first 20-year time chartering, and can be reused for many decades. Tankers represent the key constraint or opportunity in the development of world gas trade and developments in these markets cannot be overlooked. The LNG value chain today encompasses significant technology improvements for both cost reductions and safety, and environmental enhancements and protections. Overall, average cost of liquefaction, shipping, and regasification portion of the LNG chain declined from \$2.5/mmBtu to about \$1.8/mmBtu. This cost ranges from as low as \$1.5/mmBtu to as high as \$2.7/mmBtu. Upstream cost of gas, as usual, remains a significant cost risk with a range of \$0.5 to \$1/mmBtu.

The following Figure (Figure 7.1) shows the projected US EIA's wellhead price forecast versus a range for the cost to deliver LNG to the United States based on the estimates above. At projected prices, LNG projects will be commercially viable and supply cost-competitive natural gas.

Still another factor contributing to increased demand for, and use of, LNG is the development of improved technology in all phases of the LNG supply chain (including liquefication, transportation, and regasification), so that LNG can now be produced, liquefied, landed, and regasified in the United States at a cost of about \$2.50 to \$3.50 per mmBtu and perhaps as low as \$2.00. The result is the potential for a new, truly global natural gas market that no longer is limited by the reach of gas pipelines and the absence of a global marketplace.

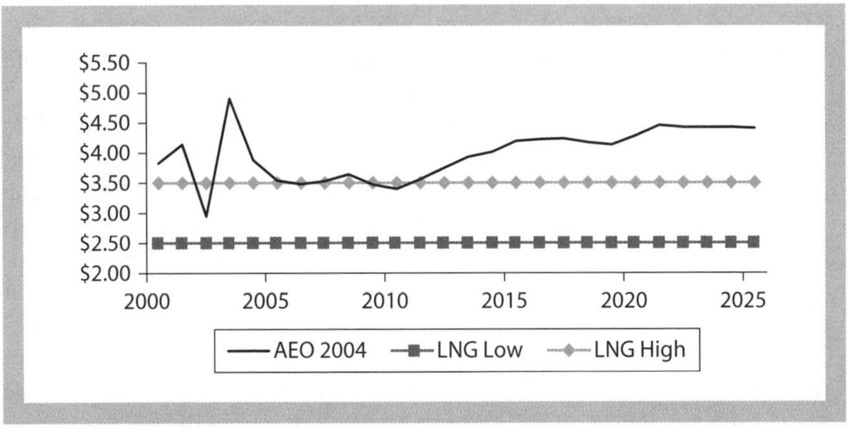

Figure 7.1 Natural gas price forecast and cost of LNG (\$/mmBtu)
Source: EIA and Industry

These factors have already dramatically increased US imports of LNG, and this trend is expected to increase geometrically. US LNG imports more than doubled from 2002 to 2003, based on preliminary estimates that show LNG imports at 540 bcf in 2003, compared to 228 bcf in 2002. The prior historic record for LNG imports was in 1979, when 256.6 bcf of LNG was imported, all of it from Algeria at that time.

Change in US government policy will drive global gas markets as the United States is the largest energy consumer in the world. The US government has made several important policy decisions in the last several years that reflect the clear intent to facilitate and increase the importation of LNG supplies. First, Congress enacted and President Bush signed the Maritime Transportation Security Act of 2002. This legislation amended the Deepwater Port Act of 1974 to include "offshore" natural gas facilities. Significantly, it transferred jurisdiction of offshore natural gas facilities from FERC to the US Maritime Administration and the US Coast Guard, both of which were at that time a part of the US Department of Transportation (DOT). The new legislation encourages construction of new offshore LNG terminals by instituting two parallel policy approaches. First, it reduces regulatory hurdles in building new offshore LNG facilities, by ending the time-consuming FERC approval process and replacing it with Maritime Administration's responsibility for reviewing the commercial aspects of the proposal, and Coast Guard's responsibility to consider safety, security, and environmental aspects. The new legislation also compels relatively quick government action. A decision is required within 365 days of receipt of an application for construction of an offshore LNG terminal. Once the final public hearing on an application has been held, it must be either approved or denied within 90 days. As acknowledged by the EIA, the ultimate impact of these provisions has both streamlined the permitting process and relaxed regulatory requirements.

The second important policy feature of the Maritime Security Transportation Act of 2002 is to provide greater financial security to developers of offshore LNG projects. Specifically, this is accomplished by allowing the owners of the offshore LNG terminal to actually own the capacity of the facility. While this principle may appear obvious to a business unencumbered by government regulation, the long-standing FERC policy had been to require the owner of an LNG terminal to allow others to bid in an "open season" for up to 100% of the capacity of the facility, with the owner offered the opportunity to recover the costs of operating the facility (plus a fair rate of return on its investment) by charging the facility users for the services provided–a classic regulated industry approach based on "cost of service" regulation. The 2002 legislation allows the owner to keep all or some of the capacity of the offshore terminal and sell the rest to bidders who will pay the owner market-determined prices for the capacity and services which such bidders buy. This is significant incentive for construction of offshore LNG receiving facilities and has now been applied to onshore facilities as well.

Shortly after President Bush signed the Maritime Transportation Security Act in November 2002, FERC applied the lead of that legislative philosophy to *onshore* LNG terminals. FERC changed significantly its policy concerning onshore LNG terminals in an order authorizing the Hackberry LNG terminal (now owned by Sempra Energy LNG Energy Group, and renamed Cameron LNG). Thus, in the December 2002 *Hackberry* decision, FERC terminated the "open season" and "open access" requirements for new onshore LNG terminals, thereby bringing parity in regulatory approaches to all LNG terminals. FERC's decision authorized Hackberry to provide services to its affiliates under rates and terms mutually agreed upon (i.e., market-based rates), rather than at regulated rates based on the costs of providing service (including a return on investment), and exempted the company from having to provide "open access" service to non-affiliates through the facilities. FERC Chairman Wood has stated that this new policy has resulted in an unprecedented movement to develop LNG facilities in the United States, by providing financial certainty for companies looking to invest the billions of dollars required to develop LNG facilities. Additionally, since the natural gas pipeline transporting regasified LNG from the facilities remains subject to FERC regulations, including open access, imposing a similar requirement on the import facilities would be redundant.

The importance of allowing an owner to operate a terminal as a proprietary facility should not be underestimated. The original four regasification facilities were all built and operated as part of the regulated interstate natural gas infrastructure. The owners were regulated entities, primarily interstate pipelines. As competitive at-risk assets, the major integrated oil companies will be interested in building, owning, and operating terminals. Given the capital requirements, participation of the majors is highly likely.

Most analysts predict the terminals that have the best chance of succeeding are the ones that line up both supply and market early. The major oils have the advantage as they typically have stakes in the gas source fields, liquefaction facilities and affiliated gas marketing organizations or large internal gas needs to ensure buyers. BP, Chevron, Conoco, Exxon, and Shell meet some or all of these criteria. Chevron and Exxon are pursuing proprietary terminal options. BP and Shell have taken space in existing facilities, though Shell is considering a proprietary project. BP is thought likely to take an equity position in one or more terminals developed by others. Conoco also is reported in talks with an independent developer for all the capacity at its proposed facility for its Qatari joint venture. For the most part, independent terminal sponsors have two business models. Either they will operate solely as tolling or fee-for-service facilities, or they will combine merchant services, in which they buy and sell LNG for their own account and tolling arrangements. These companies are all major players in Asian LNG markets on both the producer and consumer sides.

A number of new marine import terminals have been proposed. Clearly, not all of these will be built in this decade as there is no demand for all of the capacity. There is a risk of overbuilding by the importing companies between now and 2025 when all of that capacity will be needed. But, more immediate concern seems to be whether the new facilities can be built despite local community opposition even if they receive all regulatory approvals.

In mid-December, 2003, the Bush Administration held a ministerial summit on the potential growth and need for LNG in the US market. Energy ministers from several OPEC countries spoke, as well as ministers from non-OPEC countries and industry executives. There, the Bush Administration announced that up to 13 LNG facilities will be needed to supply the US market. The Administration is looking to LNG to make up the gap between domestic natural gas production and demand. Over 40 LNG terminals have been proposed, but industry and analysts acknowledge most of those proposals are unlikely to be built due to localized public opposition and the large amount of financial backing needed to construct such facilities.

US Secretary of Energy Spencer Abraham hosted the LNG Ministerial Summit, which brought together energy ministers from 24 countries to take a fresh look at the world LNG market place. The Summit served as a forum to explore global natural gas resources, size and scale of existing and proposed supply projects, export and import terminal facilities, LNG transportation routes to North America, new and growing markets, elements of the LNG value chain, new and emerging technology applications, safety and facility security, regulatory and siting challenges, and opportunities and barriers for investment in the LNG industry. Ministerial participants were from Algeria, Angola, Argentina, Australia, the Bahamas, Brazil, Brunei, Canada, Egypt, Equatorial Guinea, Italy, Mexico, Norway, Oman, Peru, Qatar, Russia, Saudi Arabia, Trinidad and Tobago, The United Arab Emirates, Venezuela, Indonesia, and United States of America. Nigeria was invited but did not attend.

In 1997, nine countries shipped less than four trillion cubic feet of LNG. Last year, 12 countries shipped 5.4 trillion cubic feet of gas. The world's producers and consumers recognize the possibilities. At least ten producing countries are either building or planning to build new gas liquefaction capacity, and another ten consuming countries are building or plan to build new regasification capacity. Based on facilities under construction, the Department of Energy (DOE) expects global LNG liquefaction capacity to increase by more than 40% by 2007. By that time, new ships joining the LNG fleet will have increased today's shipping capacity by 44%. In the United States alone, LNG imports are expected to more than double this year compared to last year, accounting for about 2% of our total natural gas consumption. The EIA forecasts that our LNG imports will increase from this year's projected 540 billion cubic feet to more than 2.2 trillion cubic feet in 2010, accounting for more than 8% of our total natural gas consumption.

LNG clearly is going to be a large factor in the world's future energy equation. The DOE estimated LNG imports would increase by 2000% in just over two decades to meet US natural gas demand. Investment in excess of $100 billion would be required to expand North American terminal capacity to handle the projected 15 bcf per day (bcf/d) by 2025.

Formatted as a series of plenary and breakout sessions, the LNG Ministerial Summit also provided a forum for the private sector to share information on the future of the LNG economy and to discuss relevant public policy issues. Industry officials generally lauded the federal government for having taken decisive actions to speed up approvals, including enactment of the Maritime Transportation Security Act giving the US Coast Guard clear jurisdiction over offshore LNG terminals, rules to expedite permits and FERC actions to allow owner discretion in terminal operations.

At the same time, industry noted that politics at the state and local levels, where key siting issues play out, are more complicated. Industry officials estimated it may take as long as five years in some cases to update or revise state laws. There may be some regions of the country, such as California, where it may be very difficult to build anything at all because of longstanding opposition to energy-related projects. To help reduce that resistance, Secretary Abraham insisted that both industry and the federal government would need to better educate the public and address environmental and safety concerns often cited by local stakeholders.

The focus of the Summit was to encourage ministerial actions to bring about long-term stability to the natural gas market. Issues at the Summit included the development of worldwide product quality standards, the development of a workable spot market mechanism, increased measures to guarantee the safety of transporting LNG, and development of solutions to issues surrounding the siting of LNG facilities that will confront both producing and consuming countries.

Analysts correctly recognize that the natural gas business is set to undergo revolutionary changes with the United States set to become a hub in the global gas trading market. With each month that passes, it is clear that the United States is joining the rest of the world in the "embrace" of LNG as a global commodity that can provide substantial assistance in meeting the growing demand for natural gas, and thereby maximizing the use of this relatively clean-burning fuel to minimize adverse environmental consequences as compared to other fossil fuels.

The United States is in the first stages of a rapid increase in the importation of LNG. The market driver is that the United States is now the world's high cost gas center. This increase is triggered by the triple combination of (1) increased use of natural gas as a relatively clean-burning fuel for new and upgraded electric power generating plants, (2) a steady increase in the price of domestically produced natural gas, and (3) the development of greatly improved technology throughout the LNG supply chain so that the delivered cost of LNG to the marketplace is much lower than in the past.

While the end result is that dozens of new LNG import projects have either been initiated or are under consideration in the United States as well as Mexico and Canada, the number of facilities and net additional capacity will depend on public acceptance and economics. Many analysts increasingly expect that only new onshore facilities relatively remote from population centers, or offshore facilities will be built. The cost associated with offshore construction will bring economics to the fore. More remote onshore facilities may have additional infrastructure costs to connect with the existing interstate pipeline grid. The current surge of interest in the importation of LNG into the United States will be tempered by the twin related factors of environmental impact and safety. As to the environment, LNG possesses the superior attribute of less harmful emissions as compared to coal and oil, especially in electric power plants. Nevertheless, an LNG import and regasification facility has its own impacts upon the local environment and has engendered active citizen opposition in certain locations. As to safety, the LNG industry has a long history of relative safety, but there are no fail-safe systems of human enterprise, as illustrated by the explosion in January 2004 at the Algerian liquefication facility. The environmental impacts and safety of LNG imports must also be contrasted with the current status and future development of the nuclear energy industry in the United States Debates concerning environmental and safety issues respecting LNG imports are comparatively small in scope and size when compared with the nuclear alternative.

NORTHEAST ASIAN TRADING HUB

Northeast Asia represents today's true LNG market with Japan, South Korea, and Taiwan taking the lion's share of global LNG supplies. Down the road, China's voracious energy appetite looms large as it constructs its first of many LNG terminals. Because of these market dynamics, it is highly likely that a Northeast Asia trading hub will occur with LNG supplies from the Middle East, Southeast Asia, the Northwest Shelf of Australia and Sakhalin Island, which brings much supply to the region. The key element that is currently missing from this equation is price discovery. Changes are already taking place and now LNG is priced with the Japanese Crude Cocktail (JCC), being challenged by Brent and Henry Hub pricing. More price discovery will create greater liquidity in this emerging market which is only tanker constrained at present. With 65 new LNG carriers being built, that dimension of world LNG trade is also becoming large.

GLOBAL PRICING PROXY

Increasingly, Henry Hub is being written into long-term LNG contracts as the pricing index for LNG liquefication and regasification facilities being developed worldwide to meet growing US demand for LNG. Market observers expect Henry Hub and the NYMEX's natural gas futures contracts to become pricing proxies for many international deals.

Trinidad, for example – responsible for 90% of US LNG imports in the first quarter of 2003 – insisted on Henry Hub-based prices in talks with Jamaica over processing its stranded gas. In the transatlantic market, players are already looking at spreads between Henry Hub and Zeebrugge, the major trading point for European pipeline gas.

While it is ultimately location that will determine price, Henry Hub will be a logical pricing point for some LNG projects proposed and under way in Louisiana and Texas. Marathon Oil says it is in talks with BG Group to use pricing linked to Henry Hub for LNG. BG Group will buy on a free-on-board (FOB) basis from Marathon's Equatorial New Guinea project.

Another active LNG pricing benchmark is likely to emerge on the US west coast. Many LNG projects are being considered for the west coast, many of which plan to trade with the Asia Pacific region. Here a SoCal benchmark, based on the natural gas pricing index on the southern California border, is expected to develop, but oil indexing is also likely to play a role.

Meanwhile, the Asian region has turned to the more liquid fuel oil or crude oil indexes as proxies for LNG, in the absence of a liquid natural gas market. There is the expectation that the Henry Hub price will become an index that will be used if not in parity then in tandem with the JCC. The JCC is a basket of crude used as a pricing benchmark for LNG in Asia and in the long term correlates well (except for a volatile freight component) with the WTI Crude Oil futures markets on NYMEX (www.nymex.com).

Volume in the JCC swaps markets could see dramatic growth during 2004, The biggest market makers being Bank of Tokyo Mitsubishi, Societe General, Goldman Sachs, Morgan Stanley, in no particular order. Tenures of these swaps are generally between 1-year up to 10-years forward. Volumes for swaps beyond 5-years forward though tend to be in the small end-user category in terms of executable volume per trade. JCC Swaps are generally traded in Yen or US Dollars.

So while global LNG trade will continue to be based on long-term contracts and relationships, the spot trade is slowly breaking new ground, with more facilities designating part of their offtake as uncommitted in order to exploit such price differentials. This year, the Malaysia LNG Tiga liquification project and Russia's Sakhalin project secured financing with a percentage of offtake not committed to long-term contracts.

But the global spot market is also hampered by the limited supply of tankers that can move spot cargo. The majority of LNG tankers are committed to, and were commissioned under, long-term contracts. As mentioned earlier in this chapter, with 65 new LNG carriers being built, that dimension of world LNG trade is also coming into place over the next two to four years to the spot market, providing more flexibility to move cargoes.

PRICING PRESSURE

Supply competition is putting downward pressure on prices and narrowing pricing disparities in more mature markets. This is clear from the Asian markets, where market power is shifting to the buyer as competition intensifies. A group of Japanese industries recently demanded lower prices for Indonesian LNG before they would agree to extend their long-term contracts. As a banker financing LNG projects, it is worth looking at hedging some cash-flows!

The move is in response to lower-priced deals recently negotiated between Indonesia and China. The Japanese cartel is paying just above $3 for LNG and wants prices in line with China's, at around $2.90. In 2002, Japan imported 75 billion cubic meters (bcm) of LNG. By comparison, Europe imported 41 bcm and the United States 6 bcm, according to Pira. Japan consumes 65% of the world's LNG.

On top of price pressures, the increasing linkage between LNG markets around the world also made itself felt this winter – particularly in respect of Japan's considerable market power and influence on US LNG. A cold spell in Korea and the shutdown of nuclear plants in Japan resulted in cargoes from the Atlantic Basin going to Korea. Hence, the United States received less spot gas.

Finally we are starting to see prices in Asia, Europe, and the United States being influenced by where cargoes go. A spot market is emerging and with this, a forward traded market could develop. For the time being we are restricted to using crude oil indexed swaps, Henry Hub swaps/futures and JCC deals to hedge our LNG exposures, but eventually we should see over the next four years regional LNG swaps markets develop off the back of an increased spot market activity.

In October 2002, the Japan-triggered US LNG shortage necessitated the diversion of more expensive cargo to the United States to compensate. By 2007, a similar supply disruption is likely to have greater consequences for the US market, given the six new and expanded LNG facilities planned for the US west coast for trade with the Asia Pacific region.

But by then, market players may leverage liquid markets based on JCC and SoCal to secure cross-commodity hedges and protect against a Japanese nuclear shutdown or the next cold Korean winter.

CHAPTER 8

Energy Risk Management in Japan

The Japanese energy market is a high cost market dependent on foreign imports for oil, gas and coal. The lack of natural resources in this highly industrialized and modern economy has brought with it a very high cost base for the energy complex. Consequently, Japanese consumers and industry are highly energy efficient already having gone through Oil shocks in 1973 and 1979; however, this situation has come at the cost of the highest energy prices in the world. High prices are an attraction to market deregulation but Japan has always been a highly protected, paternalistic market with government playing a very direct role in energy and industrial policy. Consequently, Japanese energy trading and risk management markets are very immature. Trading companies called the Shosha are actually not traditional trading companies that take on much risk but are really commodity suppliers for Japanese consumers, that is, they source raw materials for Japanese industry. Energy risk management in Japan is overshadowed by security of supply issues and an underdeveloped financial derivatives market as compared to North America or Europe. This is changing but it is the slow pace of gradual change endemic to Japanese culture not to disrupt ongoing business practices and not to upset consumers. Harmony is still the watch word in this very rich but predominantly conservative nation. Thus, energy risk management is an evolving profession and its application in Japan is nascent. While there is much interest in the topic, there is the fact that there is a fundamental lack of an entrepreneurial culture for this to take root rapidly. Energy trading is a very individualistic activity not conducive to consensual decision making.

Japan's economic stagnation since the early 1990s led to a period of consolidation in the country's energy sector. Energy demand has been stable, and Japan's energy industries, particularly the downstream oil sector, underwent a period of downsizing and consolidation. Japan remains important to the world energy sector, though, as one of the major exporters of energy-sector capital equipment, and engineering, construction, and project management services.

Oil trading is the most developed market with oil deregulation completed in March 1996.

Eight years later Japan's economic growth accelerated in 2004, continuing the recovery it began in 2003, following a decade of economic stagnation. Japan's real gross domestic product (GDP) rose by 2.5% in 2003, and it is projected to rise by 4.5% in 2004 – the fastest growth rate experienced by the Japanese economy in the last 14 years. The upturn largely reflects a surge in export demand, led by exports to China. Domestic consumer spending in Japan also has been strengthening this year.

Japan's prime minister Junichiro Koizumi, who took office in 2001, has pressed for structural reforms in Japan's economy. In one major change, Koizumi reversed the previous policy of increasing government spending to stimulate the country's economy, and has set a deficit ceiling of 30 trillion yen ($270 billion). Spending on public works projects, which had been funded as part of previous stimulus packages, has been scaled back significantly. The Bank of Japan, however, has adopted a more expansionary monetary policy, which has provided some stimulus to the economy.

Japan lacks significant domestic sources of energy and must import substantial amounts of crude oil, natural gas, and other energy resources, including uranium for its nuclear power plants. In 2002, the country's dependence on fossil fuel imports for primary energy stood at more than 80%. Oil provided Japan with 49.7% of its total energy needs, coal 18.9%, nuclear power 13.7%, natural gas 12.7%, hydroelectric power 3.7%, and renewable sources 1.1%.

Japan contains almost no oil reserves of its own (59 million barrels of proven oil reserves), but it is the world's third largest oil consumer (after the United States and China). Japan consumed an estimated 5.57 million bbl/d of oil in 2003, up from 5.30 million bbl/d in 2002. Part of the increase in oil consumption was attributable to the shutdown of a large number of nuclear power plants in 2003, which caused utilities to maximize use of oil-fired generating capacity. Most (75–80%) of this oil came from OPEC, particularly Persian Gulf countries like the United Arab Emirates, Saudi Arabia, Kuwait, Qatar, and Iran. Japan has worked – with relatively little success – to diversify its oil import sources away from the Middle East.

Until 1996, when Japan's oil consumption peaked at nearly 5.9 million bbl/d, Japanese oil consumption (and imports) had been growing steadily for years. From 1997 through 2002, Japan's oil consumption declined as its economic slump caused demand by industrial and other users to decrease. With nuclear electricity generating capacity restored, Japan's oil demand dipped in the second half 2004, despite relatively strong economic growth.

The loss of drilling rights by Japan's Arabian Oil Company (AOC) in the Saudi Arabian portion of the Neutral Zone dealt a major blow to Japan's policy of seeking overseas equity in oil projects. AOC's rights to the concession, which produced 280,000 bbl/d, expired at the end of February 2000. Japan has been trying to make up for the loss of the AOC concession in Saudi Arabia by increasing its investment in Iran. Iran announced in November 2000 that it would begin exclusive negotiations with Japex and Indonesia Petroleum (Inpex) for development rights to the huge onshore Azadegan oilfield. Azadegan has been estimated to contain 6 billion barrels of recoverable reserves. The consortium submitted a preliminary development plan for Azadegan in mid-2001, and a binding contract for the project was concluded between the Japanese firms and the National Iranian Oil Company (NIOC) in February 2004. Initial production from Azadegan is expected by 2007, with peak production of 260,000 bbl/d reached by 2012.

Apart from its interests in the Persian Gulf, Japan also has been seeking equity stakes in the Caspian Sea region. In July 1998, Mitsui purchased a 15% share, along with Azerbaijan's State Oil Company, of concessions in the Caspian Sea's Kur Dashi oil field.

Another possible source for Japanese oil imports, which has recently received increased attention, is the Russian Far East. Japan has been promoting a proposed pipeline from oilfields near Anagarsk in Siberia to an export terminal on the Pacific coast at Nakhodka. An alternate proposed route would transport the oil from Anagarsk to Daqing in China, connecting to China's existing crude oil pipeline network. A Russian export terminal on the Pacific is a very appealing idea to Japan, since it could reduce Japan's dependence on imports from the Persian Gulf. As of end 2004, it appears likely that the Nakhodka pipeline option is more likely to be built, with Japan offering financing of as much as $10 billion on favorable terms to promote its preferred pipeline route and upstream development.

As of January 2004, Japan had 4.7 million bbl/d of oil refining capacity at 32 refineries, down from 5.0 million bbl/d as recently as 2001. In recent years, as Japan's petroleum product consumption has stagnated, the country's refining industry has suffered from overcapacity. Japan also began to allow imports of petroleum products in the mid-1990s, putting additional pressure on Japanese refiners to cut costs and become internationally competitive.

In response to these pressures, Japan's refining industry went through a round of consolidations in 1999 and 2000. Nippon Oil and Mitsubishi Oil completed a merger in early 1999, forming Nippon Mitsubishi Oil. Nippon Mitsubishi then acquired Koa Oil from Caltex in September 1999, and in February 2002 merged Koa Oil with another subsidiary, Tohuku Oil. In October 1999, Nippon Mitsubishi announced a strategic alliance with another independent Japanese refiner, Cosmo Oil. The move, while not a merger, allows the two companies to coordinate distribution of refined products and to reduce costs through reduced duplication of some functions. Another similar strategic alliance was formed with Idemitsu Kosan in

December 2002. As a result of the agreement, Idemitsu shut down the 80,000 bbl/d Hyogo refinery in April 2003 and its 110,000 bbl/d Okinawa refinery in November 2003.

A second alliance coalesced around Showa Shell, Royal Dutch Shell's Japanese subsidiary, in which it owns a 50% stake. In January 1999, Showa Shell and Japan Energy announced a strategic alliance in petroleum product distribution and crude oil procurement.

GAS IN JAPAN

Japan has about 1.4 trillion cubic feet (tcf) in proven natural gas reserves, with possibly more under the seabed surrounding Japan. Because domestic natural gas production is minimal, about 97% of Japan's natural gas is imported, all in the form of liquefied natural gas (LNG). Unlike oil, demand for natural gas is still rising about 3–4% per year. Most of this LNG comes from Southeast Asia, with 28% from Indonesia, 20% from Malaysia, and 12% from Brunei. The United States also supplies a small quantity of LNG to Japan from a facility in Alaska, which accounts for slightly over 2% of Japan's natural gas consumption. Most of the LNG is used either for electric power generation or as feedstock for petrochemical plants.

Three Japanese companies, Tokyo Gas, Osaka Gas, and Toho Gas signed a binding contract in February 2002 for the import of natural gas from Malaysia's MLNG Tiga project, covering deliveries beginning in 2004. The contract is noteworthy in that it includes much more flexible terms for the purchaser than most traditional LNG contracts, which commit the purchaser to a specific volume over 15–20 years. The three firms also renewed their baseload contracts with Malaysia's first two LNG export terminals, on terms more flexible than the original contracts. Tokyo Gas and Toho Gas signed a binding contract in October 2001 for LNG purchases from Australia's North West Shelf LNG project, to begin in 2004. Three Japanese companies, Mitsubishi, Osaka Gas, and Itochu, signed contracts in June 2004 with Oman's Qalhat LNG for deliveries to begin between 2006 and 2009.

Many of Japan's existing LNG contracts date from the 1970s and 1980s, when terms were less flexible and tied to prices for crude oil. With these contracts coming up for renewal, Japanese buyers have been insisting on terms more favorable to the buyer, including volume variances, and a weakening in the pricing link to crude oil.

Japan has objected to Chinese development of natural gas resources in the East China Sea in an area where the two countries Exclusive Economic Zone (EEZ) claims overlap. Japan claims a division of the EEZ on the median line between the countries' coastlines. China claims an EEZ extending to the limits of its continental shelf. The specific development in dispute is China's drilling in the Chunxiao field, which is three miles west of the median line. But Japan contends that it may be tapping natural gas reserves that extend past the median line.

COAL

Japan is by far the world's largest importer of steam coal, mainly for power generation, paper plants, and cement production. Japan also is the world's largest importer of coking coal for its steel industry. Overall, Japan accounts for about 22% of total world coal imports. Sources of imported steam coal are Australia, South Africa, the United States, and China. Japanese coking coal imports come mainly from Australia, Canada, the United States and Russia.

Prices paid by Japanese firms for coal are currently rising, as decreased exports of coal from China put upward pressure on the market. Chinese exports has expanded rapidly in 2002 and early 2003, pushing Asian coal prices down, but increased domestic demand reversed this trend in the second half of 2003.

ELECTRICITY

Japan generated 1044 billion kiloWatthours (bkWh) of electricity on 238 gigaWatts (gW) of capacity in 2002. Of Japan's total generation in 2002, about 62% came from thermal (oil, gas, and coal) plants, 28% from nuclear reactors, 8% from hydroelectric dams, and less than 2% from geothermal, solar, and wind.

Due to the country's desire to enhance its energy security, Japan has increased its reliance on nuclear power generation. The last two years, however, have been challenging for Japan's nuclear power industry. In August 2002, it emerged that maintenance inspection findings at some nuclear reactors owned by Tokyo Electric Power (TEPCO) had not been properly reported to government regulators. This led to the shutdown of all 17 of TEPCO's nuclear reactors over the following several months. Several new reactor projects, including some proposed by other utilities, were put on hold while the issue was resolved. In the short term, this led to increases in Japan's fuel oil and LNG consumption, as generating capacity using fossil fuels has been brought online to make up for the shortage of nuclear generating capacity. TEPCO has been gradually bringing its nuclear generating units back online, as they are re-licensed, and had 13 of the 17 units in operation as of the end of June 2004. All 17 units are expected to be returned to operation by the end of August 2004.

By raising its reliance on nuclear-generated electricity, Japan is hoping to reduce its carbon dioxide emissions. Japan's current 10-year energy plan, approved in March 2002, calls for the expansion of nuclear generation by about 30% by 2011. This is expected to entail the construction of 9–12 new nuclear power plants, with 17.5 gW in new nuclear generating capacity. The Japanese government also plans to offer subsidies for nuclear power plant construction, to offset expected cost-cutting pressures on utilities due to deregulation which might lead to increased reliance on fossil fuels for electricity generation. Currently Japan ranks third worldwide in installed nuclear capacity, behind the United States and France. Japan currently has 51 reactors with an installed capacity of 45 gW. Japan's government has indicated that it is still committed to increasing nuclear power's share of generating capacity in the future, but many independent analysts think that the target of a 41% nuclear share of electric power generation by 2011 is unlikely to be achieved. Public opposition to Japan's nuclear power program has increased in reaction to a series of accidents at Japanese nuclear plants, especially the accident at the Tokaimura uranium processing plant in September 1999, the 2002 TEPCO reactor shutdowns, and an August 2004 steam pipe burst at the Mihama nuclear power plant, which killed four workers.

In August 1998, the Atomic Energy Commission approved the construction of a new light-water reactor, which will be built in Higashidori in Aomori prefecture in northern Japan. Also, in March 1999, the Japanese Nuclear Safety Commission approved plans for Hokuriku Electric Power Company to build a new nuclear power plant in the central town of Shika, which will be operational by 2006.

Japan's electricity prices are by far the highest in the OECD, and Japan has begun a program of reforms designed to make its electric utility sector more efficient. Currently, Japan is served by ten vertically integrated utilities which each have a specific geographic zone. The Japanese Diet passed a bill in May 1999 which amended the Electric Utilities Industry Law (EUIL) to allow a partial opening to competition. Beginning in March 2000, about 8000 large industrial and commercial Japanese electric power consumers, comprising roughly one-third of the Japanese power market, have been able to choose their electricity suppliers. Regional utilities currently are obligated to allow power from other suppliers to transit their grids to these large consumers. In April 2005, an additional phase of deregulation will take effect, which will extend competition to all industrial and commercial entities with peak demand over 50 kilowatts.

While a small percentage of Japan's electricity has been provided by independent power producers (IPPs) since 1995, the new deregulation is expected to generate much more investor interest in developing IPPs, though progress in this direction has been slower than expected due to weak demand.

While the Japanese electricity market is perceived by many as a closed system to foreign competition, significant changes are taking place in the world's second-largest electricity market. The major market drivers have been the need to lower power costs for industry and other consumers.

The EUIL was revised in January 1996 for the first time in 31 years. This began a process intended to open the door to competition and the internationalization of the industry. The focus of the revised law was the expansion of the number of players in the electric power generation sector as well as rate reform, and the establishment of a system for direct retail power supply.

While individual electric power companies have implemented a range of cost-reduction and efficiency programs over the past decade, the process of change has gradually accelerated over the past several years. The Japanese government has mandated reductions in rates that are forcing electric utilities to further reduce costs each year. The initially stated goal has been to reduce electric power costs by 20% by 2001. Further reforms were made by the Ministry of International Trade and Industry (MITI, now called METI) in May 1998, which allowed industrial customers to sell power to their large customers. And in May 1999 another amendment to the Electric Utilities Industry Law passed the Japanese Diet, which took effect on March 21, 2000. It allowed retail choice for large-load customers (over 2 mW) as well as require competitive bidding for thermal capacity acquisitions for the 10 regional utilities. Further regulatory reforms in the deregulation process will include allowing non-utility sales of excess power to retail customers and the creation of a pool system. The government again revised the law in 2003 as part of complete electricity restructuring which hopefully will lead to more competition and lower electricity prices. Eleven companies have applied to supply retail electric power in Japan. These competitive retailers have 2000 mW of capacity and by the end of March 2003 (the end of the Japanese fiscal year) supplied 0.89% of competitive retail markets, not a very significant amount in the huge Japanese power market. The impact of this limited competition and partial deregulation has been to have Japanese power companies to lower their prices.

The focus of industry restructuring is to expand retail competition. The deregulation plan is now to open to smaller customers of under 500 kilowatts by 2004 and to users of 50 kW by April 2005. At that point, retail competition will encompass 60% of Japanese power supply. By April 2007, the result of restructuring so far will be evaluated and full retail choice, including retail residential customers will be considered. The demise of Enron and the US merchant power section brought a chill to efforts to move deregulation aggressively and set back the market liberalization process by two years. The attitude is also fortified by the Japanese perception that US retail competition has been a failure so why rush into any significant changes now.

Another area under consideration for restructuring is the transmission sector. There is movement here to create systems operation business that will be transparent and neutral. Thus, the Japanese Power Exchange will be launched in April 2005. The exchange will be established by companies voluntarily and will manage the day ahead spot market transactions and long-term forward transactions. This wholesale power exchange will be expected to provide a price index to facilitate trading and price discovery for future investments. It remains to be seen where actual electricity trading will be substantial at that time but there is tremendous interest by Japanese electric and gas utilities. Other ideas, such as independent system operators, power exchanges, power marketing and electricity futures trading, are beginning to take hold in the Japanese power markets.

In Japan, there are ten regional investor-owned utilities, the Electricity Power Development Corporation (EPDC) now called JPower – a public power authority that is being privatized – and the government-owned Japan Atomic Power Company (JAPC). There are four large gas utilities. Both EPDC and JAPC are wholesale power companies supplying their power to the ten utilities. Tokyo Electric Power is the second largest electric utility in the world, and Osaka-based Kansai Electric Power is the sixth largest. Rounding out the total are Chubu, Tohoku, Kyushu, Hokkaido, Hokuriku, Chugoku, Shikoku, and Okinawa.

JPower will eventually be fully privatized, but its role in the past has been to supply the ten utilities with wholesale power. It has 65 generation facilities, of which 58 are hydropower (8260 mW), 6 are coal-fired (5620 mW), and 1 is geothermal (12.5 mW). The sixth-largest utility in Japan, it is expected to add 5900 mW of new capacity by 2008, including a nuclear facility. Unlike the 10 utilities, JPower has had an active slate of international technical assistance projects throughout the world since 1960. In July 1997 it established an International Power Development office to expand into IPP projects in Asia and Latin America. Japanese utilities have so far been slow to develop their international generation portfolio.

Japan has an installed capacity base of over 221,000 mW; thermal energy accounts for 138,000 mW of this total, and hydropower for 42,000 mW. The ten regional utilities own 170,000 mW; JPower, over 14,000 mW; and Japan Atomic Power, about 3000 mW. METI originally proposed a ten-year plan for changing the mix of utility generation growth that favors nuclear power and interestingly enough keeps natural gas consumption relatively flat. But a nuclear accident in September 2002 and a nuclear power scandal involving senior management at Tokyo Electric Power Company have swung the emphasis to natural gas vis a vis increased LNG imports. This is despite the environmental and efficiency benefits of combined-cycle turbine usage, and the fact that new LNG storage development is under way by both Tokyo Gas and Osaka Gas. The reason for this is to a large degree the lack of a piped gas infrastructure, and the need to protect Japanese gas utilities from the perils of competition.

The fuel profile for Japan reflects the country's lack of natural resources. Japan imports almost 100% of its oil, with 75% of that coming from the

Middle East, and almost all its natural gas. There are also undersea piped gas projects proposed from Sakhalin Island to Hokkaido and a proposed multibillion-dollar monster project from Siberia through Mongolia, China, and Korea undersea to western Japan. But ground has not been broken to construct these projects yet. Oil exports are now leaving Sakhalin and it seems more likely that LNG will be exported to Northeast Asian countries including Japan rather than the building of an undersea pipeline due to NIMBY concerns from Hokkaido fishermen. Coal imports are large, and with 90% imported, Japan continues to be the largest coal importer in the world. Japan currently has about 50 nuclear power plants in operation. It is projected that nuclear power will continue to rise from its present 35% market share, as it is primed for the greatest capacity growth, with 12 to 16 power stations under construction despite the long lead times in nuclear plants coming on line. This may not be attainable due to scandals and NIMBY issues in Japan regarding nuclear power. The renewable-fuel sector is small, but is mandated to grow to 1.4% of generation mix by 2010. Japan has an extensive hydropower system and geothermal energy, but these sources are not expected to grow due to the scarcity of available land and the fact that the best sites have been tapped. Oil still has a role – direct burn of crude oil from China and imported LSWR from Indonesia – but its market share is declining.

The potential entrance of foreign competitors may further drive competitive pressures in the Japanese power market but that is highly unlikely with the failure of Enron in Japan, the pulling out of Japan by BP, and the reluctance of foreign companies to enter a highly government-managed market, while Shell, Exxon Mobil, and others are known to be examining the Japanese market for entrance opportunities, perhaps through their refining subsidiaries, some of which cogenerate power as IPPs.

The Japanese government estimates that between 34,000 and 52,000 mW of IPP power will be needed if the current system is further liberalized. As has been mentioned previously, full fuel supply competition for power generation has not been implemented at the current time. Other companies, including Tokyo Gas, are planning to enter the electric power business. While these generated amounts may seem small, they will lead to further erosion of the past monopoly supplier system of the major electric utilities. They are also somewhat indicative of the Japanese way of doing business as a gradual change process. The ramifications are leading to more competition.

Changes in the natural gas supply market should not be understated. The Gas Utilities Industry Law was revised in March 1995, liberalizing gas supply to large-scale customers with over 2 million cubic meters per year. Already, Tokyo Electric Power and Kansai Electric Power are pursuing opportunities to supply gas from their LNG storage facilities to their largest customers. This has put tremendous competitive pressures on Tokyo Gas and Osaka Gas, and their position in the LNG market. This is evolving in the climate of the emergence of a world LNG market that will trade LNG cargoes. Japan is directly impacted by changes in LNG markets as new suppliers enter and new end-users such as the United States become more active.

Japan is the world's largest importer of LNG, with 20 active receiving terminals. Typical supply contracts are 20-year fuel procurement contracts with take-or-pay provisions. The market has developed some supply flexibility during the past few years because of reduced demand due to the Asian economic crisis, such that spot LNG cargoes have been available. Moreover, there has been a movement to develop smaller projects of 3 to 3.5 million liquefaction trains rather than the 6 to 7 million previously developed. In Asia Pacific, 40% of gas fields larger than 1 tcf have been discovered and abandoned due to the desire to develop large LNG supply sources from Australia, Indonesia, and Malaysia. That could change if newer, smaller facilities get financing.

Another very powerful market driver is the very significant embrace by Japan of the Kyoto Protocols of December 1997 for greenhouse gas emission reductions. The electric utilities are embarking on a new round of nuclear power generation and energy conservation initiatives in order to meet the 1990 emissions levels of 6% reductions from 2008 to 2012. The electric power industry has been working voluntarily since November 1996 to reduce CO_2 emissions, which it needs to reduce by 9% by 2010. The concept is to replicate the very successful model of So_2 OTC emissions trading market in the United States. This will directly impact the newer coal-fired capacity that has come on line during the past ten years and may now be required to be repowered to natural gas. It is highly likely that Japan will have an active carbon trading market before electricity and gas trading commence. Already 40 companies are participating in mock trading set up by the Japanese government.

While security of supply is still an overriding concern in Japanese policy circles, deregulation and liberalization are now under way in full force. There was even a proposal by the Basic Policy Committee of the Electric Utility Industry Council to shift to a full-scale bidding system for newly built fossil-fired power beyond 2008. But the fear was that complete liberalization would add too much risk to an increasingly fragmented market. While that proposal has been shelved at the present time, the bidding system still requires electric utilities to participate in the bidding for long-run fossil-fuel sources by themselves. This will probably change in coming years. The key change will be the emergence of true competition in the electric power markets to accelerate the market penetration of new technologies and new ways of doing business. Energy trading and risk management will take time to take hold in this overly managed market. However, these changes are already under way and are unstoppable. They are altering the nature of the energy business in Japan forever.

Western-style power markets unlikely in China and South East Asia

Asian plans for Western-style freed-up power markets are likely to founder as demand grows and investors baulk at the risks, leaving more room for fixed-price supply deals.

China alone needs $1.9 trillion of new power investment by 2030 according to International Energy Agency figures – more than a year's worth of GDP for the world's second largest electricity consumer. Along with The Philippines, Indonesia, and South Korea it is looking at creating "power pools" – where generators compete to supply electricity.

The aim is to create an efficient, transparent power market that brings lower prices and attracts more foreign investment.

Manila and Jakarta also hope that it could ease their mounting state debts by creating an alternative to Power Purchase Agreements (PPAs), the long-term deals that are currently the price of foreign power funding.

But electricity and markets are hard to mix, as shown by slow progress towards reform in Europe and post-liberalization blackouts in California. In Asia there are extra problems, not the least, the demand growth of 3.5%.

It would be surprising if the Philippines, Korea, and China implement complete deregulation and power-pool markets in the next five years. It doesn't necessarily improve these markets for consumers or investors. Leaving power prices to the market as supply tightens will only push up prices, something governments are averse to. In countries such as the Philippines and South Korea, electricity is already subsidized by the state.

Some bankers fear that if nations insist on a market-driven system, blackouts could follow as foreign investors shy away.

In countries such as the Philippines and Indonesia where regulatory regimes are murky, investors prefer PPAs.

Any reform would jeopardize existing foreign interest in the countries' multi-billion dollar power privatization programs. Foreign investors, including banks and wealthy Asian power firms such as CLP Holdings and Singapore Power and Tokyo Electric, are diversifying from their saturated home markets.

They have made a string of investments in Asia. But they are not entering volatile businesses such as merchant power plants and energy derivatives trading. This was the road to Enron Corp.'s ruin in 2001 that also forced many US power firms to sell Asian and European portfolios to repay debts.

Lights out? The Philippines and Indonesia hope a shift to power pools will ease the debt burden they have accumulated under PPAs. The Philippines' National Power Corp. (Napocor) had debts of 1.3 trillion pesos ($23 billion) at the end of 2003, a large part of which were liabilities related to PPAs, and is nearly a third of the country's gross domestic product, according to Fitch Rating.

The Philippines, Asia's largest sovereign borrower after Japan, is inviting foreign investors to buy Napocor's plants and grids to raise $4–5 billion. But the sale has attracted few serious bidders, sources close to the process said, largely because most of the plants on the block are not covered by PPA.

CHAPTER 9

Energy Developments in Southeast and South Asia

Most Southeast and South Asian countries are all net oil importers except for Indonesia and Malaysia which also export LNG. Oil trading is more active in Southeast Asia than in South Asia, but the emphasis is still on short-term trading. With constant import growth, persistent oil price volatility, and privatization and restructuring efforts underway, both regions seem ripe for the use of energy risk management financial instruments.

SOUTHEAST ASIA

The focus of most attention regarding the Southeast Asian resources has been on oil. The South China Sea region has proven oil reserves estimated at about 7 billion barrels, and oil production in the region is currently around 2.5 million bbl/d. Malaysian production accounts for almost one-half of the region's total. Total South China Sea production has increased gradually over the past few years, primarily as additional production from China, Malaysia, and Vietnam has come online. The fact that surrounding areas are rich in oil deposits has led to speculation that the Spratly Islands could be an untapped oil-bearing province located near some of the world's largest future energy consuming countries. While the Spratly Islands region will not become another Persian Gulf, some estimates suggested that potential oil resources (not proved reserves) of the Spratly and Paracel Islands could be as high as 105 billion barrels of oil.

The South China Sea is rich in natural resources such as oil and natural gas. These resources have garnered attention throughout the Asia Pacific region. Asia's economic growth rates have been among the highest in the world, and this economic growth will be accompanied by an increasing demand for energy. Between now and 2025, oil consumption in developing Asian countries is expected to rise by 3% annually on average, with more than one-third of this increase coming from China alone. If this growth rate is maintained, oil demand for these nations will increase from about 14.5 million bbl/d in 2000 to nearly 29.8 million bbl/d by 2025 putting stress on world oil markets.

Much of this additional demand will need to be imported from the Middle East and Africa. Excluding cargoes bound for South Asia, most of this volume would need to pass through the strategic Strait of Malacca into the South China Sea. Countries in the Asia-Pacific region depend on seaborne trade to fuel their economic growth, and this has led to the sea's transformation into one of the world's busiest shipping lanes.

Though sometimes overlooked, natural gas might be the most abundant hydrocarbon resource in the South China Sea. Most of the hydrocarbon fields explored in the South China Sea regions of Brunei, Indonesia, Malaysia, Thailand, Vietnam, and the Philippines contain natural gas, not oil. Estimates by the US Geological Survey and others indicate that about 60–70% of the region's hydrocarbon resources are gas.

Natural gas is expected to rise by about 4.5% annually on average through 2025 with almost half of this increase coming from China. If this growth rate is maintained, demand will exceed 21 trillion cubic feet (tcf) per year by 2025 nearly triple current consumption levels. Natural gas consumption could increase even faster if additional infrastructure is built. Proposals have been made to link the gas producing and consuming regions of the Pacific Rim region of Asia by pipeline.

Malaysia is not only the biggest oil producer in the region, it is also the dominant natural gas producer as well, and until recently has been the primary source of growth in regional gas production. The development ofnatural gas resources outside of Malaysia has been hampered by the lack of infrastructure. Despite this constraint, natural gas exploration activity elsewhere in the region has been increasing. Much of this new activity had occurred in the Gulf of Thailand, offshore China, in Indonesia around the Natuna Islands, and in Vietnam in the Nam Con Son basin southeast of Vietnam.

The bulk of the world's LNG trade passes through the South China Sea, and LNG shipments through the Sea to Northeast Asian Markets constituted well over half of the world's LNG trade in 2001. Japan is by far the world's largest consumer of LNG, with shipments to South Korea (the world's second largest consumer of LNG) and Taiwan (the world's fifth largest consumer of LNG) accounting for most of the remaining shipments through the Sea.

Thailand

Thailand is a significant net oil importer with energy consumption growing rapidly as a result of strong economic growth. The Thai electric utility and petroleum industries, which historically have been state-controlled monopolies, are currently being restructured and privatized.

Thailand has only 583 million barrels of proven oil reserves with crude oil production of about 130,000 bbl/d, which has been increasing due to investment by Chevron and Unocal in domestic oil and gas drilling. Oil consumption is over 800,000 bbl/d, and continues to grow. The Thai oil industry is dominated by PTT, formerly the Petroleum Authority of Thailand. PTT Exploration and Production (PTTEP) is the main upstream subsidiary of PTT. Thai Oil, the country's largest refiner, is also controlled by PTT. The company underwent a partial privatization in November 2001, in which 32% of its equity was sold through the Bangkok Stock Exchange. However, the Thai government still owns a 68% stake in PTT, and does not plan to sell its controlling interest in the near future.

Thailand has four oil refineries, with a combined capacity of over 700,000 bbl/d. The big three refineries are owned by Shell, Thai Oil, and Esso (a subsidiary of ExxonMobil in Thailand). There have been many proposals to turn the country into a regional processing, transportation, and trading hub for the oil industry in direct competition with Singapore which has been in decline as a transshipment center in recent years. One targeted export market would likely be cities in south-central China, which are closer to Thai ports than to the Pacific coast of China. Another proposal would see the construction of a pipeline across the isthmus of Kra, which would allow oil shipments from the Persian Gulf to East Asia to bypass the congested Strait of Malacca.

PTT is an active hedger of crude oil and petroleum products. It uses a variety of financial instruments, mostly price swaps to manage oil price risk. The key is that Thailand is net short oil and is exposed to world oil market price dynamics.

Thailand contains about 13.3 tcf of proven natural gas reserves, and produces 845 billion cubic feet (bcf) in 2001. Gas consumption continues to rise and most is used for generating electricity. In 2001, Thailand completed its program for the conversion of almost all oil-fired electric power plants to natural gas. Demand for natural gas is expected to rise at a 6% annual rate over the next five years. Thailand began imports of gas from Myanmar in late 2000, used mainly at the Ratchaburi power plant. PTT has been building an extensive gas distribution network around Bangkok, called the Bangkok Ring, which will provide fuel for power plants as well as large industrial consumers.

Planned imports of LNG from Oman and piped natural gas from Indonesia's Natuna gas fields have been postponed. Development of

Thailand's domestic natural gas resources and the imports from Burma are expected to cover anticipated Thai demand for the next several years, though LNG still remains a long-term option for Thailand.

Thailand has 21,000 mW of power generation capacity. While demand growth has recovered in step with Thailand's economic recovery, the Electricity Generating Authority of Thailand (EGAT) decided to lower its planned generating capacity reserve from 25 to 15%, which has diminished the immediate need for additional generating capacity.

The Ratchaburi power plant, Thailand's largest power project, will eventually have a capacity of 3200 mW, including 1800 mW in six combined cycle gas-fired generators. Ownership of the plant was transferred from EGAT to Ratchaburi Electric Generation in October 2000, and a successful initial public offering of stock was carried out, only the second IPO on the Thai market since the crisis of 1997–98.

One other IPP also began operation in August 2000, Tri Energy, which has a 700-mW plant at Ratchaburi. The company is owned by a consortium including Edison Mission Energy, Texaco, and local Thai firms. Additional IPP capacity may be added later in the decade, once the power generation capacity reserve ratio declines. The Thai government has stated that it plans to eventually privatize EGAT, but it is still studying the options for structuring the privatization process. Because of the slowness of the privatization process, it will be many years until a trading electric power market emerges in Thailand.

Malaysia

Malaysia is important to world energy markets because it has 75 tcf of natural gas reserves which it exports and it exports almost 300,000 bbl/d of oil. Malaysia contains proven oil reserves of 3.0 billion barrels with crude oil production remaining relatively stable in recent years, with monthly production numbers of around 700,000 bbl/d. After peaking in 2001 at 472,000 bbl/d, Malaysia's oil demand has been relatively stable, due to conservation efforts and the conversion of oil-fired power plants to natural gas. However, barring major new oil discoveries, the country could become a net oil importer around the end of the current decade joining the rest of Asia.

More than half of the country's oil production comes from the Tapis field, which contains 44° API oil with a low sulfur content. Esso Production Malaysia Inc. (EPMI), an affiliate of ExxonMobil Corporation, is the largest crude oil producer in Peninsular Malaysia, accounting for nearly half of Malaysia's crude oil production. Today, Malaysia is a viable exporter and provides one of the benchmarks for Asian oil trading in Tapis crude oil. Other producers in Malaysia include oil trading companies Shell and Amerada Hess.

As a result of declining oil reserves, Petronas, the state oil and gas company, has embarked on an international exploration and production strategy. Currently, Petronas is invested in oil exploration and production projects in Syria, Turkmenistan, Iran, Pakistan, China, Vietnam, Burma, Algeria, Libya, Tunisia, Sudan, and Angola. Overseas operations now make up nearly one-third of Petronas revenue. Malaysia exports the majority of its oil to Asian markets including Japan, Thailand, South Korea, and Singapore.

Malaysia has six refineries, with a total processing capacity of 516,000 bbl/d. The three largest are the 155,000 bbl/d Shell Port Dickson refinery and the Petronas Melaka-I and Melaka-II refineries, which each have a capacity of 95,000 bbl/d. Partners with Petronas include oil trading companies ConocoPhillips and Statoil. Petronas is an active hedger of both its crude oil refinery inputs and its petroleum product outputs.

Malaysia contains 75 tcf of proven natural gas reserves. Natural gas production has been rising steadily in recent years reaching 1.9 tcf in 2001. Natural gas consumption in 2001 was estimated at 1.1 tcf, with LNG exports of around 0.8 tcf (mostly to Japan, South Korea, and Taiwan). Malaysia accounts for approximately 14% of total world LNG exports in 2002. After much delay, Malaysia is proceeding with a long-planned expansion of its Bintulu LNG complex in Sarawak. Most of the production from the new LNG trains will be sold under term contracts to utilities in Japan as Tokyo Electric Power, Tokyo Gas, and Chubu Electric all have signed contracts for LNG from the project.

A gas pipeline will eventually combine the Thai and Malaysian gas grids. Malaysia and Thailand will eventually each take half of the gas produced, though initial production will go just to Malaysia. The emergence of a Southeast Asian gas grid is well underway as Malaysia exports 150 mcf per day to Singapore via gas pipeline as well.

Malaysia also is an importer of gas from Indonesia. Petronas signed an agreement in April 2001 with Indonesia state oil and gas company Pertamina for the import of gas from Conoco's West Natuna offshore field in Indonesian waters. The move is being seen as part of a Malaysian strategy to become a hub for Southeast Asian natural gas integration. Gas trading may come eventually. Deliveries from the pipeline commenced in mid-2003. The pipeline connected to an existing pipeline from the shore to Malaysia's offshore Duyong field, helped to minimize construction costs. There also have been preliminary discussions of a project to link gas deposits off Sarawak to the Philippines.

Malaysia currently has approximately 14,000 MW of electric power generation capacity, of which 86% is thermal and 14% is hydroelectric. The Malaysian government expects to invest in more coal-fired plants, as the Malaysian government has adopted a policy of attempting to reduce the country's heavy reliance on natural gas for electric power generation. It will have increased coal's share of electricity generation to 30% by 2006. This will add to Malaysia's environmental problems.

The Malaysian government has undertaken a 2400-mW hydropower plant in Sarawak. While electricity demand in Sarawak is modest (currently under 1 mW), the potential to use the electricity to develop a metal smelting industry in Sarawak is largely behind the renewed interest in the hydropower project.

Malaysia is considering reforms to its power sector to make it more competitive at lower costs. Currently, three state-owned utilities dominate power generation and distribution in Malaysia. The market was opened to IPPs in 1994, and 15 IPPs were licensed, though not all of the projects have been built.

In recent developments, Tenaga Nasional Berhad, the main state-owned utility, began in 1999 to divest some of its power generation units. Eventually, Malaysia expects to achieve a fully competitive power market, with generation, transmission, and distribution decoupled, but reform is still at an early stage and the exact process of the transition to a competitive market has not been decided. The issue is still under study, and cautious scrutiny due to the experiences of other electric utility systems in other countries.

Indonesia

Indonesia is important to world energy markets because of its OPEC membership and substantial, but declining, oil production. Moreover, Indonesia also is the world's largest LNG exporter.

Indonesian crude oil production averages a little over 1 million bbl/d with proven oil reserves of 5 billion barrels. Central Sumatra is the country's largest oil producing province with the location of both the large Duri and Minas oil fields. Other significant oil field development and production is located in accessible areas such as offshore northwestern Java, East Kalimantan, and the Natuna Sea. Indonesian crude oil varies widely in quality. Recent production declines are due mainly to the natural decline of aging oil fields, which recent oil discoveries have been too small to offset. Exploration and production-sharing agreement include Italian-based firm ENI and Unocal to explore for oil and gas offshore South Sulawesi. Each company holds a 50% stake. China National Offshore Oil Corporation (CNOOC) became the largest offshore oil producer in Indonesia in January 2002, after purchasing nearly all of Repsol-YPF's assets in the country for $585 million.

Companies producing from existing fields are investing in programs to increase recovery rates and to prolong the life of the fields. Caltex, which has the largest operation of any multinational oil company in Indonesia, is undertaking a steam injection project at the Duri field on Sumatra.

However, Indonesia's oil production is not likely to rise markedly, due to the continuing decline of mature fields. The country could possibly become a net oil importer by the end of the current decade.

The liberalization of Indonesia's downstream oil and gas sector has been under discussion for several years. In October 2001, the Indonesian legislature passed legislation which will remove Pertamina's monopoly on upstream oil development (which requires it to be included in all PSCs) by the end of 2003. Its monopoly on the distribution of petroleum products is to be terminated by 2004. Indonesia's Ministry of Mines and Energy will take over the function, currently carried out by Pertamina, of awarding and supervising production-sharing contracts with foreign oil companies.

Indonesia has eight refineries, with a combined capacity of 992,745 bbl/d. The largest refineries are the 348,000-bbl/d Cilacap in Central Java, the 240,920-bbl/d Balikpapan in Kalimantan, and the 125,000-bbl/d Balongan, in Java.

PT Kilang Minyak Intan Nusantara, a joint venture of Al-Banader International Group of Saudi Arabia (40%), China National Electrical Equipment Corporation (40%) and PT Intanjaya Agromegah Abadi (20%), are investing a total of $6 billion to build two Indonesian oil refineries, one in Pare-Pare, South Sulawesi and the other in Batam Island, Riau. Both projects are expected to be operational in 2005, and have identical specifications that show they will each process 300,000 bbl/d. The refineries will be export-oriented, taking Saudi crude and refining it for sale primarily to the growing Chinese market.

Indonesia has proven natural gas reserves of 92.5 tcf. Most of the country's natural gas reserves are located near the Arun field in North Sumatra, around the Badak field in East Kalimantan, in smaller fields offshore Java, the Kangean Block offshore East Java, a number of blocks in Irian Jaya, and the Natuna D-Alpha field, the largest in Southeast Asia. Despite its significant natural gas reserves and its position as the world's largest exporter of LNG, Indonesia still relies on oil to supply about half of its energy needs. About 70% of Indonesia's LNG exports go to Japan, 20% to South Korea, and the remainder to Taiwan. As Indonesia's oil production has leveled off in recent years, the country has tried to shift towards using more gas for power generation. However, the domestic natural gas distribution infrastructure still is not extensive.

A particularly significant Indonesian gas field, Natuna, is located in the South China Sea, 683 miles north of Jakarta and 140 miles northeast of Natuna Island. Partners in Natuna development include ConocoPhilips which reported a new gas discovery at West Natuna which raised reserves by about 1 tcf in 1999.

In September 2002, PT Perusahaan Gas Negara (PGN), Indonesia's natural gas pipeline operating and distribution company, announced its intention to sell a 40% stake in PT Transgasindo (a subsidiary also called Transco I) to a consortium called Trans Asia Pipeline Company for $180 million. The consortium's members include Malaysia's Petronas and ConocoPhillips. Transgindo currently owns and operates a 335 mile natural gas pipeline that connects South Sumatra to the Duri steamflood project in Central Sumatra. It also has plans to build another natural gas pipeline from South Sumatra to Singapore, which would deliver about $9 billion worth of natural gas over a 22-year period.

Also in September 2002, China awarded an $8.5 billion contract to Indonesia to supply China's planned terminal in Fujian Province with LNG for 25 years, beginning in 2007. The LNG will be supplied from the Tannguh natural gas field, which is operated by BP. Construction of the LNG terminal will begin in 2004, and be completed in 2007. Included in the deal was an agreement for BP to sell 12.5% of its stake in the Tangguh field to CNOOC.

A major related project in the planning stages is BP's Tangguh LNG project in Irian Jaya, based on over 14 tcf of natural gas reserves found onshore and offshore the Wiriagar and Berau blocks. The project would involve two trains with a combined capacity of 7 million tons per year. BP's current plans call for the project to be completed by 2007. BP announced in November 2001 that it had signed an agreement to supply LNG to the Philippines beginning in 2006, and in December 2001 announced that it had made a formal proposal to China for supplies of gas to its planned Guangdong LNG regasification terminal.

In another possible use for Indonesia's gas resources, Shell is examining the possibility of building a gas-to-liquids (GTL) plant in Indonesia. The plant, if the project goes forward, would produce 70,000 bbl/d of diesel and other middle distillates using the Fischer–Tropsch GTL process.

Indonesia has 5.92 billion short tons of recoverable coal reserves, of which 85% is lignite and 15% is anthracite. In 2001, Indonesia exported 60.6 million short (mst) tons or about 60% of its coal production. The majority of these exports are destined for Japan, South Korea, and Taiwan. Indonesia plans to double coal production over the next five years, mostly for exports to other countries in East Asia and India. The new capacity will come primarily from private mines including BHP and The Clough Group of Australia.

Indonesia has installed electrical generating capacity estimated at 21,400 mW with 87% coming from thermal (oil, gas, and coal) sources, 10.5% from hydropower, and 2.5% from geothermal sources. The Indonesian government has been unwilling to take over the commercial debts of PLN. Indonesia has plans to build a new 600-MW power plant northeast of Jakarta, in an effort to relieve power shortages in the country's main power grid, Java–Bali. In 2002, Indonesia's government undertook measures to liberalize the nation's electricity market in order to make it more interesting for foreign investment. Competition for power generation will be open on the islands of Batam, Java, and Bali by 2007. In 2008, retail competition in the electricity market will begin under the terms of the nation's new electricity law, approved in September 2002. The law requires an end to PLN's monopoly on electricity distribution within five years, after which time private companies (both foreign and domestic) will be permitted to sell electricity directly to consumers. However, all companies will need to use PLN's existing transmission network.

Philippines

The Philippines is important to world energy markets because it is a growing consumer of energy, particularly electric power, and a potential market for foreign energy firms to participate in. It also could become a significant producer of natural gas. Its electric power generation sector has active foreign participation.

The Philippines is one of the claimants to the Spratly Islands' potential oil and natural gas reserves, along with China, Taiwan, Malaysia, and Vietnam, located in the South China Sea. No exploratory drilling has been carried out due to the dispute.

The Philippines produces modest crude oil averaging over 23,000 bbl/d in 2002. The country consumed 342,000 bbl/d on average in 2002, resulting in net oil imports of 318,488 bbl/d. This oil dependence makes the Philippine economy vulnerable to sudden spikes in world oil prices. Oil consumption is expected to increase by over 5% annually over the next several years as economic growth increases demand in most sectors. Oil demand for power generation, however, is expected to decline sharply, as many aging oil-fired electric power plants are shut down or converted to burn natural gas.

The Philippines' downstream oil industry is dominated by three companies: Petron; Pilipinas Shell (Royal Dutch/Shell's Philippine subsidiary); and Caltex (Philippines). Petron is the Philippines' largest oil refining and marketing company. The company was a wholly owned subsidiary of the state-owned Philippine National Oil Company (PNOC) until 1994. Currently, the Philippine government and Saudi Aramco each own 40% of the company, with the remaining 20% held by portfolio and institutional investors, making it the only publicly listed firm amongst the three oil majors. Petron's Limay, Bataan refinery has a crude processing capacity of 180,000 bbl/d. Petron's market share as of mid-2003 is around 39%. Caltex (Philippines), a subsidiary of Caltex, the Texaco–Chevron joint venture based in Singapore, operates a 86,500-bbl/d refinery, two import terminals, and more than 1000 retail gasoline stations throughout the Philippines. Pilipinas Shell has a 153,000-bbl/d refinery, one of the largest foreign investments in the Philippines, and operates some 1000 Shell gasoline stations. Overall, Philippine refineries run at around 80% of capacity, and there is not a great deal of demand for new refinery construction.

Oil market deregulation, beginning in 1998, continues to have a significant effect on the industry. Since deregulation started, 62 new firms, including TotalfinaElf, Flying V, SeaOil (Philippines), Eastern Petroleum, Trans-Asia Energy and Unioil Petroleum Philippines Inc., have invested heavily and built several hundred new retail stations. While the three original companies still dominate the market, these firms have captured a steadily growing share of the petroleum products market, rising from around 10% in 2000 to 17% by mid-2003. These new entrants have organized the "New Players Petroleum Association of the Philippines" (NPPAP), and have been credited with putting significant downward pressure on retail fuel prices in the country. Currently, the Philippines enjoys the lowest fuel prices of any non oil-exporting Asian country. However, price swings associated with deregulation and higher world oil prices have angered many Filipinos. Despite recurring public calls for price controls, the government has remained committed to deregulation.

The Philippines has 3.8 tcf of proven natural gas reserves, but had no significant production until late 2001. The government has made expanding gas-use a priority, particularly for electric power generation, in an effort to cut oil import expenses.

The impetus for the dramatic change in the country's natural gas sector is the Malampaya offshore field involving Shell Philippines Exploration (SPEX, operator, with a 45% stake), Texaco (45%), and the PNOC (10%) to form the $4.5 billion Malampaya Deepwater Gas-to-Power Project. The Malampaya field is located in the South China Sea, off the northern island of Palawan, and contains an estimated 2.6 tcf of natural gas. A 312-mile (504-kilometer) pipeline links the field to three power plants with a combined 2700 mW of capacity in Batangas. Another field in Victoria, Tarlac, was closed because the natural gas discovered was too saturated with water for commercial production.

The Philippine government is developing a policy framework for the emerging natural gas industry that foresees the government's role as that of facilitator while attempting to ensure competition. Domestic development is to be encouraged, but competition from imported gas also is to be allowed. Gas supply to wholesale markets will have market-set prices, while prices for captive markets and small consumers will be regulated.

LNG has begun to receive added attention as a potential source of natural gas supplies. PNOC has been considering the construction of an LNG regasification terminal in Bataan, which would serve the Manila area. A letter of intent has been signed for natural gas imports into the Philippines from BP's Tangguh LNG project in Indonesia.

Energy production in the Philippines is concentrated in the electricity sector. Geothermal power accounts for the country's largest share of indigenous energy production, followed by hydropower, natural gas, coal, and oil. The Philippine government has made shifting from reliance on imported oil a major goal, and is pushing the current boom in natural gas-fired electricity development.

Electricity demand in the Philippines is expected to grow by around 9% per year through the end of the decade, necessitating as much as 10,000 MW of new installed electric capacity. The most significant event in the Philippine energy industry in recent years was the Power Industry Reform Act (PIRA) of 2001 which has three main objectives: 1) to develop indigenous resources; 2) to cut the high cost of electric power in the Philippines; and 3) to encourage foreign investment. Passage of the Act set into motion the deregulation of the power industry and the breakup and eventual privatization of state-owned enterprises. The plan is to privatize the transmission and distribution system and to encourage further IPP electricity generation development. Privatization of PNOC-EDC is also planned, though as with other generation assets, the process has progressed much slower than originally planned. The Korea Electric Power Corporation (KEPCO) began commercial operation of the 1200-mW Ilijan plant in June 2002. KEPCO will run the plant under a build-operate-transfer scheme for 20 years, after which ownership will revert to Napocor, the state-owned utility. Minority stakeholders in the plant are Southern Energy of the United States (20%) plus Mitsubishi (21%), and Kyushu Power (8%) of Japan. US company Mirant was the Philippines' largest IPP, operating five power plants in the country, before selling off its assets to other investors. Several power-generating facilities also are under extensive rehabilitation.

The Philippines, due to its geography, has problems linking all of its larger islands together into one grid and ensuring availability of electric power in rural areas. The government has set a target date of 2006 for electrification of all these villages, and also is taking steps to link together the country's three major power grids (Luzon, Visayas, and Mindanao). Where it is not economical to link small islands' grids into the national grid, separate local systems are being established around small generating plants.

The Philippines is a major developer of renewable energy and has greater potential for more renewable generation capacity. It is the world's second largest producer of geothermal power, with an available capacity of 1931 mW and will add another 990 mW, which will exceed US geothermal capacity. Geothermal power currently makes up around 16% of the Philippines' installed power generation capacity. The Philippines also appears to have a strong potential for wind generation. The US Department of Energy wind mapping survey estimates that wind resources in the Philippines have a power generation potential of as much as 70,000 mW, seven times the country's current power demand.

Privatization and power development efforts will eventually lead to power exchanges and trading in the Philippines, but at the present time, the infrastructure needs to be put in place.

Vietnam

Ongoing exploration and production efforts have led to several oil and gas discoveries in recent years in Vietnam which has the potential to become more important to world energy markets. However, much of Vietnam's large population relies heavily on non-commercial biomass energy sources such as wood, dung, and rice husks leading to Vietnam's per capita commercial energy consumption being among the lowest in Asia. However, Vietnamese energy consumption, especially natural gas, is predicted to rise substantially in coming years.

Vietnam has 600 million barrels of proven oil reserves, and further discoveries are likely. Crude oil production averaged 339,000 bbl/d in 2002. The country currently has no operating oil refineries with almost all of its oil production exported. Export markets include Japan (the largest importer of Vietnamese oil), Singapore, the United States, and South Korea. Vietnam had net exports of an estimated 153,000 bbl/d of oil in 2002.

The Vietnamese government controls both the upstream and downstream oil and natural gas industries. For upstream activities, Vietnam Oil and Gas Corporation (PetroVietnam), a government-owned company, is the only firm authorized to conduct petroleum operations. Any petroleum exploration and production activities by foreign investors must be conducted in cooperation with PetroVietnam. For downstream activities, there are several government-owned companies of which Petrolimex is the largest petroleum products importer. PetroVietnam is expected to be one of the first firms to take advantage of the new regulations because it is involved in a number of large projects (including the nation's first oil refinery) for which it needs to raise capital. About 30 energy companies, including American, European, Korean, Russian, and Japanese firms, now operate in offshore Vietnam.

The $1.3 billion Dung Quat Refinery, which is located in Quang Ngai province, will have a capacity of about 140,000 bbl/d and is currently under construction. The PetroVietnam project may not be fully operational until 2005. A second refinery project is under consideration. Mitsubishi and JGC Corporation signed a memorandum of understanding with PetroVietnam in October 2001 covering a feasibility study for the project in Ngai Son, in Thanh Hoa province.

Vietnam's natural gas consumption is rising, with further increases expected as additional fields come onstream. A South Korean consortium headed by Korea National Oil Corporation (KNOC) signed an agreement to install facilities to be used to pump and supply up to 130 mcft per day of natural gas to Vietnam. The natural gas will be bought by PetroVietnam for 23 years. Purchasing will begin in 2005, when facilities are expected to be completed. PetroVietnam is in turn expected to sell the natural gas to Electricity of Vietnam (EVN). Other projects include a pipeline, which will be built through the Asia Pacific Economic Cooperation (APEC) forum's Partnership for Equitable Growth (PEG), linking an Indonesian natural gas field with Vietnam, Malaysia, Thailand, and China. A joint venture of BP, Conoco, and ONGC (India) with PetroVietnam to develop natural gas resources in the Nam Con Son basin takes some of the gas inland to power plants.

Vietnam is a growing consumer and exporter of liquefied petroleum gas (LPG), with almost 70% of urban households using LPG for cooking and other purposes. Japan is the major consumer of Vietnamese LPG exports, receiving the country's first export shipment in May 1999. There is only one local producer of LPG in Vietnam, called the Dinh Co Plant, which is able to meet about 70% of national demand. Vietnam's LPG sector has been open to foreign companies since 1998. Saigon Petro, Elf Gas, Petrolimex, and Mobil Unique (a consortium of Mobil, Mitsui, and Unique Gas and Petrochemical), and PTT of Thailand are the major companies involved in the sector.

Vietnam contains coal reserves estimated at 165 mst, the majority of which is anthracite. In 2001, Vietnam produced just over 11 mst and has exported coal primarily to Japan. However, export markets have been shrinking during the past few years, which has exacerbated Vietnam's oversupply problem. The Vietnamese government is promoting the construction of coal-fired power plants. Vinacoal plans to build as many as seven new power plants over the next decade, with a total capacity of 2170 mW. Vietnam's coal consumption is expected to increase as it becomes a larger electricity producer, with coal-fired power plants eventually accounting for 25% of the country's total electricity production. Vietnam previously had focused much more on hydropower, and the shift to coal marks an important change in Vietnam's energy sector.

As an emerging market, Vietnam has experienced rapid commercial growth, mass migration to major cities, and rising living standards, all of which have contributed to the country's growing demand for electricity. Vietnam has a total electric generating capacity of 5000 mW. Hydropower accounts for roughly 56.4% of electricity generation, while thermal power accounts for about 43.6%. The state power company, Electricity of EVN, is working on a plan to develop a national electricity grid by 2020, patching together several regional grids. EVN also plans to increase Vietnam's natural gas consumption, using gas from offshore fields to fuel new power plants. Foreign companies are becoming involved in the growing Vietnamese power market. EVN and a consortium including TEPCO, Sumitomo, and Electricite de France (EdF) plan to construct a 715-MW plant (Phu My 2-2) in the Mekong Delta.

Vietnam has the potential to be an active oil and gas hedger for both its upstream and downstream sectors. Unfortunately, energy risk management expertise is lacking. It may take several years to create that knowledge infrastructure.

SOUTH ASIA

The South Asian region (Bangladesh, Bhutan, India, the Maldives, Nepal, Pakistan, and Sri Lanka) is notable for its large population totaling more than one-fifth of the world. While economic and population growth in South Asia have resulted in rapid increases in energy consumption in recent years, South Asia continues to average among the lowest levels of per capita energy consumption in the world.

South Asia's commercial energy mix in 2001 was 43% coal, 36% petroleum, 13% natural gas, 7% hydroelectricity, and 2% nuclear. There are significant variations within the region. Bangladesh's energy mix, for instance, is dominated by natural gas (67% in 2001), while India relies heavily on coal (51%). Sri Lanka and the Maldives are overwhelmingly dependent on petroleum (83% and 100%, respectively); Pakistan is diversified among petroleum (43%), natural gas (41%), and hydroelectricity (12%). In recent years, natural gas has been growing in importance as a source of energy in India, especially for use in power generation, fertilizer and petrochemical production. However, recent problems encountered by some developers of proposed LNG projects, and continuing tensions with Pakistan that effectively block potential natural gas pipeline routes from the Persian Gulf and Central Asia, present obstacles to the future enlargement of natural gas as a factor of India's fuel mix.

The major energy issue facing South Asian nations today is rapidly rising energy demand coupled with increasingly inadequate energy supplies. Already, most of South Asia is grappling with energy shortfalls, usually in the form of frequent, costly, and widespread electricity outages. The countries of South Asia are looking towards diversifying traditional energy supply sources (and expanding the use of indigenous energy resources), promoting additional foreign investment for energy infrastructure development, improving energy efficiency, reforming and privatizing energy sectors, and promoting and expanding regional energy trade and investment.

Another important implication of rising energy demand in South Asia is its impact of the region's level of carbon emissions. As of 2001, South Asia accounted for 4.5% of global carbon emissions. However, with the demand for coal in India projected to increase rapidly in the coming decade and the recent introduction of coal into the fuel mix of other countries in the region, the likelihood of a significant increase in emissions in the future is certain. Environmental trading of greenhouse gas emissions seems inevitable.

The region contains only 5.8 billion barrels of oil reserves, around 0.5% of the world supply. In 2001, the region consumed around 2.4 million bbl/d of oil, and produced 0.80 million bbl/d, making South Asia a net oil importer of around 1.6 million bbl/d. The vast majority of South Asia's oil production comes from India, including its offshore Bombay High field which accounts for about one-third of total Indian oil output. South Asia's oil imports are projected to more than double by 2020 as production remains about flat while demand soars. In an effort to reduce oil import dependence, a number of South Asian countries have sought to expand domestic petroleum exploration by attracting private and foreign investors. However, growing demand for transportation fuels and increased industrial power demand have been major factors behind the growth in South Asian oil consumption in recent years. Between 1990 and 2000, South Asian oil consumption, led by India, grew by about 75%.

Several South Asian countries have responded with plans to expand their refining and transportation capacity due to rising oil demand. For example, India's total refining capacity has increased to 2.1 million bbl/d by the end of 2002. The largest recent project, the Reliance Industries refinery at Jamnagar in India, began operation in late summer 1999, and has a capacity of 540,000 bbl/d. In August 2003, Bharat Petroleum Corp. Ltd. (BPCL) announced plans to expand its Mumbai refinery from 180,000 bbl/d to 240,000 bbl/d by October 2004, which would make it the second largest refinery in India after the Jamnagar facility. Petronet India, a company created in early 1998 as part of an agreement among India's three government-owned refineries (Indian Oil Corporation–IOC, Hindustan Petroleum, and BCPL) is in the process of building product pipelines that will add about 500,000 bbl/d to the existing 325,000 bbl/d (all operated by IOC) of pipeline capacity, thereby displacing rail as the main mode of transportation for petroleum products. In Pakistan, the 100,000-bbl/d "Pak-Arab" refinery came online in late 2000, helping to alleviate the country's dependence on refined product imports.

At the end of 2002, South Asia's proven natural gas reserves were estimated at 63.9 tcf, or about 1% of the world total, with potentially larger resources suspected but unproven. India's and Pakistan's reserves are roughly equal in size at 27 tcf, while the only other South Asian country with reserves, Bangladesh, contains approximately 11 tcf. Currently, there is much speculation about the actual level of Bangladeshi reserves, with foreign energy companies such as Shell and Unocal believing that the country's reserves may be higher than the official figure.

At present, all natural gas production in South Asia is consumed domestically. Natural gas is seen in the region as playing an important part in supplying new power plants in the region, plus as a means of diversifying away from expensive oil imports. As a result, natural gas usage has increased rapidly in South Asia, growing about 72% between 1991 and 2000. In 2001, the region produced and consumed around 1.98 tcf of natural gas. Around 42% of this was accounted for by Pakistan, 40% by India, and the remaining 18% by Bangladesh. An obstacle to the expansion of natural gas usage in South Asia is the region's inadequate domestic gas infrastructure. Cross-border gas pipelines also would hinge upon the successful construction of domestic gas pipeline systems first.

South Asia's coal reserves amount to 95.4 billion short tons or approximately 9% of the world total. While coal accounts for 43% of South Asia's energy consumption, nearly all of the coal in this region is produced and consumed by India, the only South Asian country with significant coal reserves (93 billion short tons), and the world's third largest coal producer after the United States and China. Power generation accounts for about 70% of India's total coal consumption. Indian coal consumption is expected to increase to 510 million tons by 2020, up 42% from 360 million tons in 2000. Largely for this reason, South Asia's carbon emissions are expected to increase sharply in coming years.

As is the case in many developing country regions, South Asia continues to rely heavily on biomass (i.e., animal waste, wood, etc.) for residential energy consumption and, particularly, in rural areas. According to the International Energy Agency (IEA) in Paris, biomass accounted for about 80% of residential energy consumption in 2000. Given that the primary enduses of biomass are cooking and heating, the expansion of electricity access, used primarily for lighting, is not expected to have a significant affect on biomass use in the future. The IEA projects that biomass use will still account for 70% of residential energy consumption in 2030.

In 2001, South Asia generated 626 billion kWh of electricity. Of this total, around 81% was from conventional thermal power plants, 17% from hydroelectric plants, 2% from nuclear, and less than 1% from "other renewables" (like wind and solar). Electricity demand in most of South Asia is currently outstripping supply and the region as a whole is characterized by chronic electricity shortages.

Electricity rates are widely subsidized in South Asia, and state electricity companies are faced with the challenge of paying IPPs their asking price for power while simultaneously providing electricity at low rates to their customers, and losing a substantial percentage to theft. Consequently, many large IPP projects in the region have been delayed or cancelled. Meanwhile, the IMF and the World Bank have encouraged liberalization of South Asian power sectors, including reduction of subsidies. Meeting future electricity demand continues to pose a major challenge for South Asia.

Energy risk management in the region is less developed than in Southeast or Northeast Asia. The rising dependency on Middle East supplies and continuous oil price volatility have focused more attention on energy risk management particularly in India. However, its development has been nascent. Gas and power risk management are essentially nonexistent.

India

India is the world's sixth largest energy consumer and plans major energy infrastructure investments to keep up with increasing demand particularly for electric power. India also is the world's third-largest producer of coal, and relies on coal for more than half of its total energy needs. Oil accounts for about 30% of India's total energy consumption. The majority of India's roughly 5.4 billion barrels in oil reserves are located in the Bombay High, Upper Assam, Cambay, Krishna–Godavari, and Cauvery basins. India's oil production averages about 750,000 bbl/d. India's oil imports were 2 million bbl/d in 2002 and are expected to rise to 3.2 million bbl/d by 2010.

India is attempting to limit its dependence on oil imports somewhat by expanding domestic exploration and production by allowing some foreign participation in its upstream sector. Niko Resources of Canada, British independent Cairn Energy, Russia's Gazprom, the US firm Mosbacher Energy, and Geopetrol of France are all active upstream oil and gas production in India. It is hoped that allowing foreign investment will bring in technology that is not available to Indian state firms, thereby increasing overall recovery rates. It is likely that most of India's easily recoverable oil has been discovered. The main cause for hope is offshore exploration, and in particular deep water exploration. Most recent drilling, however, has found natural gas rather than crude oil.

For most of the 1990s, India imported a large quantity of refined products, lacking the refining capacity to keep up with growing demand. In 1999, refinery construction allowed India to close the gap. At the end of 2002, India had a total of 2.1 million bbl/d in refining capacity, an increase of 970,000 bbl/d since 1998. In late summer 1999, Reliance Petroleum's huge 540,000 bbl/d Jamnagar refinery came onstream. Refinery construction has been encouraged by regulatory changes by the Indian government, including a five-year tax holiday for refineries completed by 2003.

Another major downstream infrastructure development is the construction of pipelines being undertaken by Petronet India, a company created by an agreement in 1998 between India's state-owned refineries, which will add 500,000 bbl/d to India's current 325,000 bbl/d capacity for pipeline transportation of refined products.

The Indian government officially ended the Administered Pricing Mechanism (APM) for petroleum product prices in April 2002. Prior to this deregulation, the Indian government had tried to offset the effects of price changes in crude oil by maintaining an Oil Pool Account, which was to build financial reserves when crude oil prices fell and release them back as increased subsidies when crude oil prices rose. In practice, though, the April 2002 reforms have not completely removed government influence on petroleum product prices. Subsidies have been maintained on some products, such as kerosene, which is commonly used as a cooking fuel by low-income households in India. State-owned downstream companies also still must submit proposed price changes to the Ministry of Petroleum and Natural Gas for approval.

The Indian government announced a decision in December 2002 to sell off majority stakes in two of the largest state-owned downstream oil companies, Hindustan Petroleum (HPCL) and BPCL. HPCL is slated to be sold off to a "strategic" buyer that is, another major oil company. BPCL's shares will be offered through a public stock offering. The Indian federal government currently owns 51% of HPCL and 66% of BPCL.

Indian consumption of natural gas has risen faster than any other fuel in recent years. Natural gas use is projected to reach 1.2 tcf in 2005 and 1.6 tcf in 2010. A major development in December 2002 was the announcement by Reliance Industries of its discovery of a large amount of natural gas in the Krishna–Godavari Basin offshore from Andhra Pradesh along India's southeast coast. New reserves from this find are estimated at about 5 Tcf. Cairn Energy also reported finds in late 2002 offshore from Andhra Pradesh as well as Gujarat, which contain reserves estimated at nearly 2 tcf.

Even with these new reserves, India's domestic natural gas supply is not likely to keep pace with the country's rising demand; thus India will have to import much of its natural gas, either via pipeline or as LNG. The US DOE's Energy Information Administration predicts a 6.1% annual growth rate in natural gas consumption. Problems with financing LNG import projects have dimmed some of the previous prospects for explosive growth in natural gas consumption in India, and helped to revive interest in pipeline import options. Financial problems in the power sector, the main consumer of natural gas, also have had a negative effect.

India is investing heavily in the infrastructure required to support increased use of natural gas. Gas Authority of India Limited (GAIL), a government-owned entity, is in the process of doubling the throughput capacity on its main Hazira–Bijaipur–Jagdishpur (HBJ) Pipeline. Work on the capacity expansion began in 2002, and will eventually raise the capacity of the line to 2.1 Bcf/d. GAIL also plans a new distribution network in West Bengal and a pipeline which would connect Calcutta with Chennai. Shell has signed a MOU with the state government of Uttar Pradesh in northern India for the development of a natural gas distribution infrastructure.

India has had an off and on again policy regarding LNG imports. Initially, India's Foreign Investment Promotion Board (FIPB) approved 12 prospective LNG import terminal projects in the1990s. However, the Indian government froze approvals of new LNG terminals in 2001 due to payment problems at the Enron-backed Dabhol Power Plant in Maharashtra. This long lasting dispute dampened enthusiasm for doing business in India's gas and power sectors and led to many questions on the financial viability of LNG import projects. Furthermore, since the main consumers of the imported gas would be power producers, the poor financial condition of most of the state power boards which purchase power and run the transmission grids, is likely to remain a major constraint on the development of LNG imports.

The largest state sector LNG projects are conducted by Petronet, a joint venture between ONGC, IOC, the GAIL, the National Thermal Power Corporation (NTPC), and Gaz de France. Petronet plans two import terminals, one at Dahej and the other at Cochin. RasGas is to begin supplying LNG to Petronet when the Dahej terminal is completed. The Dahej terminal has had advantages over some of the other proposed projects, being tied in with the main state-owned natural gas company, GAIL, and the existing HBJ pipeline network. Shell also has begun construction of its LNG import terminal at Hazira in Gujarat, and has contracted for LNG supplies from Oman. The facility is scheduled to begin operation in 2005. Like the Petronet Dahej terminal, it is to be linked into existing natural gas pipelines.

The Dabhol LNG terminal was nearly finished at the time construction was halted in June 2001, and it will be completed by another firm once a buyer is found for the now-bankrupt Enron's 65% share of the project. The problems with Dabhol led to the backing out of several other LNG projects in the second half of 2001. These LNG projects were cancelled largely in response to the Indian government's decision not to extend sovereign payment guarantees to power projects which were to have been among their largest customers.

Aside from LNG imports, imports of natural gas by pipeline may play a role eventually in satisfying India's gas needs. One possibility would supply India with natural gas from Iran's huge South Pars field via a pipeline, either subsea or through Pakistan. Iran has discussed the proposal with India and Pakistan. Australia's Broken Hill Proprietary (BHP) is the main foreign backer of the idea. Pakistan had said in early 2001 that it would allow supplies to cross its territory, and Iran would bear the contractual responsibility for assuring gas supplies to India, but the project does not appear likely to be implemented in the near future due to the obvious security concerns for India.

Another possible import route would link the natural gas reserves of Bangladesh into the Indian gas grid. Current proven reserves of natural gas in Bangladesh are at least 14 tcf. The Bangladeshi government has been reluctant to approve exports to India, however, until all questions about reserves and its domestic supply have been resolved. Foreign companies active in bringing Bangladeshi gas to India include Shell and Unocal.

India's government has been considering reforms in its natural gas pricing mechanism, which is currently set by the government. Deregulation has been delayed several times, and the recent increase in domestic reserves may lead to a tilt toward less regulation of prices, making LNG importers compete with domestic natural gas suppliers.

Coal is the dominant commercial fuel in India, satisfying more than half of India's energy demand. Power generation accounts for about 70% of India's coal consumption, followed by heavy industry. Coal consumption is projected by the IEA to 450 mst in 2010, up from 369 mst in 2000. This is a substantial increase in the rate of growth projected in previous forecasts. Indian coal generally has a high ash content and low calorific value, so most coking coal must be imported. The Indian government controls almost all coal production, which has been plagued by low productivity, distribution problems, and loss of markets to higher quality, less expensive imports. The current government has called off plans for further coal-sector liberalization in the face of strong opposition from labor unions.

India is trying to expand electric power generation capacity, as current generation is seriously below peak demand. Although about 80% of the population has access to electricity, power outages are common, and the unreliability of electricity supplies is severe enough to constitute a constraint on the country's overall economic development. The government had targeted capacity increases of 100,000 mW over the next ten years. As of January 2001, total installed Indian power generating capacity was 112,000 MW.

The drive to increase the country's generating capacity, along with the general trend toward economic liberalization in India in the 1990s, led to much interest among foreign investors in setting up IPPs in India. While dozens of projects were approved, most of the largest projects have been stalled by delays in regulatory approvals and in some cases failure to secure adequate financing. India's state electricity boards (SEB's), which run the power distribution infrastructure and own most current generating capacity, are in very poor financial shape, with many of them technically insolvent. One reason is the sale of power at subsidized rates, which does not cover costs (particularly in the agricultural sector). Other problems include the high level of transmission and distribution losses and widespread power theft. Since the SEBs would be the main purchasers of power from IPP projects, resolving their financial problems is critical to attracting the capital necessary to ensure the country an adequate supply of electric power. There is presently no national grid system in India.

In July 1998, the Indian government announced an easing of rules related to foreign investment in the power sector. Still, the financial problems of the SEBs have prevented substantial foreign investment from flowing into India's electric power sector. A large number of LNG and power projects have been cancelled in recent years.

During the past two years there has been significant interest by Indian oil companies to manage its oil price risk. Indian energy risk management has included IOC, which issues a tender seeking companies to offer assistance in the creation of a trading and price risk management unit at IOC.

Other large Indian firms like Reliance Industries for example and companies involved in the Textile industry who own their own power generation, continue to enter the risk management market and derivatives.

As regulations loosen allowing more and more oil distribution and end users exposed to oil import prices to access international energy derivatives markets for hedging, India is a big growth area.

Pakistan

Pakistan produce a little over 50,000 bbl/d of oil, and imports over 300,000 bbl/d. Pakistan's net oil imports are projected to rise substantially in coming years as demand growth outpaces increases in production. Demand for refined petroleum products also greatly exceeds domestic oil refining capacity, so nearly half of Pakistani imports are refined products. Pakistan is consistently short on petroleum products and must buy from abroad and thus has price risk exposures.

Deregulation and privatization efforts are underway in Pakistan. As part of the privatization process, the government of Pakistan is setting up the Gas Regulatory Authority (GRA) and the Petroleum Regulatory Board (PRB), which will separate out the government functions from the state-owned companies to be privatized. Pakistan's government hopes to reap significant revenues from these privatizations over the next several years.

Pakistan has 25.1 tcf of proven gas reserves, and currently produces around 0.8 tcf of natural gas per year, all of which is consumed domestically. Pakistan's demand for natural gas is expected to rise substantially in the next few years, with an increase of roughly 50% by 2006, according to Pakistan's oil and gas ministry. Pakistan plans to make gas the fuel of choice for future electric power generation projects. This will necessitate a sharp rise in production of natural gas, and also has generated interest in Pakistan in pipelines to facilitate imports from neighboring countries. Much of Pakistan's increased natural gas demand will be satisfied by increased domestic production with foreign participation by Eni, Shell, OMV, BHP, and others.

Several import schemes also have been under discussion in recent years, though recent finds now under development have made it unlikely that Pakistan will need to import natural gas within the next few years. In mid-2000, Pakistan's government stated that it would permit a natural gas pipeline linking Iran's massive reserves to rival India across Pakistani territory. Pakistan would earn transit fees for Iranian gas supplied to India and also would be able to purchase some gas from the pipeline when and if its own demand was sufficient. A pipeline from Iran to India would make sense in financial terms, as its primary justification would be sales to India, with Pakistan as only a secondary customer, but the energy security issues it raises for India make it unlikely to proceed. While Iran and Pakistan have shown great interest in the project, India has been reluctant to move forward as long as political and military tensions with Pakistan over Kashmir persist.

Another natural gas import possibility is an eventual link with the Dolphin Project, a scheme to supply gas from Qatar's North Dome gasfield to the United Arab Emirates and Oman, via a subsea pipeline from Oman. Even though Pakistan has signed a preliminary agreement to eventually purchase natural gas from Qatar, it seems increasingly unlikely that Pakistan will be included in the project in the near-term, due to its financial weakness and uncertainty about whether there will be sufficient domestic natural gas demand growth.

Pakistan has 18,000 mW of electric generating capacity. Thermal plants using oil, natural gas, and coal account for about 68% of this capacity, with hydroelectricity making up 28% and nuclear plants 2.6%. Pakistan's total power generating capacity has increased rapidly in recent years, due largely to foreign investment, leading to a partial alleviation of the power shortages Pakistan had faced earlier. Transmission losses are about 30%, due to poor quality infrastructure and a significant amount of power theft. Seasonal reductions affect the availability of hydropower, and the country faced a severe shortage in 2001. With much of Pakistan's rural areas yet to receive electric power, and less than half of the population connected to the national grid, significant power demand growth is expected in the long term.

The electric power sector in Pakistan is still primarily state-owned, but a privatization program is underway. The main state-owned utilities are the Water and Power Development Authority (WAPDA), and the Karachi Electricity Supply Corporation (KESC), which serves only Karachi and surrounding areas. WAPDA, which is made up of eight regional electricity boards, is to be split up for privatization. One regional entity, the Faisalabad Area Electricity Board, has begun the privatization process, which was scheduled to conclude in late 2002, but has been delayed for unspecified reasons. Growth in power generation in recent years has come primarily from IPP, some of which have been funded by foreign investors, and a few WAPDA hydroelectric dam projects. The UK's National Power, Saudi Arabia's Xenal and Mitsui Corporation have been involved in IPPs.

In April 2003, the Ministry of Industries and Production announced that it was planning to build coal-fired power-generation plants in export processing zones and in special industrial states to provide a less expensive source of energy. Officials hope to exploit the large, untapped coal reserves in Tharkparkar. At present, coal makes up less than a 5% share in overall energy production.

Taiwan

Taiwan lacks sufficient domestic energy sources, and is almost totally dependent on energy imports. Oil is the dominant fuel in Taiwan's energy mix, accounting for 51% of total primary energy consumption. Coal also plays an important role (32% of total energy consumption), followed by nuclear power (8%), natural gas (6%), and hydroelectric power (2%). Taiwan has very limited domestic energy resources and relies on imports for most of its energy requirements. The country's industrial sector accounts for more than half of total energy demand, but this share is expected to decline slightly, since Taiwan's economy is moving toward newer, less energy-intensive industries. The transportation sector accounts for one-quarter of total energy demand.

Chinese Petroleum Corporation (CPC), Taiwan's national oil company, is the dominant player in all sectors of the country's petroleum industry, including exploration, refining, storage, transportation, and marketing. However, significant competition began in July 2000 with the opening of a refinery a of 450,000 bbl/d Mailiao refinery owned by Formosa Petrochemical Company (FPC), a subsidiary of the private Taiwanese petrochemical firm Formosa Plastics. Prior to the construction of the FPC Mailiao refinery, Taiwan imported a significant quantity of refined petroleum products. Now the country's refining capacity exceeds its domestic consumption of petroleum products, making it an exporter. FPC signed an export agreement with China's state-owned oil trader Sinochem in December 2002, which has opened up mainland China to petroleum products from Taiwan.

Taiwan is almost 100% oil import dependent with most of its crude oil imports coming from the Persian Gulf, though West African countries also are important suppliers for Taiwan. To ensure against a supply disruption, Taiwan's refiners are under a regulatory requirement to maintain stocks of no less than 60 days of consumption. Refiner-held strategic petroleum stocks are the norm in Asia, and Taiwan's policy is similar to those of Japan and South Korea.

Taiwan's government has announced plans to further liberalize the petroleum sector. Taiwan's legislature passed the Petroleum Administration Act in September 2001, which removed CPC's quasi-governmental policy implementation functions, and which will permit the eventual sale of a majority stake in the firm. In January 2003, the Taiwanese government announced that it would accelerate the timetable for the sale, offering equity in the firm to private investors in 2003, with the process to be completed in 2004. Foreign firms will be allowed to acquire stakes in CPC on an equal basis with domestic investors.

Despite the lack of formal ties between Taipei and Beijing, Taiwan and mainland China have developed a cooperative relationship in the field of energy. CPC and Beijing's state-owned CNOOC signed a deal in 1996 to jointly explore a 5939-square-mile area in the Tainan Basin of the Taiwan Strait. Taipei officially ratified the deal in March 1998, and the first round of seismic surveys by the two companies was completed in October 1999. A joint venture agreement was signed between the two companies in May 2002, but drilling has yet to commence.

Besides oil, CPC is responsible for Taiwan's natural gas exploration, production and imports. Taiwan had net imports of 238 bcf of (LNG) in 2001 – up over 9% over the figure for 2000. Indonesia and Malaysia are Taiwan's two LNG suppliers. Total natural gas consumption in 2001 was

234 bcf. CPC operates Taiwan's only LNG receiving terminal – at Yungan, Kaohsiung. CPC anticipates an increase in natural gas demand due to the construction of additional power plants. The government plans to triple LNG consumption by 2010 for environmental reasons, as natural gas is the cleanest burning fossil fuel.

Meanwhile, Taiwan's energy sector market liberalization program has made possible the construction of competing LNG import terminals. Several private Taiwanese and Japanese firms have formed a consortium, Tung Ting Gas, to pursue an LNG regasification project in Tao-Yuan county. Construction of the terminal was started in mid-2001 by Japan's Chiyoda and Taiwan's CTCI, and it is scheduled for completion in 2006. A preliminary agreement has been signed with Qatar's RasGas for LNG supplies. Most of the natural gas from the terminal is slated to be used for electric power generation. CPC also is reportedly discussing the construction of its second LNG import terminal, which could be needed around the end of the current decade if natural gas demand in Taiwan rises as projected in the current forecast.

Taiwan Power Company (Taipower), the state-owned electric power utility, currently dominates Taiwan's electric power sector. However, Taipower's monopoly status has been undermined by a 1994 measure which allowed independent power producers (IPPs) to provide up to 20% of Taiwan's electricity. Independent power producers are required to sign power purchase agreements with Taipower, which distributes the power to consumers. However, regulations issued by the government in July 1998 allow foreign investors to play a greater role in Taiwan's electric transmission and distribution sector. The rules raised the level permitted of foreign investment in these sectors to 50%, from 30% previously.

Taiwan's first major IPP, the coal-fired Mailiao plant owned by Formosa Plastics, began operation in 1999. It currently has a capacity of 2400 mW in four 600-mW generating units, and sells about three-quarters of its output to Taipower. A second, coal-fired IPP plant, Ho-Ping Power, is to begin commercial operation of its first 660-MW unit in March 2002, with a second unit beginning operation in July 2002. Ho-Ping is a joint venture including Taiwan Cement Corporation and Hong Kong's China Power and Light Corporation. Several other IPP projects have been approved. Coal for electric power generation is imported from Australia and China.

Taipower has total installed capacity of over 30,000 mW. Taipower retains exclusive control over nuclear and hydropower plants. The government will continue to own these assets after Taipower is privatized. Taipower also has plans for a 4000-mW LNG-fired complex, the Tatan Power Plant.

A new electricity law has been under consideration in Taiwan's parliament, the major feature of which is expected to be the privatization of Taipower. Under the basic framework envisioned, Taipower would retain a monopoly on transmission and distribution networks, but Taipower's generation assets would be split into several firms. The planned privatization is to an extent the result of rapidly rising power demand in Taiwan, and Taipower's inability to build sufficient capacity to keep pace with demand, which led to a power crisis during the summer peak-demand months in 1999. The expected date for completion of Taipower's privatization was originally 2001, but several issues, most notably the controversy over nuclear power, have pushed the expected date back to 2006.

CHAPTER 10

Electronic Energy Trading in Asia

The energy industry is significantly conducive to the use of risk management tools due to its underlying price volatility, and is a logical candidate for the use of an array of electronic trading platforms. Electronic commerce, however, is only slowly transforming energy markets. The mature markets of oil and gas trading as well as the emerging markets for electric power, emissions, and weather trading are ripe for trading on electronic platforms. Both price discovery and credit risk will be enhanced using the technology of the Internet. The market drivers for the changing face of energy trading range from open outcry to screen trading for price discovery. This will be particularly true in the Asia Pacific region due to the lack of exchange-traded financial instruments for energy.

Energy e-commerce space continues to evolve albeit slower than imagined and will probably take toward the end of this decade to gain a firm foothold in the energy trading complex. Thus, the migration to the Internet will take longer than expected due to human relationships in energy trading. These relationships between traders and brokers are interwoven with added value that is, brokers provide market intelligence to traders and the ability to trade large size lots without moving the market. Screen trading can never accomplish this feat. Thus, a reconsideration is in order as to when the Internet dominates energy trading. Insights into human nature point to later rather than sooner. It is definitely not a technology problem. The area of change is of human factors, and human relationships are slow to change. Interestingly enough; however, Asia may find the ability to leapfrog the evolutionary energy market changes of the West with open outcry floor trading and then electronic applications. Asia may go totally electronic trading as is evidenced by small growth last year of the IPE/ICE platform which grew electronically in Asia from 2 to 5% of total trading volumes. It may be a harbinger of the migration to electronic energy trading first in Asia and later in Europe and North America. With Korea 98% wired and China crossing 250 million Internet users, it seems likely to be the case.

e-commerce opportunities for oil markets exist in energy trading, energy procurement, and retailing. As the energy industry is significantly conducive to the use the Internet applications because of its information intensity, e-commerce is beginning to transform energy markets. The market drivers for these changes taking place in oil markets globally include deregulation, privatization, globalization, and the need for price transparency. Asia is now set to be the next frontier for electronic energy trading and other Internet-related applications in energy. Internet penetration is the strongest in South Korea but many other Asian countries are rapidly approaching Internet saturation points so the installed technology is already there and is not an impediment to e-commerce solutions.

Oil trading began after the end of OSP programs by the major oil companies and OPEC nations after the 1973 Oil Embargo and coincided with the development of a spot market for crude oil and petroleum products. In 1978, the changing nature of the physical spot market for oil presaged the development of energy futures with the successful launch of the NYMEX heating oil futures contract which was tied to its physical delivery in New York harbor. Successive oil futures contracts and the development of an active OTC market for forward oil trading in the early 1980s brought significant structural changes to the international oil industry. In effect, price transparency accelerated both physical and financial trading of crude oil and petroleum products globally which has been integrated 24/7 market for over ten years. Other critical changes have occurred over the past 20 years; price assessment panels and index trading which failed in the late 1980s are succeeding now. A sea change in energy trading is now underway. Electronic index construction coupled with screen trading is already altering the industry globally. Electronic broking and trading platforms are emerging that will continue to change the face of energy trading are emerging. But new commodity markets for energy are also emerging for weather, coal, emissions, and LNG trading as extensions of the energy trading platform. They will most likely be on electronic platforms.

While the structure of energy trading has changed due to the demise of Enron and merchant power market makers during the past two years it has made it more conducive for short-term trading vis a vis regulated energy futures exchanges. Other critical changes have occurred over the past 20 years, price assessment panels and index trading which failed in the late 1980s and early 1990s are succeeding now. Electronic index construction coupled with screen trading is already changing the industry globally. Electronic broking and trading platforms are emerging that will continue to change the face of energy trading.

Besides energy trading, the oil industry is on the brink of dynamic and dramatic fundamental change both in the physical and financial markets around the world. Many companies entered the Internet energy space but unfortunately many failed to gain traction and have either changed their business model or disappeared over the past several years. For as the industry continues to consolidate and restructure on a larger scale like never before, margins become razor thin therefore volume becomes the key component of success. All these platforms presently lack liquidity and we have seen a major market shake out and consolidation with the emergence of two dominant e-commerce trading platforms: NYMEX and IPE/ICE. NYMEX and IPE/ICE are in many ways now standing at the crossroads of the energy trading complex but NYMEX seems to be moving ahead of the game with the introduction of its ClearPort clearing for OTC derivatives in the United States and Europe. Its just a matter of time before it goes in to Asia. NYMEX has already publicly announced during 2004, amongst others, MOUs with The Singapore Exchange, TOCOM Tokyo, SHFE, and with authorities in Dubai, to cooperate and develop markets. The IPE international petroleum exchange seems to be more inwardly focused at its own ownership and shareholding structure in the aftermath of the takeover by the Intercontinental Exchange and the mixed feelings of broker/members of the IPE over the takeover and the payout they have yet to receive.

DEREGULATION: THE DRIVING FORCE FOR TECHNOLOGICAL AND MARKET CHANGES

Energy markets are conservative in nature and thrive on security of supply. The avoidance of risk would seem to be a curious place to foster the electronic future, but the added impetus of energy deregulation as a global phenomenon is bringing the technology solution to the industry quite rapidly as a consequence of more market risk. Liberalization is the process of introducing competition and brings with it radical changes to the structure of the industry. Traditional business practices tend to disappear, as new competitive forces are unleashed. Moreover, new competitors such as Oracle, Microsoft, AT&T, British Telecommunications, and IBM will continue to make inroads into this industry for many years.

The key changes of liberalizing markets are changes in market share from monopolistic ownership, exposure to risks necessitating a new risk management infrastructure be developed for companies, and market consolidation over time. Liberalization also forces a new and very different commercial environment that brings forth new IT solutions since the business as usual model in the use of computer systems is now inadequate. The infrastructure transition from monopoly to competition focuses understanding on the need for new trading expertise, systems, and exchanges. It is definitely a new world affecting, market share, procurement patterns, and price volatility. The radical restructuring of the energy industries in oil, gas, and power across the world is accelerating. New solutions are rife. They are well positioned in Asia with its superior electronic technology and willingness to use it.

Newer commodity markets that impact on the energy industry are also appearing. The trading of weather, emissions, and water are developing as well as gas and power markets throughout the world. It seems the trading solution is taking root globally. These markets may or not be conducive to electronic trading depending on their state of development, that is, their liquidity.

Energy deregulation is creating the need for newer information systems that could support competitive markets. Deregulation shifts more risks to companies as well as creates more competition. The technological drivers of electronic trading, procurement and e-tailing will fundamentally change the structure of oil markets. In effect, the Internet is changing how the oil business is conducted and is not simply an application of new technologies to business as usual practices. The Internet has its own dynamics and has become the tool required for competing in the new oil markets where time becomes a more critical success factor. It is definitely a new world affecting, market share, procurement patterns, and price volatility. The radical restructuring of the energy industries in oil, gas, and power across the world is accelerating and simultaneously evolving with increased Internet usage by the industry.

This is a fundamental industry change, and it is irrelevant of the dotcom failures post-2000. In fact, the oil industry was late to the dotcom party, and its platforms must meet critical milestones for success, the first being the ability to create liquidity. Business-to-business (B2B) e-commerce is becoming a major part of the global oil markets including online exchanges, auctions, and retail aggregators. The next wave of electronic energy will be in the retail markets as data is aggregated, services bundled, and ancillary services. The fragmented markets of today create inefficiencies which will be consolidated by Internet applications.

For quite some time, it has been known that energy market deregulation and the transition to competitive wholesale markets would require new trading expertise, systems and exchanges. With a liquid market which has many trades, price discovery and choices, electronic trading can provide more effective risk management solutions. This factor enhances market liquidity and creates more arbitrage opportunities globally for energy trading. Electronic trading can create greater price discovery, more deal flow and more data for structured deals. It is also the driver for increased OTC market liquidity. Electronic commerce is clearly transforming other markets, and now it is transforming energy markets.

However, at the same time, there has been a softening in energy markets due to Enron's demise, the California energy crisis, the loss of many major energy market makers in North America and Europe, and the demise of many electronic platforms. The major repercussions felt in electronic trading markets has been a dramatic falling off of trading and a lack of liquidity. In fact, 16 of the top 20 gas and power marketers in the United States have either exited trading or dramatically scaled back their trading operations during the past two years. As EnronOnline, DynegyDirect and other Internet energy platforms fell by the wayside, and energy merchants came under increased scrutiny and essentially left the markets, trading volumes dried up both on electronic platforms and on OTC markets. Ironically, this has hardly impacted the Asian trading markets since they were not as active as North American or European markets. Moreover, these markets are currently in the rebuilding stage where major financial institutions will take the place of energy trading companies, something akin to the Wall Street refiners of the late 1980s who are now entering the electric power business on the physical side.

The threat of more oversight and regulation of the OTC markets has further damaged liquidity and brought a fundamental structural change to energy trading. Trading devolved to using hedging instruments to balance supply risk. The tenor of trading also changed to more short-term trading (less than a year) from the former structures trading for five, ten or twenty years. Massive power price volatility also hammered liquidity in electricity markets. Few if any company could manage 200 to 300% annualized power price volatility. While it could be argued that this volatility can generate hedging interest, few counterparties (energy merchants) had strong enough balance sheets to take on the risk of these speculative trades.

The market meltdown has compounded a more basic problem. The adoption of electronic energy trading is really not a technology issue nor a problem of illiquid markets as they can recover. The difficulty lies in human resistance to changing their trading practices. This is especially true in the energy trading space which has very strong human relationships, particularly between traders and brokers. These relationships are based on the ability to obtain via human contact market intelligence and execute trading strategies that can never be found on a computer screen. Nowhere is this more true of traditional business practices than in Asia. Trading is an entrepreneurial skill set. Screen trading can never take the place of human beings who can play golf, go to sporting events, and take clients out to dinner. While the Internet can enhance trading, electronic trading platforms need to overcome the obstacle of no human interaction, and especially quell people's fear of change. Technology has not been the impediment to electronic energy trading especially with the cheaper solutions that are currently offered. It is human factors that will drive these changes or lack thereof.

Since the beginning of 1999, over 60 new energy Internet trading platforms have been launched. Many have consolidated, transformed into another service, or disappeared. However, we are also seeing renewed interest in the energy sector from other venture capital groups. Evaluating their ultimate success or failure may be premature as many of these platforms are now particularly focused on the physical trading of oil, gas, or electric power, but clearly the NYMEX versus Intercontinental Exchange competition is going forward at full force.

THE VALUE OF THE TRADING FLOOR

While the Internet was initially over hyped, so was its demise. It is not over yet. This is the beginning of change for both electronic media and the trading floor. However, the value of a floor trading operation has been overlooked over the past several years due to the Internet hysteria phase of market development.

The floor appears to the layman to be a bunch of people jumping up and down. There is much more there than meets the eye. One could argue that it is capitalism in its purest form. Commodities exchanges have been around for hundreds of years. They obviously offer price discovery, liquidity, the ability to do size, and execute trading strategy. In the energy industry, however, they are a relatively new phenomenon as energy trading only began in 1978. Before that time, NYMEX was known as the butter and egg exchange. Its transition to become the premier energy exchange and media for global price discovery for oil and gas is amazing. No one place has such influence on the formation of energy prices globally.

The energy commodity complex is very different from the New York Stock Exchange or for that matter financial futures for foreign exchange and interest rates. There is a very large physical component to energy trading. That physicality has practical applications on the NYMEX floor in that events drive physical energy markets. These events can be weather-related, political, or economic. Supply and demand also factor into energy price formation. The floor has the capability of interpreting all that news into financial terms.

While there are changes underway in the energy complex due to market deregulation in many countries, more financial risk means that more energy risk management techniques are needed. For the energy business is consolidating, restructuring, and concentrating on a larger scale like never before. Margins are razor thin; therefore volume becomes the only game in town and the need to move more barrels, molecules, or electrons is paramount to viable trading. Trading liquidity at NYMEX reflects that growth trajectory quite well. It will only get larger in the future as newer and less traditional players enter energy trading and new commodity markets form.

It should always be remembered that energy hedging is still in its infancy with most producers and consumers not hedging. Deregulation shifts more risks to companies so that more trading and hedging is inevitable.

Moreover, the technological drivers of electronic trading and the Internet will fundamentally change the structure of energy markets that will inevitability enhance market liquidity across the energy complex and around the world. Energy trading is still on an upward slope, and has not fully matured by any stretch of the imagination.

Energy deregulation created the need for newer information systems that could support competitive markets since more data was needed on customers, procurement practices, and fuel risks. The Internet has become the tool required for the next generation of energy trading which is faster, has higher volume, and needs IT to be successful. This fundamental change will affect energy trading because of the dynamism of the global markets. It works in tandem with the floor. But this will be a slow process of migration from the floor to electronic markets. Electronic news information, greater volumes of data, and the need for more real time price discovery are further factors pushing the electronic trading envelope. NYMEX and IPE/ICE will be in the center of this market evolution.

WHERE ENERGY TRADING IS TODAY

The energy industry was a little late to the dotcom party, but was not damaged from the dotcom crash of spring 2000. While slow to embrace electronic commerce, the energy industry is very information-intensive and today very conducive to Internet applications. However, electronic energy trade will firmly take hold for oil, gas, and power trading later rather than sooner due to the complexity of the business and the overriding human element in its business model. Human beings still make the trading decisions, and because of this fact, the trading floor is a valuable piece of real estate for a very information-intensive industry.

While the oil and gas industry has been gradually using risk management tools to manage its financial risks over the past two decades, the unprecedented price volatility in oil and gas markets experienced over the past four years is accelerating industry adoption of both financial instruments and more energy trading. Much of this trading has migrated to the NYMEX and IPE trading floors. While liquidity today remains low on the Internet, the movement to Internet trading will create its own liquidity such that the paper markets for oil, gas and power will migrate to the web. It will enhance liquidity for the exchange. Moreover, the other industry trends of consolidation, market liberalization, and privatization are creating a tsunami of risk that must be managed more proactively.

While the number of Internet platforms continued to ramp up and then collapsed despite their valiant public relations efforts, most of these platforms were in dire financial straits and have not built trading liquidity. Ultimately, most failed; what appears inevitable is that some will dominate the Internet trading space while others will perform well in niche market functions.

What the floor offers

Energy exchanges offer safe harbor in the continuing storm over nonregulated energy derivatives, their oversight by the regulatory agencies, and the market performance of their clearing offer that OTC traders and market makers could not control in the wake of Enron's collapse and the subsequent collapse of the merchant energy sector. Longer-term oil and gas trading also collapsed as the loss of so many market makers drained trading liquidity. This structural change also plays to NYMEX's and IPE's strength in that trading is much more short-term oriented than the past. Today, energy futures contract rule the market.

Because of the strong element of human relationships in energy trading, energy e-commerce solutions will evolve at a much slower pace than imagined during the dot-coms' glory days. That is because the human relationships between brokers and traders add value. From those relationships, traders get market intelligence and the ability to trade large-size lots without moving the market. Screen trading can't do that as well since they are essentially order filling matching systems. Moreover, screens can't play golf, drink beer, and go to sporting events. They never will.

The technology is not the problem as costs have come down and been more reliable. But Internet energy trading is an adjunct to the floor not a replacement to the floor. NYMEX now has the opportunity to dominate the Internet space due to the continued viability of its floor operation. In effect, the floor makes NYMEX stronger to penetrate the Internet world of energy trading. NYMEX can offer both the floor and the Internet for trading. The same is true of IPE/ICE.

The race for first place: ICE vs. NYMEX

The grand race for first place in the global energy electronic trading and clearing arena has begun. During the years 2000 and 2001, the energy industry witnessed a "black gold" rush with a new electronic energy exchange being launched somewhere on the internet nearly every month with each new exchange pronouncing itself as "The" global answer to online energy trading. Since the end of the dotcom era of the 1990s, combined with the demise of Enron and with it, EnronOnline in the fourth quarter of 2001 when the company entered bankruptcy, the majority of these "global" electronic energy exchanges have disappeared as quickly as they had entered the e-trading space.

After a period of consolidation in this electronic trading space during early 2002 until the present time, two contenders have taken a clear lead ahead of all other potential competition. The top two contenders are:

- Intercontinental Exchange/International Petroleum Exchange
- New York Mercantile Exchange (NYMEX)

NYMEX caught up to ICE by launching OTC Clearing services in late 2002, and is now viewed by the energy trading market as being side by side in the race with ICE. NYMEX launched its new online, Internet based trading platform called NYMEX ClearPort in early 2003. ClearPort currently allows companies to trade and clear OTC energy deals. ClearPort received Financial Services Authority (FSA) regulatory approval during the first quarter of 2003 from the UK authorities which means it will be competing head to head with the IPE (ICE's energy futures exchange) on its home turf. NYMEX has mentioned verbally to its membership that ClearPort will supersede NYMEX ACCESS (electronic futures trading) as well. Today, ACCESS has 1,500 users. This means that in the very near future, NYMEX will be able to offer trading for its full suite of successful energy futures contracts (WTI, Heating Oil, Gasoline, and Henry Hub Natural Gas) as well as a wide range of OTC Energy contracts all on one online Internet-based trading platform with one single back-end trade confirmation and clearing solution. NYMEX is clearly positioned to lead in the battle for first place, and is focused on OTC Clearing in Asia through relationships with Tocom and the Singapore Exchange.

NYMEX is already gearing up the promotion of this single futures and OTC clearing, and by pooling credit risks, exchanges such as NYMEX have another advantage over ICE in attracting more participants, which in turn increases volume and therefore liquidity.

ICE and the IPE relationship

Following the ICE's purchase of the IPE on June 18, 2001, the IPE is now making a very substantial contribution to the underlying percentage profit of the ICE as record growth continues on the IPE exchange. However the process of going electronic and replacing traditional "pit" style floor trading with electronic futures trading on the ICE platform has been very slow.

In addition, the market seems to hold a general view that ICE really needs to find a strategic clearing service partnership, one that works, and it needs to happen in the very near future or ICE will be in second place to NYMEX. ICE did launch OTC clearing services first with the London Clearing House (LCH), but that relationship has been disappointing for ICE as well as for many market participants. ICE appears frustrated by the lack of speed at which LCH has been able to list OTC contracts for clearing.

People close to the LCH clearing relationship with ICE have indicated that the LCH was not happy with the business culture or approach of ICE. An indication of friction in the relationship between LCH and ICE was last year's move by ICE to offer OTC American Power clearing via the Chicago Board of Trade Clearing Corporation (BOTCC). Moreover, there is the prospect of the IPE being forced to go totally electronic and to scrap pit trading altogether. This presents NYMEX with a major opportunity to open a London trading floor operation if the IPE closes its floor operation which now seems unlikely.

Characteristics of oil trading

Oil markets are conservative in nature and thrive on security of supply concerns particularly in Asian markets. The avoidance of risk would seem to be a curious place to foster this electronic future, but the added impetus of energy deregulation as a global phenomenon is bringing the technology solution to the industry quite rapidly as a consequence of greater market risk. Liberalization is the process of introducing competition and brings with it radical changes to the structure of the industry. Traditional business practices tend to disappear, as new competitive forces are unleashed. The e-Business model not only reduces customer service costs, but also a means to retain and attract customers. It improves the quality of the customer service. Incidentally, Internet back office applications like billing and customer care are becoming much more central to the energy business.

While today Internet technologies are still prone to problems regarding reliability, speed and performance, the transformation into a medium that is fast, reliable, and convenient is rapidly emerging with seamless access to the Internet. The impact on Internet energy trading will be instantaneous access in real time from anywhere in the world. The movement toward broadband technologies with text, voice, video, and graphics will widen applications even more and move past current Internet gridlock.

e-commerce and Internet energy applications are still just beginning. Many of the new exchanges, procurement sites, and retail services will fail since many provide duplicative functions. But the key is not to forget that this is the beginning of how the oil industry reinvents itself into an IT-centric, information responsive modality. Time becomes compressed, decision making accelerated, and globalization enhanced. Industry information impacts trading, investment, procurement, and customer services. The sure way to fail is to try to do too much in this complex space. The better way is to succeed in a defined, market niche, and build on that success record.

The question here is whether the physical oil market is ready or willing to embrace online trade. The challenges are certainly daunting, from a diverse market structure that cannot be standardized to resistance from the entrenched trading community. The handful of early players have found the going especially tough. Yet the size of the prize is too powerful for some to resist. While many firms want to change the way the whole physical market goes about its trade, it seems that physical oil may be a poor candidate for electronic trade. Many electronic markets in financial instruments such as swaps, for example, aim to cut costs by standardizing products and tightening margins, streamlining an otherwise efficient business process. The physical oil industry, by contrast, is made up of fragmented sub-markets, each dominated by a small group of players. Every cargo is unique, and requires its own auction which leaves little scope for standardization. Those targeting physical oil have so far failed due to the market's very inefficiency.

Physical platforms are not seeking to trade huge volumes of standardized products, but to match parties more efficiently. An electronic process can capture great value. There should be some efficiency gain in physical trade, although it won't be as much as on the financial side. The question is whether people will change their practices. It seems not to be very quick if at all there is any change.

Oil traders thrive in an opaque market, and tend to regard electronic exchanges with suspicion, even hostility. For the broker, the dealer, and the trader, a lack of transparency is something that can work to their advantage. It is not necessarily to the advantage of the consumer or producer, who cannot be certain that they are getting the best deal. Those intermediaries are crucial to business getting done. Most of the time, producers are looking to sell high and consumers are looking to buy low. Producers are typically looking to scale up and consumers to scale down. Nothing gets done until a trader is involved on the other side. Altra, which was established in early 1993, saw little liquidity on its crude oil platform until the year 2000 because of this phenomenon, and actually was initially successful in the much smaller market niche of LPG trading for many years.

Otherwise, big oil companies have been conspicuous by their absence from the online physical market. They have basically dabbled in the market in the past through Altra, Enbridge, and Houston Street, with their focus firmly on North American crude oils, which move in pipeline-based batches but have not committed large physical volumes of crude oil or products. The thought was that electronic trade would foster some standardization in this market, but that has been challenged by the fact that that oil pipeline trade is not a uniform business. For example, Enbridge Petroleum at one time had 52 separate descriptors for the type of product that you put in their pipeline. Shell, for example, has over 70 grades of gasoline. Moving into the larger cargo markets may offer opportunities but also poses more variables and challenges.

It was believed that the application of computer power to this extremely complicated industry would happen quickly. This sheer complexity is the key to opportunity in that it breeds vast inefficiencies. While a lot of other business-to-business projects are based on disintermediating an otherwise efficient supply chain, what you have in the oil industry is an extremely inefficient supply and demand allocation problem, which is today being resolved by nineteenth-century technology that is, people talking on the telephone. The physical oil industry is not just the largest real marketplace in the world. But it is also the industry most resistant to change. While the market's size at $3 trillion or so in annual transactions should attract massive competition, it has not been conducive to change due to the pre-established human relationships. It may take decades to implement that change.

The Russian oil market is expected to change substantially soon, with a new set of financial market laws working its way through the DUMA government. These laws are expected to be promulgated. These new financial market laws will implement big changes creating the required legal and tax structures for commodity futures and OTC Swaps trading and settlement under Russian jurisdiction. A special DUMA committee in Russia has even requested assistance from the ISDA organization to advise it upon laws and legislation covering Swaps trading in Russia. Therefore, Russia should be monitored for oil futures and eventually power trading contracts in 2004.

China seems primed to be in the thick of electronic energy trading. On March 1, 2004, China promulgated new rules for derivatives. The need for rule of law will facilitate foreign participation in a large and emerging energy market.

The next generation of e-commerce is beginning to emerge with the use of more seamless technology. Electronic Data Interchange (EDI) and other standards are beginning to emerge which are better encrypted and more secure. But the reality is that today, the energy electronic commerce solution is focused on the building of infrastructure rather than exploiting more powerful network applications. In a sense, they are first and second generation technologies. Once the networks are more established and robust, even more competitive solutions and applications will emerge. B2B e-commerce in energy will be forced to move to real time with next hour gas markets following electric power markets. Aggregators will provide more bundled services. And a true multicommodity warehouse of oil, gas, coal, power, emissions, weather, and bandwidth will be available in the trading equation as a one-stop shop.

Features of successful trading system

The key features that make trading systems successful revolve around the following two factors:

- Liquidity, for the trader on the front end
- Proven clearing and trade guarantee solution, for the management and Chief Financial officer (CFO) of the company

Since desktop acreage is limited, traders want one screen to access all markets. This demand is being serviced by Independent Software Vendors (ISVs) offering front end trading solutions which connect in to all the exchanges that the traders need to access. Some exchanges are not yet available via ISVs and these exchanges are putting themselves at a disadvantage not to allow their exchanges to be accessible via trading terminals already in place on traders' desks. The future will have the connectivity of the Internet to most platforms on a global basis.

At the backend, the administration and credit side of the energy business also need to be serviced. The online energy trading platforms that are expected to succeed in attracting and holding liquidity against the fierce competition are the ones who successfully bolt on efficient and cost effective clearing and trade guarantee mechanisms.

In the capital-intensive and highly capital-inefficient energy markets, energy trading companies and banks are becoming more aware of the fact that they are paying a high price in terms of capital usage to support their energy trading operations. Thus, companies want to pool their energy portfolio in to a single highly credit worthy clearing mechanism in order to benefit from position and margin offsets, reducing capital and collateral requirements for trading operations.

We think that exchanges that have liquidity now, may ultimately lose out to exchanges that have successful and efficient, cost competitive and effective clearing and trade guarantee platforms bolted on. This could be a reason why we are hearing rumors of the Intercontinental Exchange talking with EUREX (Deutsche Borse) in order to stay competitive on clearing with NYMEX and its ClearPort system.

This is why NYMEX with its large pool of liquidity, international recognition, and reputation, combined with its new ClearPort system is expected to command an extremely strong position, and in fact, take liquidity away from ICE in the coming years.

One strategic advantage NYMEX's ClearPort has been promoting from day one, over and above ICE which is now trying to catch up, was the ability for brokers to be involved in the whole trade execution process and clearing process of the ClearPort product.

ICE system initially was closed to brokers, then only open to the FCMs who were members of the LCH and then only to clear trades. Recently ICE has been trying to attract broker participation in the execution side, but it is playing catch up with NYMEX's ClearPort trading system which from day one welcomed OTC and FCM participation in brokering and clearing OTC energy deals.

NYMEX is also now well positioned to create the global energy futures complex which will continue to have a vibrant floor in New York. ClearPort has brought Nymex into the center of energy clearing with its $5 billion credit facility. It will enhance the global reach of NYMEX into markets and other energy-related commodities such as weather, emissions, renewable energy, and freight derivatives markets that don't have robust futures exchanges in place. Many countries are now liberalizing and privatizing energy markets yet they have no effective exchanges or trading liquidity. NYMEX brings that element to them in spades without the fear of nonperformance nor credit risk.

ICE has tried to move in the direction of working with more voice brokers to create more liquidity on its platform. ICE announced some collaboration with Prebon Yamane brokers in February 2003.

The question now is when electronic trading will transform the energy markets. While exchange clients are not techno-phobic, it will take more time than anyone realizes to gravitate to new trading solutions based on their ease of access, low cost, and reliability of the emerging electronic trading platforms. Energy brokers are in the middle of this transitional phase. They are trying to forestall the implementation of electronic trading by pooling their trading data which is a good business for them to be in. In fact, due to the present financial debacles of energy trading of both California and Enron, broker-assisted networks for electronic trading (the so-called hybrid trading model) may be around with us for some time to come. ICE and Bloomberg's Powermatch have both moved to the broker-assisted hybrid-trading model. NYMEX will continue to use this system as it inches toward allowing access trading during floor trading hours.

As a result, the timetable for Internet domination of energy trading is still five to ten years away. The important points to note are that the process of electronic energy trading is now a decade old (when the first trading platforms were initially introduced in 1993), and that these platforms will coexist with exchange floors and brokers for some time to come. Thus, while it appears that pit-traded futures contracts may be under siege globally by the rise of screen trading, the reality is that the US market will remain the last bastion of "open outcry" trading. The demise of EnronOnline, DynegyDirect, and the OTC energy market liquidity crisis have actually enhanced the role of NYMEX which is government regulated and has neither credit nor counterparty issues. Regulated futures exchanges are very oriented to the short-term nature of current energy trading which may change if the markets can be rebuilt. Thus, existing futures exchanges are trying to move to electronic trading without disrupting or cannibalizing their existing face-to-face open outcry floor business. The exchanges in both New York and Chicago (for other commodities) are offering electronic trading after hours. The Chicago Options Exchange will begin offering electronic trading this summer during trading hours. They will gradually transform their electronic "hybrid" system to allow electronic trading by the end of the year but keep the floor as the dominant trading system. They recognize that there will always be in a trading floor in the United States.

Futures exchange offer safe harbor in the continuing storm over OTC market trading. NYMEX has seen trading volumes and open interest more than double in the last year as the demise of Enron and other market makers have brought the exchange more liquidity than ever before. NYMEX OTC clearing has in fact created quasi-futures contracts since they now fall under government regulation. Its seat prices have risen to a record high of $1.3 million. It also cannot be denied that the fact that NYMEX is regulated by the US Commodities Future Trading Commission is a very important factor in the present energy trading complex. Recently NYMEX relaunched its electricity futures contracts on both the trading floor (PJM) and in electronic space (NYISO). Both contracts are succeeding, proving that each media can work both together and separately, that is, the trading floor or the Internet.

NYMEX's web-enabled ACCESS will give way to a successful Internet trading platform. Another question to consider is when will NYMEX offer 24/7 trading. That seems to be a way-off as the exchange "Locals" are still reluctant to offer customers the option of trading both on the floor and on the internet. Pit trading on NYMEX has remained much more popular than electronic energy trading on the Internet.

The past two years have been turbulent in the world of North American and European electronic energy trading. A pattern of normal market development whereby market maturity breeds consolidated market depth has not occurred and it has been replaced by turmoil. While the demise of Enron and EnronOnline would have negative impacts on market liquidity, the fact is that this was coupled with continued negative publicity about energy trading companies that have been forced to scale back both their market making function and trading activities. The dubious trading practices have severely damaged market liquidity. The pattern of wash trading, that is buying and selling the commodity at the same market price with the same counterparty, has destroyed much market credibility. These trades seemed particularly suited to online energy trading exchanges due to the anonymous nature of this type of trading as well as low or no transaction costs. The pattern of market gaming that spread across the energy trading complex has led to widespread calls for more government regulation and oversight that NYMEX and other futures exchange must live by. Restrictive regulation is not an impetus for electronic trading. It is in fact a barrier to start ups from entering the market.

The NYMEX trading floor is still evolving. Traders are already using technology in the trading pits such as hand-held wireless devices. Eventually, NYMEX will offer trading simultaneously on the floor and in cyberspace. Trading will grow in other regions of the globe and clearly on NYMEX. Order execution will flow through NYMEX enhancing the value of exchange seats and creating new techniques for energy risk management. The past two years post-Enron has shown that regulated futures exchanges can cope with a colossal meltdown in liquidity and daily trading volumes.

Much of the shorter-term OTC natural gas swaps markets migrated to NYMEX in that period as noticed by the large uptick in natural gas trading volumes and open interest. Nymex offered safe harbor in this period of tumult. The floor performed very well. Down the road, the floor will grow with newer commodities on both electronic trading platforms clearing on NYMEX and arbitraging in the trading pits.

Today, we are obviously in a transitional period to the emerging market of Internet energy trading. Voice brokering is still strong with brokers bundling their deals with data, consulting, and other value-added services. The end game for electronic energy trading is the creation of market liquidity. It is not here yet, and in fact, we are still in the beginning phase of market development. However, the greatest hurdle for significant breakthroughs in electronic trading will be human not technological. Today's trading platforms are only the beginning of a sea of change in energy trading. Newer and cheaper technologies will be developed and slowly gain liquidity in the energy trading space. Best of all, since the energy trading complex is global, the transition to the Internet will open up new markets throughout the world as the energy industry remains very conducive to Internet trading. It just will take more time than anyone imagined.

Electronic regulation

New electronic exchanges were not envisioned under the regulatory structures of open outcry trading floors. While traditional risks of mishandling of accounts and floor trading market manipulation will recede, new types of regulatory oversight will be needed. Record keeping requirements for pit trading will become obsolete, but electronic audit trails will be needed to be maintained. Market surveillance from watchdog agencies such as the US Commodity Futures Trading Commission and Securities and Exchange Commission will change as well. In effect, new regulatory structures will have to evolve since they have not been envisioned as of yet. Of course, self-regulation which now applies to the OTC derivatives market by the money center banks may become the standard as electronic energy commerce matures.

Turning to the European Union, Europe is struggling with the same problem and is trying to pass legislation to govern e-commerce on the Internet across Europe. Individual countries don't wish to delegate this authority to Brussels at the present time since it is an evolving situation and may have to be decided on a country by country basis each with its own set of laws and regulatory structure.

At present, there do not appear to be significant barriers for Asian energy trading on the technology side. The issue will be more focused on credit and counterparty performance issues.

Down the road, barriers to e-commerce will fall as the authority to regulate the Internet is borderless and will eventually shift to the broadest possible governmental authority. The economic imperatives of globalization and the Internet will eventually force states and federal governments to cede power to the larger national or international authority whether that is the US Government or the EU. The need for simplicity which rules e-commerce mandates those changes. Then, a set of common rules can be established. The Internet is obviously changing politics as well as economics but this is only the first wave of many more changes to come.

Rapid growth of electronic trading is forcing fundamental, structural changes in the energy markets and in the energy industry. The model of global energy trading is being irrevocably changed. Better transaction data, more price transparency, reduced trading fees, and access to better information will create more liquidity but lower margins. Volume will surge, and newer players will be engaging in the business of energy risk management and energy trading. But the process is going to take another two to five years on the road to market maturity.

It is predicted that the spread of the Internet and electronic commerce will give rise to price destruction on manufactured goods and fundamentally change the manufacturing industry. While e-commerce is already becoming the main distribution channel for the energy industry, it is increasingly obvious to many that both the old manufacturing/industrial economy and the new information economy will exist side by side. Thus, Internet platforms in energy trading must not discard what is viable and works, but enhance those features that already work. Reinventing an endless wheel is not how to effectively harness the power of the web. The change rate is accelerating as energy trading takes hold throughout the industry. It is only the beginning of this fundamental change process.

While today Internet technologies are still prone to problems regarding reliability, speed, and performance, the transformation into a medium that is fast, reliable, and convenient is rapidly emerging. Already hand-held wireless devices for cellular phones, and notebook computers are under commercial development and will use Wireless Applications Protocol (WAP). This change will bring seamless access to the Internet. The impact on Internet energy trading will be instantaneous access in real time from anywhere in the world.

The movement toward broadband technologies with text, voice, video, and graphics will widen applications even more and move past current Internet gridlock. DSL and cable modems will move more data, that is, financial transactions thus adding the technological capability to enhance market liquidity. Moreover, speech recognition and translation technologies will be more finely developed which will further globalize Internet-based trading. These new speech recognition algorithms will improve the interface with the network creating the virtual global trading floor.

Some energy market players are in fact waiting for greater technological developments before they launch their electronic trading platforms. They will use the technologically advanced edge to gain market share.

Looking at other financial markets today, the aggressive move of the Deutsche Borse to trade stocks, options, and futures in the United States, and NASDAQ's push into the European markets signal that the global stock exchanges are not that far off in the future. The globalization of electronic energy trading may be only a vision today, but the reality is that global trading platforms can be launched and become functional very quickly. This technological advantage may be the key to the development of a global electronic emissions trading market since carbon reduction for global warming mitigation requires a global solution under the Kyoto Protocols. In effect, electronic commodity exchanges can either be an extension of existing futures exchanges or new rivals.

The Internet has been called a near perfect tool for capital markets and offers other advantages such as the cheaper alternative to physical markets. The Internet also allows the real time dissemination of financial information including pricing, spreads, and yields on a computer screen.

Obviously, the new technologies harnessed by the Internet challenge "open outcry" exchanges as electronic communications networks (ECNs) are even cheaper than established electronic exchanges such as NASDAQ. It should not be forgotten that over five years ago the very high telecommunications cost was a major impediment to greater market penetrations of Williams Chalkboard oil trading system, the first electronic energy trading system back in 1993.

Electronic energy trading may be a double-edged sword. It may lead to more trading liquidity with more individual investors (the so-called doctors and dentists who trade the NYMEX), but it could lead to higher price volatility since active day traders try to exploit tiny price discrepancies in the market. Market fragmentation thus becomes a risk worth monitoring as so many electronic markets develop. This trend is already in evidence in US stock trading as a "volatility influence" exists. For the energy complex, which are the most volatility commodities ever created, it probably means even more volatility fueled by day traders. This phenomenon is already in evidence and influenced by NYMEX floor traders who trade for their own account on a daily basis.

As established markets consolidate and demutualize in response to the new technologically advanced competitors, the role of existing exchanges changes to that of listed companies. In effect, the NYMEX and IPE become commodities. As the NYMEX is the oil and gas futures exchange, and continues to grow every year in those two commodities, private investors and companies can buy a share of NYMEX. This is significant since the oil and gas contracts are robust.

The overall impact of electronic energy trading system is that traditional floor exchanges are fighting for survival in the wake of technological change and global financial integration. More refinement and technological improvement will come as there is recognition that gas markets in the United States particularly must trade on a next hour basis to match the power trading requirements. Real-time will really be in real-time in the future with 24-hour markets everyday of the year. They must adapt or be superceded with the next generation of technology.

FUTURE DEVELOPMENTS: TAKING TRADING TO THE NEXT LEVEL

To date the scope of electronic trading platforms in the energy sector has been restricted to North America and Europe. By 2005, Europe may have a highly efficient, electronically traded convergent energy market. The market driver for Asia is Internet market penetration and usage.

And it is not just geographical markets where opportunities exist. The emerging ancillary markets of emissions, weather, and bandwidth are becoming part of a convergent energy market and will be traded on electronic platforms which are essentially extensions of the energy trading complex. These new electronic exchanges are perfectly positioned for these emerging markets since they can be constructed quickly and at minimal costs.

The emerging Internet energy market is going to have to come to grips with the human factors part of the equation. Voice broking is still strong among a consolidating OTC brokerage community. It is estimated that energy broking accounts for $300 million in annual commissions. That sector is not going away without a fight, and probably will not go away at all. Brokers are bundling their deals into data, offering consulting services, and continue to provide value-added services for clients. Brokers provide more flexibility over screens, market intelligence, better handling of fast markets and personal contact. It should never be forgotten that human beings are transacting with human beings and not artificial intelligence. The hybrid model of voice broking and electronic trading may provide part of the solution.

The end game for electronic energy trading is the creation of market liquidity. It is not there yet. In fact, the financial markets for electric power in the United States are still dominated by physical at 95% rather than financial power. Thus, outside of the well-established oil and gas futures complex on the NYMEX and oil complex on the IPE, there exists tremendous opportunity to create the electronic platforms for the emerging market of electric power, emissions, weather, coal, and LNG trading.

The hunt for liquidity for B2B energy exchanges is still the key to the success or failure of any electronic exchange. This cannot be masked by saying we have 200 users or have traded one billion dollars of a commodity. The reality is that this is still the beginning of a market, and it requires that brokers be actively involved in the process to facilitate trading on electronic platforms. This has been true from the beginning of the transition to electronic platforms with Williams' Chalkboard and later with Alta. The model thus becomes one of broker-assisted energy commodities trading on these platforms.

Finally, it is worth remembering that electronic trading is an infinite market since the development of new technology is only dependent on time. The current electronic systems are only the beginning. The rate of advancement in electronic trading technology will make current systems redundant in the next few years no matter how scalable they appear today. The challenge to improve the systems on offer is immense and will increase as trading demands increase. More refinement and technological improvement will come, as there is recognition, for example, that gas markets in the United States particularly must trade on a next-hour basis to match the power trading requirements. Real-time will really be in real-time in the future with 24-hour markets everyday of the year. The older business conventions of yesterday will be replaced by a new era of continuous change at an accelerated pace. Today's platforms are only the beginning of a sea change in energy trading with the best yet to come as the Internet access penetrates the entire energy world.

It should always be remembered that energy hedging is still in its infancy with most producers and consumers not hedging. Deregulation shifts more risks to companies so that more trading and hedging is inevitable. Moreover, the technological drivers of electronic trading and the Internet will fundamentally change the structure of energy markets that will inevitability enhance market liquidity across the energy complex and around the world.

Electronic trading also can reduce transaction costs through greater economies of scale, an advantage over both futures exchanges and brokers. Electronic energy trading will also be integrated into a robust price risk and transaction management system so that real time trading operations can be integrated into a company's front to back office. This still will require the appropriate software technology applications and systems integration.

Energy deregulation created the need for newer information systems that could support competitive markets. The Internet has become the tool required for the next generation of energy trading which is faster, has higher volume, and needs IT to be successful. This fundamental change will affect energy trading because of the dynamism of the global markets.

The key market driver is the changing nature of energy markets due to deregulation, privatization, and liberalization schemes for oil, gas, and power. Coupled with the rise of competitive markets are technological changes rapidly driven by the spread of the Internet, personal and network systems, and new telecommunications technology. Electronic news information, greater volumes of data, and the need for more real time price discovery are further factors pushing the electronic trading envelope.

Moreover, the other industry trends of consolidation, market liberalization, and privatization are creating a tsunami of risk that must be managed more proactively, and the Internet will be the medium for that trade particularly in Asia.

CHAPTER 11

ISDA 2002, The ISDA Master Agreement Ten Years On

OTC DERIVATIVES LEGAL DOCUMENTATION

In 1992 the "ISDA Master Agreement" revolutionized the documentation and legal contract process surrounding swaps trading across all markets including energy. The 1992 version, the first version, remains the most popular and is widely used in energy trading markets (especially oil price index swaps).

THE ISDA AGREEMENT

ISDA agreements are made up of two important parts: the ISDA Master Agreement is a standard format which does not change (an example is included at the end of this chapter as Appendix 1 for your reference) and the ISDA Schedule to the Master Agreement. The Schedule is the part that is negotiated between counterparties and contains information such as procedures on settlement, early termination, default, netting arrangements (if any), and banking details for both organizations party to the Master Agreement. Sometimes the Credit Support Annex is attached to this, an example of which is also included as Appendix 2 at the end of this chapter.

The majority of crude oil, petroleum products, and financial power and gas OTC derivatives (i.e. derivatives that are money settled not involving any physical delivery of the commodity – OTC Swaps/Options) use the *1992 ISDA Master Swaps Agreement Multi-currency Cross-border* version. In addition to this, counterparties in the market generally use this Master Swaps agreement with 1993 ISDA Commodity Derivatives definitions and the 2000 supplement to the 1993 ISDA commodity derivatives definitions.

ISDA's 2003 Operational Benchmarking Survey found that the use of master agreements has been steadily increasing. ISDA members reported that signed master agreements are in place with around 90% of their OTC derivatives counterparties, compared to around 92% in 2002 and 85% in 2001 (www.isda.org).

Development in markets and derivative disasters like the collapse of Enron prompted a major review of the ISDA Master Agreement. In January 2003 the ISDA which is the global trade association that represents leading participants in the privately negotiated derivatives industry issued its first full revision of the 1992 Master Agreement (Multicurrency, Cross-border version). The product of several months' consultation and amendment, the 2002 Master Agreement (ISDA 2002) builds upon and amends many of the provisions of its predecessor. Practically speaking not many companies have yet adopted the 2002 ISDA Master Agreement, but it is slowly being introduced by energy market participants, so it is important for us to understand the key differences between the 1992 and 2002 version.

For this reason in this chapter we will focus on:

1. A more detailed breakdown of the still market-dominant ISDA 1992 agreement.
2. The main differences between ISDA 2002 and ISDA 1992 Master Agreements.
3. The procedure to follow in order to upgrade an existing 1992 ISDA Master Agreement that may be placed with another counterpart to a 2002 ISDA Master Agreement.

THE ISDA MASTER AGREEMENT

Any non-legal manager taking his first look at an ISDA agreement usually has a shock. It is a voluminous document and consists of 14 sections, as follows:

1. Interpretation
2. Obligations
3. Representations
4. Agreements
5. Events of default and termination events (An event is anything that has to happen to trigger some action in the contract. For example, when a counterparty goes bankrupt , it is considered to be an event and this may then allow certain action to be taken under the ISDA agreement.)

6. Early termination
7. Transfer
8. Contractual currency (In the energy industry this is normally always US dollars)
9. Miscellaneous
10. Offices
11. Expenses
12. Notices
13. Governing law and jurisdiction (normally English law)
14. Definitions

USEFUL ISDA PUBLICATIONS

ISDA publishes some other very useful books to help business managers understand the meanings of the contract sections of its agreements, in particular the meaning of the 1993 and 2000 Supplementary ISDA agreements and terms.

1. *1993 ISDA Commodity Derivatives Definitions:* These definitions are designed to facilitate the documentation of commodity transactions under the 1992 Master Agreements. Sample forms of confirmation are included.

2. *2000 Supplement to the 1993 ISDA Commodity Derivatives Definitions:* The Supplement is an update of the 1993 ISDA Commodity Derivatives Definitions (the "1993 Definitions"), which many participants in the OTC commodity derivatives markets have incorporated into existing confirmations or other agreements. As is the case with the 1993 Definitions, the Supplement is designed for use by participants in the markets for commodity derivatives transactions in documenting cash-settled commodity swaps, options, caps, collars, floors, and swaptions or such other cash-settled commodity derivatives transactions as the parties' desire.

The Supplement includes additional commodity reference prices for energy, metals and paper. The Supplement may not include all the commodity reference prices available for a particular commodity and used by market participants, but it adds significantly to the number of commodity reference prices set forth in the 1993 Definitions and includes the Commodity Reference Price Framework from the 1993 Definitions, which facilitates the definition of a commodity reference price that is not set forth in the Supplement. In addition to an expanded Commodity Reference Price Section, the Supplement allows parties to incorporate price materiality into the Price Source Disruption Event defined in Section 7.4.

3. *2000 ISDA Definitions and Annex:* This is what the majority of players in the energy market are using at the moment, although this may change in the not-too-distant future.

PRE-CONFIRMATIONS AND LONG-FORM CONFIRMATIONS

Banks and financial institutions aim to have ISDA Agreements negotiated and signed off within three months although it can often take between three and six months to have an ISDA put in place with a counterpart. Because of the time it takes to set up an ISDA, it is common to see counterparties trading with one another on the basis of an ISDA being put in place eventually (or under negotiation whilst trading). Most risk management policies prohibit any trading before an ISDA has been signed off by both parties; however, the commercial need to trade sometimes takes precedence over this policy (with management approval). But trading without an agreement does add considerable legal risk to a business and if trading must go ahead with a counterparty it may be better to use what is termed a "pre-confirmation" or a "long-form confirmation."

A "pre-confirmation" states the terms of the derivatives transaction and choices of provisions that would appear in the ISDA Master Agreement. The idea behind this is to commit counterparties to this wording before the agreement is signed. However, these are becoming less common due to a tightening of risk management policies over documentation and controls over trading prior to ISDA Master Agreements.

These days "long-form confirmations" are far more frequently used. (They get their name from the fact that they usually consist of about nine feet of telex roll or fax paper!) Basically, this is a one-off derivatives contract for a specific deal which covers all the main eventualities. This type of confirmation is probably best for dealing with entities which are not regular trading partners and so do not warrant the legal cost of creating an ISDA. It can also be helpful in situations in which there is an urgent need to trade, but an ISDA has not been signed off yet. "Long-form" contracts should be used for short dated "Plain vanilla" derivatives, with a counterpart in a familiar jurisdiction.

ISDA DOCUMENTATION PROCESSING

When entering into an ISDA agreement, one of the counterparties will usually take the initiative and send its standard ISDA Schedule draft wording for the other party to review and comment on. As mentioned earlier, the ISDA Master Agreement is not changed by counterparties; the ISDA Schedule is the negotiated document.

At this stage of proceedings, no negotiation has begun on the specific terms in the ISDA Schedule. Prior to negotiation on terms, the credit department must first process the counterpart details and pass the details of internally approved credit terms to the legal department who need this for inclusion in the ISDA Schedule; this also affects whether or not Credit Support Annexes are required.

Before rushing into the expense of processing legal documentation with a new OTC counterpart, it is useful to check the memorandum and articles of association of the counterparty's organization. These are known as the "M and As" and provide the legal incorporation details of the organization, specifying what business functions it can carry out and sometimes what it is prohibited from doing. It is very important to check that there is nothing in the M and As of the firm that prevents it from entering into OTC derivative contracts with other companies. If the M and As are satisfactory then both parties should be ready to put together an ISDA agreement.

Although the ISDA Master Agreement is a standard document there are areas of it which give rise to different types of risk for counterparties and are therefore often areas of negotiation in the Schedule. (Remember that the Schedule is where counterparties make the choices of how certain areas of the Master Agreement will affect their derivatives transactions.) These areas are as follows:

(Following notes refer to the ISDA 1992 Master Agreement which is still the key agreement offered by energy counterparties at the time of writing this book.)

- Legal risk
  - *Section 1(b) Inconsistency:* Where there is any inconsistency between the ISDA Master Agreement text and the ISDA Schedule (which is negotiated between the counterparties to the agreement) the Schedule will prevail. Also a key point is that if there is any conflict between a Confirmation and the ISDA Master and the Schedule, the Confirmation will prevail for the trade the Confirmation is recapping. This can contribute to operational risk, so trade confirmations must go out correctly.
  - *Section 1(c) Single agreement:* If trades are closed out, this section makes sure the values of all trades between the two counterparties are calculated and netted off against each other, so only one payment is required between the two counterparties. This avoids a situation called "Cherry picking" where if a company has gone bankrupt, the liquidator can call in payments on trades that are profitable for the bankrupt client, but refuse to pay out on trades which are not profitable. For example, imagine that counterparty A and counterparty B do two derivatives trades, with counterparty A making US$2 million dollars on one deal (it is a zero-sum game, so counterparty B is losing US$2 million), and on the other deal counterparty B is making US$1.5 million dollars (with counterparty A losing US$1.5 million dollars). In this situation, if counterparty B went bankrupt and Section 1(c) was not in place (because it had been deliberately excluded via the wording in the ISDA Schedule), then counterparty A could end up being forced to pay to counterparty B

US$1.5 million dollars (even though the Net position is that counterparty B owes counterparty A US$500,000). The single agreement concept reinforces the position that a liquidator cannot do this. It collapses and nets out the entire portfolio of derivatives trades into one single payment due to one counterparty or the other.

■ *Section 5(a) Events of default is a key area:* This covers a party's failure to make any payment or delivery under Section 2 of the Master agreement which covers the counterparty's obligations. In the past, the energy industry adopted a grace period of three days, however this is increasingly being shortened to sometimes just one day grace period on payments. The section also covers credit support default, misrepresentation, default under specified transactions (we look at this in more detail in the ISDA Schedule example later in this chapter), cross default, bankruptcy, merger, illegality and credit event upon merger.

■ *Section 7 Transfer of the agreement:* Normally, counterparties are not allowed to transfer the ISDA Agreement or any rights and obligations under it without written consent from the other party. There are a few exceptions to this rule but these are rare instances where a counterparty wants to transfer the agreement to avoid an "event" (e.g., illegality, tax event, certain cases surrounding a merger) and a counterparty transfers the close-out money payable to it by a defaulting counterparty to another firm.

■ *Section 8 Contractual currency:* This protects counterparties from foreign exchange losses on settlement and close-out payments.

■ *Section 9(d) Miscellaneous (remedies cumulative):* When a counterparty is faced with another counterparty defaulting, it should not forget that the termination of derivatives trades is not the only course of action. A counterparty can leave the trades open or even sue for damages, if it chooses to do so.

■ *Section 13 Governing law and jurisdiction:* The majority of energy derivatives trades under ISDA outside the United States, even with American companies, are conducted under English Law and the jurisdiction of the English courts. Under ISDA there is a choice between English Law and English Courts or State of New York Law and the jurisdiction of the courts of the State of New York and the US District Court located in the borough of Manhattan in New York.

■ Counterparty risk

■ *Section 5 Events of default and termination events:* This is examined from a practical standpoint in the ISDA Schedule example later in this chapter.

■ Market risk

■ *Section 6 ISDA Master Agreement:* This covers early termination especially with automatic early termination. We look at this in the ISDA Schedule example later in this chapter.

- Documentation risk

  - *Section 4 Agreements:* This covers the agreement of what documents both counterparties agree to provide one another (e.g., company certificates of incorporation, copies of licenses and renewals). It also covers an agreement that in some cases counterparties must maintain certain licenses and also pay any stamp duty taxes on any agreements etc.

- Payment on settlement risk

  - *Section 2:* This key area is where counterparties agree on details of how payments are to be made, how netting is performed, and it also covers provisions protecting counterparties against withholding tax deductions.

TRADING BEFORE AN ISDA IS SIGNED

There is a documentation risk in the time period between the execution of an OTC derivatives trade and an agreement being agreed upon and signed. If a trade does take place prior to an ISDA being signed between the two counterparties (which is not advisable unless there are considerable commercial pressures to put a hedge on very quickly) then the Trade Confirmation sent out will normally state that both counterparties to the deal must use "best endeavors" (a legal term as to the amount of effort used to achieve an agreement) to enter into an ISDA agreement. In the Confirmation it usually states that the derivatives trade is subject to the terms of an ISDA Master Agreement without a Schedule, so it is basically unamended.

The lack of a Schedule, though, means that the two counterparties cannot make their own choices over key issues in the Master Agreement. These issues would include: choices over what triggers automatic early termination of derivatives deals, payment netting and methods, what happens if a company merges with another, termination currency, tax representations (regarding withholding taxes on settlement payments), credit support (any parent companies willing to support the credit exposure on the derivatives trades) and which entities are included in Specified Entities (the other companies that are included in the agreement for the purposes of triggering a default).

The biggest risk for an organization if it trades without an ISDA Agreement is that if the other counterparty goes into bankruptcy or liquidation, a liquidator could end up "cherry picking" any profitable deals.

ISDA MASTER AGREEMENT SCHEDULE

The ISDA Master Agreement Schedule basically states which sections of the Master Agreement will be in force between the two parties to the agreement. As this is the case, it is often the center of much discussion and negotiation. Although ISDA Schedules will differ slightly from one another in commercial terms, there are still key parts that turn up again and again, so in this chapter we will go through an example of an ISDA Master Agreement between a bank and a nonfinancial institution energy trader.

The ISDA Schedule is always executed (signed off) on the same date as the Master Agreement it refers to. If an organization updates a Master Agreement Schedule at a later date and it has some OTC derivatives currently outstanding with the other firm under its old agreement, it is common practice for energy trading companies to backdate the new ISDA Schedule agreement with the same date as the old one so that old transactions are covered by the updated ISDA Schedule.

The Schedule is made up of the following core sections:

- Termination provisions
- Tax representations
- Agreement to deliver documents,
- Miscellaneous provisions, and
- Other provisions.

In the following section, we go through an ISDA Master Agreement Schedule and note some of the key areas.

Step by step explanation of a typical ISDA master agreement schedule between a trader and a bank

Agreement dated as of June 26, 2004 between
Corex Trading Limited (Party A)
and XYZ Bank Limited (Party B).

[First of all, the Schedule names the two counterparties to the agreement: the two organizations (or groups) that want to trade with one another.]

Part 1: Termination

In this Agreement:

1. "Specified Entity" means in relation to Party A for the purpose of:

Section 5(a)(v):	[Default under specified transactions]
Section 5(a)(vi):	[Cross Default]
Section 5(a)(vii):	[Bankruptcy]
Section 5(b)(iv):	[Termination event – credit event upon merger]

"Specified Entity" means in relation to Party B for the purpose of:

Section 5(a)(v):	Not applicable
Section 5(a)(vi):	Not applicable
Section 5(a)(vii):	Not applicable
Section 5(b)(iv):	Not applicable

[This is about Party B getting as much credit cover as possible against Party A in the event of defaults. In this example Section 5 XYZ Bank Ltd does not have to give these assurance back to Corex Trading Ltd. Corex Trading Ltd though is basically agreeing that if it defaults on any OTC contract with XYZ Bank, XYZ bank has the right to close out all transactions under this agreement. Note that Credit Support providers of Corex Trading Ltd (e.g. its parent company) are automatically joined to this provision in the 1992 ISDA Master Agreement.

The aim of the specified entity provision is to draw in those organizations whose capital are closely correlated to those of Corex Trading Ltd. Banks rarely offer this Specified Entity provision because most of the assets of its group will be in the bank itself and they see little point in opening themselves to the risk of Corex Trading Ltd, for example, closing out trades under this agreement through the default of a small bank subsidiary in another agreement with Corex Trading Ltd or one of its specified entities.]

2. "Specified Transaction" will have the meaning specified in Section 14 of this Agreement.

[Section 14 is in the Master Agreement and unless it states otherwise , which in this example it does not, it means any OTC derivative transaction existing in another agreement between the parties to this Schedule or their affiliates or specified entities. The bottom line is , if Corex Trading Ltd has lots of swaps and OTC options positions with XYZ Bank Ltd, and a subsidiary of Corex Trading Ltd called EFG Trader decides under another agreement with XYZ Bank Ltd to enter into a Swap with XYZ Bank Ltd, and this subsidiary EFG Trader then goes bust and defaults then, under this agreement, XYZ Bank Ltd could go back and close out ABC's positions ! Changes in Specified Transaction provisions are being proposed which could widen the scope beyond OTC transactions being in default to allow the party not in default to close out all transactions with the defaulting party.]

3. "Cross Default" means that The provisions of Section 5(a)(vi) will apply to Party A and Party B.

[This provision catches contractual terms and payment defaults in relation to borrowed money in agreements between the two parties to this ISDA agreement and their specified entities or credit support providers with any third party. Such a default has to exceed a defined limit, termed the threshold amount. This means that if Corex Trading Ltd or any of its companies in its group, or any company that is providing credit support in this agreement to permit trading between ABC and XYZ, defaults on any agreement under which it has borrowed money, then XYZ Bank Ltd can close out the transactions under this ISDA Agreement.]

"Specified Indebtedness" will have the meaning specified in Section 14 of this Agreement except that (i) such term shall not include obligations in respect of deposits received in the ordinary course of a party's banking business and (ii) there shall be added at the end thereof "or any money otherwise raised whether by means of issue of notes, bonds, commercial paper, certificates of deposit or other debt instruments, under financial leases, deferred purchase schemes or under any currency or interest rate swap or exchange agreement of any kind whatsoever or otherwise."

[In this schedule XYZ Bank Ltd is extending what the borrowing of money is related to for example, noted, bonds, commercial paper ... or financial leases ... XYZ Bank Ltd wants to protect itself against the higher risk of Corex Trading Ltd, working on the notion that a default somewhere else in some loan or lease etc. may be the early warning signs of a bankruptcy on its way. XYZ Bank Ltd then has the ability to close out its OTC positions and control its losses. In this section XYZ Bank has excluded the banking deposits it may receive from its bank customers, which is quite common. Technically, these deposits are money borrowed by the bank from its customers so some may argue over this. The usual problem faced by a bank is that its customer bank account deposits are very large and would easily breach any threshold amount level.]

"Threshold Amount" means with respect to Party A an amount of US$10,000,000 or the US dollar equivalent of any obligations stated in any other currency, currency unit, or combination thereof, with respect to Party B, an amount equal to 5% of stockholders equity as of the end of its most recently completed fiscal year (or its equivalent in any currency).

[The threshold amount is the amount of money or limit of specified indebtedness, below which XYZ Bank Ltd cannot trigger its close-out rights under this agreements' cross default clause. In this case, for Corex Trading Ltd, the limit is US$10,000,000. XYZ Bank Ltd is a huge entity and its capital base can be very variable so instead of a fixed monetary amount, a formula base on a percentage of stockholders' equity is used. This is quite common for Wall Street refiners that is, financial institutions trading in the energy derivatives markets.]

4. "Credit event upon merger": The provisions of Section 5(b)(iv) will apply to Party A and Party B as amended in the following paragraph:

Whether, for the purposes of Section 5(b)(iv) of this Agreement, the resulting, surviving or transferee entity (hereinafter "Y") is "materially weaker" shall be a matter to be determined in the reasonable discretion of the other party. Notwithstanding the foregoing, the creditworthiness of Y shall not be determined to be materially weaker if Y agrees to and does within two local business days of demand provide eligible credit support (as defined in the Credit Support Annex) in an amount equal to or in excess of the delivery amount (as defined in the Credit Support Annex) on the basis that the threshold for Y shall be zero notwithstanding anything to the contrary in the Credit Support Annex and thereafter maintains such eligible credit support in accordance with the Credit Support Annex as amended by this provision.

[Sometimes, to avoid dispute, parties to an ISDA Schedule will be specific as to what "Materially weaker" actually means for the purposes of their Schedule agreement. for example, "If either Corex Trading Ltd or XYZ Bank Ltd fails to maintain a long term, unsecured, and unsubordinated debt rating of at least BBB as determined by Standard & Poor's Ratings Group, or Baa3 as determined by Moody's investors Service Inc." These ratings are used because anything below these ratings is generally considered non-investment grade or perhaps even junk bond status. Terminology like this may be used in a Schedule between two large entities, perhaps two large banks. Enron almost certainly suffered as a result of OTC transactions being closed out when its rating was lowered, because others who had only put in their schedule, cover against default on a trade or borrowing of money had to wait whilst they saw Enron going down fast, but not defaulting on loans as banks tried to bail them out. Needless to say what defines a "Default" has been under great scrutiny in the world of OTC derivatives since Enron.]

A credit event shall also occur if

(a) any person or entity acquires directly or indirectly the beneficial ownership of equity securities having the power to elect a majority of the board of directors of X, any credit support provider of X or any applicable specified entity of X or otherwise acquires directly or indirectly the power to control their policy making decisions; or
(b) X, any credit support provider of X or any applicable specified entity of X enters into any agreement providing for any of the credit events specified in Section 5(b)(iv) of the Agreement or in clause (a) above.

5. The "Automatic early termination" provision of Section 6(a) will apply to Party A and Party B.

[Automatic early termination impacts events of default on bankruptcy. The effect of this provision is that all transactions under the agreement are deemed terminated as of a date immediately before a winding-up order is presented against the defaulting party and immediately at the time bankruptcy proceedings are instituted against the defaulting party in all other cases. This means that the non-defaulting party can exercise its rights outside the insolvency proceedings. Including this section in a Schedule is a choice 80% of the time. There are some countries though where it is advisable to use this section 6(a) – a fully updated list of countries is available from ISDA. www.isda.org]

6. Payments on early termination. For the purpose of Section 6(e) of this Agreement:

(i) The market quotation method will apply;
(ii) The loss method will apply; and
(iii) The second method will apply.

[In the energy markets there are three choices on how to calculate the amount owed between the counterparties in the event that contracts are terminated early and payment is required. The market quotation is very popular as it is simple to use for plain vanilla instruments such as fixed for floating swaps where there is typically good liquidity. It involves obtaining a series of usually three or four quotations from market makers (not brokers) for the replacement value of the derivatives to be terminated. If the derivatives to be terminated are more complex than plain vanilla swaps, you could encounter problems obtaining reasonable quotes from the market makers, in this circumstance loss could be used as a fallback and put in the Schedule as a fallback provision. Loss is the non-defaulting party's "good faith" determination of its losses and costs (minus its gains) in respect of replacing terminated transactions. Last but not least, the second method basically means the defaulting party has to pay anything it owes to the non-defaulting party, but if the non-defaulting party owes the defaulting party money it has no obligation to pay any amount to the defaulting party until it has received confirmation that all transactions have been terminated under this schedule, and that all obligations (matured or unmatured) of the defaulting party or any of its affiliates to the non-defaulting party or any affiliate of the non-defaulting party has been made.]

7. "Termination Currency" means the currency selected by the party which is not the defaulting party or the affected party, as the case may be, or where there is more than one affected party the currency agreed by Party A and Party B. However, the termination currency shall be one of the currencies in which payments are required to be made in respect of transactions. If the currency selected is not freely available, or where there are two affected parties and they cannot agree on a termination currency, the termination currency shall be United States Dollars.

[Simply, it is the currency into which all derivatives transactions are converted to on close out and settlement. The above section 7 illustrates very common wording in ISDA Schedules. It allows the non-defaulting to choose the currency. If the currency chosen for any reason is not freely available then the Schedule defaults to US Dollars.]

8. "Additional termination event" shall apply as given in paragraphs following the interpretation.

[Additional termination events include change of control, ratings downgrade (like in the case of Enron), even death or resignation of key men (if you are dealing with a small entity or one controlled perhaps by key management), breach of agreements, and sovereign event (maybe if you are dealing with a company that is based in a politically less stable region). This example Schedule shows wording for change of ownership and ratings downgrade.]

Change of ownership : Mega Corporation either directly or indirectly ceases to own directly or indirectly 51% of the issued share capital of ABC Small Traders Ltd carrying voting rights in ordinary circumstances in a general meeting of shareholders, or a comparable meeting of Corex Trading Ltd or otherwise directly or indirectly ceases to control the board of directors of Corex Trading Ltd and/or Corex Trading Ltd ceases to be a fully consolidated subsidiary of Mega Corporation.

Downgrade:

(i) S&P, or Moody's, or both rate the long term, unsecured, unsubordinated debt obligations of Corex Trading Ltd or XYZ Bank Ltd at least three modifiers (a modifier being 1,2,or 3 for Moody's, or plus, neutral, minus for S&P) lower than the highest rating which had previously applied (from the date of this agreement) to the long term unsecured, unsubordinated debt obligations of Corex Trading Ltd, or XYZ Bank Ltd.

(ii) Corex Trading Ltd or XYZ Bank Ltd cease to be rated by both S&P and Moody's. For the purposes of the foregoing termination event, the affected party shall be the party that was downgraded or ceased to be rated. [This is self explanatory: if the rating gets too badly affected then OTC derivatives contracts under this agreement can be terminated by the "affected" party.]

Part 2: Tax Representations

[Tax representations are left over from the early years of OTC derivatives when there was even uncertainty in the United States as to whether a payer's tax authority would levy a withholding tax on settlement payments made on OTC swaps transactions. The ISDA agreement covers both counterparties against any withholding tax ever being required to be paid on any derivative settlements via Section 2(d) (i) (4) of the Master Agreement which makes it the responsibility of the payer (the company sending the payment) to ensure that the payee (the company receiving the payment) gets full payment. The payer must gross up the payment to the payee so that the payee receives, after deduction of the payer's jurisdictional withholding tax, the full settlement required on the derivatives trade. I have only come across one such jurisdiction where there was a clear withholding tax issue for energy derivatives, that was Thailand. Any organization entering into an ISDA agreement with a new counterparty should get a legal opinion on the country that they are going to be dealing with.]

Payer tax representations

1. For the purpose of Section 3(e) of this Agreement, both parties make the following representation:

It is not required by any applicable law, as modified by the practice of any relevant governmental revenue authority, of any Relevant Jurisdiction to make any deduction or withholding for or on account of any Tax from any payment (other than interest under Section 2(e), 6(d)(ii), or 6(e) of this Agreement) to be made by it to the other party under this Agreement.

[Relevant jurisdiction in the ISDA Schedule refers to the payer's home jurisdiction, where the office actually executing the trades is based, the jurisdiction where it executed the Agreement and also the jurisdiction from which it makes payments including settlement payments for any transactions under this agreement.]

In making this representation, it may rely on

(i) the accuracy of any representation made by the other party pursuant to Section 3(f) of this Agreement;
(ii) the satisfaction of the agreement of the other party contained in Section 4(a)(i) or 4(a) and the accuracy and effectiveness of any document provided by the other party pursuant to Section 4(a)(i), or 4(a)(iii) of this Agreement; and
(iii) the satisfaction of the agreement of the other party contained in Section 4(d).

Provided that it shall not be a breach of this representation where reliance is placed on Clause (ii) and the other party does not deliver a form or document under Section 4(a)(iii) by reason of material prejudice to its legal or commercial position.

[The payer tax representation actually does not include default interest payments or any interest that could be charged due to an early termination payment. This payer tax representation section is very standard, and there are a few jurisdictions where ISDA may not have been tested and some where overseas payment and or tax regulations have been outpaced by the local adoption of derivatives instruments usage. If it does not appear in an ISDA Schedule you are being asked to agree to, query it!]

Payee tax representations

2. For the purpose of Section 3(f), both parties make the following representation:

Each payment received or to be received by it in connection with this Agreement relates to the regular business operations of the party (and not to an investment of the party).

[This section is not always included because of the existence of many double tax treaties around the world which have income and interest provisions giving protection against withholding taxes.]

Other representations

1. Each party represents and warrants to the other (which shall be deemed to be repeated by each party on each date on which a transaction is entered into) that (a) there has been no material adverse change in its financial condition since the last day of the period covered by its most recently prepared audited financial statement and that "Accuracy of specified information" as provided for in Section 3(d) will apply to the financial information which a party is required to deliver to the other party under this Schedule, and (b) It is entering into this Agreement and each transaction as principal (and not as agent or in any other capacity, fiduciary or otherwise).

2. Each party will be deemed to represent to the other party on the date on which it enters into a transaction that (absent a written agreement between the parties that expressly imposes affirmative obligations to the contrary for that transaction) (a) It is acting for its own account, and it has made its own independent decisions to enter into that Transaction and as to whether that Transaction is appropriate or proper for it based upon its own judgment and upon advice from such advisers as it has deemed necessary. It is not relying on any communication (written or oral) of the other party as investment advice or as a recommendation to enter into that transaction; it being understood that the information and explanations related to the terms and conditions of the transaction shall not be considered investment advice or a recommendation to enter into that Transaction. No communication (written or oral) received from the other party shall be deemed to be an assurance or guarantee as to the expected results of that transaction; that (b) it is capable of assessing the merits of and understanding (on its own behalf or through independent professional advice), and understands and accepts, the terms, conditions, and risks of that transaction. It is also capable of assuming, and assumes, the risks of that transaction; and that (c) the other party is not acting as a fiduciary for or an adviser to it in respect of that transaction.

3. Absence of litigation. Section 3(c) of the Agreement is hereby amended by limiting the definition of "affiliate" for the purposes of this representation to such affiliates, if any, as may be a specified entity for purposes of Section 5(a)(v).

Part 3: Documents to be delivered

For the purpose of Section 4(a)(i) and (ii) of this Agreement each party agrees to delivery of the following documents, as applicable:

[Below is a standard list of documents often required by banks entering into an ISDA Agreement with a corporate entity before trading begins. Here it will also note what documents are exchanged after each derivatives trade/ transaction. A certified copy of a board resolution authorizing execution of the agreement is very important to get hold of, otherwise trade conducted may not be enforceable on one or both parties to the agreement. In practical terms, counterparties may say that it will take three months or more to get a Board resolution due to the infrequency of the Board of Directors meeting, but it is worth waiting for.]

Party required to deliver document	Form/document/ certificate	Date by which to be delivered	Covered by Section 3(d) representation
Party A	A certified copy of a board resolution authorizing the execution, delivery, and performance of this Agreement and each Confirmation executed hereunder together with the names, titles, and specimen signatures of the persons entitled to execute this Agreement and each Confirmation executed hereunder.	On or before execution hereof and if any change in authority has occurred prior thereto, on or before the execution of each Confirmation.	Yes
Party A	In respect of each transaction an accepted Confirmation signed by an authorized signatory.	Within 24 hours of receipt of the relevant Confirmation from Party B.	Yes
Party A	A capacity certificate in the form attached to this Agreement as Appendix A.	On or before execution hereof.	Yes

Part 4: Miscellaneous provisions

[Don't be fooled by the term "Miscellaneous," it is still important. In Part 4 parties set out their contact details for notices, mainly for administrative purposes.]

1. Address for notices. For the purpose of Section 12(a):

Address for notices or communications to Party A: Corex Trading Ltd
Address: 27 Old Gloucester Street, London, WC1N 3XX, United Kingdom

Attention:

Telex No: 12345 Answerback: ABCSTrader

Facsimile No: +44 207 681 2076 Telephone No:

Address for notices or communications to Party B: XYZ Bank Limited,
Address: Bank of England Road, London, United Kingdom.

Attention: Swaps Back Office (Confirmations only)
Mr Paul French (All other notices or communications)

Telex No: 98238 XYZ

Facsimile No: +44 123456 7890 Telephone No: +44 207 12345678

2. Process agent. For the purpose of Section 13(c):

[A process agent will usually need to be appointed if a party is not incorporated in England, if the ISDA is under English Law (which is the preferred industry norm for majority of OTC energy contracts outside the United States) or not incorporated in New York for a New York Law based agreement. So if an organization does not have an office or is not incorporated in these jurisdictions, it will need to nominate an organization or lawyer in London or New York to act on its behalf. A process agent receives writs, termination notices, or other legal documentation associated with the ISDA agreement.]

Party A appoints as its Process Agent:
Party B appoints as its Process Agent: Not applicable

[Not applicable for Party B indicated that XYZ Bank Ltd is incorporated in England (as this example is under English law), or it would indicate that it was incorporated under New York law if this contract was under New York Law. XYZ Bank can accept legal notices directly; it does need a process agent.]

3. Offices. The provision of Section 10 (a) will not apply.

[Section 10 (a) provides that if one of the companies signing this Schedule enters into a derivatives trade through one of its branches, its obligations will be the same as if it had executed the trade through its head office.]

4. Multibranch party. For the purpose of Section 10(c):

Party A is not a multibranch party.
Party B is not a multibranch party.

[If Section 10(c) did apply then it would mean that both companies signing this Schedule were effectively providing an implied payment guarantee for any derivatives trades that their branch offices entered into. The benefits of multibranch, is that an organization via one ISDA agreement with its head office can permit all is branches to trade with the other counterparty to this ISDA Schedule.

It would read like this:-
"(d) Multibranch party. For the purposes of Section 10 (c) of this agreement: Party A is a Multibranch and may act through the following Offices: (-)Tokyo, Singapore, Frankfurt, London, New York, Houston." Party B can also put down whether it wants to use multibranch clause or not.]

5. Calculation agent. The calculation agent is Party B, unless otherwise specified in a Confirmation in relation to the relevant transaction.

[This is the counterparty in the agreement that has to determine the floating rate values and calculate payments. It is usual for a financial institutional trader like a bank to insist that it is the calculation agent where the agreement is with a corporate hedger or nonfinancial institution trader. Whoever is not the calculation agent will always have to double check the calculation agent's figures and can dispute any big differences. Most of the time with Platts price-related energy derivatives, any difference in calculations often arises from the calculation agent simply not picking up on a change of the Platts price for a particular day, as the correction of the price may have been published much later in the contract month. If two counterparties cannot agree on who will be the calculation agent, they can agree to both being calculation agents, that is, co-calculation agents. The calculation agent also has to establish whether a "market disruption event" has occurred and remedy it (see point 12 under part 5 in this example Schedule).]

6. Credit support document. Details of any credit support document

In respect of Party A: Parental Guarantee Dated December 10, 2002
In respect of Party B: Not applicable

[This is where any form of unconditional and irrevocable credit support against derivatives transactions under this ISDA Schedule is specified. For example, in OTC Energy Swaps, the majority of companies utilize "irrevocable standby letters of credit (LC's)" from a bank, "bank guarantee" or less often parental guarantees from their parent holding company, if a subsidiary. In this example Party A which is Corex Trading Ltd is offering a parental guarantee from its Parent "Mega Corporation".]

7. Credit support provider

Credit support provider means in relation to Party A: Mega Corporation [Mega Corporation is the parent company offering the Parental Guarantee noted in paragraph 6 above so it is named here.]

Credit support provider means in relation to Party B: Not applicable

8. Governing law. This Agreement will be governed by and construed in accordance with the laws of England.

[This example is showing English law – as mentioned earlier in the chapter the two key laws and jurisdictions used are English and New York State in the United States. Any other jurisdiction should be avoided unless an organization is prepared to get legal advice on the fact that the new jurisdiction's law will not have an adverse impact on ISDA provisions and the Master Agreement. ISDA contracts are already well tested under English and New York State law. For reference, if this example ISDA Schedule were under New York Law, paragraph 8 would read "This Agreement will be governed by and construed in accordance with the laws of the State of New York (without reference to choice of law doctrine).]

9. Netting of payments. Subparagraph (ii) of Section 2(c) of the Agreement will not apply to all transactions under this Agreement starting from the date of this Agreement.

[This provision is where the counterparties choose the scope of payment netting to be applied to the Agreement. The wording that is chosen is often limited by how advanced their risk management systems are. An organization should not feel pressurized into any complex netting of payment wordings. Organizations should liaise with their back office to ensure systems can automate the netting required, or if not, that they are prepared to allocate human resources to process it.

The wording in this example is the standard chosen by default by the majority of banks and traders in the energy derivatives arena. When Subparagraph (ii) of Section (c) applies (as above) it means that "Single Transaction Netting" applies. Single Transaction Netting = Same product, same currency, and same value date. This means that the two parties to this Schedule do not have to make payments to each other, but the one who owes the most money has to pay the difference between the two amounts to the counterparty.

The other choices organizations can make on payment/settlement netting are

- Cross-product netting
  - For more than one derivatives trade, for different products, in the same currency and due for payment on the same date.
- Multiple transaction netting
  - For more than one derivatives trade of the same type, in the same currency and due for payment on the same date.

If an organization wants to leave its options open, starting with the simplest form of netting and then, if it can handle it operationally later on, move on to more complex netting, it could agree with its counterparty on the following wording "Netting of Payments. (i) Subparagraph (ii) of Section 2 (c) will apply to all transactions under this agreement unless otherwise specified in a Confirmation in relation to the relevant transaction."]

Part 5: Other provisions

The following changes are made to this Agreement:

1. Definitions. This Agreement incorporates, and is subject to and governed by, unless otherwise specified in a Confirmation, the 2000 ISDA Definitions published by the International Swaps and Derivatives Association, Inc. (the "2000 Definitions") and the 1993 ISDA Commodity Derivatives Definitions ("1993 Definitions"). In the event of any inconsistency between the provisions of this Agreement and the 2000 Definitions and/or the 1993 Definitions, this Agreement will prevail. In the event of any inconsistency between the provisions of the 2000 Definitions and the 1993 Definitions, the 1993 Definitions will prevail. In the event of any inconsistency between the provisions of any Confirmation and this Agreement or the 2000 Definitions or the 1993 Definitions, such Confirmation will prevail for the purpose of the relevant transaction. In the event of any inconsistency between the provisions of this Schedule and the Agreement this Schedule shall prevail.

[Earlier in the chapter some of ISDA's booklets were mentioned, some of which have a listing of definitions. This example Schedule operates under the latest year 2000 ISDA definitions and the 1993 ISDA Commodity Derivatives provisions which covers energy OTC derivatives transactions/trades.]

2. Change of account. At the end of Section 2(b) add the following words:

"provided that, if any new account of the notifying party is not in the same jurisdiction as the original account, the other party shall not be obliged to pay any greater amount and shall not receive any lesser amount as a result of such change than would have been the case if such change had not taken place."

[Under ISDA Master Agreement, both parties can give each other 5 local business day's notice of a change of their banking account details for payments. The reason this Paragraph 2 has been included in this schedule example is to protect both parties from potential withholding tax charges and Foreign Exchange controls that might arise from the other counterparty moving its bank account to another jurisdiction.]

3. Pari passu. Party A hereby agrees that it will ensure that its payment and delivery obligations under this Agreement rank at all times at least pari passu in all respects with all of its other unsecured and unsubordinated obligations (except for those which are mandatorily preferred by operation of law).

[In this example XYZ Bank is getting Corex Trading Ltd to ensure that any unsecured debt it owes to XYZ Bank through settlement payments due on trades under this ISDA contract will rank equally with other unsecured and unsubordinated obligations in any winding up (liquidation) of Corex Trading Ltd. It is very important for corporates to understand this clause as it can only be given if it is true. Advice should be taken on this clause if it turns up in a Schedule being proposed by another counterparty.]

4. Confirmations. Each confirmation shall be in the standard form used by Party B from time to time or in such other form as the parties may agree. With respect to each transaction, Party B shall on, or promptly after the trade date, send Party A a Confirmation. Party A shall promptly sign and return a copy of the Confirmation or advise any discrepancy between the Confirmation and Party A's own records whereupon the parties will promptly agree on the text of a replacement Confirmation for signature by Party A.

[Self explanatory. However it is worth noting that more and more wording for the acceptance of Electronic confirmations in the energy trading industry is being placed into ISDA Schedules. Several organizations have electronic confirmations systems for energy swaps deals. These include Intercontinental Exchange (www.intcx.com) who has also launched an electronic confirmation system for trades executed via its ICE platform. NYMEX (www.nymex.com) has electronic confirmation of OTC deals registered via its online system, ClearPort.

Example wording to allow acceptance of electronic confirmations: "Electronic Confirmations. Where a Transaction is confirmed by means of an electronic messaging system that the parties have elected to use to confirm such transaction such confirmation will constitute a 'Confirmation' as referred to in this agreement."]

5. Automatic early termination. If automatic early termination is specified as applying to a party in Part 1 point 5 above, that Party shall upon the occurrence of an event of default notify it immediately to the other Party and provided further that automatic early termination shall not apply to either party if the event of default concerned is the presentation of a winding up petition which is withdrawn without advertisement. In the event of absence of such notice on the day of the occurrence of the event of default, the defaulting Party shall fully indemnify the non-defaulting Party on demand against all expense, loss, damage, or liability that the non-defaulting Party may incur in respect of this Agreement and each transaction as a consequence of movements in interest, currency, exchange, or other relevant rates or prices between the early termination date and the local business day on which the non-defaulting Party first becomes aware that the darly termination date has occurred under Section 6 (a). The non-defaulting Party may for this purpose convert any expense, loss, damage, or liability to the termination currency.

6. Early Termination. At the end of Section 6 add the following Sections 6(f) and (g):

"(f) *Conditions of certain payments*. Notwithstanding the provisions of Section 6(e), the non-defaulting Party shall have no obligation to make any payment on early termination to the defaulting Party unless and until the non-defaulting Party shall have received confirmation satisfactory to it in its sole discretion (which may include an unqualified opinion of its counsel) that (i) in accordance with Section 6(c)(ii) of the Agreement, no further payments or deliveries under Section 2(a)(i) or 2(e) in respect of terminated transactions will be required to be made and (ii) each specified transaction shall have terminated pursuant to its specified termination date or through the exercise by a party of a right to terminate and all obligations owing under each such specified transaction shall have been fully and finally performed; and

(g) (i) Without affecting the provisions of this Agreement requiring the calculation of certain net payment amounts, all payments under this Agreement will be made without set-off or counterclaim; provided, however that any amount (the "early termination amount") payable to one party (the Payee) by the other party (the Payer) under Section 6 (e) in circumstances where there is a defaulting Party or one affected Party in the case where a termination event under Section 5 (b) (i) to (v) inclusive has occurred, will, at the option of the party ("X") other than the defaulting Party or the affected Party (and without prior notice to the defaulting Party or affected Party), be reduced by its set-off against any amount(s) (the "other agreement amount") payable (whether at such time or in the future or upon occurrence of a contingency) by the Payee to the Payer (irrespective of the currency, place of payment, or booking office of the obligation) under any other agreement(s) between the Payee and the Payer or instrument(s) or undertaking(s) issued or extended by one party to, or in favor of, the other party (and the other agreement amount will be discharged promptly and in all respects to the extent it is so set-off). X will give notice to the other party of any set-off effected under this Section.

(ii) For this purpose, either the early termination amount or the other agreement amount (or the relevant portion of such amounts) may be converted by X into the currency in which the other is denominated at the rate of exchange at which X would be able, acting in a reasonable manner and in good faith, to purchase the relevant amount of such currency.

(iii) If an obligation is unascertained, X may in good faith estimate that obligation and set-off in respect of the estimate, subject to the relevant party accounting to the other when the obligation is ascertained.

(iv) Nothing in this Section 6(g) shall be effective to create a charge or other security interest. This Section 6(g) shall be without prejudice and in addition to any right of set-off, combination of accounts, lien, or other right to which any party is at any time otherwise entitled (whether by operation of law, contract, or otherwise)."

7. Transfer. Rights and obligations under this Agreement or any Transaction may not be transferred, in whole or in part, except upon the prior written consent of both parties and any such transfer made without such consent shall be void.

[Often counterparties, for reassurance that the other party will accept a reasonable transfer of rights and obligations under the ISDA Agreement, will insert the following sentence. "which consent shall not be unreasonably withheld."]

8. Default rate. The default rate shall mean 1% over LIBOR compounded on a daily basis where "LIBOR" on any day shall mean the one-month London Interbank Offered Rate as reported in *The Financial Times* or if *The Financial Times* ceases publication temporarily or permanently, such other newspaper published in London as Party B may determine.

[If one of the Counterparties defaults on a payment then the other counterparty is entitled to charge interest on monies owed.]

9. Physical delivery. Unless specifically stated to the contrary in a signed Confirmation, no physical delivery by either party shall take place under

the terms of this Agreement and transactions entered into hereunder shall be settled in cash only.

[ISDA OTC derivatives trades in energy are all cash–settled.]

10. Telephone recording. Each party to this Agreement acknowledges and agrees to the electronic recording of telephone conversations between the parties (including any director, officer, employee, agent, or representative thereof) and whether by one or other or both of the parties and that any such recording may be submitted in evidence to any court or in any proceedings for the purpose of establishing any matters pertinent to any transaction.

[Electronic trading platforms are making progress in penetrating the OTC Energy market, but outside the United States, the market practice is still generally to trade over the telephone. Consent has to be given to telephone recordings if they are to be used for any legal purposes in the future.]

11. Designated account Details for US dollar payments.

(a) In the case of Party A: As specified by Party A when returning the Confirmation from Party B.

    [or the counterparty can state its banking details under this Agreement and it can change them in the future by giving 5 local business days' notice.]

(b) In the case of Party B:

    Name of bank : XYZ Bank Ltd
    Account number: 08231-89178236-73624-02
    Account name : XYZ Bank derivatives receipts

12. "Market Disruption Event" means the occurrence of any of the following events in the reasonable determination of the calculation agent:

(a) Price source disruption;
    [If a settlement price is not available for some reason, for example, not published by the reference agency like Platts on a day it would normally be available.]
(b) Trading suspension;
    [A look-a-like swap would settle, for example, against a futures market settlement price each day during the pricing period, if the futures market was suspended.]
(c) Disappearance of commodity reference price;
    [If a publisher stops publishing the price reference counterparties are using as the floating price reference on a derivative trade.]
(d) Material change in formula;
(e) Material change in content; and
(f) Trading limitation.

13. Disruption fallbacks relating to commodity transactions:

The following disruption fallbacks (as defined in the 1993 Commodity Definitions) shall be applicable in each case in the order in which they appear:

(i) In respect of any transaction having a calculation period or calculation periods which are greater than or equal to one calendar month:

(a) Average daily price disruption, with maximum days of disruption equal to five;
(b) Fallback reference price;
(c) Negotiated fallback;
(d) The Parties shall appoint a single independent expert to determine an alternative pricing method. If the parties fail to agree on the appointment of an expert, the Chairman for the time being of the Institute of Petroleum in the United Kingdom shall be requested by either party to make such appointment within two days of request. An expert, if appointed, shall be deemed not to be an arbitrator but shall render his decision as an expert and his determination shall be final and binding upon both parties save in the event of manifest error or fraud; and
[In this example Schedule, where everything else fails, both Parties will in the end approach the Chairman of the Institute of Petroleum to be an expert to establish the price.]
(e) No fault termination.

(ii) In respect of any transaction having a calculation period or calculation periods which are less than one calendar month:

(a) Average daily price disruption, provided that the maximum days of disruption shall be zero where the calculation period is less than or equal to two commodity business days; one, where the calculation period is between three and five commodity business days inclusive; two where the calculation period is between six and ten commodity business days inclusive; three, where the calculation period is between 11 and 15 commodity business days inclusive; and four, where the calculation period is greater than 16 commodity business days inclusive;
(b) Fallback reference price;
(c) Negotiated fallback;
(d) The Parties shall appoint a single independent expert to determine an alternative pricing method. If the parties fail to agree on the appointment of an expert, the Chairman for the time being of the Institute of Petroleum in the United Kingdom shall be requested by either party to make such appointment within two days of request. An expert, if appointed, shall be deemed not to be an arbitrator but shall render his decision as an expert and his determination shall

be final and binding upon both parties save in the event of manifest error or fraud; and

(e) No fault termination.

All determinations and calculations hereunder by the calculation agent shall be made in good faith, in the exercise of its commercially reasonable judgment and only after consultation with the other party.

14. Commencement date. This Agreement is deemed to have come into effect on December 15, 2002.

ABC Small Trader Limited	XYZ Bank Limited
By:	By:
Name:	Name:
Title:	Title:
By:	By:
Name:	Name:
Title:	Title:

ADDITIONAL NOTES

Withholding tax and ISDA

Counterparties should do detailed legal and tax analysis at the start of their business relationship to ensure that no withholding tax is likely to be charged in any of the jurisdictions through which the counterparty proposes to trade OTC derivatives. ISDA's legal infrastructure makes provisions against being caught out withholding tax by making the counterparty pay the net amount (Net of any taxes payable in their home country).

Netting and ISDA agreements

The ISDA Master Agreement has established international contractual standards governing privately negotiated derivatives transactions that reduce legal uncertainty and allow for reduction of credit risk through netting of contractual obligations. Ensuring the enforceability of the netting provisions of the ISDA Master Agreement remains a key initiative for ISDA, because of its importance in reducing the credit risk arising from the OTC derivatives business. ISDA's work in this area has resulted in a series of laws being passed in various countries that ensure legal certainty surrounding the process of netting in those nations.

Around 36 countries have already confirmed acceptance of netting procedures in OTC transactions via the ISDA Master Agreement and this number continues to grow. See ISDA's website www.isda.org for regular updates on country legal opinions and results of their operational surveys and swaps trading volumes reported by ISDA members which are conducted annually.

The main differences between ISDA 2002 and the ISDA 1992 Master agreement

Although ISDA 2002 and ISDA 1992 are similar agreements in many ways, substantial revisions have been made to some of the more fundamental provisions of ISDA 1992.

Executive summary

- The reduction in grace period for failure to pay and other events of default, including bankruptcy;
- A new event of default for repudiation of the agreement;
- A redrafting of the cross-default event of default;
- The amendment of the illegality termination event;
- The introduction of a force majeure termination event;
- An amended hierarchy of events where circumstances arise which are capable of giving rise to an illegality and/or force majeure, or some other termination event or an event of default;
- The replacement of first method and second method, market quotation and loss with a single valuation method for payments on early termination – the close-out amount;
- The incorporation of a set-off provision; and the consolidation of the various interest provisions.

In terms of operations relating to ISDA-based swaps deals, the most interesting development is *Confirmations*. Some people think it is just a fairly technical difference between ISDA 2002 and ISDA 1992 but it is really worth noting that while Confirmations can finally now (welcome to the twenty-first century!) be executed and delivered by counterparties by exchange of *e-mails*, please note that only the Agreement can be executed and delivered by counterparties including by fax or electronic messaging system (which ISDA 2002 appears to differentiate from e-mails). Notices or other communications in respect of events of default, termination events and early termination may not be given by either e-mail or electronic messaging system.

Other key changes

ISDA 2002 contains similar events of default to ISDA 1992, although there have been some changes to the description of some of these events of default.

- *Failure to pay or deliver:* A failure to pay or deliver must be remedied within one local business day (or one local delivery day in the case of deliveries) of notice of such failure being given to the relevant party in order to avoid an event of default. ISDA 1992 allowed a three local business day grace period.
- *Breach of agreement; repudiation of agreement:* ISDA 2002 incorporates a new subsection giving rise to an event of default if a party disaffirms, disclaims, repudiates, or rejects, in whole or in part, or challenges the validity of, the Master Agreement, any confirmation or any transaction evidenced thereby. This subsection is similar to, and is in addition to, the credit support default under 5(a)(iii)(3) of ISDA 1992 in respect of credit support documents.
- *Credit support default:* The failing or ceasing of any security interest granted by a party or a credit support provider to the other party pursuant to a credit support document can give rise to an event of default.
- *Default under specified transaction:* This section has been amended to separate (i) defaults in making payment on the last payment or exchange date (or any payment on an early termination) (ii) defaults in making any delivery (iii) any other defaults (other than delivery) and (iv) disaffirming, disclaiming, repudiating, rejecting, or challenging the validity of a specified transaction. Delivery default and other defaults require the subsequent liquidation or acceleration of obligations under the relevant specified transaction (in respect of all defaults excepting delivery) or all transactions outstanding under documentation applicable to that specified transaction (in respect of delivery default only). Final payment default allows a grace period of one day but requires no further knock-on effects in order to constitute an event of default. Each of the defaults except for final payment default now refers expressly to a default under any credit support arrangement relating to a specified transaction as being capable of giving rise to an event of default under this heading. The definition of specified

transaction under ISDA 2002 expressly excludes transactions under the Agreement.

■ *Cross-default:* The first paragraph of this event of default has been amended to clarify that the threshold amount relates to the size of the aggregate principal amount of the agreements or instruments in respect of which there has been a default, event of default etc. Whereas this is probably what was intended by ISDA 1992 as well, there was perhaps room for debate as to whether the threshold amount applied to the size of the specified indebtedness or the size of amounts involved in the default.

■ *Bankruptcy:* Although the provisions are largely the same in ISDA 2002 as they were in ISDA 1992, there have been changes made to the applicable grace periods. Where a party institutes, or has instituted against it by a regulator, supervisor, or any similar insolvency officer insolvency or bankruptcy proceedings it would appear that an event of default will arise immediately, without reference to any grace period or the entering of any judgment. Where proceedings are instituted against it by any other entity, such proceedings can give rise to an event of default if either (i) they are not dismissed within 15 days or (ii) judgment is entered. The grace period under ISDA 1992 was 30 days. Also a reduction in grace period has been made with respect to circumstances where a secured party takes steps to enforce its credit security.

■ *Termination events:* The principal differences between the termination events in ISDA 1992 and ISDA 2002 are the expanded section concerning illegality and the inclusion of force majeure. Unlike ISDA 1992, ISDA 2002 does not make express reference to a change in law or interpretation and merely requires that the illegality be due to an event or circumstance (other than any action taken by a party or, if applicable, a credit support provider of such party) occurring after a transaction has been entered into. The subsection dealing with illegality of a transaction has been changed to make it clear that the illegality should affect the office through which payments and deliveries are effected in respect of a transaction, and that the ability to take receipt of payments and deliveries is also included. The subsection dealing with illegality in respect of a credit support document has been restricted to cover only obligations to make or receive payments or deliveries or compliance with any other material provision of the affected credit support document.

■ *Force majeure:* ISDA 2002 includes a provision dealing with force majeure. It is basically like the optional "Impossibility" provision, which was suggested within the user's guide to ISDA 1992. Force majeure, like illegality, has been made office-specific and expressly includes the ability to take receipt of deliveries and payments as well as the ability to make them. Of potential concern to counterparties to the ISDA 2002 is the expansion of force majeure to include not just circumstances where performance is pretty much impossible, but also where the affected trading office is prevented from performance or where performance is impracticable. Like illegality, force majeure can arise in respect of a transaction or in respect of a credit support document; the provision is split into two subsections, each covering one of the two options. The principal difference between the operation of force majeure and illegality is that force majeure requires not only that the relevant cause be out of the control of the affected office, party, or credit support provider but will only apply if such office, party, or credit support provider could not overcome the prevention, impossibility, or impracticability having used reasonable efforts such as would not require such party etc. to incur more than incidental losses. You have to work hard to make sure that you really cannot get around the problems faced by your trading office that is affected.

■ *Credit event upon merger:* This termination event has been amended in two ways; first, by a redrafting of the section by reference to separate designated events (the first of which being the equivalent ISDA 1992 termination event), the inclusion of an express requirement to take account of any credit support document and by the expanding of the equivalent ISDA 1992 wording to include the transfer of a substantial part of a party's assets, as well as reorganization, reincorporation, and reconstitution. Second, by the addition of two, new, designated events. The first being the acquisition of an ownership interest in a party by any person, related to an entity enabling such person to control that party. The second being the making by a party of any substantial change in its capital structure by means of the issuance, incurrence, or guarantee of debt or the issue of either (i) preferred stock or other securities convertible into debt or preferred stock, or (ii) an ownership interest in that party. These new designated events were not previously included in the ISDA 1992 and do seem open to a fairly broad interpretation.

■ *Deferral of payments:* ISDA 2002 introduces deferral provisions which will be effective upon the occurrence of an illegality or force majeure. The new provisions defer any payment or delivery obligations under a transaction affected by illegality or force majeure so that such obligation does not become due until the earlier of (i) the first local business day (or local delivery day in the case of deliveries) after the applicable waiting period, and (ii) the date on which the event or circumstance giving rise to the illegality or force majeure ceases to exist. The waiting periods are set out in ISDA 2002 as three local business days in respect of illegality and eight local business days in respect of force majeure. However, this will be reduced to zero in each case in respect of illegality or force majeure affecting credit support documents where delivery or payment is actually required on the relevant day.

■ *Close out netting–early termination:* Although the principal difference between the early termination provisions of ISDA 1992 and ISDA 2002 is the differing method of valuation, there are a number of other changes, many of which build upon the newly expanded illegality and the newly introduced force majeure termination events.

■ *Rights to terminate contracts:* The provisions relating to the right to terminate following an event of default in ISDA 2002 are unchanged from ISDA 1992. Also the provisions relating to the right to terminate following a termination event (save for the exclusion of illegality from the list of termination events giving rise to an obligation to transfer or reach agreement) remain unchanged. ISDA 2002 contains two new provisions that relate solely to illegality and force majeure. Unlike in respect of the other termination events, except in certain limited circumstances, either party may designate an early termination date in respect of all or less than all affected transactions. If one party serves notice terminating less than all affected transactions, the other party may respond designating the same early termination date in respect of all affected transactions. In the case of illegality and force majeure affecting credit support documents, only the non-affected party can serve an initial notice terminating either all or less than all affected transactions. However, if less than all affected transactions have been terminated, the affected party does have the right to respond with a designation of an early termination date in respect of all affected transactions.

■ *Payments on early termination:* Unlike ISDA 1992 which allowed parties to elect either first method or second method, market quotation or loss, and set out different methods of calculating the early termination amount owing depending on that election, ISDA 2002 only permits parties to use the close-out amount valuation method. The mechanics of arriving at an early termination amount owing once the close-out amount is established are similar in operation to calculating an amount owing on an early termination date once a settlement amount has been determined in accordance with the second method and market quotation election under ISDA 1992. The early termination amount will generally be equal to the sum of the close-out amount determined by the determining Party (or half the difference between the close-out amounts determined by each party in the case of a termination following a termination event with two affected parties) and any unpaid amounts owing between the parties.

■ *Set-off:* This provision is included for the first time within ISDA 2002, however it is substantially similar to the suggested "Set-Off" provisions in the user's guide to ISDA 1992. The effect of the provision is to enable the non-defaulting party or non-affected party (provided that all outstanding transactions are affected transactions) in circumstances where there is one such party to elect that any early termination amount owing be reduced to the extent of any other amounts owing between the parties. In order to satisfy the requirement for mutuality between the parties in order for set-off to apply, ISDA 2002 also incorporates a representation that parties are dealing as principals in respect of all transactions.

■ *Office multibranches:* The provisions dealing with multibranch arrangements have been expanded in ISDA 2002. Counterparties are expressly prevented from having recourse to the head office of a multibranch party in respect of deliveries or payments deferred in accordance with the provisions of ISDA 2002 following an illegality or force majeure for so long as those deliveries or payments are so deferred. New deeming provisions have also been included whereby a party will be deemed to have entered into a transaction through its head office, unless otherwise specified in the applicable confirmation or Agreement between the parties.

APPENDIX

[LETTERHEAD OF SIGNATORY]

[Insert counterparty contact details]

Re: Amendment Agreement to the 1992 ISDA Master Agreement

Dear [insert name]:

I enclose a form of bilateral Amendment Agreement recently published by the International Swaps and Derivatives Association. The purpose of the Amendment Agreement is to replace Market Quotation and Loss, the measure of damages provisions from the 1992 ISDA Master Agreement, with a new single measure of damages provision, Close-out Amount. By executing the Amendment Agreement, parties will obtain the benefit of the new single measure of damages contained in the 2002 ISDA Master Agreement, without having to replace their existing 1992 Master Agreement. The Amendment replaces "Market Quotation" and "Loss" with Close-out Amount and makes other corollary changes such as updating Section 6(e) Payments on Early Termination and dropping the First Method approach.

Please review the Amendment Agreement and have it executed by an authorized signatory and returned to me.[1] Please contact me if you have any further questions.

Yours sincerely,

[Signatory's Name]

Enc.

[1] Parties may wish to add references to any additional formalities or documentation that they deem appropriate.

MARCH 2003

ISDA®

International Swaps and Derivatives Association, Inc.

AMENDMENT[1]

dated as of ....

to the

ISDA MASTER AGREEMENT

dated as of ....

between

.... and ....

(the "Agreement")

The parties have previously entered into the Agreement and have now agreed to amend the Agreement by the terms of this Amendment (this "Amendment").

The International Swaps and Derivatives Association, Inc. ("ISDA") has published the 2002 Master Agreement. The parties wish to modify the Agreement to reflect certain provisions of the 2002 Master Agreement. The specific modifications that the parties wish to incorporate in the Agreement are set forth in the Attachment to this Amendment (the "Attachment"). The purpose of this Amendment is to amend the Agreement on the terms set forth in the Attachment.

Accordingly, in consideration of the mutual agreements contained in this Amendment, the parties agree as follows:

1. Amendment of the Agreement

The Agreement is amended in accordance with the amendments set forth in the Attachment.

2. Representations

Each party represents to the other party in respect of the Agreement, as amended pursuant to this Amendment, that all representations made by it pursuant to the Agreement are true and accurate as of the date of this Amendment.

3. Miscellaneous

(a) ***Entire Agreement; Restatement***.

(i) This Amendment constitutes the entire agreement and understanding of the parties with respect to its subject matter and supersedes all oral communication and prior writings (exc ept as otherwise provided herein) with respect thereto.

(ii) Except for any amendment to the Agreement made pursuant to this Amendment, all terms and conditions of the Agreement will continue in full force and effect in accordance with its provisions on the date of this Amendment. References to the Agreement will be to the Agreement, as amended by this Amendment.

(b) ***Amendments***. No amendment, modification or waiver in respect of the matters contemplated by this Amendment will be effective unless made in accordance with the terms of the Agreement.

(c) ***Counterparts***. This Amendment may be executed and delivered in counterparts (including by facsimile transmission), each of which will be deemed an original.

(d) ***Headings***. The headings used in this Amendment are for convenience of reference only and are not to affect the construction of or to be taken into consideration in interpreting this Amendment.

(e) ***Governing Law***. This Amendment will be governed by and construed in accordance with [English law][the laws of the State of New York (without reference to choice of law doctrine)].[2]

IN WITNESS WHERE OF the parties have executed this Amendment on the respective dates specified below with effect from the date specified first on the first page of this Amendment.

....	....
(Name of Party)	(Name of Party)
By:	By: ....
Name:	Name:
Title:	Title:
Date:	Date:

ATTACHMENT

Amendments to Master Agreement

1. The terms of Section 6(d)(i) of the Agreement are amended in their entirety as follows:

"(d) ***Calculations; Payment Date.***

(i) Statement. On or as soon as reasonably practicable following the occurrence of an Early Termination Date, each party will make the calculations on its part, if any, contemplated by Section 6(e) and will provide to the other party a statement (1) showing, in reasonable detail, such calculations (including any quotations, market data or information from internal sources used in making such calculations), (2) specifying (except where there are two Affected Parties) any Early Termination Amount payable and (3) giving details of the relevant account to which any amount payable to it is to be paid. In the absence of written confirmation from the source of a quotation or market data obtained in determining a Close-out Amount, the records of the party obtaining such quotation or market data will be conclusive evidence of the existence and accuracy of such quotation or market data."

2. The terms of Section 6(e) of the Agreement are amended in their entirety as follows[3]:

"(e) ***Payments on Early Termination***. If an Early Termination Date occurs, the amount, if any, payable in respect of that Early Termination Date (the "Early Termination Amount") will be determined pursuant to this Section 6(e) and will be subject to any Set-off.

(i) ***Events of Default***. If the Early Termination Date results from an Event of Default, the Early Termination Amount will be an amount equal to (1) the sum of (A) the Termination Currency Equivalent of the Close-out Amount or Close-out Amounts (whether positive or negative) determined by the Nondefaulting Party for each Terminated Transaction or group of Terminated Transactions, as the case may be, and (B) the Termination Currency Equivalent of the Unpaid Amounts owing to the Non-defaulting Party less (2) the Termination Currency Equivalent of the Unpaid Amounts owing to the Defaulting Party. If the Early Termination Amount is a positive number, the Defaulting Party will pay it to the Non-defaulting Party; if it is a negative number, the Non-defaulting Party will pay the absolute value of the Early Termination Amount to the Defaulting Party.

(ii) ***Termination Events***. If the Early Termination Date results from a Termination Event:?

(1) *One Affected Party*. If there is one Affected Party, the Early Termination Amount will be determined in accordance with Section 6(e)(i), except that references to the Defaulting Party and to the Non-defaulting Party will be deemed to be references to the Affected Party and to the Nonaffected Party, respectively.

(2) *Two Affected Parties*. If there are two Affected Parties, each party will determine an amount equal to the Termination Currency Equivalent of the sum of the Close-out Amount or Close-out Amounts (whether positive or negative) for each Terminated Transaction or group of Terminated Transactions, as the case may be, and the Early Termination Amount will be an amount equal to (A) the sum of (I) one-half of the difference between the higher amount so determined (by party "X") and the lower amount so determined (by party "Y") and (II) the Termination Currency Equivalent of the Unpaid Amounts owing to X less (B) the Termination Currency Equivalent of the Unpaid Amounts owing to Y. If the Early Termination Amount is a positive number, Y will pay it to X; if it is a negative number, X will pay the absolute value of the Early Termination Amount to Y.

(iii) ***Adjustment for Bankruptcy***. In circumstances where an Early Termination Date occurs because "Automatic Early Termination" applies in respect of a party, the Early Termination Amount will be subject to such adjustments as are appropriate and permitted by applicable law to reflect any payments or deliveries made by one party to the other under this Agreement (and retained by such other party) during the period from the relevant Early Termination Date to the date for payment determined under Section 6(d)(ii).

(iv) ***Pre-Estimate***. The parties agree that an amount recoverable under this Section 6(e) is a reasonable pre-estimate of loss and not a penalty. Such amount is payable for the loss of bargain and the loss of protection against future risks and except as otherwise provided in this Agreement neither party will be entitled to recover any additional damages as a consequence of the termination of the Terminated Transactions."

3. The term "Termination Currency Equivalent" in Section 14 of the Agreement is hereby amended by replacing "Market Quotation or Loss (as the case may be)" with "Close-out Amount".

4. The following terms are added to Section 14 of the Agreement in the appropriate alphabetical position:

""Close-out Amount" means, with respect to each Terminated Transaction or each group of Terminated Transactions and a Determining Party, the amount of the losses or costs of the Determining Party that are or would be incurred under then prevailing circumstances (expressed as a positive number) or gains of the Determining Party that are or would be realised under then prevailing circumstances (expressed as a negative number) in replacing, or in providing for the Determining Party the economic equivalent of, (a) the material terms of that Terminated Transaction or group of Terminated Transactions, including the payments and deliveries by the parties under Section 2(a)(i) in respect of that Terminated Transaction or group of Terminated Transactions that would, but for the occurrence of the relevant Early Termination Date, have been required after that date (assuming satisfaction of the conditions precedent in Section 2(a)(iii)) and (b) the option rights of the parties in respect of that Terminated Transaction or group of Terminated Transactions.

Any Close-out Amount will be determined by the Determining Party (or its agent), which will act in good faith and use commercially reasonable procedures in order to produce a commercially reasonable result. The Determining Party may determine a Close-out Amount for any group of Terminated Transactions or any individual Terminated Transaction but, in the aggregate, for not less than all Terminated Transactions. Each Close-out Amount will be determined as of the Early Termination Date or, if that would not be commercially reasonable, as of the date or dates following the Early Termination Date as would be commercially reasonable.

Unpaid Amounts in respect of a Terminated Transaction or group of Terminated Transactions and legal fees and out-of-pocket expenses referred to in Section 11 are to be excluded in all determinations of Close-out Amounts.

In determining a Close-out Amount, the Determining Party may consider any relevant information, including, without limitation, one or more of the following types of information:?

(i) quotations (either firm or indicative) for replacement transactions supplied by one or more third parties that may take into account the creditworthiness of the Determining Party at the time the quotation is provided and the terms of any relevant documentation, including credit support documentation, between the Determining Party and the third party providing the quotation;

(ii) information consisting of relevant market data in the relevant market supplied by one or more third parties including, without limitation, relevant rates, prices, yields, yield curves, volatilities, spreads, correlations or other relevant market data in the relevant market; or

(iii) information of the types described in clause (i) or (ii) above from internal sources (including any of the Determining Party's Affiliates) if that information is of the same type used by the Determining Party in the regular course of its business for the valuation of similar transactions.

The Determining Party will consider, taking into account the standards and procedures described in this definition, quotations pursuant to clause (i) above or relevant market data pursuant to clause (ii) above unless the Determining Party reasonably believes in good faith that such quotations or relevant market data are not readily available or would produce a result that would not satisfy those standards. When considering information described in clause (i), (ii) or (iii) above, the Determining Party may include costs of funding, to the extent costs of funding are not and would not be a component of the other information being utilised. Third parties supplying quotations pursuant to clause (i) above or market data pursuant to clause (ii) above may include, without limitation, dealers in the relevant markets, end-users of the relevant product, information vendors, brokers and other sources of market information.

Without duplication of amounts calculated based on information described in clause (i), (ii) or (iii) above, or other relevant information, and when it is commercially reasonable to do so, the Determining Party may in addition consider in calculating a Close-out Amount any loss or cost incurred in connection with its terminating, liquidating or re-establishing any hedge related to a Terminated Transaction or group of Terminated Transactions (or any gain resulting from any of them).

Commercially reasonable procedures used in determining a Close-out Amount may include the following:?

(1) application to relevant market data from third parties pursuant to clause (ii) above or information from internal sources pursuant to clause (iii) above of pricing or other valuation models that are, at the time of the determination of the Close-out Amount, used by the Determining Party in the regular course of its business in pricing or valuing transactions between the Determining Party and unrelated third parties that are similar to the Terminated Transaction or group of Terminated Transactions; and

(2) application of different valuation methods to Terminated Transactions or groups of Terminated Transactions depending on the type, complexity, size or number of the Terminated Transactions or group of Terminated Transactions."

""Determining Party" means the party determining a Close-out Amount."

""Early Termination Amount" has the meaning specified in Section 6(e)."

""Non-affected Party" means, so long as there is only one Affected Party, the other party."

5. The following terms in Section 14 of the Agreement are deleted in their entirety: "*Loss*", "*Market Quotation*", "*Reference Market-makers*" and "*Settlement Amount*"[4].

6. Part 1(f) of the Schedule is deleted in its entirety and the subsequent paragraphs are renumbered sequentially. In case the parties have used another designation for the paragraph of the Schedule specifying the selection of Market Quotation or Loss and First Method or Second Method, the reference herein to Part 1(f) of the Schedule shall be deemed a reference to that paragraph.

CHAPTER 12

Derivative Hedge Accounting

These days, no one doubts the importance of accurate reporting of derivatives in a company's accounts. The scandal associated with the sudden reported large losses with China Aviation Oil in Singapore in November 2004 highlighted the importance of proper management accounting and reporting of derivatives positions to shareholders and relevant regulatory authorities.

Everyone who trades in the physical or derivatives world of energy takes counterparty credit risk at some point in time. Without the implementation of solid accounting standards, showing not just the physical side of deals but the derivatives hedges and speculative trades as well, energy sector companies can not properly and fairly evaluate the credit risk they are being exposed to.

In the past, derivatives accounting was, at best, a quagmire of non-standards, inconsistent guidelines, and general confusion. Developments in the derivatives market seemed to consistently outpace the development of financial regulations and accounting standards to control and account for them. This lack of clear accounting standards meant that users of derivatives had to interpret GAAP (Generally Accepted Accounting Practices) to cover derivatives as best they could and sometimes, in doing so, opened themselves up to criticism. The area that caused particular difficulties was how to account for hedges (derivatives used to control the price risk in commodity inventory / stock , oil cargoes, forward cost of production / consumption).

However, an accounting standard has emerged that finally began to clarify matters: the IAS 39 (from the London-based International Accounting Standards Committee) and this standard is focused on in this chapter. IAS 39 becomes mandatory for consolidated financial statements of all EU listed equity groups for financial years commencing January 1, 2005. European listed companies have to prepare accounts in line with the IASC standards by the year 2005, but nothing stops them from adopting them now. IAS 39 requires derivatives to be marked-to-market (MTM – obtaining fair value) and reported on the balance sheet.

Of course some risk managers and accounting staff are concerned about the implications of these new accounting standards. Since accounting regulations sometimes do not allow assets and liabilities to be marked-to-market, volatility in the income statement of an organization could be increased due to the addition of the derivatives hedge, P+L now having to be added to the income statement in certain circumstances.

In fact some top 100 global natural resource companies have not implemented IAS 39 accounting for "hedge accounting", instead choosing to explain to investors that additional balance sheet volatility could be created by not adopting IAS 39, but at the end of the day it means more money to shareholders and less spent in costly IAS 39 implementation. If your investors are happy about it then it is ok.

In the past, the majority of users of derivatives (even end-users such as airlines and utilities) marked to market their derivatives positions, which entailed taking the buy/sell position executed price and comparing that to the current day's value for the same contract. Through this process, companies could keep informed of unrealized profit or loss on their derivatives book (positions). With the new standard, the difference is that they have to report these figures on their balance sheet.

For example, if company ABC buys an OTC jet fuel swap and pays a fixed price of US$20 for 100,000 barrels a month over 12 months (total 1.2 million barrels), the notional value (NV) of this trade is US$ 24 million. (100,000 bbls per month × 12 × fixed price US$20 = US$24 million NV) So the traded price is the fixed price of US$20 per barrel and the MTM value is the difference between the trade price and the current or last known market price. If the jet fuel price goes down to US$18 dollars , then the derivative position's MTM value is now negative US$2.4 million dollars. (100,000 barrels × 12 months) × MTM of US$ −2 per barrel = US$−2.4 million.

Before IAS 39, companies would not have had to report this US$2.4 million unrealized loss anywhere in their balance sheet. The derivative and, in turn, its unrealized loss would stay "off-balance sheet" until its expiry and settlement or when the position was closed out by a trader. At this stage, the amount paid out or received by the company on the derivative position would have been subtracted or added to the company's earnings statement. This is no longer the case, as the new accounting regulations require companies using derivatives to report their portfolio's MTM value. This means that companies have to report the unrealized loss or profit from derivatives on their balance sheet rather than just the final cash figure that is paid out or received at settlement of the transaction. If you were hedging against some physical energy risk and having to report your derivatives hedge

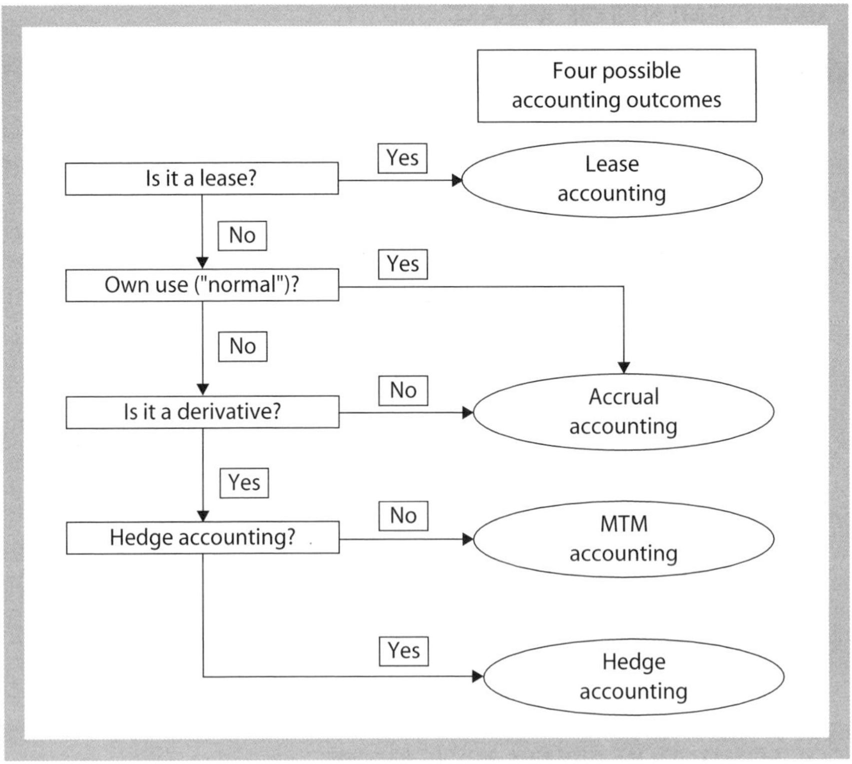

Figure 12.1 The IAS 39 framework

P+L in your balance sheet, it could create counter-productive volatility in your company' s statements. For this reason, IAS 39 goes into a lot of detail on special "hedge accounting" methods to handle reporting of derivatives if they are used as a hedging tool against some physical energy transaction. However, if you are just investing in the market and trading derivatives for speculation and profitable gain, the unrealized P+L of your derivatives portfolio needs to go straight to the balance sheet, whatever accounting standard the company chooses to follow. Hedge accounting under these new accounting rules is certainly much clearer (see Figure 12.1).

Various types of contracts are excluded from IAS 39. These include lease contracts and "normal" purchase and sales contracts.

The lease and normal purchase/sales exclusions are the most applicable for commodity contracts. Lease assessment is a critical issue for commodities companies managing PPAs (Power purchase agreements), processing/tolling agreements, transportation, and storage capacity agreements. They are important because leases are subject to other types of accounting standards, that is, IAS 17. Also, if subject to lease criteria, many of these contracts would be considered financing leases. Unfortunately there is little clear guidance to determine when a contract is a lease.

THREE ELEMENTS OF A LEASE

- Asset to be used is specified
- The purchaser controls the right to use the asset for a specific period through direct control over operations, or by taking "substantially all" the output produced by the asset
- The purchaser's obligation to make payments is not based on the actual use of the asset

The rest of this chapter takes a derivative user's and management viewpoint on how to interpret the new accounting standards sweeping across the industry.

It focuses on the key accounting scenarios that the majority of companies may face. Of course, all companies already involved in or looking to embark on the use of derivatives for trading or hedging purposes should get expert advice from accountants, or auditors for their specific derivatives usage. Such advice is particularly crucial for organizations which are hedging for risk management purposes due to the greater complexity of hedge account regulations.

CONSOLIDATION AND CLARIFICATION OF ACCOUNTING STANDARDS SINCE 2001

The main work on the consolidation and clarification of standards has been done by the International Accounting Standards Committee (IASC) in the United Kingdom. This organization has made clear progress in creating standards for derivatives market participants and both accounting standards provide useful guidelines for management to work from.

IAS 32 and 39 – International Accounting Standards Commmittee

- http://www.iasc.org.uk
- IASC framework expected to become the international standard on derivatives and hedge accounting.
- IAS 39

Before IAS 32 and 39 were introduced, GAAP only created enhanced footnote disclosures footnote refers to the note of reference, explanation, or comment (usually placed below the main accounting report entries). They did not focus on the actual issue of accounting for derivatives and, as a consequence, many derivatives contracts remained off the balance sheet.

Under the new accounting rules for derivatives, users of derivative instruments (contracts) not only have to report accounting entries for derivatives but also have to be able to answer key questions about

- What derivative instruments they choose for their hedging practices? and
- How they calculate that these instruments are effective hedges?

These have been the two biggest issues for corporations to administer since most banks and financial institutions have always written detailed internal papers on their derivatives usage because of bank and financial regulator regulations and guidelines. The upside for the industry as a whole is that it forces all participants at all levels to take a serious look at the derivatives they are using and the reasons for using them.

Of key concern from a risk management perspective is how to conduct proper accounting for hedges (derivative transactions entered into for the purposes of reducing price risk exposure). In the past, this has been a grey area due to lack of standardization. Before IAS 32 and 39, GAAP had different accounting methods for different types of hedge, depending on the types of underlying energy risk. Hedge accounting is a key issue because if you are hedging using derivatives you wish to illustrate in your financial statements that you are reducing or eradicating certain price risk exposures. However if you are speculating with derivatives that could be gearing up your company for a potentially big gain or big loss; this risk needs to be properly reported so that management and investors can monitor it and properly control it.

THE BASICS OF HEDGE ACCOUNTING

Why hedge?

- To match risk or reduce exposure
- To reduce exposure to fair value movements in asset or liability
  - fair value hedging
- To reduce exposure to variability in cash flows
  - cash flow hedging

Hedge accounting is matching of P&L recognition of gains and losses of both hedged item and hedging instrument but it has the onerous responsibility to get hedge accounting to stop abuse of principles.

The purpose of using derivatives

The use of derivatives falls under one of the following categories:

- For speculative purposes
  - In this case, derivatives gains and losses must be marked to market and will be recognized in the "current earnings" of the financial statement.

- To hedge the exposure associated with the price fluctuations of an asset, liability, or firm commitment
  - The carrying value of the item being hedged – the asset, liability, or firm commitment is adjusted to reflect the change in its market value due to the risk being hedged, and this change is posted to earnings. Corresponding profits or losses on the derivatives used to hedge the risk are also posted to earnings, just as they are for non-hedge derivatives applications.
- To hedge the exposure associated with an uncertain forecasted cash flow.
  - For cash flow hedges, derivatives results must be evaluated and a determination made as to how much of the result is "effective" and how much is "ineffective." The ineffective component of the hedge result must be realized and posted in current income. The new derivatives accounting regulations recognizes hedges as ineffective for accounting purposes only when the hedge effects exceed the effects of the underlying forecasted cash flow (on a cumulative basis).

The "fair value" accounting method is used for fair value hedges, which are derivatives used to hedge an underlying energy production or consumption. The accounting treatment of the hedge (the derivatives position) follows the accounting treatment of the asset (the energy production or consumption). Both are marked to market and the cash flows from both the derivatives hedge and the physical energy exposure are recognized in current earnings and recorded in earnings.

One new burden for corporate users of derivatives for hedging is that they have to show that the derivative instruments they are using for hedging show a close correlation with the underlying physical energy they are hedging.

Cash flow hedge accounting is the most common hedge used in the commodities industry. In cash flow hedging a firm is hedging the exposure of price movements in future cash flows (i.e., forecasted transactions).

Accounting

- Fair value of contract booked on the balance sheet and through equity with ineffectiveness recorded in earnings.
- Only the change in hedging instrument is adjusted.
- No accounting for the hedged item.
- Amounts recorded in equity are moved into the income statement when the hedged item impacts profit/loss.

For up to date news on accounting developments with International Accounting Standards, you can access www.iasplus.com

Example of a hedge

If the derivatives hedge is making a profit of US$1,000,000 but the physical energy position is losing US$750,000, then there is US$250,000 that has to be reported straight onto the current income/earnings statements. The other US$750,000 would be posted to the OCI (Other Comprehensive Income statement) until the overall trade has been completed.

In energy markets we often see unstable price correlation patterns caused by seasonal effects or political problems/issues in the Middle East. Under FASB rules, it is important to remember that you need to prove that the price reference of your derivatives hedge is closely correlated with the underlying that you are hedging. Any user of derivatives is going to want to have effective hedges because, as shown earlier, any ineffectiveness is reflected immediately in income/earnings statements and can cause additional volatility in a company's overall balance sheet.

When assessing effectiveness of a derivative market for hedging

- Take historical data of the physical energy market you are hedging and analyze the correlation between the price index your derivative contract is linked to and your physical energy market.
- If outside 80–125% correlation, the entire hedge does not qualify for hedge accounting.
- Even if inside 80–125%, some ineffectiveness occurs unless 100% effective.
- Ineffectiveness = 80–99% and 101–125%.
- Ineffective part of hedge is to be recognized in income statement immediately.

INTERNATIONAL ACCOUNTING STANDARDS BOARD (IASB) WWW.IASC.ORG.UK, WWW.IASB.ORG.UK

IAS 32 – financial instruments disclosure and presentation

Before looking at the IAS 39 accounting standards for derivatives, it is necessary first to clarify what a derivative contract is for the purposes of IAS 39. In the IAS 32 guidelines, it defines a financial instrument as "any contract that gives rise to both a financial asset of one entity and a financial liability or equity instrument of another entity." It goes on to define financial instruments by saying that they include "… derivative instruments such as financial options, futures and forwards … swaps." Derivative financial instruments (e.g., swaps and options) meet IAS 32's definition and are subject to this accounting standard.

"Derivative financial instruments," in terms of definition, should create rights and obligations that have the effect of transferring between the parties to the contract one or more of the financial risks inherent in an underlying primary financial instrument. In energy markets, the main underlying financial risk is the market price. Derivative financial instruments do not generally result in a transfer of the underlying primary financial instrument on inception (just like an oil price swap under ISDA Master Agreement which is cash-settled, so no exchange of the physical oil takes place, nor is the full notional value of the contract ever transferred) and such a transfer does not necessarily take place on settlement or closing out of the contract.

The latest proposed amendments to IAS 32 (dated June 2002) say that if a trader buys or sells a nonfinancial item, for example, a commodity futures contract that has physical delivery of the commodity as its final settlement on expiry, for a fixed price and at a future date, this will not meet the definition of a "financial instrument" under IAS 32. In the context of energy futures markets, this means that a firm's derivatives futures position does not fall under IAS 32 reporting requirements, if it is using a derivative futures instrument that can go to physical delivery on final settlement. So it is worth noting what contracts should be excluded from these derivative accounting regulations under the latest proposed amendments to IAS 32:

- NYMEX–WTI crude futures
    - Heating oil NYMEX futures
    - Unleaded gasoline
    - Henry Hub gas
    - Electricity
- IPE Gas oil
- IPE Nat. gas NBP

IPE Brent, for example, is excluded from this list since it is a cash-settled futures contract and no physical delivery can take place via the futures expiry/settlement. An organization's positions would also fall under IAS 32 reporting guidelines if it regularly settles its futures contracts by trading out of them with an offsetting buy/sell futures position, and/or is usually taking delivery of the physical commodity and sells out of it within a short period after delivery for the prime reason of generating a profit from short-term market price movements. This would indicate the futures contract is entered into for speculative/trading purposes and not for its own physical purchase, sale or usage requirements.

Under IAS 32 all ISDA-based swaps specify settlement through cash payments, determined according to a formula in the contract. The swap is indexed to a commodity price but is settled only in cash. Therefore ISDA-based swaps on energy prices constitute a financial instrument and must be disclosed.

[Further reading on this can be found in the June 2002 Exposure Draft of proposed amendments to IAS 32 published by International Accounting Standards Board in London, UK, www.iasb.org.uk]

IAS 39 financial instruments: recognition and measurement

IAS 39 became effective from the financial year beginning on or after January 1, 2001 and all listed companies in Europe may be required to produce accounts in accordance with IAS during 2005. IAS 39 is a supplement to the disclosure requirements of IAS 32 for financial instruments. Although companies can opt out of IAS 39 hedge accounting for derivatives. The impact of doing so can add substantial earnings volatility on your company's balance sheet. This would require large investor education effort to explain to them why they can expect to see volatility on the balance sheet even though the company is hedging. Why would this happen? You would not be accounting for the derivatives and the MTM of physical in the same manner and they would not be offset with one another.

Under IAS 39, all financial assets and financial liabilities are recognized on the balance sheet, including all derivatives. They are initially measured at cost, which is the fair value. After the initial recognition on the balance sheet, all derivatives are re-valued on a fair value (MTM) basis.

It is quite similar in many respects to FAS 133 and organizations looking to implement IAS 39 can learn from their American cousins as to the issues at hand. In fact, International Accounting Standards Board is working on the convergence of IAS 39 standards with FAS 133 more and more each year.

Implementing IAS 39

The first step that a firm needs to take is to educate itself on IAS 39, as it contains some of the most complicated rules introduced so far. A firm will then have to look at implementing a formal risk management policy. Basically, a firm needs to be able to give a lot of detail on its hedging activities in order to be able to book derivatives as hedge transactions. Many users of derivatives may find that for the first time they need to implement an automated accounting/risk management system in order to deliver required IAS 39 documentation for accounts on, for example, MTM valuation of derivatives positions (current market value of the derivative). They will also have to produce documentation on the derivative positions, and provide "effectiveness testing" of how effective a hedge is. If it is not within certain parameters then it will not qualify for hedge accounting.

What is a hedge item under IAS 39?

A hedged item can be an asset or liability, a firm commitment, or a highly probable forecasted future transaction that exposes the company to a risk of changes in fair value or future cash flows. For example, a buyer of LPG Cargoes which bottles the LPG for retail re-sale may normally just buy its LPG on a spot basis and have no contractual commitments to take regular cargoes from anyone. This organization may, however, have a highly probable forecast future purchase of LPG to resell on to a retail network and unless it uses derivatives to hedge its price risk it could face competitive risk against other suppliers, not to mention profit exposure.

Under this standard, a hedge qualifies for hedge accounting

- If the hedge relates to a specific and identified risk, and not merely an overall business risk, and it must ultimately affect the organization's profit or loss
- If the hedge is expected to be highly effective in achieving offsetting changes in fair value or cash flows (If the derivatives contract moves in line with the underlying asset or the cash flow it is trying to protect)
- If an organization at the beginning of the hedge has put together internal documentation of the risk management objective and the strategy for the hedge
  - This documentation shall include identification of the hedging instrument (the type of derivative the organization is planning to use to hedge the underlying energy exposure)
  - Details of the energy exposure being hedged
  - The nature of the risk being hedged
  - How the organization is going to assess the derivatives' effectiveness for hedging the changes in the hedged item's fair value or the hedged transactions' cash flows that is attributable to the hedged risk.
  - Effectiveness of hedging should be assessed at a minimum when the organization prepares its annual or interim financial statements.

What is considered a highly effective hedge under this accounting standard?

As discussed earlier in this chapter a hedge is regarded as highly effective if, throughout the life of the hedge, the organization should expect changes in the fair value or cash flows of the hedged item to be almost fully offset by the changes in the fair value or cash flows of the derivatives instrument creating the hedge. This should be evaluated at a minimum at the time the user prepares its annual or interim financial statements. If the key terms of the derivatives instruments and the hedged asset or liability or hedged forecasted transaction are the same, an organization can conclude that changes in fair value or cash flows of the price risk being hedged are expected to offset each other fully at execution of the hedge and on an ongoing basis. For example, an organization may assume that in the case of a derivatives hedge on a forecast purchase of some physical oil, gas, power, etc. with a futures or swap which has the same pricing reference as the underlying oil, gas, or power being hedged, that the hedge will be highly effective and that there will be no ineffectiveness in profit or loss protection.

This is the benefit of OTC derivatives, as more often than not you can obtain a swap or options contract that is priced against the same reference price as the physical energy you are trying to hedge. Then there is only the timing basis risk, if the timing of the derivatives contract does not match the underlying physical energy which is being hedged.

Although IASB does not specify a single method for assessing a hedge effectiveness in its IAS 39 documentation it does give an example to work from. If the organization using the derivatives for hedging can expect changes in the fair value/cash flows of the hedged item to be almost fully offset (protected) by the changes in the fair value/cash flows of the derivatives hedge and if actual results of effectiveness assessments are within a range of 80–125% the organization can conclude that the hedge is highly effective. For example, if the loss on the hedging instrument is $120 and the gain on the energy price being hedged is $100, the offset/level of protection/correlation can be measured by 120/100 = 120% or by 100/120 which is 83%. Both results are within the 80–125% range so this could be covered as an effective hedge.

If a fair value hedge meets these conditions it would be accounted for under IAS 39 in the following way:

- The gain or loss from MTM revaluation of the hedging instrument at fair value (for a derivative hedging contract) should be recognized immediately in profit or loss.
- The profit or loss on the hedged item (the underlying energy exposure) attributable to the hedged risk should adjust the carrying amount of the hedged item and be recognized immediately in profit or loss (the underlying energy exposure).

Since the value of derivatives hedges and the hedged item are both reported to profit and loss it is important that the user chooses wisely the type of derivatives for hedging. Ineffective hedges will certainly add volatility to a user's balance sheet.

What is evidence of fair value for marked to market?

Currently IAS 39 states that a "quoted price normally being the best evidence of fair value." It has been proposed though that this wording will be amended in the future to "quoted market price is the best evidence of fair value."

IAS 39 is generally similar to US GAAP and the IASB continues to propose amendments that will reduce further or eliminate altogether any differences.

CLOSING NOTE

Now more than ever before, companies that hold assets (maybe an oil well or a power station) are encouraged and required to use MTM accounting principles. These new accounting regulations that demand fair value assessment (MTM valuations) of derivative positions and assets (if hedged) are great in theory but in practice, they can be abused. Some derivative contracts or assets in the energy business do not have unambiguous market prices, and sometimes a lot of judgment must be exercised when producing a suitable price for MTM fair value reporting purposes. Financial auditors are supposed to make sure that these MTM valuations are credible and at least reasonable. In the collapse of Enron at the end of 2001, and the subsequent downfall of its auditors, Andersen's, it would appear this auditing and control function was clearly defective.

Accounting standards aim to produce transparency of an organization's activities and financial position. However, any accounting standard is only really as effective as the control functions surrounding it in an organization and the external controls offered by truly independent auditing firms.

CHAPTER 13

GreenTrading™: Managing Financial Risk for the Environment in Asia

The energy business is already globalized and multinational as large energy companies operate in more than two hundred countries. This globalized business coupled with the spread of information across borders through media such as the Internet, CNN, and television have significantly changed public perception about the environment. In effect, pollution cannot be exported across borders any more as a new, globally conscious environmentalism has been created over the past decade. This global environmentalism is even more true of greenhouse gas emissions, which affect the entire planet. With carbon content increasing in the atmosphere at 4 ppm per year, the fear is that inaction will only lead to ecological disaster. Thus, the potential for web-based emissions trading is beginning as the web is borderless and international trading platforms are global. However, before this changes, we need to review where we are today and the emissions trading experience that has evolved so far.

In the past environmental protection in many countries has followed the heavy-handed command and control approach that has proved to be expensive and cumbersome. Instead, more cost effective market-based incentives using tradable permits have been gathering momentum over the past decade. The initial successes to date have been the trading of chlorofluorocarbons under the Montreal Protocol of 1987 to save the ozone layer, and the United States emissions trading scheme for sulfur dioxide (SO_2) for acid rain abatement, which began in 1995. The key has been the introduction of tradable permits combined with sanctions for noncompliance. It is a system that works in reducing air emissions.

The private sector will take the lead on the development of emissions trading markets since they have a vested commercial interest in emissions reductions. There are strong beliefs that markets will form first, thus creating an emissions trading marketplace, and that governments should not inhibit such growth. This new marketplace would motivate firms with surplus emission rights to trade or supply those rights to the market. In effect, despite the risk of uncertainty on future rules, there are merits in moving forward early. It seems evident that industry-driven trading schemes for early action on greenhouse gas (GHG) emissions will be grandfathered in the future as rules are more clearly defined. Thus, industry can now create its own domestic and international portfolio of emissions allowances and credits. Compliance responsibility, however, will rest with the government.

The GHG emissions reduction environment now offers the next commercial opportunity for commoditization, and ironically mimics US oil market developments in the late 1970s except that this time the market maturation process will be done on a global basis. Large financial institutions are now acknowledging the need to manage the financial risk of owning generation assets and are developing their internal emissions trading expertise. Moreover, large oil and gas companies recognize these increasing risks already and are beginning to create a profit and loss statement for managing their carbon liabilities. This is a business opportunity that is growing, not contracting, and also rising as a corporate board issue each year.

Since European, Japanese, and US-based companies are now moving ahead to develop pilot programs, there exists a first mover advantage in this field since waiting for regulatory approval may prove more costly in the future. Emissions rights may be traded through bilateral transaction, listing on exchanges or through brokerage houses.

In the Kyoto Protocol, it was envisioned that three international mechanisms would enable Annex 1 to reduce emissions to reach Kyoto targets beginning in 2008 through 2012. These mechanisms included emissions trading, joint implementation (JI), and the clean development mechanism (CDM).

All three modes are currently being used. It is thought that bilateral trade between countries would be the most effective means to trade emissions initially. The emissions unit to be traded is one ton of carbon dioxide (CO_2) equivalent for the six greenhouse gases. Nitrous oxides (NO_x) and CH_4 (methane) emissions, two other greenhouse gases are more difficult to quantify in many countries. The United States has already established an OTC market for both NOx emissions which began in 1999 and CO_2 emissions. It has also completed cross-border trades with Canada.

Since trading mechanisms will be part of any long-term approach to limiting GHG emissions, the emissions market is going forward on many fronts without Kyoto approval or US participation in Kyoto. It is thought that actions taken today will most likely be grandfathered into the future revised treaty. Kyoto was meant to be flexible and allow market-based solutions to trading GHG as a carbon reduction strategy and as a means to influence the spread of energy efficiency technologies for industry. Governments also expect industry to make the largest GHG reductions and this falls heavily on electric and gas utilities, manufacturing, and automakers.

THE US EMISSIONS TRADING EXPERIENCE: RAMIFICATIONS FOR ASIA

Despite the fact that many countries continue to propose emissions trading schemes in the form of green certificates, the reality is that the United States is the only country that has successfully developed an emissions trading market that has worked well for the past nine years. It is the model for a cap and trade system. As initially proposed by the Environmental Defense Fund (a US environmental organization now called Environmental Defense) to the first Bush Administration for the trading of sulfur dioxide (SO_2) credits, the emissions trading market has been successful beyond what its architects envisioned. Basically, the US Environmental Protection Agency (EPA) runs an emissions auction during March of each year that is supervised by the Chicago Board of Trade, a commodity futures exchange. Under Phase I which began on January 1, 1995, the 110 highest emitting utility plants were mandated to reduce their annual SO_2 emissions by 3.5 million tons. This process was begun in 1995 for SO_2 and extended to NO_x in 1999. Today, half of the United States is under the NO_x trading program. The OTC forward markets for SO_2 trade these vintage credits through to the year 2030. Several OTC energy brokers are involved in brokering these credits including Evolution Markets, Natsource, and Cantor Fitzgerald's CO_2e, and over one million trades per year occur. Thus, the market is liquid and has created emissions credits that are a fungible financial product. It has also saved $1 billion per year over command and control strategies. Under Phase II, which began on January 1, 2000, a more stringent standard calling for an additional annual reduction of 5 million tons of SO_2 was required, and the program was expanded to another 700 utility plants throughout the United States.

Under the SO_2 program, utilities are given one allowance for each metric ton of SO_2 emitted. The utilities are given flexibility on how they meet the mandated targets, and can switch to fuels with lower sulfur content, install pollution control equipment, or buy allowances in order to comply with the law. In order to buy allowances, other utilities must reduce their emissions below their emissions limit. These emissions allowances are fully marketable once they are allocated through an EPA auction and can be bought, sold, and banked. The allowances are allocated in phases. The later phases tighten the limits on previously impacted sources of pollution and are also imposed on smaller cleaner units. Compliance is assured through continuous emissions monitoring at plants and regular reports to the EPA. Fines are assessed if companies don't comply with the law. It is a mandatory government-regulated program.

The system has an allowance trading system. All transfers are recorded and posted on the Internet. Serial numbers allow the tracking of each allowance's trading history, and an inventory for all accounts is provided. The most interesting phenomenon from this market-based solution to pollution has been that from 1995 to 1999 the market not only met its emissions reduction targets but was 30% under compliance. This approach has exceeded expectations by lowering emissions below the announced targets because some companies demonstrated unexpected behavior such as banking rather than selling emissions credits.

THE GREENTRADING MARKET TODAY

The existing green trading market can be characterized as having the following characteristics: opaque prices, little trading, few participants, poor liquidity, tremendous inefficiency, and wide arbitrage opportunities. If these attributes sound familiar, they are the primary factors of each emerging market. Having seen the emergence and maturation of oil, gas, power, weather, and coal as fungible commodity trading markets, the environment is now well positioned to be the next financial commodity trading market. More uniquely it will explode simultaneously throughout the world. Similar to oil market developments *c.* 1978, we are now seeing the emergence of global carbon market (CO_2) as a fungible commodity trading market trading in metric tonnes. Moreover, it will emerge simultaneously throughout the world – something that has never happened before.

Moreover, the other unique aspect of this market is that this is a government-mandated market despite the claims of voluntary trading in the United States. In fact, the United States created the carbon template if one looks at the trading regime of the SO_2 allowance market, which began in 1995 and has vintage credits upto the year 2030. A true carbon regime will have a span of 50 to 100 years. This is envisioned after 2012 for Kyoto Protocol and work at the governmental level is already underway to create the longer-term market.

While the private sector will take the lead in the development of emissions trading markets wherever it has a vested commercial interest in emissions reductions, compliance responsibility will rest with governments. There are strong beliefs that markets will form first, thus creating an emissions-trading marketplace, and that governments should not inhibit such growth. This new marketplace would motivate firms with surplus emissions rights to trade or supply those rights to the market. In effect, despite the risk of uncertainty on future rules, there are merits to moving forward early. It seems evident that industry-driven schemes will be grandfathered in the future as rules are more clearly defined. Thus, industry can create its own domestic and international portfolio of emissions allowances or credits.

The environment today is coming to be framed as a corporate financial issue. Greater financial disclosure of corporate environmental risks including climate change has raised the issue of environment as a corporate fiduciary responsibility. Corporate boards are increasingly concerned as shareholders question their environmental practices. Companies such as Innovest Strategic Advisors, the so-called Green Moodys, highlight these environmental financial risks and that concept is now beginning to resonate in corporate boardrooms. Moreover, it is an issue that is gaining momentum. Environmental performance and financial performance of companies are increasingly intertwined. This directly impacts automobile manufacturers, electric utilities, oil and gas companies, banks, and insurance companies. Automakers are concerned about carbon dioxide (CO_2) emissions per vehicle produced and sold. Electric utilities are paying more attention to reducing their GHG emissions footprint as part of their air emissions reductions. Oil and gas companies are increasingly concerned about emissions as production, refining, transportation, and distribution liabilities. Bank share valuation could fall if they do not have adequate carbon risk management strategies. And insurance and reinsurance companies are now at the forefront of confronting these financial risks such as the catastrophic risk of crop failure due to climate change, and health-related risks due to the linkage of climate change and infectious disease. These new financial risks for insurance and reinsurance companies may lead to them dropping coverage for certain companies. These new financial risks and liabilities will become the market drivers for change and market creation.

As the Kyoto Protocol nears ratification, energy markets and many private companies are already moving forward under their own initiatives to comply with the treaty. Under the Kyoto Protocol, it was envisioned that three international mechanisms would enable developed countries (Annex 1) to reduce emissions to reach the Kyoto standards. Beginning in 2008 and upto 2012 for all countries that have signed the Kyoto Protocol emissions trading, JI and a CDM are the means to achieve Kyoto compliance. The latter two require more international cooperation and the rules are still being formulated as many CDM projects have been rejected this year. However trading emissions presents a near-term viable alternative. So far, the greatest activity to create emissions trading markets has been in the United States, Canada, Japan, and Europe. Many believe actions taken today are likely to be grandfathered into the future revised treaty. The highly successful and pioneering markets for SO_2 and now also nitrous oxide (NOx) are providing the financial template to be applied for global CO_2 markets.

There are several parallels between the development of emissions trading schemes, and the dual process of electric power industry liberalization in many countries. Emissions trading and electric power deregulation intersect since the power industry contributes to GHG emissions.

EXCHANGE OPPORTUNITIES

Since almost all environmental financial contracts such as SO_2 or CO_2 are traded on the OTC markets, there is an opportunity for exchanges like the New York Mercantile Exchange (NYMEX) to offer OTC clearing which would effectively make them quasi-futures contracts under government oversight. This could help make them more acceptable to risk managers. NYMEX could also supplement this effort by launching environmental futures contracts such as SO_2, NOx, CO_2 and Renewable Energy Credits (RECs). Currently NYMEX trades WTI crude oil, heating oil, gasoline, natural gas, electric power, and coal futures, which are directly linked with emissions. These efforts are under consideration by the Exchange. There is also an opportunity for the IPE in London to trade emissions in the EU.

In Japan, both the Tocom and Tokyo Stock Exchange are considering launching carbon derivatives contracts. Presently, the ground rules in Japan are in a state of flux between a "cap and trade" market and a baseline market. There is also a movement emerging to create the next trading regime beyond 2012 and the Kyoto Protocol to include developing giants such as China, India, and Indonesia.

The Chicago Climate Exchange (CCX) is following another route to GHG market maturation and launched a voluntary carbon exchange in the fall of 2003. This voluntary carbon exchange will be centered on the United States and Canada and currently has many participating multinational companies such as IBM, Rolls Royce AEP and other corporations. It is the first exchange conducting daily carbon trading to launch in a time of changing US attitudes on global warming and it is a precursor to other North American exchanges that may wish to enter this emerging market space.

The GHG market has been estimated at $2.3 billion by the Council of Foreign Relations, a noted foreign policy advisory group based in New York, and they may have underestimated its potential size. This market sizing attracts capital. Typically, commodity contracts trade at six to twenty times the physical underlying market. To put this in perspective, the US SO_2 market has been estimated at $6 billion. The energy derivatives markets, both exchange-traded futures contracts and OTC price swaps, have been estimated at about $2 to 3 trillion. The global foreign exchange and interest rate swaps market is over $120 trillion in NV.

Exchanges may be established quickly on the Internet following the model of the CCX. Internet-based emissions trading would allow immediate disclosure for market players and would have low costs of operation. As the market matures, it is envisioned that Internet-based trading will be the platform that allows quickly evolving global emissions trading schemes and seamless cross-border carbon trading.

ENTER AGRICULTURE!

The agricultural sector is beginning to realize the market potential and financial benefits of renewable energy, not just in the form of rents from siting large wind towers but from self-generation with wind and biomass. The utilization of plant and animal farm waste can produce additional cash crops to be "harvested" and commercialized for their environmental attributes. This is a particularly hot commercial topic in Asian biomass markets where agriculture can meet an electric power generation need. The energy and agricultural sectors can join forces to develop new energy supplies while reducing externalities and creating new industries in America that can be exported throughout the world.

Together energy and agriculture are the world's largest businesses. They are also the most deeply liquid commodity markets. Financial engineering on environmental financial products will grow cross-commodity arbitrage opportunities for energy and agricultural commodities and GHG, renewable energy and efficiency. The inflexion point for this sea change is during the next two years.

PROJECT FINANCE IMPLICATIONS

Another emerging trend that may hold the key to GHG emissions liquidity is the structured finance market, that is, "Green Finance." A fuel type shift to greener and cleaner fuels such as natural gas in preference to coal or oil is becoming embedded in the fabric of new power station project financing. Since these plants have a useful life of 30–40 years, they will bring a stream of emissions credits that can be banked or used up front. They are unlocking another avenue for market evolution. This type of thinking is just beginning at investment and commercial banks in New York, London, and Tokyo.

Moreover, it can be envisioned that an environmental checklist is emerging in the green or environmental finance arena, yet another area where financial engineering can bring about market development and liquidity. There is no time to fight past demons. Forward-thinking and globally based energy participants should embrace the inevitability that international policy on greenhouse gases is being set by both media and public perceptions. In this context, the rational response by enlightened industry participants is to develop and support market-based solutions to global pollution.

In an imperfect world, this is the reality. In order to reduce CO_2 emissions, emissions trading will act as the catalyst of change in the transition of world economies toward renewables and accelerated transfer of more efficient and greener technologies.

Ironically, the global market that now seems best positioned for trading is the REC market. Renewable energy has undergone a quantum technology shift in terms of increased efficiency and lower costs with few financial players focusing on the new factors that drive this market. The technology for wind, solar, biomass, and waste-to-energy is many generations more efficient than even two to three years ago, although financial analysts have only just started to follow the sector. Once again, government mandates, called Renewal Portfolio Standards in the United States, are driving market maturation. But in the physical market, wind and solar power are growing at 40% and 30% per annum globally with costs now competitive with gas and coal. Tax subsidies for waste-to-energy and biomass power generation will move the equation further. Looking at a small installed base of renewable power generation today misses the fact that the ramping-up of this technology is global. These power stations are also getting bigger with wind turbines of 2.5 to 5.5 mW and multiple siting of 300 to 400 mW wind farms being developed. More importantly, they have created another fungible commodity market that can be traded cross-border as the credits are measured in megaWatt hours. Such green power initiatives will create a highly fungible market for RECs.

NEED FOR PRICE INDICES

Markets in environmental financial derivatives are positioned for rapid growth due to political initiatives and business opportunities, but these markets will reach their full potential only if based on reliable indices widely accepted by the trading community. To focus solely on GHG emissions misses the opportunity to capture the benefits of other energy/ environmental market-based solutions to global pollution such as RECs or energy efficiency (mW) trading. Therefore, in order to maximize the business opportunity for an established exchange, several environmental products for various geographic markets must be traded using regional environmental indices as the underlying benchmarks. The composite of these financial indices will contribute to a global index as well. The need is to establish exchange-traded derivatives products for SO_2, nitrous oxides (NOx), CO_2, RECs, megaWatts (energy efficiency), mercury and other environmental verticals, with the first step being the creation of several tradable indices in North America, Europe, and Asia.

Because government mandates are the primary market driver for environmental financial products, the scope of activity has been limited to a small number of players. Nonetheless the growth of emission trading and profit opportunities are attracting a new generation of traders in the market. Commodity traders from the world's largest banks and financial institutions are responding to these opportunities by opening trading operations on both sides of the Atlantic. The inhibiting factor is the lack of a reliable index, which has so far muted their effort to create a liquid market. The current trading environment is handicapped by the operational complexity of having adequate allowance inventory on hand to complete a trade, so that there are still more sellers than buyers of carbon. This limits access to those with ample allowances or those who can borrow allowances. Furthermore it takes time to transfer allowances from one party to another and the process can take weeks, limiting traders' ability to enter or exit the market with ease. An index would remove this impediment making it possible to attract more players into the market, by allowing more trade structures, and by turning the environmental market into a cash-settled operation. This would have the added benefit of improving cap and trade policy. Because of the potential for improving regulatory policy we expect close cooperation between government regulatory agencies and any exchange seeking to use the indices as underlying benchmarks for trading financial products.

Many countries have renewable energy, energy efficiency, and greenhouse gas programs. Some coordination to provide consistency needs to take place, but most such programs today are and have been independently developed. Consistent methodologies for measuring emissions, including GHG, renewable and efficiency efforts would facilitate project investment. Consistency would facilitate development of project templates thereby reducing costs and gaining rapid dissemination of the learning gained from early projects. National and international markets for GHG credit trading would offer the liquidity necessary to return value to projects and thereby financing. To function efficiently such markets require assurance of integrity – clear definitions, avoidance of double counting, verification, and liquidity. At this point in market development, it is critical to build some consensus around the development of common metrics for the private sector and for policymakers to analyze opportunities at the regional, national, and international levels. Greenhouse gas registries managed by a third party, non-governmental entity could serve as a model at both the state level as in California or at the federal level as in most EU countries.

Today, we have a one-off market with many companies not acting on what will ultimately benefit them financially. A few innovators are proactive, but the reality is that the environment is emerging as a financial liability of multinational corporations globally. These liabilities are the market drivers for change. The quantification of these risks will keep analysts and mathematicians busy for many years as the dynamic models have yet to be built.

CREATION OF THE GREENTRADING MARKETPLACE

Because of the ability to establish exchanges quickly on the Internet, it is thought that this may be a desired outcome for emissions trading. Internet-based emissions trading would allow immediate disclosure for market players and has low costs of operation. The concept behind the allowances was to foster the implementation of demand side efficiencies or use of renewable energy. These concepts are tailored to the developing CO_2 market and the use of the Internet as the means to implement change.

The thought is that the creation of a marketplace for emissions trading will motivate firms with surplus emissions rights to supply them to the market. In effect, there are merits in moving forward early, despite the risk of uncertainty on future rules. It seems evident that industry-driven schemes will be grandfathered in the future as the rules are more clearly defined. Thus, industry can create its own domestic and international portfolio of emissions allowances or credits. The argument today is that to do it early will probably be less costly than in the future. Using GHG emissions allowances now is a form of insurance for industry participants. Moreover, emissions trading delivers significant environmental reductions (as reduced compliance costs) as well as promoting environmental technologies.

The global energy industry is severely affected by these new financial risks related to climate change. With growing energy demand particularly for oil, gas, and electric power in the Asia Pacific region, market-based mechanisms for reducing carbon intensity offer a cost-effective solution to global pollution. There are several similarities between emissions trading schemes, and electric power industry liberalization in many countries. Emissions trading and electric power deregulation intersect since the power industry contributes to the GHG emissions. The GreenTrading markets today are still embryonic, but are starting to accelerate in the market maturation process. Despite the apparent obstacles to creating viable green trading markets, the timing is now right as the political momentum shifts toward moving forward, with both developed and developing countries creating a regional and a global market.

There is a clear market opportunity for GreenTrading. The market characteristics for commoditization are there and the cross-border dimension is inevitable. The essential elements for trading are also growing, the technology is available and the timing is right, even though the financial risk is real and leadership is lacking. Most importantly, the financial engineering and risk management tools are in place, with the affected parties willing to participate. It is the most effective public–private partnership available since government must set the rules for the market development by business. The next few years promise to be the breakthrough time for the first financial market since oil to emerge globally.

CHAPTER 14

What's on the Horizon for Asian Energy Markets

This book has introduced the reader to a variety of emerging commodity market trading developments in Asia that are being driven by global changes in energy industry regulatory structures, privatization efforts, and competitive market forces. The good news is that as world energy markets are open to new competitive risks, there are now more risk management techniques as well as risk mitigation techniques. These include more sophisticated options strategies and models, and more flexible and web-based risk management software solutions that are available or under development. Weather, LNG, emissions, and renewable energy markets will follow the more traditional oil, gas, and power markets in trading and risk management arbitrage in Asia. As trading liquidity grows in the global market place, the Internet-based trading platforms will absorb much of this trading liquidity and enhance its growth. Asia is primed to be the next emerging market for energy trading.

Today, we are seeing the beginning of convergence to the multicommodity market founded on over two decades of oil trading and risk management. The extension of energy commodity trading expertise for natural gas began in North American markets in 1990 and in Europe since the late 1990s. The beginning of physical and financial markets for electric power in North America, Europe, and Australia surfaced in the mid-1990s. An active emissions trading market began in 1995 in North America. Now Asia is set to enter center stage due to its voracious energy appetite. These markets are in various states of emergence and maturity. But the key fact is that they are growing, and extending the energy risk management platform. Moreover, Internet trading of these commodities, which began as proprietary electronic trading in 1993, is now moving forward rapidly, offering lower transaction costs and global access.

The oil and gas industry has been using energy risk management tools to manage its financial risks over the past two decades, but the unprecedented price volatility in oil, gas, and electric power markets experienced since late 1998 is accelerating the industry's adoption of both financial instruments and Internet energy trading. While liquidity on the Internet today remains low, the movement to Internet trading will create its own liquidity and force the OTC paper markets for oil, gas, and power to migrate to the web. Moreover, other industry trends of consolidation, market liberalization, and privatization are creating greater risks that must be managed more proactively. The Internet will be the medium for that trade, too.

Commoditization has been accelerating into many new markets through the innovative efforts of companies who act as market makers and absorb risk. The good news is that commodity markets need more players to develop fungible financial products and provide liquidity. The world's financial institutions and major oil companies are up to the challenge.

LNG TRADING

LNG trading and hedging is following the development of a global market similar to the track that oil trading followed over 20 years ago. Growing spot trading in LNG since 1999 and the development of global gas markets have brought about the opportunity for LNG hedging. The development of the LNG spot market has been stimulated by the expiration of some 20-year supply contracts, new market entrants on the producing side, the availability of LNG tankers and LNG capacity creep (excess capacity over nameplate). The first significant hedging of LNG was for cargoes delivered into Taiwan by Mobil Oil in 1999. Since those initial market developments, trading houses and market makers are setting up structuring desks to hedge LNG cargoes. Basically, this involves using oil OTC contracts as surrogates for the natural gas, and either deconstructing the crude cocktail on which east Asian LNG prices are based or using the NYMEX Henry Hub natural gas delivery point as a price marker. In effect, the optionality of the contracts is extracted.

The new suppliers of LNG have made the market much more competitive. While east Asia still takes 75% of LNG supply, many new countries such as Spain, Turkey, France, Belgium, Germany, and the United Kingdom are adding more diversity on the consuming side. The same is true on the supply side with more suppliers including Qatar, Egypt, and Trinidad. Moreover, the re-emergence of the United States as an LNG consumer with the reactivation and expansion of its four receiving terminals (with many new ones proposed) and others have created more cargo movements and liquidity in the market. Particular interest has been seen in the North American West Coast receiving terminals in Baja, Mexico, which now brings the United States into both Atlantic and Pacific basin LNG trade. Today, the United States is the high cost gas market, and this will drive much of the LNG trading and hedging down the road.

The hedging of LNG cargoes is giving suppliers and end-users flexibility and greater efficiency in a very capital-intensive industry. It is also another application of innovative financial engineering to commoditize a new market.

ELECTRONIC TRADING: SET TO TAKE OFF

As most energy trading platforms have failed, it now seems obvious that the two that will dominate the Internet trading space will be NYMEX and IPE/ICE. They are both poised for future growth in Asia, although other Internet energy trading platforms will perform well in niche market functions. Something has radically changed in energy trading markets, and that is the age of electronic trading coupled with the OTC market flexibility, which usurped exchange-traded futures contracts. The futures exchanges were initially slow to react to this Internet phenomenon but now have risen to the challenge and will dominate the Internet trading space.

The Asian Internet energy markets have evolved more slowly but that is beginning to change. The Singapore Exchange will now only launch electronic energy contracts in the future as its oil futures contracts for Brent mutual offset and fuel oil have fallen by the wayside. While Platts Global 190 trades oil electronically, it seems to be there by default and by a lack of trade interest. There is an interesting play in open spec naphtha (e-OSN.com) in the East Asian markets that will probably work since it has had an active and liquid forward OTC market for over a decade. E-Osn.com acts as broker to all market participants; however, the site is a niche market play. It does, however, demonstrate the potential viability of niche market segments for energy trading on the web. The Tocom energy contracts for gasoline is gaining some liquidity but the contract volume in kiloliters is quite small. However, Tocom has agreements with NYMEX and should ramp up as the Japanese acquire a greater appetite for risk.

One of the obstacles in Asian market development has been that Asian Internet growth lags behind worldwide usage although it should accelerate over the next several years. China and India will undergo rapid growth as the Internet usage currently is under 25% of their populations. India has the world's largest electronic exchange (for equity trading). Both countries may embrace Internet energy trading in a big way by leapfrogging technology. South Korea trades the most derivatives and is 98% wired.

The death of the Internet has been greatly exaggerated just as its entrance was. The key barriers today are not technological but changing human behavior to use the Net and break away from human relationships, which are still a strong part of the energy trading complex. No one doubts there is a need to attract more liquidity, create methods for more price discovery, create adequate controls and systems to handle credit risk, clearing, and settlement. Asian energy trading will embrace the Internet as the barriers to entry are not technology but human behavior.

The fragmented markets of today will lead to the consolidated trading markets of tomorrow with several dominant global players and regional and niche players relegated to the sidelines. This is what is occurring now. Parsing and weaving the best of other platforms for other commodities related to energy such as emissions and bandwidth will create a multicommodity warehouse that will have clearing and settlement taken care of by the major banks that are already part of a global consortium. The platforms will have better functionality as the technologies improve. Buying customers and technology, the front, middle, and back office will be Web-enabled so that the exchanges can provide seamless trading opportunities on a 24/7, borderless basis. Pricing will become more transparent and liquidity will grow exponentially.

The energy industry is the nexus for the application of the Internet not only for energy trading, but also for procurement and e-tailing. A global business packed with information would seem to be the place to catalyze Internet applications.

EMERGING MARKETS

Emissions, LNG, and electronic energy trading are coming on strong in global financial markets because these commodities are global and moved by global market drivers. These markets are becoming established on the Internet where time compression increases and the maturation process decreases. They are real world applications of financial engineering techniques. One key change will be the use of energy project finance. We will see some of this application in the creation of clean development mechanism credits in the emissions markets and that will bring liquidity to the GHG emissions market. Such green finance will be embraced by investment banks and traders to hedge environmental risk and securitize energy projects.

The future holds endless applications of financial engineering, commoditization, and risk management for global energy markets, and energy risk management has now become a fiduciary responsibility of energy companies. Energy hedging is still in its infancy, and there will be greater growth over the next decade even in the mature oil trading markets and a broadening of the energy trading platform to electric power, LNG, coal, and emissions. Asia is the target of all this new growth in energy risk management. The ride will be fast!

APPENDIX 1

ISDA – A SURVEY – 2004

ISDA

INTERNATIONAL SWAPS AND DERIVATIVES ASSOCIATION

A SURVEY OF FINANCE PROFESSORS' VIEWS ON DERIVATIVES

Survey Conducted by
The International Swaps and Derivatives Association
March 2004

19TH ANNUAL GENERAL MEETING
CHICAGO

INTRODUCTION

As part of its mission to encourage the prudent and efficient development of privately negotiated derivatives activity, the International Swaps and Derivatives Association actively seeks to advance public understanding of these instruments and their role in the financial marketplace.

To that end, ISDA conducted a survey in March 2004 of finance professors at the top 50 business schools* worldwide to explore perceptions of derivatives, as well as their impact on the global financial system. In some questions, we asked participants to rate their agreement or disagreement with a statement related to derivatives. In others we asked participants for their opinions on specific issues.

In conducting the survey, a web-based questionnaire was sent to finance professors at the top 50 business schools. A total of 84 professors, at 42 institutions, provided responses. Participants were able to choose whether they wished to have their quotes attributed or to remain anonymous.

We asked participants whether they strongly agreed, agreed, somewhat agreed, somewhat disagreed, disagreed or strongly disagreed with statements 1 through 6, and to respond to questions 7 through 9:

1. Managing financial risk more effectively is a way for companies to build shareholder value.

2. Derivatives help companies manage financial risk more effectively.

3. Derivatives will continue to grow in use and application.

4. Derivatives have not created new types of risk; they simply allow existing risks to be managed better.

5. The impact of derivatives on the global financial system is beneficial.

6. The risks of using derivatives have been overstated.

7. What contribution do derivatives make to the stability of the global financial system?

8. What are the most important benefits that derivatives offer companies?

9. Which areas will benefit most from innovations in derivatives in the next five years?

Respondents were also provided an opportunity to offer any additional insights they believed to be relevant.

*Financial Times, January 26, 2004

We would like to thank the following institutions for participating in the survey:

City University: Cass Business School
College of William and Mary
Columbia University: Columbia Business School
Cornell University: Johnson
Dartmouth College: Tuck
Duke University: Fuqua School of Business
Georgetown University: McDonough
Harvard Business School
IESE Business School
Institute for Management Development
Instituto de Empresa
London Business School
Manchester Business School
Massachusetts Institute of Technology: Sloan
McGill University
Michigan State University: Broad
Northwestern University: Kellogg School of Management
New York University: Stern School of Business
Northwestern University: Kellogg School of Management
Ohio State University: Fisher
Purdue University: Krannert
Rotterdam School of Management
Scuola di Diezione Aziendale dell' Universita Bocconi
University of California Los Angeles: Anderson
University of Chicago: Graduate School of Business
University of Illinois at Urbana-Champaign
University of Iowa: Tippie
University of Maryland: Smith
University of Michigan Business School
University of North Carolina: Kenan-Flagler
University of Oxford: Said Business School
University of Pennsylvania: Wharton
University of South Carolina: Moore School of Business
University of Southern California: Marshall
University of Texas at Austin: McCombs
University of Toronto: Rotman
University of Virginia: Darden Business School
University of Western Ontario: Ivey
Warwick Business School
Washington University: Olin School of Business
Yale School of Management
York University: Schulich School of Business

EXECUTIVE SUMMARY

Outlined below are the major findings of the ISDA Academic Survey:

SECTION I:

- Ninety-eight percent of respondents agreed that managing financial risk more effectively is a way for companies to build shareholder value.
- Respondents unanimously agreed that derivatives help companies manage financial risk more effectively.
- All respondents agreed that derivatives will continue to grow in use and application.
- Over half the respondents agreed that derivatives have not created new types of risk; they simply allow existing risks to be managed better.
- Ninety-nine percent of respondents agreed that the impact of derivatives on the global financial system is beneficial.
- Eighty-one percent of respondents agreed that the risks of using derivatives have been overstated.

SECTION II:

- The use of derivatives by companies as a quick and efficient way to manage risks was commonly cited as a contribution to the stability of the global financial system.
- The flexibility derivatives offer in customizing a company's risk profile was commonly cited as a benefit the instruments offer companies. Many also noted that derivatives allow companies to assume only the risks that add value and enable them to concentrate on their primary products. Others described derivatives as important risk management tools that are inexpensive to utilize.
- Several respondents consider credit risk the area most likely to benefit from innovations in derivatives in the next five years. Other areas cited included financial services and international and emerging markets.

SURVEY RESPONSES

Participants were asked to rate each statement on a scale of "Strongly Agree" to "Strongly Disagree."

Managing financial risk more effectively is a way for companies to build shareholder value.

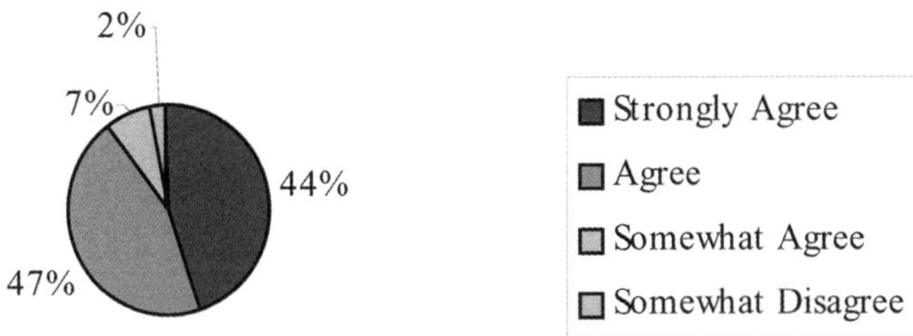

Base: 81 responses

Ninety-eight percent of respondents agreed with the above statement.

Of the respondents, 44 percent strongly agreed, 47 percent agreed and seven percent somewhat agreed. Two percent of respondents somewhat disagreed.

Insights of value included:

"The transfer of risk from those parties who bear it at high cost to those who can bear it at a lower cost releases value. Those gains from trade in risk are massive and they are utterly dependent on properly functioning derivatives markets."
-- Samuel Wylie, Assistant Professor, Dartmouth College: Tuck

Derivatives help companies manage financial risk more effectively.

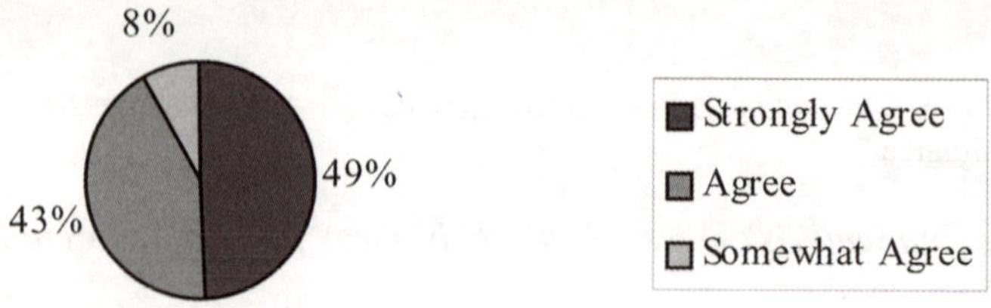

Base: 84 responses

100 percent of respondents agreed with the above statement.

Of the respondents, 49 percent strongly agreed, 43 percent agreed and eight percent somewhat agreed.

Comments from respondents emphasized the key benefits provided by the use of derivatives. The most commonly cited benefit was the ability of companies to use derivatives to customize their risk profile and to assume only those risks that add value. Participants noted that by serving as effective risk management tools, derivatives enable companies to concentrate on their business operations:

"Derivatives allow companies to bear or assume only the risks that they want to take."
-- James Angel, Associate Professor of Finance, Georgetown University: McDonough

"The flexibility to match the financial risks a firm takes and the risk appetite of the firm."
-- Ronald Huisman, Assistant Professor, Rotterdam School of Management

"Flexibility -- being able to target the risk that needs to be managed without having to devise a high-frequency hedging strategy."
-- Michael W. Brandt, Associate Professor of Finance, Duke University: Fuqua School of Business

"Flexibility to alter risk profiles without changing underlying exposures."
-- Jan Ericsson, Assistant Professor of Finance, McGill University

"[Derivatives] allow companies (with forex, industry, local or global interest rate, product or commodity price exposures arising in operations or in financing) to focus on their primary business or core competence instead of worrying about fluctuations in financial markets."
-- Mo Chaudhury, Faculty Lecturer in Finance, McGill University

"Derivatives allow companies to focus on their primary products and allow financial experts to control their financial risks in the interest rate and foreign exchange markets."
-- Robert Geske, Professor, University of California Los Angeles: Anderson

"Derivatives allow firms to eliminate those risks that they do not control and in doing so allows them to take additional risks that they believe contributes to their firm's values."
-- Sheridan Titman, Professor, University of Texas at Austin: McCombs

Quick and inexpensive risk management was another benefit noted by participants.

Derivatives will continue to grow in use and application.

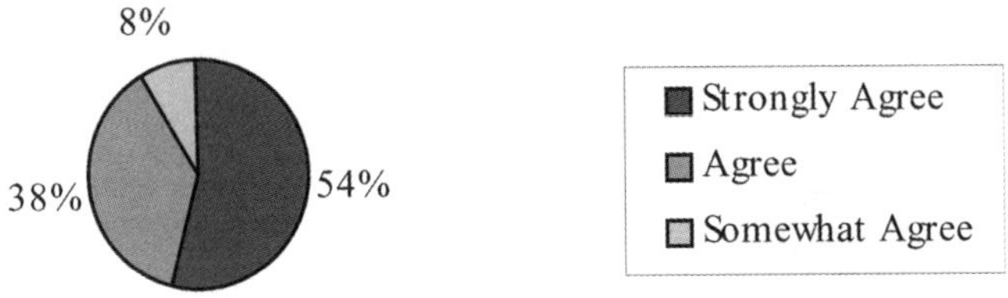

Base: 84 responses

100 percent of respondents agreed with the above statement.

Of the respondents, 54 percent strongly agreed, 38 percent agreed and eight percent somewhat agreed.

The majority of participants who provided feedback cited credit risk as the area most likely to benefit from innovations in derivatives in the next five years:

"The credit derivatives market is likely to continue to grow. This will primarily benefit financial institutions. We can expect to see the pace of innovation in derivatives markets continue. Possibly there will be more products aimed at allowing private individuals to manage risk. At the other extreme we may see products aimed at managing the risks faced by governments."

"The management of exposure to credit risk will benefit from additional innovations and continued growth in the market for credit derivatives."

"FX, energy, and interest rate risk management are the traditional uses for derivatives, but newer products (e.g. weather derivatives and credit derivatives) will also provide major benefits."
-- James Angel, Associate Professor of Finance, Georgetown University: McDonough

Other respondents chose to indicate an industry that will benefit from innovations in derivatives, rather than a specific product area, and cited financial institutions, including the banking and insurance industries:

"Financial institutions and banking industry."
Javad Kashefi, Visiting Professor of Finance, University of Southern California: Marshall

"Pension funds, insurance."
-- Roel Oomen, Lecturer in Finance, Warwick Business School

"Banking, real estate, insurance."

A few others cited international and emerging markets as areas likely to benefit from innovations in derivatives:

"Liquidity management in international markets, European capital markets."

"Small firms, firms in developing countries. As these products become more understood and therefore the markets more liquid, the benefits will be realized by these groups as well."

Derivatives have not created new types of risk; they simply allow existing risks to be managed better.

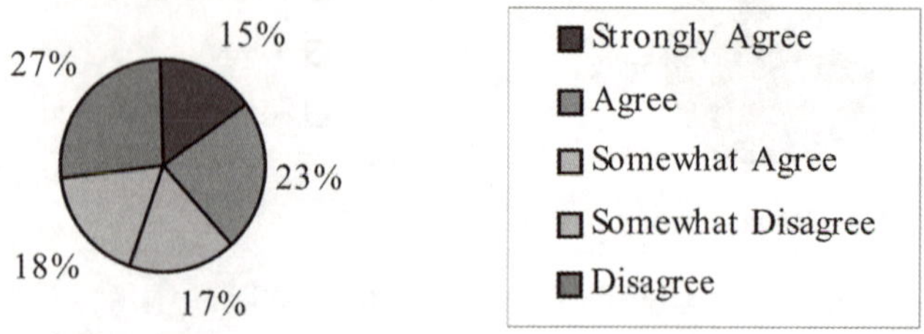

Base: 84 responses

55 percent of respondents agreed with the above statement.

Of the respondents, 15 percent strongly agreed, 23 percent agreed and 17 percent somewhat agreed. Eighteen percent of respondents somewhat disagreed and 27 percent disagreed.

The question did not specify types of "new" risk, leaving it to the respondents to interpret. For example, it did not distinguish between the risk inherent in the bilateral relationship (i.e., counterparty credit risk) and other types of risk, particularly macroeconomic ones that are sometimes attributed to derivatives. In this regard, the virtually unanimous agreement on the question on the beneficial impact of derivatives on the global financial system and the strong belief of the respondents that the risks of using derivatives have been overstated are indications that, whatever the risks the respondents believe may arise in using derivatives, there is not cause for concern.

"On net derivatives are effective at better distributing financial risks. These benefits are largely outside the financial system. On net the benefits of derivatives are also positive for the financial system but there are additional (new) risks that need to be considered."

"Derivatives with high counterparty credits allow intermediaries and dealers to hedge their positions much more effectively, at a much lower cost and in a speedier fashion. This greatly reduces the insolvency/liquidity risk of intermediaries and dealers thereby adding stability to the global financial system."
-- Mo Chaudhury, Faculty Lecturer in Finance, McGill University

The impact of derivatives on the global financial system is beneficial.

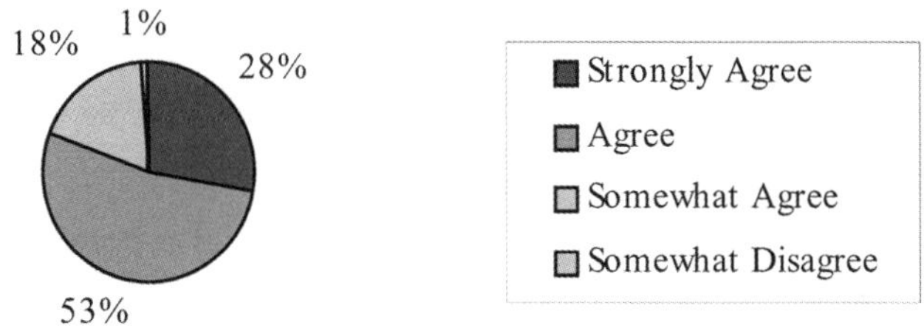

Base: 83 responses

Ninety-nine percent of respondents agreed with the above statement.

Of the respondents, 28 percent strongly agreed, 53 percent agreed and 18 percent somewhat agreed. One percent of respondents somewhat disagreed with the statement.

Respondents commonly cited the use of derivatives by companies as a cost-effective means of risk transfer to be the key contribution derivatives make to the stability of the global financial system:

"Widely used derivatives offer the opportunity to transfer risk quickly and efficiently, providing the markets liquidity and less volatility."
-- Juan Fernandez, MD of Portfolio Management, Instituto De Empresa

"By allowing for a more efficient management of risk derivatives have resulted in a more efficient allocation of capital. An efficient allocation of our resources, including capital, allows for more rapid global economic growth. It is through economic growth that each generation has the ability to live better than past generations. Thus, an expanded efficient use of derivatives is an important component for future economic growth."
-- Michael Brandl, Lecturer, University of Texas at Austin: McCombs

"[Derivatives] manage routine risks more efficiently, and by securitization make it possible to spread risks more widely."
-- Geoffrey Heal, Professor, Columbia Business School

"They allow financial and non-financial corporations to manage their risks in a way that would not otherwise be possible. Sound risk management leads to more predictability and therefore more stability in the global financial system."

"By facilitating the transfer of risks from those who don't wish to bear risks to those who are willing to bear risks, derivatives make financial markets less volatile."

"By allowing firms to manage risks, they are no longer as susceptible to changes in market prices for currencies, commodities, etc. This has brought a lot more stability (esp. in smaller markets, like Canada, where these risks can have a big negative impact)."
-- Craig Dunbar, Associate Professor, University of Western Ontario: Ivey

"They allow the transfer of risk from parties that don't want to bear risk to parties that can. For example, credit derivatives make the banking system safer."
-- James Angel, Associate Professor of Finance, Georgetown University: McDonough

The risks of using derivatives have been overstated.

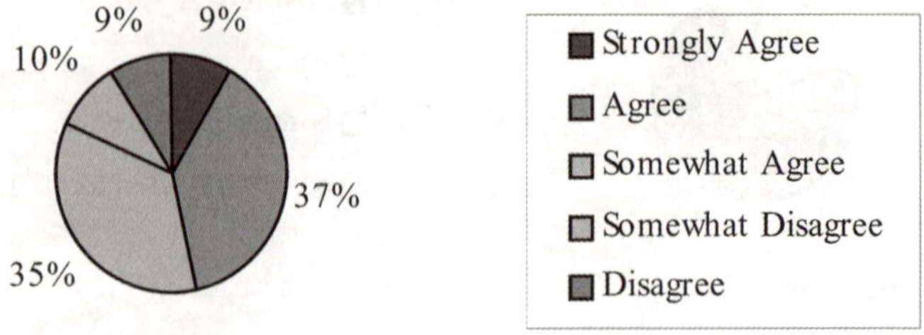

Base: 82 responses

Eighty-one percent of respondents agreed with the above statement.

Of the respondents, Nine percent strongly agreed, 37 percent agreed and 35 percent somewhat agreed. Ten percent of respondents somewhat disagreed and nine percent disagreed.

Some respondents offered comments to support their agreement with the above statement:

"The problem is not with derivatives but with some market participants that use them extensively without a reasonable understanding of financial markets and especially derivatives."
-- Zvi Wiener, Visiting Professor, University of Southern California: Marshall

"As above, derivatives do not create risk; they merely enable its better management."
-- Dr. Paul Dawson, Senior Lecturer in Financial Derivatives, City University: Cass Business School

The need for better understanding of derivatives and their benefits among market participants was a common theme found in additional feedback submitted by respondents:

"Companies need a better understanding of the economics that should drive derivative use. In general companies understand that lower risk is a good thing but they need a better understanding of exactly what the benefits are. Many still believe they can gain significantly from trying to time markets with hedges."

APPENDIX 2

ISDA 2002 – Chinese Version

ISDA®

International Swaps and Derivatives Association, Inc.

2002 MASTER AGREEMENT

dated as of ....

______________________ and ______________________

have entered and/or anticipate entering into one or more transactions (each a "Transaction") that are or will be governed by this 2002 Master Agreement, which includes the schedule (the "Schedule"), and the documents and other confirming evidence (each a "Confirmation") exchanged between the parties or otherwise effective for the purpose of confirming or evidencing those Transactions. This 2002 Master Agreement and the Schedule are together referred to as this "Master Agreement".

Accordingly, the parties agree as follows:—

1. Interpretation

(a) ***Definitions.*** The terms defined in Section 14 and elsewhere in this Master Agreement will have the meanings therein specified for the purpose of this Master Agreement.

(仅供参考)*

ISDA®

国际掉期及衍生工具协会

2002年主协议

______年______月______日

______________________与______________________

之间已进行及/或预期进行受本2002年主协议约制(或将为其约制)的一项或多项交易(均称为" 交易")；本主协议包括附件(以下简称" 附件")以及各方之间交换的或为确认或证明该些交易而生效的文件和其他确认证据(均称为" 确认书")。本2002年主协议及其附件统称为" 主协议" 。

据此，双方同意如下：－

1. 释义

(a) *定义。*就本主协议而言，第14条以及本主协议其他部分所定义的词汇将具有其所特定的含义。

* This Chinese translation is for reference only. Parties should always execute the English original in conducting transactions. Although every effort has been made to ensure the accuracy of this translation, due to differences in grammar and legal terminologies, the possibility that terms or words used in the Chinese translation may have different meanings or connotations from the English original cannot be ruled out. Therefore, this Chinese translation should not be relied upon by any person in making any decision or taking any action. If there exists any difference between this Chinese version and the English version, the English version should govern.

本翻译稿仅用于参考。虽然译者已尽力使该中文译本准确反映英文原文，但由于中英文用词、语法结构及法律术语之不同，中文译义不可避免与英文本存有一些差异，因此交易者不应仅依赖于本译本而做出任何决定或采取任何行动，中英文本不一致之处，应以英文本为准。

(b) ***Inconsistency.*** In the event of any inconsistency between the provisions of the Schedule and the other provisions of this Master Agreement, the Schedule will prevail. In the event of any inconsistency between the provisions of any Confirmation and this Master Agreement, such Confirmation will prevail for the purpose of the relevant Transaction.

(b) *不一致。*若附件的条款与本主协议的其他条款有不一致之处，以附件为准。若任何确认书与本主协议之条款有不一致之处，就有关交易而言，以确认书为准。

(c) ***Single Agreement.*** All Transactions are entered into in reliance on the fact that this Master Agreement and all Confirmations form a single agreement between the parties (collectively referred to as this "Agreement"), and the parties would not otherwise enter into any Transactions.

(c) *单一协议。*所有交易的进行乃基於本主协议以及所有确认书构成双方之间的单一协议(统称" 协议")这一事实，否则双方不会进行任何交易。

2. Obligations

2. 义务

(a) ***General Conditions.***

(a) *一般条件。*

(i) Each party will make each payment or delivery specified in each Confirmation to be made by it, subject to the other provisions of this Agreement.

(i) 受本协议的其他条款约束，双方应按各份确认书的规定进行各项付款或交付。

(ii) Payments under this Agreement will be made on the due date for value on that date in the place of the account specified in the relevant Confirmation or otherwise pursuant to this Agreement, in freely transferable funds and in the manner customary for payments in the required currency. Where settlement is by delivery (that is, other than by payment), such delivery will be made for receipt on the due date in the manner customary for the relevant obligation unless otherwise specified in the relevant Confirmation or elsewhere in this Agreement.

(ii) 本协议项下的付款应於到期日在有关确认书所规定的帐户所在地或按本协议其他规定另行支付；款项应以自由可转让资金以及所需货币付款的通用方式支付。若结算以交付形式进行(即付款之外的方式)，该交付应於到期日按有关义务的通用方式进行，有关确认书或本协议另有规定者除外。

(iii) Each obligation of each party under Section 2(a)(i) is subject to (1) the condition precedent that no Event of Default or Potential Event of Default with respect to the other party has occurred and is continuing, (2) the condition precedent that no Early Termination Date in respect of the relevant Transaction has occurred or been effectively designated and (3) each other condition specified in this Agreement to be a condition precedent for the purpose of this Section 2(a)(iii).

(iii) 第2(a)(i)条下各方的每项义务取决於以下先决条件：(1)对方没有发生及持续存在的违约事件或潜在违约事件；(2)就有关交易而言尚未出现或尚未有效地指定提前终止日；以及(3)本协议规定的作为本第2(a)(iii)条先决条件的其他各项条件。

(b) ***Change of Account.*** Either party may change its account for receiving a payment or delivery by giving notice to the other party at least five Local Business Days prior to the Scheduled Settlement Date for the payment or delivery to which such change applies unless such other party gives timely notice of a reasonable objection to such change.

(b) *更改帐户。*除非另一方及时发出通知对帐户更改提出合理的反对意见，任何一方可在付款或交付的预定结算日前至少五个当地营业日通知对方变更接收款项或交付的帐户。

(c) ***Netting of Payments.*** If on any date amounts would otherwise be payable:—

(c) *付款净额结算。*若任何日期双方均须：-

(i) in the same currency; and

(i) 以相同货币；及

(ii) in respect of the same Transaction,

(ii) 就相同交易，

by each party to the other, then, on such date, each party's obligation to make payment of any such amount will be automatically satisfied and discharged and, if the aggregate amount that would otherwise have been payable by one party exceeds the aggregate amount that would otherwise have been payable by the other party, replaced by an obligation upon the party by which the larger aggregate amount would have been payable to pay to the other party the excess of the larger aggregate amount over the smaller aggregate amount.

向另一方付款，双方支付该款项的义务将於当日自动地完成及解除，若一方本应支付的总额高於对方本应支付的总额，支付较大总额一方的付款义务则为向另一方缴付两者之间的差额。

The parties may elect in respect of two or more Transactions that a net amount and payment obligation will be determined in respect of all amounts payable on the same date in the same currency in respect of those Transactions, regardless of whether such amounts are payable in respect of the same Transaction. The election may be made in the Schedule or any Confirmation by specifying that "Multiple Transaction Payment Netting" applies to the Transactions identified as being subject to the election (in which case clause (ii) above will not apply to such Transactions). If Multiple Transaction Payment Netting is applicable to Transactions, it will apply to those Transactions with effect from the starting date specified in the Schedule or such Confirmation, or, if a starting date is not specified in the Schedule or such Confirmation, the starting date otherwise agreed by the parties in writing. This election may be made separately for different groups of Transactions and will apply separately to each pairing of Offices through which the parties make and receive payments or deliveries.

双方可就两项或以上的交易选择就该些交易於同一日期以相同货币支付的所有付款进行净额结算及履行付款义务，不论此等付款是否关於同一笔交易。该选择可於附件或任何确认书上作出，并规定" 多项交易付款？额结算" 适用於该选择所指定的交易(在此情况下上述第(ii)款将不适用於此等交易)。如多项交易付款？额结算适用的话，其生效日期为附件或确认书中规定的开始日期；如附件或确认书中未规定生效日期，则由双方书面另行约定开始日期。此选择可就不同组别的交易分别作出并分别适用於双方用以交接款项或交付的每一组办事处。

(d) ***Deduction or Withholding for Tax.***

(d) *税务的扣除或预提。*

(i) ***Gross-Up.*** All payments under this Agreement will be made without any deduction or withholding for or on account of any Tax unless such deduction or withholding is required by any applicable law, as modified by the practice of any relevant governmental revenue authority, then in effect. If a party is so required to deduct or withhold, then that party ("X") will:—

(i) *所扣税项补足。*本协议项下的所有付款应不因任何税项而予以扣除或预提，除非此扣除或预提是按当时有效的并经有关政府税务机关的惯例加以修正的适用法律之要求而做出。若一方被要求扣除或预提任何款项，该方("X方")应： -

(1) promptly notify the other party ("Y") of such requirement;

(1) 及时将该要求通知另一方("Y方")；

(2) pay to the relevant authorities the full amount required to be deducted or withheld (including the full amount required to be deducted or withheld from any additional amount paid by X to Y under this Section 2(d)) promptly upon the earlier of determining that such deduction or withholding is required or receiving notice that such amount has been assessed against Y;

(2) 当确定需要支付该扣除或预提款项或收到通知获悉已向Y方评核该款项(二者之较早发生者)时，应及时向有关政府机关支付所需扣除或预提的全部款项(包括按本第2(d)条要求从X方付给Y方的任何额外款项中扣除或预提的全部款项)；

(3) promptly forward to Y an official receipt (or a certified copy), or other documentation reasonably acceptable to Y, evidencing such payment to such authorities; and

(3) 及时向Y方发出正式收据(或经认证的副本)，或Y方能合理接受的其他文件，证明已向有关政府机关付款；以及

(4) if such Tax is an Indemnifiable Tax, pay to Y, in addition to the payment to which Y is otherwise entitled under this Agreement, such additional amount as is necessary to ensure that the net amount actually received by Y (free and clear of Indemnifiable Taxes, whether assessed against X or Y) will equal the full amount Y would have received had no such deduction or withholding been required. However, X will not be required to pay any additional amount to Y to the extent that it would not be required to be paid but for:—

(4) 若该税为可获补偿税项，则除了支付给Y方其在本协议项下应得的款项外，还应向Y方支付额外款项，使Y方实得的净额(不包括向X方或Y方评估的可获补偿税项)相等於在不需要扣除或预提款项时其应得的全部款项，但是如果X方的支付义务是由以下事件所引发的，则X方无须向Y方支付任何额外款项： -

(A) the failure by Y to comply with or perform any agreement contained in Section 4(a)(i), 4(a)(iii) or 4(d); or

(A) Y方未能遵守或履行第4(a)(i)、4(a)(iii)或4(d)条所载的任何协议；或

(B) the failure of a representation made by Y pursuant to Section 3(f) to be accurate and true

(B) Y方按第3(f)条所作的陈述为不准确及不真实，除非该陈述是由于：(I)在进行某项交易以

unless such failure would not have occurred but for (I) any action taken by a taxing authority, or brought in a court of competent jurisdiction, after a Transaction is entered into (regardless of whether such action is taken or brought with respect to a party to this Agreement) or (II) a Change in Tax Law.

後，税务机关采取的行动或在有管辖权的法庭内提出的诉讼(不论该行动或诉讼是否就本协议一方提出)，或(II)税法的变更而变得不准确及不真实。

(ii) ***Liability.*** If:—

(1) X is required by any applicable law, as modified by the practice of any relevant governmental revenue authority, to make any deduction or withholding in respect of which X would not be required to pay an additional amount to Y under Section 2(d)(i)(4);

(2) X does not so deduct or withhold; and
(3) a liability resulting from such Tax is assessed directly against X,

then, except to the extent Y has satisfied or then satisfies the liability resulting from such Tax, Y will promptly pay to X the amount of such liability (including any related liability for interest, but including any related liability for penalties only if Y has failed to comply with or perform any agreement contained in Section 4(a)(i), 4(a)(iii) or 4(d)).

(ii) ***责任***。如果：-

(1) 因按经有关政府税务机关的惯例加以修正的任何适用法律之要求，X方需作出任何扣除或预提，但按第2(d)(i)(4)条之规定，X方无须向Y方支付任何额外款项；

(2) X方没有扣除或预提款项；并且
(3) 税务责任直接加於X方，

则Y方除非已承担或将承担该税务所引致的责任外，Y方应及时向X方支付有关该责任的款项(包括任何有关利息，但仅在Y方未能遵守或履行第4(a)(i)、4(a)(iii)或4(d)条所载的任何协议时才包括任何有关惩罚性责任)。

3. Representations

Each party makes the representations contained in Sections 3(a), 3(b), 3(c), 3(d), 3(e) and 3(f) and, if specified in the Schedule as applying, 3(g) to the other party (which representations will be deemed to be repeated by each party on each date on which a Transaction is entered into and, in the case of the representations in Section 3(f), at all times until the termination of this Agreement). If any "Additional Representation" is specified in the Schedule or any Confirmation as applying, the party or parties specified for such Additional Representation will make and, if applicable, be deemed to repeat such Additional Representation at the time or times specified for such Additional Representation.

3. 陈述

各方向另一方作出第3(a)、3(b)、3(c)、3(d)、3(e)和3(f)条以及(如按附件规定适用时的)第3(g)款所载的陈述(这些陈述将被视为在每次进行交易当日为各方复述，按第3(f)条所作的陈述将被视为直至本协议终止前不断为各方所复述)。如任何"其他陈述"按附件或确认书的规定适用时，该陈述中规定的一方或各方将于该陈述规定的时候作出或被认为在重复(如适用的话)这一其他陈述。

(a) ***Basic Representations.***

(i) ***Status.*** It is duly organised and validly existing under the laws of the jurisdiction of its organisation or incorporation and, if relevant under such laws, in good standing;

(ii) ***Powers.*** It has the power to execute this Agreement and any other documentation relating to this Agreement to which it is a party, to deliver this Agreement and any other documentation relating to this Agreement that it is required by this Agreement to deliver and to perform its obligations under this Agreement and any obligations it has under any Credit Support Document to which it is a party and has taken all necessary action to authorise such execution, delivery and performance;

(iii) ***No Violation or Conflict.*** Such execution, delivery and performance do not violate or conflict with any law applicable to it, any provision of its constitutional documents, any order or judgment of any court or other agency of government applicable to it or any of its assets or any contractual restriction binding on or affecting it or any of its assets;

(iv) ***Consents.*** All governmental and other consents that are required to have been obtained by it with respect to this Agreement or any Credit Support

(a) ***基本陈述***。

(i) ***地位***。其为适当地组成并按其成立或组织的司法管辖区之法律有效存续以及，如与该等法律相关的话，处于良好的状态；

(ii) ***权力***。其有权签署本协议以及其为一方的与本协议有关的其它任何文件，有权按本协议有关交付的要求交付本协议及有关本协议的任何其它文件，及有权履行本协议项下的义务以及任何以其为一方的信用支持文件下的义务，并已采取所有必要行动授权此等签署、交付及履行；

(iii) ***无违反或？触***。此等签署、交付及履行并无违反或？触任何适用的法律，符合其组织章程性文件的任何规定，符合适用於该方或其资产的任何法庭或政府机关所颁布的法令或判决，或任何约束或影响该方或其资产的合同约定；

(iv) ***同意***。已获取有关本协议或其为一方的任何信用支持文件所需的一切政府同意及其它同意；此等同意已全面生效并且有关同意生效的所有条件已获遵守；以及

Document to which it is a party have been obtained and are in full force and effect and all conditions of any such consents have been complied with; and

(v) ***Obligations Binding.*** Its obligations under this Agreement and any Credit Support Document to which it is a party constitute its legal, valid and binding obligations, enforceable in accordance with their respective terms (subject to applicable bankruptcy, reorganisation, insolvency, moratorium or similar laws affecting creditors' rights generally and subject, as to enforceability, to equitable principles of general application (regardless of whether enforcement is sought in a proceeding in equity or at law)).

(v) *义务的约束。*其在本协议及其为一方的任何信用支持文件项下的义务均构成其合法、有效及有约束力的义务，并可按该些文件的有关条款强制执行(受限於适用的破产、重组、无偿还能力、延期偿还或通常影响债权者权利的类似法律，并在有关执行方面受限於普遍适用的衡平原则(无论该执行是诉诸于衡平法或普通法))。

(b) ***Absence of Certain Events.*** No Event of Default or Potential Event of Default or, to its knowledge, Termination Event with respect to it has occurred and is continuing and no such event or circumstance would occur as a result of its entering into or performing its obligations under this Agreement or any Credit Support Document to which it is a party.

(b) *不存在某些事件。*没有任何已经发生及持续的违约事件或潜在的违约事件，或据其所知并无有关该方的终止事件，并且签署或履行本协议或其为一方的任何信用支持文件下的义务，不会引致该终止事件或情况的发生。

(c) ***Absence of Litigation.*** There is not pending or, to its knowledge, threatened against it, any of its Credit Support Providers or any of its applicable Specified Entities any action, suit or proceeding at law or in equity or before any court, tribunal, governmental body, agency or official or any arbitrator that is likely to affect the legality, validity or enforceability against it of this Agreement or any Credit Support Document to which it is a party or its ability to perform its obligations under this Agreement or such Credit Support Document.

(c) *不存在诉讼。*没有任何待决的，或据其所知，没有任何对其或其任何信用支持提供者或其任何有关特定机构购成威胁的基於普通法或衡平法或於任何法庭、裁判所、政府实体、代理人、官员或仲裁者前进行的诉讼、控告或起诉将可能影响本协议或其为一方的任何信用支持文件的合法性、有效性或可执行性，或其履行本协议或该些信用支持文件下的义务之能力。

(d) ***Accuracy of Specified Information.*** All applicable information that is furnished in writing by or on behalf of it to the other party and is identified for the purpose of this Section 3(d) in the Schedule is, as of the date of the information, true, accurate and complete in every material respect.

(d) *指定资料的准确性。*以书面形式由其发出或以其名义发给另一方，并为本第3(d)条的目的在附件上指明的所有适用资料，於该资料的日期在各重要方面均为真实、正确及完整。

(e) ***Payer Tax Representation.*** Each representation specified in the Schedule as being made by it for the purpose of this Section 3(e) is accurate and true.

(e) *付款人税务陈述。*其为本第3(e)条目的在附件中所作的陈述均为正确及真实。

(f) ***Payee Tax Representations.*** Each representation specified in the Schedule as being made by it for the purpose of this Section 3(f) is accurate and true.

(f) *受款人税务陈述。*其为本第3(f)条目的在附件中所作的陈述均为正确及真实。

(g) ***No Agency.*** It is entering into this Agreement, including each Transaction, as principal and not as agent of any person or entity.

(g) *无代理。*其作为本人而非任何人或机构的代理人订立本协议。

4. Agreements

4. 协议

Each party agrees with the other that, so long as either party has or may have any obligation under this Agreement or under any Credit Support Document to which it is a party:—

双方彼此同意，当任何一方在本协议或其为一方的任何信用支持文件下负有或可能负有任何义务时：－

(a) ***Furnish Specified Information.*** It will deliver to the other party or, in certain cases under clause (iii) below, to such government or taxing authority as the other party reasonably directs:—

(a) *提供指定资料。*其将向另一方，或在下面第(iii)款的某些情形下向另一方合理地指示的政府或税务机关提供：－

(i) any forms, documents or certificates relating to taxation specified in the Schedule or any Confirmation;

(i) 附件或任何确认书规定的有关税务的表格、文件或证书；

(ii) any other documents specified in the Schedule or any Confirmation; and

(ii) 附件或任何确认书规定的任何其他文件；以及

(iii) upon reasonable demand by such other party, any form or document that may be required or reasonably requested in writing in order to allow such other party

(iii) 按另一方的合理要求，提供可能需要或以书面合理地要求的任何表格或文件，使该另一方或其信用支持提供者在按本协议或任何适用的信用支持文件付款时无需就任何税务支

or its Credit Support Provider to make a payment under this Agreement or any applicable Credit Support Document without any deduction or withholding for or on account of any Tax or with such deduction or withholding at a reduced rate (so long as the completion, execution or submission of such form or document would not materially prejudice the legal or commercial position of the party in receipt of such demand), with any such form or document to be accurate and completed in a manner reasonably satisfactory to such other party and to be executed and to be delivered with any reasonably required certification,

付扣除或预提款项，或以减低比率支付此等扣除或预提款项(只要是该表格或文件的完成、签署或递交不会严重地损害接受该要求一方的法律或商业地位)，此等表格或文件应准确地并按使另一方合理满意的方式填妥，签署後再附上任何合理要求的证明予以交付，

in each case by the date specified in the Schedule or such Confirmation or, if none is specified, as soon as reasonably practicable.

以上各项义务需按附件或该确认书规定的日期，或者如无规定，则以合理可行的最快时间予以完成。

(b) ***Maintain Authorisations.*** It will use all reasonable efforts to maintain in full force and effect all consents of any governmental or other authority that are required to be obtained by it with respect to this Agreement or any Credit Support Document to which it is a party and will use all reasonable efforts to obtain any that may become necessary in the future.

(b) ***维持授权。***应尽一切合理的努力使本协议或其为一方的任何信用支持文件中要求该方从政府或其它机关获取的一切同意维持充分的效力，并将尽一切合理的努力，获取日後可能必要的其它同意。

(c) ***Comply With Laws.*** It will comply in all material respects with all applicable laws and orders to which it may be subject if failure so to comply would materially impair its ability to perform its obligations under this Agreement or any Credit Support Document to which it is a party.

(c) ***遵守法律。***应在一切重要方面遵守对其有约束力的所有适用法律及法令，如果不遵守该等法律、法令将会严重影响其履行本协议或其为一方的任何信用支持文件下的义务的能力。

(d) ***Tax Agreement.*** It will give notice of any failure of a representation made by it under Section 3(f) to be accurate and true promptly upon learning of such failure.

(d) ***税务协议。***当该方得悉其按第3(f)条所作的陈述有不准确及不真实之处，应及时就此发出通知。

(e) ***Payment of Stamp Tax.*** Subject to Section 11, it will pay any Stamp Tax levied or imposed upon it or in respect of its execution or performance of this Agreement by a jurisdiction in which it is incorporated, organised, managed and controlled or considered to have its seat, or where an Office through which it is acting for the purpose of this Agreement is located ("Stamp Tax Jurisdiction"), and will indemnify the other party against any Stamp Tax levied or imposed upon the other party or in respect of the other party's execution or performance of this Agreement by any such Stamp Tax Jurisdiction which is not also a Stamp Tax Jurisdiction with respect to the other party.

(e) ***印花税的缴付。***除第11条另有规定外，应缴付其成立、组织、被管理、被控制的司法管辖区，或视该方拥有一席位，或为履行本协议的某个办事处所在的司法管辖区对该方或就其签署或履行本协议所徵收的印花税(" 印花税司法管辖区")，并当某印花税司法管辖区对非处於该印花税司法管辖区的一方或就其签署或履行本协议徵收印花税时对另一方作出赔偿。

5. Events of Default and Termination Events

5. 违约事件和终止事件

(a) ***Events of Default.*** The occurrence at any time with respect to a party or, if applicable, any Credit Support Provider of such party or any Specified Entity of such party of any of the following events constitutes (subject to Sections 5(c) and 6(e)(iv)) an event of default (an "Event of Default") with respect to such party:—

(a) ***违约事件。***任何时候，当一方或，如适用的话，该方的任何信用支持提供者或该方的任何特定机构发生以下任何事件，将构成(受第5(c)和第6(e)(iv)条限制)该方的违约事件(以下简称" 违约事件")：-

(i) ***Failure to Pay or Deliver.*** Failure by the party to make, when due, any payment under this Agreement or delivery under Section 2(a)(i) or 9(h)(i)(2) or (4) required to be made by it if such failure is not remedied on or before the first Local Business Day in the case of any such payment or the first Local Delivery Day in the case of any such delivery after, in each case, notice of such failure is given to the party;

(i) ***未能付款或交付。***该方未能於到期日按本协议付款或按第2(a)(i)、第9(h)(i)(2)或(4)条的规定履行交付义务，并且在向该方发出逾期通知后的首个当地营业日(适用于付款)或首个当地交付日(适用于实物交付)或之前仍不予以纠正；

(ii) ***Breach of Agreement; Repudiation of Agreement.***

(1) Failure by the party to comply with or perform any agreement or obligation (other than an obligation to make any payment under this Agreement or delivery under Section 2(a)(i) or 9(h)(i)(2) or (4) or to give notice of a Termination Event or any agreement or obligation under Section 4(a)(i), 4(a)(iii) or 4(d)) to be complied with or performed by the party in accordance with this Agreement if such failure is not remedied within 30 days after notice of such failure is given to the party; or

(2) the party disaffirms, disclaims, repudiates or rejects, in whole or in part, or challenges the validity of, this Master Agreement, any Confirmation executed and delivered by that party or any Transaction evidenced by such a Confirmation (or such action is taken by any person or entity appointed or empowered to operate it or act on its behalf);

(iii) ***Credit Support Default.***

(1) Failure by the party or any Credit Support Provider of such party to comply with or perform any agreement or obligation to be complied with or performed by it in accordance with any Credit Support Document if such failure is continuing after any applicable grace period has elapsed;

(2) the expiration or termination of such Credit Support Document or the failing or ceasing of such Credit Support Document, or any security interest granted by such party or such Credit Support Provider to the other party pursuant to any such Credit Support Document, to be in full force and effect for the purpose of this Agreement (in each case other than in accordance with its terms) prior to the satisfaction of all obligations of such party under each Transaction to which such Credit Support Document relates without the written consent of the other party; or

(3) the party or such Credit Support Provider disaffirms, disclaims, repudiates or rejects, in whole or in part, or challenges the validity of, such Credit Support Document (or such action is taken by any person or entity appointed or empowered to operate it or act on its behalf);

(iv) ***Misrepresentation.*** A representation (other than a representation under Section 3(e) or 3(f)) made or repeated or deemed to have been made or repeated by the party or any Credit Support Provider of such party in this Agreement or any Credit Support Document proves to have been incorrect or misleading in any material respect when made or repeated or deemed to have been made or repeated;

(v) ***Default Under Specified Transaction.*** The party, any Credit Support Provider of such party or any applicable Specified Entity of such party:—

(ii) ***违反协议；否认协议。***

(1) 该方未能按本协议规定遵守或履行其应该遵守或履行的任何协议或义务(但不包括本协议第2(a)(i)、第9(h)(i)(2)或(4)条下的付款义务或交付义务，或发出终止事件通知的义务，或第4(a)(i)款、第4(a)(iii)款或4(d)条项下的任何协议或义务)，并且在向该方发出违约通知後的三十天内仍不予以纠正；或

(2) 该方取消、否认、放弃或拒绝全部或部分的本主协议、由该方签订和交付的任何确认书或此等确认书证明的任何交易，或对本主协议、上述确认书或交易的有效性提出异议(或该行动由经委派或授权管理该方的任何个人或实体作出或代表其作出)；

(iii) ***信用支持违约。***

(1) 该方或该方的任何信用支持提供者未能按任何信用支持文件的规定遵守或履行其应该遵守或履行的任何协议或义务，并在任何适用的宽限期过后仍然不予以纠正；

(2) 未经另一方书面同意，在该方未就此等信用支持文件所涉及的每项交易履行所有义务前，此等信用支持文件届满或终止，或此等信用支持文件或该方或其信用支持提供者根据任何此等信用支持文件给予另一方的任何担保权益未能保持为本协议目的之充分效力(以上任一情况均不包括按协议条文的正常失效)；或

(3) 该方或该方的信用支持提供者取消、否认、放弃或拒绝全部或部分的信用支持文件，或对该信用支持文件的有效性提出异议(或该行动由经委派或授权管理该方的任何个人或实体作出或代表其作出)；

(iv) ***错误的陈述。***该方或该方的任何信用支持提供者於本协议或任何信用支持文件下作出或复述的，或被视为作出或复述的陈述(按第3(e)或3(f)条所作的陈述除外)被证实在作出、复述或被视为作出或复述之时在重要方面为错误或带有误导成分；

(v) ***特定交易项下的违约。***某方、该方的任何信用支持提供者或该方的任何适用特定机构：－

(1) defaults (other than by failing to make a delivery) under a Specified Transaction or any credit support arrangement relating to a Specified Transaction and, after giving effect to any applicable notice requirement or grace period, such default results in a liquidation of, an acceleration of obligations under, or an early termination of, that Specified Transaction;

(2) defaults, after giving effect to any applicable notice requirement or grace period, in making any payment due on the last payment or exchange date of, or any payment on early termination of, a Specified Transaction (or, if there is no applicable notice requirement or grace period, such default continues for at least one Local Business Day);

(3) defaults in making any delivery due under (including any delivery due on the last delivery or exchange date of) a Specified Transaction or any credit support arrangement relating to a Specified Transaction and, after giving effect to any applicable notice requirement or grace period, such default results in a liquidation of, an acceleration of obligations under, or an early termination of, all transactions outstanding under the documentation applicable to that Specified Transaction; or

(4) disaffirms, disclaims, repudiates or rejects, in whole or in part, or challenges the validity of, a Specified Transaction or any credit support arrangement relating to a Specified Transaction that is, in either case, confirmed or evidenced by a document or other confirming evidence executed and delivered by that party, Credit Support Provider or Specified Entity (or such action is taken by any person or entity appointed or empowered to operate it or act on its behalf);

(vi) ***Cross-Default.*** If "Cross-Default" is specified in the Schedule as applying to the party, the occurrence or existence of:—

(1) a default, event of default or other similar condition or event (however described) in respect of such party, any Credit Support Provider of such party or any applicable Specified Entity of such party under one or more agreements or instruments relating to Specified Indebtedness of any of them (individually or collectively) where the aggregate principal amount of such agreements or instruments, either alone or together with the amount, if any, referred to in clause (2) below, is not less than the applicable Threshold Amount (as specified in the Schedule) which has resulted in such Specified Indebtedness becoming, or becoming capable at such time of being declared, due and payable under such agreements or instruments before it would otherwise have been due and payable; or

(2) a default by such party, such Credit Support Provider or such Specified Entity (individually or collectively) in making one or more payments

(1) 於特定交易或有关特定交易的任何信用支持安排下违约(未能履行交付义务除外)，而在任何适用的通知要求或宽限期生效后，该违约导致该特定交易的清算、加速偿还、或提前终止的情形；

(2) 於任何适用的通知要求或宽限期生效后，未能在特定交易的最后付款或交换日到期时履行任何付款的义务，或未能支付有关特定交易的提前终止的款项(或如无适用的通知要求或宽限期，该违约持续至少一个当地营业日)；

(3) 未能履行特定交易或有关特定交易的任何信用支持安排项下的任何交付义务(包括最后付款日或交换日到期的任何交付义务)，并在适用的通知要求或宽限期生效后，该违约导致有关特定交易的文件下所有未完成交易的清算、加速偿还、或提前终止的情形；或

(4) 全部或部分取消、否认、放弃或拒绝由该方、其信用支持提供者或特定机构签订和交付的文件或其他确认证据确认或证明的特定交易或有关特定交易的任何信用支持安排，或对特定交易或有关特定交易的任何信用支持安排的有效性提出异议(或该行动由经委派或授权管理该方的任何个人或实体作出或代表其作出)；

(vi) ***交叉违约***。若" 交叉违约" 在附件中被指定为适用於某方，发生或存在以下事件：－

(1) 该方、该方的任何信用支持提供者或该方的任何适用特定机构(单独的或总体的)就有关任何一方特定债务的一份或多份协议或文件发生违约、违约事件或其它类似的情况或事件(不论如何描述)，该协议或文件下的累计本金金额与以下第(2)款所述的金额(如有的话)分别或累计达到适用的起点金额(如附件中定义)，从而使特定债务在原定到期及应缴付的期限之前已按此等协议或文件得以宣告到期及应缴付或能够被宣告为到期及应缴付，或

(2) 该方、该信用支持提供者或该特定机构(单独的或总体的)未能在付款到期日(在任何适用的通知要求或宽限期生效后)按上述协议或文件付款，并且其累计金额

under such agreements or instruments on the due date for payment (after giving effect to any applicable notice requirement or grace period) in an aggregate amount, either alone or together with the amount, if any, referred to in clause (1) above, of not less than the applicable Threshold Amount;

单独地或与以上第(1)款所述的金额(如有的话)分别或一并计算达到适用的起点金额；

(vii) ***Bankruptcy.*** The party, any Credit Support Provider of such party or any applicable Specified Entity of such party:—

(1) is dissolved (other than pursuant to a consolidation, amalgamation or merger); (2) becomes insolvent or is unable to pay its debts or fails or admits in writing its inability generally to pay its debts as they become due; (3) makes a general assignment, arrangement or composition with or for the benefit of its creditors; (4)(A) institutes or has instituted against it, by a regulator, supervisor or any similar official with primary insolvency, rehabilitative or regulatory jurisdiction over it in the jurisdiction of its incorporation or organisation or the jurisdiction of its head or home office, a proceeding seeking a judgment of insolvency or bankruptcy or any other relief under any bankruptcy or insolvency law or other similar law affecting creditors' rights, or a petition is presented for its winding-up or liquidation by it or such regulator, supervisor or similar official, or (B) has instituted against it a proceeding seeking a judgment of insolvency or bankruptcy or any other relief under any bankruptcy or insolvency law or other similar law affecting creditors' rights, or a petition is presented for its winding-up or liquidation, and such proceeding or petition is instituted or presented by a person or entity not described in clause (A) above and either (I) results in a judgment of insolvency or bankruptcy or the entry of an order for relief or the making of an order for its winding-up or liquidation or (II) is not dismissed, discharged, stayed or restrained in each case within 15 days of the institution or presentation thereof; (5) has a resolution passed for its winding-up, official management or liquidation (other than pursuant to a consolidation, amalgamation or merger); (6) seeks or becomes subject to the appointment of an administrator, provisional liquidator, conservator, receiver, trustee, custodian or other similar official for it or for all or substantially all its assets; (7) has a secured party take possession of all or substantially all its assets or has a distress, execution, attachment, sequestration or other legal process levied, enforced or sued on or against all or substantially all its assets and such secured party maintains possession, or any such process is not dismissed, discharged, stayed or restrained, in each case within 15 days thereafter; (8) causes or is subject to any event with respect to it which, under the applicable laws of any jurisdiction, has an analogous effect to any of the events specified in clauses (1) to (7) above (inclusive); or (9) takes any action in furtherance of, or indicating its consent to, approval of, or acquiescence in, any of the foregoing acts; or

(vii) *破产。*若一方、该方的任何信用支持提供者或该方的任何适用特定机构：—

(1)解散(因联合、合并或兼并的除外)；(2)资不抵债或无力偿还债务，或以书面承认其总体上无力偿还到期债务；(3)向其债权人、或为其债权人利益作出一般的转让、安排或和解清偿；(4)(A)在该方成立或组建的司法管辖区或其总部或总办事处的司法管辖区内，对其拥有主要破产、重整或监管权的管理者、监督者或任何其他同类官员针对该方提出或已提出法律程序，按任何破产或无力偿付法律或影响债权人权利的其它类似法律寻求无力偿付或破产判决或任何其它救济方法，或该方、其管理者、监督者或同类官员提交关于业务结束或清算的请求，或(B)已经提出法律程序，按任何破产或无力偿付法律或影响债权人权利的其他类似法律寻求无力偿付或破产判决或任何其他救济方法，或就其业务结束或清算提交请求，并且该诉讼或请求并非由以上(A)款中的人士或机构提出，并且这一诉讼或请求：(I)导致无力偿付或破产之判决或救济命令，或其业务结束或清算的命令，或(II)该诉讼或请求在提出後十五天内未被驳回、撤销、中止或禁止；(5)就其业务结束、官方管理或清算(因联合、合并或兼并的除外)通过决议；(6)就该方或各方或其大部分的资产寻求任命或任命破产管理人、临时清算者、监护人、破产事务官、受托人、保管人或其它类似官员或受该类任命约束；(7)担保权益持有人取得其所有或大部分资产的占有权，或对其所有或大部分资产提起或强制执行扣押、执行、查封、强制保管或其他法律程序，并且该担保权益持有人持续占有此等资产，或在其后十五日内该法律程序未被驳回、撤销、中止或禁止；(8)受制於在任何司法管辖区适用法律下产生与任何上述第(1)至(7)款(包括该条款)所指事件有类似效果的事件或促使该事件的发生；或(9)就上述任何行为采取支持行动、或对其表示同意、批准或默许；或

(viii) ***Merger Without Assumption.*** The party or any Credit Support Provider of such party consolidates or amalgamates with, or merges with or into, or transfers all or substantially all its assets to, or reorganises, reincorporates or reconstitutes into or as, another entity and, at the time of such consolidation, amalgamation, merger, transfer, reorganisation, reincorporation or reconstitution:—

(viii) *不承担债务的合并。*一方或该方的任何信用支持提供者与另一实体联合、合并或兼并，或将其所有或大部分的资产转移给另一实体，或重组、再设立或改组成为另一实体；而在该联合、兼并、合并、转让、重组、再设立或改组时：-

(1) the resulting, surviving or transferee entity fails to assume all the obligations of such party or such Credit Support Provider under this Agreement or any Credit Support Document to which it or its predecessor was a party; or

(1) 最终的、续存的或受让的实体未能承担该方或该方信用支持提供者或其前任者在本协议下或任何信用支持文件下的所有义务；或

(2) the benefits of any Credit Support Document fail to extend (without the consent of the other party) to the performance by such resulting, surviving or transferee entity of its obligations under this Agreement.

(2) 任何信用支持文件的利益(在未得到另一方同意前)未能延伸以涵盖该最终的、续存的或受让的实体在本协议下的履约行为。

(b) ***Termination Events.*** The occurrence at any time with respect to a party or, if applicable, any Credit Support Provider of such party or any Specified Entity of such party of any event specified below constitutes (subject to Section 5(c)) an Illegality if the event is specified in clause (i) below, a Force Majeure Event if the event is specified in clause (ii) below, a Tax Event if the event is specified in clause (iii) below, a Tax Event Upon Merger if the event is specified in clause (iv) below, and, if specified to be applicable, a Credit Event Upon Merger if the event is specified pursuant to clause (v) below or an Additional Termination Event if the event is specified pursuant to clause (vi) below:—

(b) *终止事件。*一方，(如适用的话)该方的任何信用支持提供者、或该方的任何特定机构在任何时候若发生以下(i)款所述的事件将构成(除第5(c)条另有规定外)非法，若发生(ii)款所述的事件将构成不可抗力事件，若发生以下(iii)款所述的事件将构成税务事件，若发生(iv)款所述的事件将构成构成因合并造成的税务事件，若指定为适用的话，发生以下(v)款所述的事件将构成因合并造成的信用事件，发生以下(vi)款所述的事件将构成其它终止事件：-

(i) ***Illegality.*** After giving effect to any applicable provision, disruption fallback or remedy specified in, or pursuant to, the relevant Confirmation or elsewhere in this Agreement, due to an event or circumstance (other than any action taken by a party or, if applicable, any Credit Support Provider of such party) occurring after a Transaction is entered into, it becomes unlawful under any applicable law (including without limitation the laws of any country in which payment, delivery or compliance is required by either party or any Credit Support Provider, as the case may be), on any day, or it would be unlawful if the relevant payment, delivery or compliance were required on that day (in each case, other than as a result of a breach by the party of Section 4(b)):—

(i) *非法。*在运用了有关确认书或本协议其他部分规定的任何适用条款、中断保障或补偿条款后，因交易进行之後发生的任何事件或情况(一方或(如适用)该方的信用支持提供者采取的任何行动除外)使得以下行为按照任何适用法律(包括但不限于任何一方或任何信用支持提供者(视情况而定)需进行付款、交付和遵守协议时所在地国家的法律)于任何一日成为非法，或使得有关付款、交付和遵守协议如作出时将会成为非法(因违反第4(b)条导致上述后果的除外)：-

(1) for the Office through which such party (which will be the Affected Party) makes and receives payments or deliveries with respect to such Transaction to perform any absolute or contingent obligation to make a payment or delivery in respect of such Transaction, to receive a payment or delivery in respect of such Transaction or to comply with any other material provision of this Agreement relating to such Transaction; or

(1) 该方(即受影响方)就该交易交接款项或交付的办事处为该交易进行支付或交付而履行任何无条件或附条件义务，或接受支付或交付，或就该交易遵守本协议的任何其它重要条款；或

(2) for such party or any Credit Support Provider of such party (which will be the Affected Party) to perform any absolute or contingent obligation to make a payment or delivery which such party or

(2) 该方或该方的任何信用支持提供者(即受影响方)为作出该交易有关的信用支持文件中规定的该方或信用支持提供者的支付或交付而履行任何无条件或附条件义务，或接受该信用支持文件项下的支付或交付，或遵守

Credit Support Provider has under any Credit Support Document relating to such Transaction, to receive a payment or delivery under such Credit Support Document or to comply with any other material provision of such Credit Support Document;

该信用支持文件的任何其他重要条款；

(ii) ***Force Majeure Event.*** After giving effect to any applicable provision, disruption fallback or remedy specified in, or pursuant to, the relevant Confirmation or elsewhere in this Agreement, by reason of force majeure or act of state occurring after a Transaction is entered into, on any day:—

(ii) ***不可抗力事件。***在运用了有关确认书或本协议其他部分规定的任何适用条款、中断保障或补偿条款后，因交易进行之后发生的不可抗力或政府行为，于任何一日：—

(1) the Office through which such party (which will be the Affected Party) makes and receives payments or deliveries with respect to such Transaction is prevented from performing any absolute or contingent obligation to make a payment or delivery in respect of such Transaction, from receiving a payment or delivery in respect of such Transaction or from complying with any other material provision of this Agreement relating to such Transaction (or would be so prevented if such payment, delivery or compliance were required on that day), or it becomes impossible or impracticable for such Office so to perform, receive or comply (or it would be impossible or impracticable for such Office so to perform, receive or comply if such payment, delivery or compliance were required on that day); or

(1) 该方(即受影响方)就该交易交接款项或交付的办事处不能为该交易进行支付或交付而履行任何无条件或附条件的义务，或不能接受支付或交付，或不能就该交易遵守本协议的任何其他重要条款(或如该日提出该付款、交付或遵守协议的要求而不能做到)，或该办事处的履行、接受付款或遵守协议变得不可能或不可行(或如该日提出支付款项、交付或遵守协议的要求而该办事处按要求履约不可能或不可行)；或

(2) such party or any Credit Support Provider of such party (which will be the Affected Party) is prevented from performing any absolute or contingent obligation to make a payment or delivery which such party or Credit Support Provider has under any Credit Support Document relating to such Transaction, from receiving a payment or delivery under such Credit Support Document or from complying with any other material provision of such Credit Support Document (or would be so prevented if such payment, delivery or compliance were required on that day), or it becomes impossible or impracticable for such party or Credit Support Provider so to perform, receive or comply (or it would be impossible or impracticable for such party or Credit Support Provider so to perform, receive or comply if such payment, delivery or compliance were required on that day),

(2) 该方或该方的任何信用支持提供者(即受影响方)不能履行该方或该信用支持提供者在有关该等交易的任何信用支持文件项下无条件或附条件的支付或交付义务，或不能接受支付或交付，或不能就该交易遵守本协议的任何其他重要条款(或如该日提出该付款、交付或遵守协议的要求而不能做到)，或该方或该信用支持提供者的履行、接受付款或遵守协议变得不可能或不可行(或如该日提出支付款项、交付或遵守协议的要求而该方或该信用支持提供者按要求履约不可能或不可行)，

so long as the force majeure or act of state is beyond the control of such Office, such party or such Credit Support Provider, as appropriate, and such Office, party or Credit Support Provider could not, after using all reasonable efforts (which will not require such party or Credit Support Provider to incur a loss, other than immaterial, incidental expenses), overcome such prevention, impossibility or impracticability;

只要这一不可抗力或政府行为超出该办事处、该方或该信用支持提供者(视情况而定)的控制范围，并且该办事处、该方或信用支持提供者在尽所有合理努力(但该努力不应使该方或信用支持提供者承受损失，但不重要及附带开支以外的损失除外)之後仍无法克服上述不能，不可能或不可行的情况；

(iii) ***Tax Event.*** Due to (1) any action taken by a taxing authority, or brought in a court of competent jurisdiction, after a Transaction is entered into (regardless of whether such action is taken or brought

(iii) ***税务事件。***由於：(1)在交易进行以後税务机关采取行动或在有合法管辖权的法庭提出的任何诉讼(不论该诉讼是否与本协议一方有关)，或(2)因税法的变更，一方(即受影响方)将或有极大可能，於下一个预定结算日：(A)须按第

with respect to a party to this Agreement) or (2) a Change in Tax Law, the party (which will be the Affected Party) will, or there is a substantial likelihood that it will, on the next succeeding Scheduled Settlement Date (A) be required to pay to the other party an additional amount in respect of an Indemnifiable Tax under Section 2(d)(i)(4) (except in respect of interest under Section 9(h)) or (B) receive a payment from which an amount is required to be deducted or withheld for or on account of a Tax (except in respect of interest under Section 9(h)) and no additional amount is required to be paid in respect of such Tax under Section 2(d)(i)(4) (other than by reason of Section 2(d)(i)(4)(A) or (B));

2(d)(i)(4)条就可获补偿税项向另一方支付额外款项(有关第9(h)条的利息除外)，或(B)收取一项需从该项付款中扣除或预提税款之款项(有关第9(h)条的利息除外)，而无权按第2(d)(i)(4)条之规定要求对方支付额外款项(基於第2(d)(i)(4)(A)或(B)条的原因除外)；

(iv) ***Tax Event Upon Merger.*** The party (the "Burdened Party") on the next succeeding Scheduled Settlement Date will either (1) be required to pay an additional amount in respect of an Indemnifiable Tax under Section 2(d)(i)(4) (except in respect of interest under Section 9(h)) or (2) receive a payment from which an amount has been deducted or withheld for or on account of any Tax in respect of which the other party is not required to pay an additional amount (other than by reason of Section 2(d)(i)(4)(A) or (B)), in either case as a result of a party consolidating or amalgamating with, or merging with or into, or transferring all or substantially all its assets (or any substantial part of the assets comprising the business conducted by it as of the date of this Master Agreement) to, or reorganising, reincorporating or reconstituting into or as, another entity (which will be the Affected Party) where such action does not constitute a Merger Without Assumption;

(iv) ***因合并造成的税务事件。***在下一个预定结算日，一方(" 有负担方")将：(1)就第2(d)(i)(4)条下的可获补偿税项支付额外款项(有关第9(h)条有关的利息除外)，或(2)收取一项已在该付款中扣除或预提任何税款的款项，而另一方不须就该税款支付额外款项(基於第2(d)(i)(4)(A)或(B)条的原因除外)，以上任何一情况，皆由於一方将与另一实体联合、合并或兼并，或将其所有或大部份资产(或本主协议日期起其从事的商业行为中运用的大部分资产)转移给另一实体，或重组、再设立或改组为另一实体(称为受影响方)所导致，并且该行动不构成不承担债务的合并；

(v) ***Credit Event Upon Merger.*** If "Credit Event Upon Merger" is specified in the Schedule as applying to the party, a Designated Event (as defined below) occurs with respect to such party, any Credit Support Provider of such party or any applicable Specified Entity of such party (in each case, "X") and such Designated Event does not constitute a Merger Without Assumption, and the creditworthiness of X or, if applicable, the successor, surviving or transferee entity of X, after taking into account any applicable Credit Support Document, is materially weaker immediately after the occurrence of such Designated Event than that of X immediately prior to the occurrence of such Designated Event (and, in any such event, such party or its successor, surviving or transferee entity, as appropriate, will be the Affected Party). A "Designated Event" with respect to X means that:—

(v) ***因合并造成的信用事件。***若附件中规定" 因合并造成的信用事件" 适用於某方，而该方、该方的任何信用支持提供者或该方的任何适用特定机构(各为" X方")发生指定事件(定义如下)，并且该指定事件不构成不承担债务的合并，而X方，或(如适用的话)X方的继承的、存续的或受让的实体的资信情况，在考虑任何适用的信用支持文件之后仍严重低于指定事件发生之前X方的资信情况(在任何此等情况下，该方或其继承的、存续的或受让实体，视情况而定将成为" 受影响方")。有关X方的" 指定事件" 是指：—

(1) X consolidates or amalgamates with, or merges with or into, or transfers all or substantially all its assets (or any substantial part of the assets comprising the business conducted by X as of the date of this Master Agreement) to, or reorganises, reincorporates or reconstitutes into or as, another entity;

(1) X方与另一实体联合、合并或兼并，或将其所有或大部份资产(或本主协议日期起其从事的商业行为中运用的大部分资产)转移给另一实体，或重组、再设立或改组为另一实体；

(2) any person, related group of persons or entity acquires directly or indirectly the beneficial ownership of (A) equity securities having the power to elect a majority of the board of directors

(2) 任何人、相关联的人或实体直接或间接获得：(A)选举X方董事会(或同类机构)大多数成员的股权的受益权，或(B)使其能对X方行使控制权的任何其他所有权的受益权；或

(or its equivalent) of X or (B) any other ownership interest enabling it to exercise control of X; or

(3) X effects any substantial change in its capital structure by means of the issuance, incurrence or guarantee of debt or the issuance of (A) preferred stock or other securities convertible into or exchangeable for debt or preferred stock or (B) in the case of entities other than corporations, any other form of ownership interest; or

(3) X方通过发债、负债或保证的方式对其资本结构进行重大改变，或(A)以发行优先股或可转换或交换成债券或优先股的其他证券，或(B)如X方并非公司，发行其他形式的所有权的方式对其资本结构进行重大改变；或

(vi) ***Additional Termination Event.*** If any "Additional Termination Event" is specified in the Schedule or any Confirmation as applying, the occurrence of such event (and, in such event, the Affected Party or Affected Parties will be as specified for such Additional Termination Event in the Schedule or such Confirmation).

(vi) *其他终止事件*。若附件或任何确认书规定" 其他终止事件" 适用时，发生该些事件(在此情况下，受影响方或各受影响方将视附件或该确认书中有关其他终止事件的规定而定)。

(c) ***Hierarchy of Events.***

(c) *事件的等级*。

(i) An event or circumstance that constitutes or gives rise to an Illegality or a Force Majeure Event will not, for so long as that is the case, also constitute or give rise to an Event of Default under Section 5(a)(i), 5(a)(ii)(1) or 5(a)(iii)(1) insofar as such event or circumstance relates to the failure to make any payment or delivery or a failure to comply with any other material provision of this Agreement or a Credit Support Document, as the case may be.

(i) 任何构成或导致非法或不可抗力事件的事件或情况，如在其存续期间与未能付款或未能交付或未遵守本协议或信用支持文件(视情况而定)的任何其他重大规定有关，则将不构成或导致第5(a)(i)、第5(a)(ii)(1)或第5(a)(iii)(1)条下的违约事件。

(ii) Except in circumstances contemplated by clause (i) above, if an event or circumstance which would otherwise constitute or give rise to an Illegality or a Force Majeure Event also constitutes an Event of Default or any other Termination Event, it will be treated as an Event of Default or such other Termination Event, as the case may be, and will not constitute or give rise to an Illegality or a Force Majeure Event.

(ii) 除上述(i)款规定的情况外，若任何可构成或导致非法或不可抗力事件的事件或情况，亦构成违约事件或任何其他终止事件，该事件或情况将被视作违约事件或其他终止事件(视情况而定)，而不构成或导致非法或不可抗力事件。

(iii) If an event or circumstance which would otherwise constitute or give rise to a Force Majeure Event also constitutes an Illegality, it will be treated as an Illegality, except as described in clause (ii) above, and not a Force Majeure Event.

(iii) 若任何可构成或导致不可抗力事件的事件或情况亦构成非法，该事件或情况将被视作非法(上述第(ii)款规定的情况除外)，而非不可抗力事件。

(d) ***Deferral of Payments and Deliveries During Waiting Period.*** If an Illegality or a Force Majeure Event has occurred and is continuing with respect to a Transaction, each payment or delivery which would otherwise be required to be made under that Transaction will be deferred to, and will not be due until:—

(d) *等待期间的迟延付款及交付*。如就任何交易已发生非法或不可抗力事件且非法或不可抗力处于持续状态，该交易下须履行的每项付款或交付迟延至以下时间方才到期：—

(i) the first Local Business Day or, in the case of a delivery, the first Local Delivery Day (or the first day that would have been a Local Business Day or Local Delivery Day, as appropriate, but for the occurrence of the event or circumstance constituting or giving rise to that Illegality or Force Majeure Event) following the end of any applicable Waiting Period in respect of that Illegality or Force Majeure Event, as the case may be; or

(i) 有关非法或不可抗力事件(视情况而定)适用的等待期之后的首个当地营业日，在交付的情况下为首个当地交付日(或若无非法或不可抗力事件(视情况而定)的发生本应为当地营业日或当地交付日(视情况而定)的首日)；或

(ii) if earlier, the date on which the event or circumstance constituting or giving rise to that Illegality

(ii) 如更早的话，构成或导致非法或不可抗力事件的事件或情况终止之日，或如该日不是当地营业日或就交付而言并非

or Force Majeure Event ceases to exist or, if such date is not a Local Business Day or, in the case of a delivery, a Local Delivery Day, the first following day that is a Local Business Day or Local Delivery Day, as appropriate.

当地交付日，则下一个构成当地营业日或当地交付日(视情况而定)之日。

(e) ***Inability of Head or Home Office to Perform Obligations of Branch.*** If (i) an Illegality or a Force Majeure Event occurs under Section 5(b)(i)(1) or 5(b)(ii)(1) and the relevant Office is not the Affected Party's head or home office, (ii) Section 10(a) applies, (iii) the other party seeks performance of the relevant obligation or compliance with the relevant provision by the Affected Party's head or home office and (iv) the Affected Party's head or home office fails so to perform or comply due to the occurrence of an event or circumstance which would, if that head or home office were the Office through which the Affected Party makes and receives payments and deliveries with respect to the relevant Transaction, constitute or give rise to an Illegality or a Force Majeure Event, and such failure would otherwise constitute an Event of Default under Section 5(a)(i) or 5(a)(iii)(1) with respect to such party, then, for so long as the relevant event or circumstance continues to exist with respect to both the Office referred to in Section 5(b)(i)(1) or 5(b)(ii)(1), as the case may be, and the Affected Party's head or home office, such failure will not constitute an Event of Default under Section 5(a)(i) or 5(a)(iii)(1).

(e) ***总部或总办事处不能履行分支的义务。***如(i)发生第5(b)(i)(1)或第5(b)(ii)(1)条下的任何非法或不可抗力事件，而有关办事处并非受影响方的总部或总办事处，(ii)第10(a)条适用，(iii)另一方要求受影响方的总部或总办事处履行有关义务或遵守有关规定，并且(iv)某一事件或情况导致受影响方的总部或总办事处未能按要求履约，而若该受影响方通过该总部或总办事处就有关交易进行付款和交付，该事件会构成或导致非法或不可抗力事件，而且该未能履约的行为可构成该方第5(a)(i)或第5(a)(iii)(1)条下的违约事件，则在第5(b)(i)(1)或5(b)(ii)(1)条(视情况而定)所述办事处及受影响方的总部或总办事处皆持续存在有关事件或情况的整个期间，该未能履约的行为不构成第5(a)(i)或第5(a)(iii)(1)条下的违约事件。

6. Early Termination; Close-Out Netting

6. 提前终止；终止交易时的净额结算

(a) ***Right to Terminate Following Event of Default.*** If at any time an Event of Default with respect to a party (the "Defaulting Party") has occurred and is then continuing, the other party (the "Non-defaulting Party") may, by not more than 20 days notice to the Defaulting Party specifying the relevant Event of Default, designate a day not earlier than the day such notice is effective as an Early Termination Date in respect of all outstanding Transactions. If, however, "Automatic Early Termination" is specified in the Schedule as applying to a party, then an Early Termination Date in respect of all outstanding Transactions will occur immediately upon the occurrence with respect to such party of an Event of Default specified in Section 5(a)(vii)(1), (3), (5), (6) or, to the extent analogous thereto, (8), and as of the time immediately preceding the institution of the relevant proceeding or the presentation of the relevant petition upon the occurrence with respect to such party of an Event of Default specified in Section 5(a)(vii)(4) or, to the extent analogous thereto, (8).

(a) ***违约事件发生后的终止权利。***在任何时侯发生有关一方(以下简称"违约方")的违约事件并持续存在，另一方(以下简称"守约方")可以用通知期不超过二十天的通知形式通知违约方有关违约事件，并将不早於通知生效的日期指定为有关所有未完成的交易的提前终止日。但是，如果附件上规定"自动提前终止"适用於一方，则该方发生第5(a)(vii)(1)、(3)、(5)、(6)条规定，或第5(a)(vii)(8)条规定的类似的违约事件之时，或在该方发生第5(a)(vii)(4)条所规定或第5(a)(vii)(8)条规定的类似的违约事件后提出有关诉讼或请求状之前，有关所有未完成交易的提前终止日立即生效。

(b) ***Right to Terminate Following Termination Event.***

(b) ***终止事件后的终止权利。***

(i) ***Notice.*** If a Termination Event other than a Force Majeure Event occurs, an Affected Party will, promptly upon becoming aware of it, notify the other party, specifying the nature of that Termination Event and each Affected Transaction, and will also give the other party such other information about that Termination Event as the other party may reasonably require. If a Force Majeure Event occurs, each party will, promptly upon becoming aware of it, use all reasonable efforts to notify the other party, specifying the nature of that Force Majeure Event, and will also give the other party such other information about that Force Majeure Event as the other party may reasonably require.

(i) ***通知。***若发生不可抗力事件以外的终止事件，受影响方应在获悉该事件後立即通知另一方，说明该终止事件的性质及每项受影响交易，并按另一方合理的要求把有关终止事件的其他资料通知另一方。如发生不可抗力事件，每一方应在获悉该事件后立即尽所有合理的努力通知另一方，说明该不可抗力事件的性质，并按另一方合理的要求把有关不可抗力事件的其他资料通知另一方。

(ii) ***Transfer to Avoid Termination Event.*** If a Tax Event occurs and there is only one Affected Party, or if a Tax Event Upon Merger occurs and the Burdened Party is the Affected Party, the Affected Party will, as a condition to its right to designate an Early Termination Date under Section 6(b)(iv), use all reasonable efforts (which will not require such party to incur a loss, other than immaterial, incidental expenses) to transfer within 20 days after it gives notice under Section 6(b)(i) all its rights and obligations under this Agreement in respect of the Affected Transactions to another of its Offices or Affiliates so that such Termination Event ceases to exist.

(ii) ***为避免终止事件而转让***。若发生税务事件，而只有一个受影响方，或发生因合并造成的税务事件而有负担方是受影响方，受影响方作为拥有第6(b)(iv)条下指定提前终止日的权利之条件，应尽所有合理的努力(但该努力不应使该方承受损失，但不重要及附带开支以外的损失除外)在按第6(b)(i)条发出通知後的二十天内将其在本协议下就该受影响交易的所有权利和义务转让给其他办事处或关联企业，以避免有关终止事件。

If the Affected Party is not able to make such a transfer it will give notice to the other party to that effect within such 20 day period, whereupon the other party may effect such a transfer within 30 days after the notice is given under Section 6(b)(i).

若受影响方未能作出以上转让，应在二十天内通知另一方，而另一方可於收到第6(b)(i)条下的通知後三十天内进行上述转让。

Any such transfer by a party under this Section 6(b)(ii) will be subject to and conditional upon the prior written consent of the other party, which consent will not be withheld if such other party's policies in effect at such time would permit it to enter into transactions with the transferee on the terms proposed.

一方按第6(b)(ii)条所作的任何转让均须取得另一方的事前书面同意，如另一方届时生效的政策容许其与受让方按提出的条件进行交易时，另一方不得拒绝同意该转让。

(iii) ***Two Affected Parties.*** If a Tax Event occurs and there are two Affected Parties, each party will use all reasonable efforts to reach agreement within 30 days after notice of such occurrence is given under Section 6(b)(i) to avoid that Termination Event.

(iii) ***两个受影响方***。若发生税务事件而有两个受影响方时，各方应在第6(b)(i)条下有关事件发生的通知作出后三十天内尽一切合理的努力达成协议，以避免该终止事件的发生。

(iv) ***Right to Terminate.***

(iv) ***终止的权利***。

(1) If:—

(1) 如果：－

(A) a transfer under Section 6(b)(ii) or an agreement under Section 6(b)(iii), as the case may be, has not been effected with respect to all Affected Transactions within 30 days after an Affected Party gives notice under Section 6(b)(i); or

(A) 受影响方在发出第6(b)(i)条下的通知后三十天内，未能就所有受影响交易进行第6(b)(ii)条下的转让或达成第6(b)(iii)条下的协议(视情况而定)；或

(B) a Credit Event Upon Merger or an Additional Termination Event occurs, or a Tax Event Upon Merger occurs and the Burdened Party is not the Affected Party,

(B) 发生因合并造成的信用事件或其他终止事件，或发生因合并造成的税务事件而有负担方并非受影响方，

the Burdened Party in the case of a Tax Event Upon Merger, any Affected Party in the case of a Tax Event or an Additional Termination Event if there are two Affected Parties, or the Non-affected Party in the case of a Credit Event Upon Merger or an Additional Termination Event if there is only one Affected Party may, if the relevant Termination Event is then continuing, by not more than 20 days notice to the other party, designate a day not earlier than the day such notice is effective as an Early Termination Date in respect of all Affected Transactions.

发生因合并造成的税务事件情况下的有负担方，发生税务事件或其他终止事件并且有两个受影响方情况下的任何受影响方，或发生因合并造成的信用事件或其他终止事件并且仅有一个受影响方的情况下的不受影响方，可在有关终止事件正在持续的情况下，用通知期不超过二十天的通知形式通知另一方，指定该通知生效后的一日作为所有受影响交易的提前终止日。

(2) If at any time an Illegality or a Force Majeure Event has occurred and is then continuing and any applicable Waiting Period has expired:—

(A) Subject to clause (B) below, either party may, by not more than 20 days notice to the other party, designate (I) a day not earlier than the day on which such notice becomes effective as an Early Termination Date in respect of all Affected Transactions or (II) by specifying in that notice the Affected Transactions in respect of which it is designating the relevant day as an Early Termination Date, a day not earlier than two Local Business Days following the day on which such notice becomes effective as an Early Termination Date in respect of less than all Affected Transactions. Upon receipt of a notice designating an Early Termination Date in respect of less than all Affected Transactions, the other party may, by notice to the designating party, if such notice is effective on or before the day so designated, designate that same day as an Early Termination Date in respect of any or all other Affected Transactions.

(B) An Affected Party (if the Illegality or Force Majeure Event relates to performance by such party or any Credit Support Provider of such party of an obligation to make any payment or delivery under, or to compliance with any other material provision of, the relevant Credit Support Document) will only have the right to designate an Early Termination Date under Section 6(b)(iv)(2)(A) as a result of an Illegality under Section 5(b)(i)(2) or a Force Majeure Event under Section 5(b)(ii)(2) following the prior designation by the other party of an Early Termination Date, pursuant to Section 6(b)(iv)(2)(A), in respect of less than all Affected Transactions.

(2) 如任何时候非法和不可抗力事件发生并持续存在，而适用的等待期已经届满：-

(A) 除下述(B)款另有规定外，任何一方可以用通知期不超过二十天的通知形式通知另一方，(I)就所有受影响交易指定该通知生效日之後的一天作为提前终止日，或(II)在通知中说明其指定提前终止日的受影响交易，就部分受影响交易指定该通知生效日两个当地营业日之後的一天作为提前终止日。另一方在收到仅就部分受影响交易指定提前终止日的通知后可以通知指定方(该通知须于指定的提前终止日或之前生效)就任何或所有其他受影响交易指定同日为提前终止日。

(B) 任何受影响方(如非法或不可抗力事件与该方或该方的任何信用支持提供者履行有关信用支持文件下支付或交付的义务有关，或与遵守有关信用支持文件任何其他重要条款有关)仅在另一方根据第6(b)(iv)(2)(A)条就部分受影响交易指定提前终止日之后，方有权按第6(b)(iv)(2)(A)条就第5(b)(i)(2)条下的非法或第5(b)(ii)(2)条下的不可抗力事件造成的结果指定提前终止日。

(c) ***Effect of Designation.***

(i) If notice designating an Early Termination Date is given under Section 6(a) or 6(b), the Early Termination Date will occur on the date so designated, whether or not the relevant Event of Default or Termination Event is then continuing.

(ii) Upon the occurrence or effective designation of an Early Termination Date, no further payments or deliveries under Section 2(a)(i) or 9(h)(i) in respect of the Terminated Transactions will be required to be made, but without prejudice to the other provisions of this Agreement. The amount, if any, payable in respect of an Early Termination Date will be determined pursuant to Sections 6(e) and 9(h)(ii).

(c) *指定的效力。*

(i) 如果按第6(a)或6(b)条发出通知指定提前终止日，则不论有关的违约事件或终止事件仍否持续，该提前终止日将於指定的日期生效。

(ii) 当提前终止日来临或被有效指定时，无须再就已终止交易进行第2(a)(i)或第9(h)(i)条下的付款或交付，但本协议的其它规定将不受影响。有关提前终止日应支付的款项(如有的话)将按第6(e)和第9(h)(ii)条确定。

(d) ***Calculations; Payment Date.***

(i) ***Statement.*** On or as soon as reasonably practicable following the occurrence of an Early Termination Date,

(d) *计算；付款日。*

(i) *报告。*在提前终止日或之后合理可行的最短时间内，各方应按第6(e)条的规定计算其帐目，并向另一方提交一份报

each party will make the calculations on its part, if any, contemplated by Section 6(e) and will provide to the other party a statement (l) showing, in reasonable detail, such calculations (including any quotations, market data or information from internal sources used in making such calculations), (2) specifying (except where there are two Affected Parties) any Early Termination Amount payable and (3) giving details of the relevant account to which any amount payable to it is to be paid. In the absence of written confirmation from the source of a quotation or market data obtained in determining a Close-out Amount, the records of the party obtaining such quotation or market data will be conclusive evidence of the existence and accuracy of such quotation or market data.

告：(1)合理详细地说明此等计算(包括计算中使用的任何报价、市场数据或内部信息)，(2)说明应付的任何提前终止款项(有两个受影响方的情况除外)，以及(3)详细说明其应收款项应存入的有关帐户。若在确定结算款项的过程中，就一项报价或市场数据无法从其来源得到书面确认，则获取该报价或市场数据一方的记录将成为该报价或市场数据存在和准确性的结论性证明。

(ii) ***Payment Date.*** An Early Termination Amount due in respect of any Early Termination Date will, together with any amount of interest payable pursuant to Section 9(h)(ii)(2), be payable (1) on the day on which notice of the amount payable is effective in the case of an Early Termination Date which is designated or occurs as a result of an Event of Default and (2) on the day which is two Local Business Days after the day on which notice of the amount payable is effective (or, if there are two Affected Parties, after the day on which the statement provided pursuant to clause (i) above by the second party to provide such a statement is effective) in the case of an Early Termination Date which is designated as a result of a Termination Event.

(ii) ***付款日。***就任何提前终止日所计算的提前终止款项将连同根据第9(h)(ii)(2)条应付的任何利息款项(1)当因违约事件指定提前终止日时，在付款通知书生效当日支付，及(2)当因终止事件指定提前终止日时，在付款通知书生效日后的第二个当地营业日支付(或如有两个受影响方，在第二方根据第(i)款所提供的报告生效日之后支付)。

(e) ***Payments on Early Termination.*** If an Early Termination Date occurs, the amount, if any, payable in respect of that Early Termination Date (the "Early Termination Amount") will be determined pursuant to this Section 6(e) and will be subject to Section 6(f).

(e) ***提前终止的付款。***如出现提前终止日，就提前终止日应缴付的款项(如有的话)(以下简称"提前终止款项")将根据本第6(e)条确定并须遵守第6(f)条的规定。

(i) ***Events of Default.*** If the Early Termination Date results from an Event of Default, the Early Termination Amount will be an amount equal to (1) the sum of (A) the Termination Currency Equivalent of the Close-out Amount or Close-out Amounts (whether positive or negative) determined by the Non-defaulting Party for each Terminated Transaction or group of Terminated Transactions, as the case may be, and (B) the Termination Currency Equivalent of the Unpaid Amounts owing to the Non-defaulting Party less (2) the Termination Currency Equivalent of the Unpaid Amounts owing to the Defaulting Party. If the Early Termination Amount is a positive number, the Defaulting Party will pay it to the Non-defaulting Party; if it is a negative number, the Non-defaulting Party will pay the absolute value of the Early Termination Amount to the Defaulting Party.

(i) ***违约事件。***如提前终止日因违约事件产生，提前终止款项等于(1)以下(A)项与(B)项之和：(A)为守约方就每一项终止交易或一组终止交易(视情况而定)决定的结算款项(无论是正数还是负数)的终止货币等值额；(B)为欠守约方的未付款项终止货币等值额，减去(2)欠违约方的未付款项的终止货币等值额。如该提前终止款项为正数，应由违约方向守约方支付；如该提前终止款项为负数，守约方应向违约方支付该金额的绝对值。

(ii) ***Termination Events.*** If the Early Termination Date results from a Termination Event:—

(ii) ***终止事件。***如提前终止日因终止事件产生：－

(1) *One Affected Party.* Subject to clause (3) below, if there is one Affected Party, the Early Termination Amount will be determined in accordance with Section 6(e)(i), except that references to the Defaulting Party and to the Non-defaulting Party will be deemed to be references to the Affected Party and to the Non-affected Party,

(1) *一个受影响方。*除下述第(3)款另有规定外，如只有一个受影响方，提前终止款项应按第6(e)(i)条决定，但有关违约方和守约方的指称将分别被视为对受影响方和非受影响方的指称。

respectively.

(2) *Two Affected Parties*. Subject to clause (3) below, if there are two Affected Parties, each party will determine an amount equal to the Termination Currency Equivalent of the sum of the Close-out Amount or Close-out Amounts (whether positive or negative) for each Terminated Transaction or group of Terminated Transactions, as the case may be, and the Early Termination Amount will be an amount equal to (A) the sum of (I) one-half of the difference between the higher amount so determined (by party "X") and the lower amount so determined (by party "Y") and (II) the Termination Currency Equivalent of the Unpaid Amounts owing to X less (B) the Termination Currency Equivalent of the Unpaid Amounts owing to Y. If the Early Termination Amount is a positive number, Y will pay it to X; if it is a negative number, X will pay the absolute value of the Early Termination Amount to Y.

(2) *两个受影响方*。除下述第(3)款另有规定外，如有两个受影响方，各方将就每一项终止交易或一组终止交易(视情况而定)决定一笔相等于结算款项(无论是正数还是负数)的终止货币等值额，而提前终止款项将等于(A)以下(I)项与(II)项之和：(I)为(由"X"方)确定的较高的金额与(由"Y"方)确定的较低金额的差额的一半；(II)为欠X方的未付款项的终止货币等值额，减去(B)欠Y方的未付款项的终止货币等值额。如提前终止款项为正数，Y方应向X方支付；如提前终止款项为负数，X方应向Y方支付该金额的绝对值。

(3) *Mid-Market Events*. If that Termination Event is an Illegality or a Force Majeure Event, then the Early Termination Amount will be determined in accordance with clause (1) or (2) above, as appropriate, except that, for the purpose of determining a Close-out Amount or Close-out Amounts, the Determining Party will:—

(3) *市场中间价事件*。如该终止事件是非法或不可抗力事件，则提前终止款项将根据上述第(1)和第(2)款(视情况而定)决定，但决定方在确定结算款项时应当：–

(A) if obtaining quotations from one or more third parties (or from any of the Determining Party's Affiliates), ask each third party or Affiliate (I) not to take account of the current creditworthiness of the Determining Party or any existing Credit Support Document and (II) to provide mid-market quotations; and

(A) 若从一个或以上的第三方(或从决定方的任何关联公司)获取报价，则要求第三方或关联公司：(I)不考虑决定方目前的资信情况或任何现存的信用支持文件，及(II)提供中间市场报价；及

(B) in any other case, use mid-market values without regard to the creditworthiness of the Determining Party.

(B) 在其他情况下，使用市场中间价，并且不须考虑决定方的资信情况。

(iii) ***Adjustment for Bankruptcy.*** In circumstances where an Early Termination Date occurs because Automatic Early Termination applies in respect of a party, the Early Termination Amount will be subject to such adjustments as are appropriate and permitted by applicable law to reflect any payments or deliveries made by one party to the other under this Agreement (and retained by such other party) during the period from the relevant Early Termination Date to the date for payment determined under Section 6(d)(ii).

(iii) ***破产调整***。如提前终止日因自动提前终止适用於一方而产生，提前终止款项将根据适用法律允许作出适当的调整，以反映在有关提前终止日起至第6(d)(ii)条决定的付款日止一段期间内，一方在协议项下向另一方支付(并为该方保留的)的任何款项或其它支付。

(iv) ***Adjustment for Illegality or Force Majeure Event.*** The failure by a party or any Credit Support Provider of such party to pay, when due, any Early Termination Amount will not constitute an Event of Default under Section 5(a)(i) or 5(a)(iii)(1) if such failure is due to the occurrence of an event or circumstance which would, if it occurred with respect to payment, delivery or compliance related to a Transaction, constitute or give rise to an Illegality or a Force Majeure Event. Such amount will (1) accrue interest and otherwise be treated as an Unpaid Amount owing to the other party if subsequently an Early

(iv) ***就非法或不可抗力事件作出的调整。***一方或该方的信用支持提供者未能於到期日支付任何提前终止款项，并且这一未能按期付款的事件或情况如发生于有关交易下的付款、交付或遵守协议的义务时将会构成或导致非法或不可抗力事件，这一行为将不构成第5(a)(i)、或5(iii)(1)条下的违约事件。该款项将：(1)累计利息，如随後由於有关违约事件、因合并造成的信用事件或其他终止事件使所有未完成交易变成受影响交易而导致提前终止日的到来，应被当作欠另一方的未付款项；并(2)根据第9(h)(ii)(2)条计算利息。

Termination Date results from an Event of Default, a Credit Event Upon Merger or an Additional Termination Event in respect of which all outstanding Transactions are Affected Transactions and (2) otherwise accrue interest in accordance with Section 9(h)(ii)(2).

(v) ***Pre-Estimate.*** The parties agree that an amount recoverable under this Section 6(e) is a reasonable pre-estimate of loss and not a penalty. Such amount is payable for the loss of bargain and the loss of protection against future risks, and, except as otherwise provided in this Agreement, neither party will be entitled to recover any additional damages as a consequence of the termination of the Terminated Transactions.

(v) *预先估计*。双方同意，在按第6(e)条支付的款项是对亏损的合理预先估计而非罚款，支付该数额的目的是为了补偿交易的未能实现和预防风险安排的丧失。除非本协议另有规定，任何一方均无权因终止交易的终止而收取任何额外赔偿。

(f) ***Set-Off.*** Any Early Termination Amount payable to one party (the "Payee") by the other party (the "Payer"), in circumstances where there is a Defaulting Party or where there is one Affected Party in the case where either a Credit Event Upon Merger has occurred or any other Termination Event in respect of which all outstanding Transactions are Affected Transactions has occurred, will, at the option of the Non-defaulting Party or the Non-affected Party, as the case may be ("X") (and without prior notice to the Defaulting Party or the Affected Party, as the case may be), be reduced by its set-off against any other amounts ("Other Amounts") payable by the Payee to the Payer (whether or not arising under this Agreement, matured or contingent and irrespective of the currency, place of payment or place of booking of the obligation). To the extent that any Other Amounts are so set off, those Other Amounts will be discharged promptly and in all respects. X will give notice to the other party of any set-off effected under this Section 6(f).

(f) *抵销*。在出现违约方或发生因合并造成的信用事件而产生一个受影响方的情况下，或发生任何其他终止事件而所有未完成交易变成受影响交易时，一方(以下简称"付款人")应向另一方(以下简称"收款人")支付的任何提前终止款项将按守约方或不受影响方(视情况而定，以下简称"X"方)的选择(并在无需事先通知违约方或受影响方(视情况而定)的情况)下用於扣减抵销收款人应向付款人支付的任何其他款项(以下简称"其他款项")(无论其是否是本协议下产生的、是到期的还是或有的，亦无论该债务的货种、支付地点或债务入册的地点如何)。在任何其他款项以此方式抵销时，此等其他款项将被立即全面解除。X方将通知另一方根据本第6(f)条实施的任何抵销。

For this purpose, either the Early Termination Amount or the Other Amounts (or the relevant portion of such amounts) may be converted by X into the currency in which the other is denominated at the rate of exchange at which such party would be able, in good faith and using commercially reasonable procedures, to purchase the relevant amount of such currency.

为此目的，X方可以使用按诚信原则以合理的商业程序购得相关数额该种货币时的汇率将提前终止款项或其他款项(或这些款项的相关部分)兑换成另一款项票面所使用的货币。

If an obligation is unascertained, X may in good faith estimate that obligation and set off in respect of the estimate, subject to the relevant party accounting to the other when the obligation is ascertained.

如果一项债务尚未确定，X方可以按诚信原则预估该债务并就该预估数目进行抵销，只要该债务确定后由有关交易方向交易对方交帐即可。

Nothing in this Section 6(f) will be effective to create a charge or other security interest. This Section 6(f) will be without prejudice and in addition to any right of set-off, offset, combination of accounts, lien, right of retention or withholding or similar right or requirement to which any party is at any time otherwise entitled or subject (whether by operation of law, contract or otherwise).

本第6(f)条的规定不具有设立抵押或其他担保权益的效力。本第6(f)条不影响，并且额外存在于任何一方可能随时享有或受到的(法律、合同或其他规定下的)任何抵销权、充抵权、合并帐户权、留置权、保留权或预扣或类似的权利或要求。

7. Transfer

7. 转让

Subject to Section 6(b)(ii) and to the extent permitted by applicable law, neither this Agreement nor any interest or obligation in or under this Agreement may be transferred (whether by way of security or otherwise) by either party without the prior written consent of the other party, except that:—

受第6(b)(ii)条的限制并在适用法律允许的范围内，未经另一方事先书面同意，本协议任何一方不可转让本协议或本协议项下任何权益或义务(不论以担保或其它方式)，下列情况除外：－

(a) a party may make such a transfer of this Agreement pursuant to a consolidation or amalgamation with, or merger with or into, or transfer of all or substantially all its assets to, another entity (but without prejudice to any other right or remedy under this Agreement); and

(a) 一方可通过与另一实体联合或合并，兼并另一实体或并入另一实体，或向另一实体转让其所有或大部份资产以转让本协议(但不影响本协议下任何其它权利或补救措施)；及

(b) a party may make such a transfer of all or any part of its interest in any Early Termination Amount payable to it by a Defaulting Party, together with any amounts payable on or with respect to that interest and any other rights associated with that interest pursuant to Sections 8, 9(h) and 11.

(b) 一方可转让违约方应向其支付的任何提前终止款项的全部或部分的权益，以及其根据第8、第9(h)和第11条就上述款项享有的利息及任何其他权利。

Any purported transfer that is not in compliance with this Section 7 will be void.

与第7条不符的任何转让均为无效。

8. Contractual Currency

8. 合同货币

(a) ***Payment in the Contractual Currency.*** Each payment under this Agreement will be made in the relevant currency specified in this Agreement for that payment (the "Contractual Currency"). To the extent permitted by applicable law, any obligation to make payments under this Agreement in the Contractual Currency will not be discharged or satisfied by any tender in any currency other than the Contractual Currency, except to the extent such tender results in the actual receipt by the party to which payment is owed, acting in good faith and using commercially reasonable procedures in converting the currency so tendered into the Contractual Currency, of the full amount in the Contractual Currency of all amounts payable in respect of this Agreement. If for any reason the amount in the Contractual Currency so received falls short of the amount in the Contractual Currency payable in respect of this Agreement, the party required to make the payment will, to the extent permitted by applicable law, immediately pay such additional amount in the Contractual Currency as may be necessary to compensate for the shortfall. If for any reason the amount in the Contractual Currency so received exceeds the amount in the Contractual Currency payable in respect of this Agreement, the party receiving the payment will refund promptly the amount of such excess.

(a) *以合同货币进行的支付*。本协议项下各款项均以本协议规定的有关货币(以下简称"合同货币")支付。在适用法律许可的范围内，本协议项下以合同货币付款的任何义务如果通过使用合同货币以外的其它货币偿付，不被视作已清偿或满足，但是，若该等偿付款项被应收款方按诚信原则以合理的商业程序把本协议项下应付的所有数额全数兑换为合同货币并实际收讫，则不受此限。如因任何原因，所收合同货币少於本协议项下应付的合同货币额，按要求付款一方应在适用法律许可的范围内，立即以合同货币支付该等额外数额以补足缺额。如因任何原因，所收合同货币超过本协议项下应付的合同货币额，收款方应立即把该等超出额退回。

(b) ***Judgments.*** To the extent permitted by applicable law, if any judgment or order expressed in a currency other than the Contractual Currency is rendered (i) for the payment of any amount owing in respect of this Agreement, (ii) for the payment of any amount relating to any early termination in respect of this Agreement or (iii) in respect of a judgment or order of another court for the payment of any amount described in clause (i) or (ii) above, the party seeking recovery, after recovery in full of the aggregate amount to which such party is entitled pursuant to the judgment or order, will be entitled to receive immediately from the other party the amount of any shortfall of the Contractual Currency received by such party as a consequence of sums paid in such other currency and will refund promptly to the other party any excess of the Contractual Currency received by such party as a consequence of sums paid in such other currency if such shortfall or such excess arises or results from any variation between the rate of exchange at which the Contractual Currency is converted into the currency of the judgment or order for the purpose of such judgment or order and the rate of exchange at which such party is able, acting in good faith and using commercially reasonable

(b) *判决*。在适用法律许可的范围内，如任何判决或命令中明示以合同货币以外的货币支付：(i)本协议项下所欠任何款项；(ii)有关本协议任何提前终止的任何款项或(iii)另一法院作出的有关支付上述第(i)或第(ii)款所载款项的判决或命令，则请求补偿的一方在收取其根据判决或命令有权获得的总金额後，有权立即从另一方获得该方因以其它货币付款而少收的合同货币，或立即向另一方退回因以其它货币付款而多收的合同货币，如果该缺额或超出是因合同货币为该判决或命令的目的兑换为判决或命令中的货币时的汇率，与该方按诚信原则以合理的商业程序在用实际收到的判决或命令中的货币款项购买合同货币时能够实际获得的汇率不同而引致或产生的。

procedures in converting the currency received into the Contractual Currency, to purchase the Contractual Currency with the amount of the currency of the judgment or order actually received by such party.

(c) ***Separate Indemnities.*** To the extent permitted by applicable law, the indemnities in this Section 8 constitute separate and independent obligations from the other obligations in this Agreement, will be enforceable as separate and independent causes of action, will apply notwithstanding any indulgence granted by the party to which any payment is owed and will not be affected by judgment being obtained or claim or proof being made for any other sums payable in respect of this Agreement.

(c) *独立赔偿。*在适用法律许可的范围内，本第8条的赔偿权构成分别和独立的义务，有别於本协议项下其它义务，并将作为分别和独立的案由而执行，无论应收款一方是否授予任何宽容均得到适用，并不受就本协议下应付的任何其他款项而获得的判决或作出的要求或提供的证明所影响。

(d) ***Evidence of Loss.*** For the purpose of this Section 8, it will be sufficient for a party to demonstrate that it would have suffered a loss had an actual exchange or purchase been made.

(d) *亏损的证明。*为本第8条的目的，如一方可证明若实际发生兑换或购买，该方将会蒙受损失，则该方视作已满足对亏损的证明责任。

9. Miscellaneous

9. 其它规定

(a) ***Entire Agreement.*** This Agreement constitutes the entire agreement and understanding of the parties with respect to its subject matter. Each of the parties acknowledges that in entering into this Agreement it has not relied on any oral or written representation, warranty or other assurance (except as provided for or referred to in this Agreement) and waives all rights and remedies which might otherwise be available to it in respect thereof, except that nothing in this Agreement will limit or exclude any liability of a party for fraud.

(a) *完整协议。*本协议构成双方就本协议下事宜的全部协议和谅解。各方承认其在签订本协议时并无依赖任何口头或书面的陈述、担保或其他保证(本协议中规定或提及的除外)，并就以上所述放弃原本可以享有的一切权利和补救，但本协议的内容不得限制或排除一方的任何欺诈责任。

(b) ***Amendments.*** An amendment, modification or waiver in respect of this Agreement will only be effective if in writing (including a writing evidenced by a facsimile transmission) and executed by each of the parties or confirmed by an exchange of telexes or by an exchange of electronic messages on an electronic messaging system.

(b) *修订。*除非以书面形式(包括有传真证明的书面文件)作出并经双方签署，或经交换电传或通过电子信息系统交换的电子信息所确认，任何与本协议有关的修订、修改或放弃均为无效。

(c) ***Survival of Obligations.*** Without prejudice to Sections 2(a)(iii) and 6(c)(ii), the obligations of the parties under this Agreement will survive the termination of any Transaction.

(c) *义务的续存。*在不影响第2(a)(iii)条和第6(c)(ii)条的情况下，双方在本协议下的义务在任何交易终止後仍然有效。

(d) ***Remedies Cumulative.*** Except as provided in this Agreement, the rights, powers, remedies and privileges provided in this Agreement are cumulative and not exclusive of any rights, powers, remedies and privileges provided by law.

(d) *累积补救。*除本协议另有规定外，本协议规定的权利、权力、补救及特权具累积性，并不排除法律规定的任何权利、权力、补救及特权。

(e) ***Counterparts and Confirmations.***

(e) *复本和确认。*

(i) This Agreement (and each amendment, modification and waiver in respect of it) may be executed and delivered in counterparts (including by facsimile transmission and by electronic messaging system), each of which will be deemed an original.

(i) 本协议(及有关本协议的各修订、修改和弃权)可以复本签署和交付(包括以传真及电子信息系统发送的复本)，各复本均被视为正本。

(ii) The parties intend that they are legally bound by the terms of each Transaction from the moment they agree to those terms (whether orally or otherwise). A Confirmation will be entered into as soon as practicable and may be executed and delivered in counterparts (including by facsimile transmission) or be created by an exchange of telexes, by an exchange of electronic

(ii) 双方自其同意各交易的条款起，受各交易条款的法律约束(不论以口头或其它方式作出的)。在实际可行的情况下，应尽早签署交易之确认书，并可签署和交付复本(包括以传真发送的)，或由交换电传或通过电子信息系统交换电子信息或交换电子邮件而建立确认书，上述各种方式均足以证明具有约束力的协议补充文件之存在。双方在该通讯中或通过

messages on an electronic messaging system or by an exchange of e-mails, which in each case will be sufficient for all purposes to evidence a binding supplement to this Agreement. The parties will specify therein or through another effective means that any such counterpart, telex, electronic message or e-mail constitutes a Confirmation.

另一有效途径规定，任何该等复本、电传、电子信息或电子邮件均构成一项确认书。

(f) ***No Waiver of Rights.*** A failure or delay in exercising any right, power or privilege in respect of this Agreement will not be presumed to operate as a waiver, and a single or partial exercise of any right, power or privilege will not be presumed to preclude any subsequent or further exercise, of that right, power or privilege or the exercise of any other right, power or privilege.

(f) ***不放弃权利。***未能或延迟行使与本协议有关的任何权利、权力或特权不被视作弃权，单独或部份行使任何权利、权力或特权不视作放弃对以后或进一步对该权利、权力或特权的行使，或任何其它权利、权力或特权的行使。

(g) ***Headings.*** The headings used in this Agreement are for convenience of reference only and are not to affect the construction of or to be taken into consideration in interpreting this Agreement.

(g) ***标题。***本协议所用标题只为方便参考，并不影响本协议的构成或用作解释本协议。

(h) ***Interest and Compensation.***

(h) ***利息和补偿。***

(i) ***Prior to Early Termination.*** Prior to the occurrence or effective designation of an Early Termination Date in respect of the relevant Transaction:—

(i) ***提前终止之前。***就有关交易出现或有效地指定提前终止日之前：－

(1) *Interest on Defaulted Payments.* If a party defaults in the performance of any payment obligation, it will, to the extent permitted by applicable law and subject to Section 6(c), pay interest (before as well as after judgment) on the overdue amount to the other party on demand in the same currency as the overdue amount, for the period from (and including) the original due date for payment to (but excluding) the date of actual payment (and excluding any period in respect of which interest or compensation in respect of the overdue amount is due pursuant to clause (3)(B) or (C) below), at the Default Rate.

(1) *违约付款的利息。*如一方未能履行付款义务，该方应在适用法律允许范围内并受限于第6(c)条的规定，(於判决之前及之后)在另一方要求时，向另一方就逾期款项按违约利率以与欠款相同的货币支付利息，计息的期间为从原定付款到期日(包括当日)起至实际付款日(不包括当日)为止(但不包括按以下第(3)(B)或第(C)款就逾期款项支付利息或补偿的期间)。

(2) *Compensation for Defaulted Deliveries.* If a party defaults in the performance of any obligation required to be settled by delivery, it will on demand (A) compensate the other party to the extent provided for in the relevant Confirmation or elsewhere in this Agreement and (B) unless otherwise provided in the relevant Confirmation or elsewhere in this Agreement, to the extent permitted by applicable law and subject to Section 6(c), pay to the other party interest (before as well as after judgment) on an amount equal to the fair market value of that which was required to be delivered in the same currency as that amount, for the period from (and including) the originally scheduled date for delivery to (but excluding) the date of actual delivery (and excluding any period in respect of which interest or compensation in respect of that amount is due pursuant to clause (4) below), at the Default Rate. The fair market value of any obligation referred to above will be determined as of the originally scheduled date for delivery, in good faith and using commercially reasonable procedures, by the party that was

(2) *违约交付的补偿。*如一方未能履行任何交付义务，该方应在另一方要求时：(A)须按有关确认书或本协议的其他规定向另一方作出补偿，并且(B)除有关确认书或本协议另有规定外，在适用法律允许范围内并受限于第6(c)条的规定，(於判决之前及之后)向另一方按违约利率就交付义务的公平市值并以与该款项相同的货币支付利息，计息的期间为从原定交付日(包括当日)起至实际交付日(不包括当日)为止(但不包括根据以下第(4)款就过期款项支付利息或补偿的期间)。以上所述的公平市值由有权接收交付的一方从原定交付日起，依据诚信原则以合理的商业程序确定。

entitled to take delivery.

(3) *Interest on Deferred Payments.* If:—

(A) a party does not pay any amount that, but for Section 2(a)(iii), would have been payable, it will, to the extent permitted by applicable law and subject to Section 6(c) and clauses (B) and (C) below, pay interest (before as well as after judgment) on that amount to the other party on demand (after such amount becomes payable) in the same currency as that amount, for the period from (and including) the date the amount would, but for Section 2(a)(iii), have been payable to (but excluding) the date the amount actually becomes payable, at the Applicable Deferral Rate;

(B) a payment is deferred pursuant to Section 5(d), the party which would otherwise have been required to make that payment will, to the extent permitted by applicable law, subject to Section 6(c) and for so long as no Event of Default or Potential Event of Default with respect to that party has occurred and is continuing, pay interest (before as well as after judgment) on the amount of the deferred payment to the other party on demand (after such amount becomes payable) in the same currency as the deferred payment, for the period from (and including) the date the amount would, but for Section 5(d), have been payable to (but excluding) the earlier of the date the payment is no longer deferred pursuant to Section 5(d) and the date during the deferral period upon which an Event of Default or Potential Event of Default with respect to that party occurs, at the Applicable Deferral Rate; or

(C) a party fails to make any payment due to the occurrence of an Illegality or a Force Majeure Event (after giving effect to any deferral period contemplated by clause (B) above), it will, to the extent permitted by applicable law, subject to Section 6(c) and for so long as the event or circumstance giving rise to that Illegality or Force Majeure Event continues and no Event of Default or Potential Event of Default with respect to that party has occurred and is continuing, pay interest (before as well as after judgment) on the overdue amount to the other party on demand in the same currency as the overdue amount, for the period from (and including) the date the party fails to make the payment due to the occurrence of the relevant Illegality or Force Majeure Event (or, if later, the date the payment is no longer deferred pursuant to Section 5(d)) to (but excluding) the earlier of the date the event or circumstance giving rise to that Illegality or Force Majeure Event ceases to exist and the date during the period upon which an Event of Default or Potential Event of Default with respect to that party

(3) *迟延付款的利息。*如：–

(A) 一方不支付若非第2(a)(iii)条的规定则原应支付的任何款项的话，该方应在适用法律允许范围内并受限于第6(c)条和以下第(B)和第(C)款的规定，(於判决之前及之后)在另一方要求时(在该款项应予支付时)以与该款项相同的货币按适用的迟延利率支付利息，计息期间从若非第2(a)(iii)条的规定则原应支付款项之日(包括当日)起，至实际应予支付之日(不包括当日)为止；

(B) 若某项付款按第5(d)条的规定迟延支付的话，本须支付该款项的一方将在适用法律允许范围内并受限于第6(c)条的规定，在该方未发生及持续存在违约事件或潜在的违约事件的整个期间内，(於判决之前及之后)在另一方要求时(在该款项应予支付时)以与该迟延款项相同的货币就迟延款项按适用的迟延利率支付利息，计息的期间为从若非第5(d)条规定则原应支付款项之日(包括当日)起，至该付款根据第5(d)条规定不再迟延交付或该方在迟延期间发生违约事件或潜在的违约事件之日(以较早的日期为准，不包括当日)为止；或

(C) 如一方(於以上第(B)款下的任何迟延期生效后)因发生非法或不可抗力事件不能支付任何款项，该方将在适用法律允许范围内并受限于第6(c)条的规定，在导致非法或不可抗力事件的事件或情况持续存在并且该方没有发生并持续存在的违约事件或潜在的违约事件的整个期间，(於判决之前及之后)在另一方要求时以与该逾期款项相同的货币就欠款按适用的迟延利率支付利息，计息的期间为从该方因非法或不可抗力事件无法付款之日(或更迟的话，该付款根据第5(d)条规定不再推迟支付之日)(包括当日)起，至导致该非法或不可抗力事件的事件或情况不复存在之日或该方在迟延期间发生违约事件或潜在的违约事件之日(以较早的日期为准，不包括当日)为止(但不包括有关逾期款项的利息或补偿根据以上(B)款支付的期间)。

occurs (and excluding any period in respect of which interest or compensation in respect of the overdue amount is due pursuant to clause (B) above), at the Applicable Deferral Rate.

(4) *Compensation for Deferred Deliveries.* If:—

(A) a party does not perform any obligation that, but for Section 2(a)(iii), would have been required to be settled by delivery;

(B) a delivery is deferred pursuant to Section 5(d); or

(C) a party fails to make a delivery due to the occurrence of an Illegality or a Force Majeure Event at a time when any applicable Waiting Period has expired,

the party required (or that would otherwise have been required) to make the delivery will, to the extent permitted by applicable law and subject to Section 6(c), compensate and pay interest to the other party on demand (after, in the case of clauses (A) and (B) above, such delivery is required) if and to the extent provided for in the relevant Confirmation or elsewhere in this Agreement.

(4) *迟延交付的补偿。*如：–

(A) 一方不履行若非第2(a)(iii)条的规定则原应交付的义务；

(B) 交付根据第5(d)条推迟；或

(C) 一方在任何适用的等待期届满之后因非法或不可抗力事件而无法进行交付，

按要求(或按要求本应)进行交付的一方应在适用法律允许范围内并受限于第6(c)条的规定，按有关确认书或本协议其他规定在另一方要求时(在以上(A)条和(B)款的情况下，在该交付被要求之后)向另一方作出补偿并支付利息。

(ii) ***Early Termination.*** Upon the occurrence or effective designation of an Early Termination Date in respect of a Transaction:—

(1) *Unpaid Amounts.* For the purpose of determining an Unpaid Amount in respect of the relevant Transaction, and to the extent permitted by applicable law, interest will accrue on the amount of any payment obligation or the amount equal to the fair market value of any obligation required to be settled by delivery included in such determination in the same currency as that amount, for the period from (and including) the date the relevant obligation was (or would have been but for Section 2(a)(iii) or 5(d)) required to have been performed to (but excluding) the relevant Early Termination Date, at the Applicable Close-out Rate.

(2) *Interest on Early Termination Amounts.* If an Early Termination Amount is due in respect of such Early Termination Date, that amount will, to the extent permitted by applicable law, be paid together with interest (before as well as after judgment) on that amount in the Termination Currency, for the period from (and including) such Early Termination Date to (but excluding) the date the amount is paid, at the Applicable Close-out Rate.

(ii) ***提前终止。***就有关交易出现或有效地指定提前终止日之时：–

(1) *未付款项。*在确定有关交易的未付款项时，在适用法律允许范围内，应就任何应付款项或交付义务的公平市值以该款项相同的货币按适用的结算利率支付利息，计算利息的期间为有关义务须(或若非按第2(a)(iii)条或第5(d)条规定应当)予以履行之日(包括当日)至有关提前终止日(不包括当日)为止。

(2) *提前终止款项的利息。*如提前终止款项于该提前终止日到期，该款项将在适用法律允许范围内，与以终止货币在该提前终止日(包括当日)至该款项实际支付之日(不包括当日)的期间内，按适用的结算利率计算的利息(於判决之前及之后)一起支付。

(iii) ***Interest Calculation.*** Any interest pursuant to this Section 9(h) will be calculated on the basis of daily compounding and the actual number of days elapsed.

(iii) ***利息的计算。***任何根据本第9(h)条支付的利息将按每日复式利率以及实际过期的日数计算。

10. Offices; Multibranch Parties

(a) If Section 10(a) is specified in the Schedule as applying, each party that enters into a Transaction through an Office other than its head or home office represents to and agrees with the other party that, notwithstanding the place of booking or its jurisdiction of incorporation or organisation, its obligations are the same in terms of recourse against it as if it had entered into the Transaction through its head or home office, except that a party will not have recourse to the head or home office of the other party in respect of any payment or delivery deferred pursuant to Section 5(d) for so long as the payment or delivery is so deferred. This representation and agreement will be deemed to be repeated by each party on each date on which the parties enter into a Transaction.

(b) If a party is specified as a Multibranch Party in the Schedule, such party may, subject to clause (c) below, enter into a Transaction through, book a Transaction in and make and receive payments and deliveries with respect to a Transaction through any Office listed in respect of that party in the Schedule (but not any other Office unless otherwise agreed by the parties in writing).

(c) The Office through which a party enters into a Transaction will be the Office specified for that party in the relevant Confirmation or as otherwise agreed by the parties in writing, and, if an Office for that party is not specified in the Confirmation or otherwise agreed by the parties in writing, its head or home office. Unless the parties otherwise agree in writing, the Office through which a party enters into a Transaction will also be the Office in which it books the Transaction and the Office through which it makes and receives payments and deliveries with respect to the Transaction. Subject to Section 6(b)(ii), neither party may change the Office in which it books the Transaction or the Office through which it makes and receives payments or deliveries with respect to a Transaction without the prior written consent of the other party.

11. Expenses

A Defaulting Party will on demand indemnify and hold harmless the other party for and against all reasonable out-of-pocket expenses, including legal fees, execution fees and Stamp Tax, incurred by such other party by reason of the enforcement and protection of its rights under this Agreement or any Credit Support Document to which the Defaulting Party is a party or by reason of the early termination of any Transaction, including, but not limited to, costs of collection.

12. Notices

(a) ***Effectiveness.*** Any notice or other communication in respect of this Agreement may be given in any manner described below (except that a notice or other communication under Section 5 or 6 may not be given by electronic messaging system or e-mail) to the address or number or in accordance with the electronic messaging system or e-mail details provided (see the Schedule) and will be deemed effective as indicated:—

10. 办事处；拥有多个办事处的交易方

(a) 如附件规定第10(a)条适用，则通过办事处而非总部或总办事处达成交易的一方向另一方声明并约定：尽管登记交易的办事处地点与其成立或组成的司法管辖区不同，但就追索权而言该方的义务与通过总部或总办事处达成交易情况下的义务相同，但根据第5(d)条迟延履行的付款或交付则例外，在这种例外情况下，在迟延的整个期间内一方对另一方的总部或总办事不拥有追索权。本声明和约定将被视作在双方达成交易的每一日由每一方重述。

(b) 如附件规定一方为拥有多个办事处的交易方，依下述第(c)款的规定，该方可通过在附件中列明的任何办事处达成交易、登记交易、作出或接受任何交易项下的款项或交付(除非双方另有书面约定则不可使用其他办事处)。

(c) 一方达成交易的办事处即是有关确认书中为该方指定的或由双方另外书面约定的办事处，如该方的办事处未在有关确认书中指定或由双方另外书面约定，则是其总部或总办事处。除双方另有书面约定外，一方达成交易的办事处亦是其登记交易的办事处以及其作出或接收任何交易项下的款项或交付的办事处。除依第6(b)(ii)条的规定外，未经另一方事先书面同意，任何一方不可更改其登记交易的办事处以及其作出或接收任何交易项下的款项或交付的办事处。

11. 开支

违约方将按要求，向另一方赔偿并报销其一切合理的开支，包括该方因执行和保障违约方为一方当事人之本协议或任何信贷支持文件项下的权利所产生的律师费、签署费及印花税，或因任何交易提前终止而产生的费用，包括但不限於催收费用。

12. 通知

(a) *生效*。有关本协议的任何通知或其它通讯可以下列所述任何方式送达下列地址或号码(第5条或第6条项下的通知或其它通讯不得以电子信息或电子邮件送达者除外)或根据提供的电子信息系统或电子邮件送达(详见附件)，通知的生效日期如下：－

(i) if in writing and delivered in person or by courier, on the date it is delivered;

(ii) if sent by telex, on the date the recipient's answerback is received;

(iii) if sent by facsimile transmission, on the date it is received by a responsible employee of the recipient in legible form (it being agreed that the burden of proving receipt will be on the sender and will not be met by a transmission report generated by the sender's facsimile machine);

(iv) if sent by certified or registered mail (airmail, if overseas) or the equivalent (return receipt requested), on the date it is delivered or its delivery is attempted;

(v) if sent by electronic messaging system, on the date it is received; or

(vi) if sent by e-mail, on the date it is delivered,

unless the date of that delivery (or attempted delivery) or that receipt, as applicable, is not a Local Business Day or that communication is delivered (or attempted) or received, as applicable, after the close of business on a Local Business Day, in which case that communication will be deemed given and effective on the first following day that is a Local Business Day.

(b) ***Change of Details.*** Either party may by notice to the other change the address, telex or facsimile number or electronic messaging system or e-mail details at which notices or other communications are to be given to it.

13. Governing Law and Jurisdiction

(a) ***Governing Law.*** This Agreement will be governed by and construed in accordance with the law specified in the Schedule.

(b) ***Jurisdiction.*** With respect to any suit, action or proceedings relating to any dispute arising out of or in connection with this Agreement ("Proceedings"), each party irrevocably:—

(i) submits:—

(1) if this Agreement is expressed to be governed by English law, to (A) the non-exclusive jurisdiction of the English courts if the Proceedings do not involve a Convention Court and (B) the exclusive jurisdiction of the English courts if the Proceedings do involve a Convention Court; or

(2) if this Agreement is expressed to be governed by the laws of the State of New York, to the non-exclusive jurisdiction of the courts of the State of New York and the United States District Court located in the Borough of Manhattan in New York City;

(ii) waives any objection which it may have at any time to the laying of venue of any Proceedings brought in any such court, waives any claim that such

(i) 如用书面方式及通过专人或速递服务交付，则为交付当日；

(ii) 如用电传发送，则为收到收件人的回讯之日；

(iii) 如用传真发送，则为收件方之负责员工收到字迹清楚的传真当日(双方同意，发件方承担收件方是否收到该通知的举证责任，发件方传真机列印的传真报告将不满足该举证责任)；

(iv) 如用挂号邮递(如在外国，则为空邮)或同等的邮递方式发出(需送件收据)，则为邮件交付或试图交付当日；

(v) 如用电子信息传送，则为收到电子信息当日；或

(vi) 如用电子邮件传送，则为交付当日，

如果交付(或试图交付)或收件当日(按情况适用)并非当地营业日或该讯息在当地营业日结束后才交付(或试图交付)或收到(按情况适用)，则该讯息将视作在该日之後的第一个当地营业日送达和生效。

(b) ***更改详情。***双方可向另一方发通知，更改收取通知或其它通讯的地址、电传或传真号码或电子讯息系统或电子邮件。

13. 管辖法律和司法管辖区

(a) ***管辖法律***。本协议受附件规定的法律管辖并按该等法律解释。

(b) ***司法管辖区***。就与本协议中产生的或相关的任何争议有关的任何诉讼、法律行动或程序(以下简称"诉讼")，各方不可撤销地遵守下列规定：-

(i) 接受管辖：-

(1) 如本协议明确规定由英国法律管辖，(A)而该诉讼不涉及公约法院，则接受英国法院的非排他性管辖，及(B)而该诉讼涉及公约法院，则接受英国法院的排他性管辖；或者

(2) 如本协议明确规定由纽约州法律管辖，则接受纽约州法院及位於纽约市曼哈顿区的美国联邦地方法院的非排他性管辖；

(ii) 放弃任何对该等法院选择的诉讼地点提出异议的权利，放弃因该等诉讼在不方便的法院进行而作出请求，并放弃基于该等法院就有关诉讼对该方没有管辖权的反对权，及

Proceedings have been brought in an inconvenient forum and further waives the right to object, with respect to such Proceedings, that such court does not have any jurisdiction over such party; and

弃基于该等法院就有关诉讼对该方没有管辖权的反对权；及

(iii) agrees, to the extent permitted by applicable law, that the bringing of Proceedings in any one or more jurisdictions will not preclude the bringing of Proceedings in any other jurisdiction.

(iii) 同意在适用法律允许范围内在任何一个或多个司法管辖区提起诉讼不排除在任何其它司法管辖区提起诉讼的权利。

(c) ***Service of Process.*** Each party irrevocably appoints the Process Agent, if any, specified opposite its name in the Schedule to receive, for it and on its behalf, service of process in any Proceedings. If for any reason any party's Process Agent is unable to act as such, such party will promptly notify the other party and within 30 days appoint a substitute process agent acceptable to the other party. The parties irrevocably consent to service of process given in the manner provided for notices in Section 12(a)(i), 12(a)(iii) or 12(a)(iv). Nothing in this Agreement will affect the right of either party to serve process in any other manner permitted by applicable law.

(c) ***送达法律程序文件***。双方不可撤销地委派附件指定的与其名对列的传票代理人(如有的话)替其并代表其在任何诉讼中接收传票。如因任何原因，任何一方的传票代理人未能履行上述工作，该方应立即通知另一方，并在三十日内委派另一方接受的替代传票代理人。双方不可撤销地同意以第12(a)(i)条、第12(a)(iii)或第12(a)(iv)条规定的通知方式送达法律程序文件。本协议的规定不影响任何一方以适用法律许可的任何其它方式送达传票的权利。

(d) ***Waiver of Immunities.*** Each party irrevocably waives, to the extent permitted by applicable law, with respect to itself and its revenues and assets (irrespective of their use or intended use), all immunity on the grounds of sovereignty or other similar grounds from (i) suit, (ii) jurisdiction of any court, (iii) relief by way of injunction or order for specific performance or recovery of property, (iv) attachment of its assets (whether before or after judgment) and (v) execution or enforcement of any judgment to which it or its revenues or assets might otherwise be entitled in any Proceedings in the courts of any jurisdiction and irrevocably agrees, to the extent permitted by applicable law, that it will not claim any such immunity in any Proceedings.

(d) ***放弃豁免权***。在适用法律许可的范围内，各方不可撤销地放弃有关其本身、其收入和资产(不考虑其用途或试图用途)的基於主权或其他类似权利而享有的所有下列豁免权：(i)诉讼，(ii)任何法院的司法管辖，(iii)禁止令或实际履行或收回财产的命令，(iv)扣押资产(不论在判决之前或之后)及(v)任何司法管辖区内任何针对其本身的收入或资产判决的执行或强制执行，并且双方不可撤销的同意，在适用法律许可的范围内，其不会在任何诉讼中要求该等豁免。

14. Definitions

14. 定义

As used in this Agreement:—

在本协议内，下列词语有如下定义：–

"Additional Representation" has the meaning specified in Section 3.

"其他陈述" 具有第3条规定的含义。

"Additional Termination Event" has the meaning specified in Section 5(b).

"其他终止事件" 具有第5(b)条规定的含义。

"Affected Party" has the meaning specified in Section 5(b).

"受影响方" 具有第5(b)条规定的含义。

"Affected Transactions" means (a) with respect to any Termination Event consisting of an Illegality, Force Majeure Event, Tax Event or Tax Event Upon Merger, all Transactions affected by the occurrence of such Termination Event (which, in the case of an Illegality under Section 5(b)(i)(2) or a Force Majeure Event under Section 5(b)(ii)(2), means all Transactions unless the relevant Credit Support Document references only certain Transactions, in which case those Transactions and, if the relevant Credit Support Document constitutes a Confirmation for a Transaction, that Transaction) and (b) with respect to any other Termination Event, all Transactions.

"受影响交易" 指(a)对於那些由非法行为、不可抗力事件、税务事件或因合并造成的税务事件所构成的任何终止事件，指所有受该终止事件影响的交易(第5(b)(i)(2)条的非法或第5(b)(ii)(2)条的不可抗力事件下的受影响交易指所有交易，除非有关信用支持文件仅提及某些交易，在信用支持文件将受影响交易限定为某些交易时，指这些被限定的交易，如有关信用支持文件构成一项交易的确认书，指这项交易)及(b)对於任何其他终止事件，指所有交易。

"Affiliate" means, subject to the Schedule, in relation to any person, any entity controlled, directly or indirectly, by the person, any entity that controls, directly or indirectly, the

"关联企业" 除非附件另有规定，就某一实体或人而言，指直接或间接对其进行控制、直接或间接受其控制、或直接或间接与其共处同一控制之下的任何实体或人。本定义中"控制"任何实体

person or any entity directly or indirectly under common control with the person. For this purpose, "control" of any entity or person means ownership of a majority of the voting power of the entity or person.

共处同一控制之下的任何实体或人。本定义中"控制"任何实体或人指拥有该实体或人的大部份投票权。

"Agreement" has the meaning specified in Section 1(c).

*"协议"*具有第1(c)条规定的含义。

"Applicable Close-out Rate" means:—

*"适用的结算利率"*指：－

(a) in respect of the determination of an Unpaid Amount:—

(a) 在确定以下的未付款项时：－

(i) in respect of obligations payable or deliverable (or which would have been but for Section 2(a)(iii)) by a Defaulting Party, the Default Rate;

(i) 对於违约方应支付或交付的义务(或若非第2(a)(iii)条之规定则应支付或交付的义务)，指违约利率；

(ii) in respect of obligations payable or deliverable (or which would have been but for Section 2(a)(iii)) by a Non-defaulting Party, the Non-default Rate;

(ii) 对於应由守约方支付或交付的义务(或若非第2(a)(iii)条之规定，则应支付或交付的义务)，指守约利率；

(iii) in respect of obligations deferred pursuant to Section 5(d), if there is no Defaulting Party and for so long as the deferral period continues, the Applicable Deferral Rate; and

(iii) 对于根据第5(d)条而迟延履行的义务，如无违约方，在迟延期内指适用的迟延利率；及

(iv) in all other cases following the occurrence of a Termination Event (except where interest accrues pursuant to clause (iii) above), the Applicable Deferral Rate; and

(iv) 在发生终止事件(除按上述第(iii)款累计利息的情况外)后的其它一切情况，则指适用的迟延利率；及

(b) in respect of an Early Termination Amount:—

(b) 对於提前终止款项指：－

(i) for the period from (and including) the relevant Early Termination Date to (but excluding) the date (determined in accordance with Section 6(d)(ii)) on which that amount is payable:—

(i) 从有关提前终止日(包括当日)至该款项应付之日为止(根据第6(d)(ii)条确定)(不包括当日)的期间内：－

(1) if the Early Termination Amount is payable by a Defaulting Party, the Default Rate;

(1) 如应由违约方支付提前终止款项，指违约利率；

(2) if the Early Termination Amount is payable by a Non-defaulting Party, the Non-default Rate; and

(2) 如应由守约方支付提前终止款项，指守约利率；

(3) in all other cases, the Applicable Deferral Rate; and

(3) 在其情况下，则指适用的迟延利率；及

(ii) for the period from (and including) the date (determined in accordance with Section 6(d)(ii)) on which that amount is payable to (but excluding) the date of actual payment:—

(ii) 从该款项应付之日(根据第6(d)(ii)条确定)(包括当日)至实际付款日(不包括当日)的期间内：－

(1) if a party fails to pay the Early Termination Amount due to the occurrence of an event or circumstance which would, if it occurred with respect to a payment or delivery under a Transaction, constitute or give rise to an Illegality or a Force Majeure Event, and for so long as the Early Termination Amount remains unpaid due to the continuing existence of such event or circumstance, the Applicable Deferral Rate;

(1) 造成一方不能支付提前终止款项的事件或情况是因为发生于某项交易下的付款或交付会构成或导致非法或不可抗力事件，当该提前终止款项因该事件或情况的持续存在而仍未支付时，指适用的迟延利率；

(2) if the Early Termination Amount is payable by a Defaulting Party (but excluding any period in respect of which clause (1) above applies), the Default Rate;

(2) 如应由违约方支付提前终止款项(但不包括上述(1)款适用的期间)，指违约利率；

(3) if the Early Termination Amount is payable by a Non-defaulting Party (but excluding any period in respect of which clause (1) above applies), the Non-default Rate; and

(3) 如应由守约方支付提前终止款项(但不包括上述(1)款适用的期间)，指守约利率；及

(4) in all other cases, the Termination Rate.

(4) 在其它一切情况，则指终止利率。

"Applicable Deferral Rate" means:—

"适用的迟延利率" 指：-

(a) for the purpose of Section 9(h)(i)(3)(A), the rate certified by the relevant payer to be a rate offered to the payer by a major bank in a relevant interbank market for overnight deposits in the applicable currency, such bank to be selected in good faith by the payer for the purpose of obtaining a representative rate that will reasonably reflect conditions prevailing at the time in that relevant market;

(a) 就第9(h)(i)(3)(A)条的目的而言，指有关付款人认证的有关银行同业市场上一家主要银行就相关货币隔夜存款给予付款人的利率，该银行由付款人按诚信原则选择以便获得可合理反映该有关市场当时状况的有代表性的利率；

(b) for purposes of Section 9(h)(i)(3)(B) and clause (a)(iii) of the definition of Applicable Close-out Rate, the rate certified by the relevant payer to be a rate offered to prime banks by a major bank in a relevant interbank market for overnight deposits in the applicable currency, such bank to be selected in good faith by the payer after consultation with the other party, if practicable, for the purpose of obtaining a representative rate that will reasonably reflect conditions prevailing at the time in that relevant market; and

(b) 就第9(h)(i)(3)(B)条和适用的结算利率的定义中第(a)(iii)款的目的而言，指有关付款人认证的为有关银行同业市场上一家主要银行就相关货币隔夜存款给予主要银行的利率，该银行由付款人经与另一方(如可行)协商后按诚信原则选择以便获得可合理反映该有关市场当时状况的有代表性的利率；及

(c) for purposes of Section 9(h)(i)(3)(C) and clauses (a)(iv), (b)(i)(3) and (b)(ii)(1) of the definition of Applicable Close-out Rate, a rate equal to the arithmetic mean of the rate determined pursuant to clause (a) above and a rate per annum equal to the cost (without proof or evidence of any actual cost) to the relevant payee (as certified by it) if it were to fund or of funding the relevant amount.

(c) 就第9(h)(i)(3)(C)条以及适用的结算利率的定义中第(a)(iv)、第(b)(i)(3)和第(b)(ii)(1)款的目的而言，指根据以上(a)款确定的利率和有关收款人(经其认证的)如获得有关金额须付的资金成本的年利率(无需提供任何实际成本的证明或证据)的算术平均值。

"Automatic Early Termination" has the meaning specified in Section 6(a).

"自动提前终止" 具有第6(a)条规定的含义。

"Burdened Party" has the meaning specified in Section 5(b)(iv).

"有负担方" 具有第5(b)(iv)条规定的含义。

"Change in Tax Law" means the enactment, promulgation, execution or ratification of, or any change in or amendment to, any law (or in the application or official interpretation of any law) that occurs after the parties enter into the relevant Transaction.

"税法变更" 指在双方达成有关交易之后制定、发布、执行、批准、变更或修订法律(或任何法律的适用或官方解释)。

"Close-out Amount" means, with respect to each Terminated Transaction or each group of Terminated Transactions and a Determining Party, the amount of the losses or costs of the Determining Party that are or would be incurred under then prevailing circumstances (expressed as a positive number) or gains of the Determining Party that are or would be realised under then prevailing circumstances (expressed as a negative number) in replacing, or in providing for the Determining Party the economic equivalent of, (a) the material terms of that Terminated Transaction or group of Terminated Transactions, including the payments and deliveries by the parties under Section 2(a)(i) in respect of that Terminated Transaction or group of Terminated Transactions that would, but for the occurrence of the relevant Early Termination Date, have been required after that date (assuming satisfaction of the conditions precedent in Section 2(a)(iii)) and (b) the option rights of the parties in respect of that Terminated Transaction or group of

"结算款项" 对於每项终止交易或每组终止交易及某一决定方而言，指为决定方替换或提供与(a)、(b)项相同的经济效果在当时的情况下决定方所付或将付的损失或费用(以正数表达)，或由决定方所实现或将实现的收益(以负数表达)：(a)该项终止交易或该组终止交易的主要条款，包括关于该终止交易或该组终止交易若未出现提前终止日时，根据第2(a)(I)款的规定本应由各方在此日之后作出的付款或交付(假设已满足第2(a)(iii)条中规定的先决条件)；以及(b)各方对於该终止交易或该组终止交易的期权。

Terminated Transactions.

Any Close-out Amount will be determined by the Determining Party (or its agent), which will act in good faith and use commercially reasonable procedures in order to produce a commercially reasonable result. The Determining Party may determine a Close-out Amount for any group of Terminated Transactions or any individual Terminated Transaction but, in the aggregate, for not less than all Terminated Transactions. Each Close-out Amount will be determined as of the Early Termination Date or, if that would not be commercially reasonable, as of the date or dates following the Early Termination Date as would be commercially reasonable.

决定方(或其代理人)将按诚信原则并按合理的商业程序确定任何结算款项，以达到合理的商业效益。决定方可为任何一组终止交易或一项终止交易(但总数不得少于所有被终止交易)确定结算款项。每笔结算款项应在提前终止日确定，或如果这一日期在商业上不合理可行的话，亦可按提前终止日之後商业上合理之日确定。

Unpaid Amounts in respect of a Terminated Transaction or group of Terminated Transactions and legal fees and out-of-pocket expenses referred to in Section 11 are to be excluded in all determinations of Close-out Amounts.

在决定结算款项时不应考虑有关一项终止交易或一组终止交易的未付款项和第11条所指的律师费及实付费用。

In determining a Close-out Amount, the Determining Party may consider any relevant information, including, without limitation, one or more of the following types of information:—

决定方可在确定结算款项时参考任何有关信息，包括但不限于以下一类或多类信息：—

(i) quotations (either firm or indicative) for replacement transactions supplied by one or more third parties that may take into account the creditworthiness of the Determining Party at the time the quotation is provided and the terms of any relevant documentation, including credit support documentation, between the Determining Party and the third party providing the quotation;

(i) 一个或多个第三方提供的有关替换交易的(确定的或指示性的)报价，第三方在提供这些报价时可以考虑决定方在提供报价之时的资信状况以及决定方与提供报价的第三方之间的任何有关文件，包括信用支持文件的条款；

(ii) information consisting of relevant market data in the relevant market supplied by one or more third parties including, without limitation, relevant rates, prices, yields, yield curves, volatilities, spreads, correlations or other relevant market data in the relevant market; or

(ii) 一个或多个第三方提供的相关市场数据的资料，包括但不限于相关利率、价格、收益率、收益率曲线、波动性、利差、相关性以及相关市场的其他相关市场数据；或

(iii) information of the types described in clause (i) or (ii) above from internal sources (including any of the Determining Party's Affiliates) if that information is of the same type used by the Determining Party in the regular course of its business for the valuation of similar transactions.

(iii) 源于内部的(包括源于决定方的任何关联公司)的以上(i)和(ii)款所述类型的资料，但该资料应是决定方在评估同类交易的日常商务过程中使用的同类资料。

The Determining Party will consider, taking into account the standards and procedures described in this definition, quotations pursuant to clause (i) above or relevant market data pursuant to clause (ii) above unless the Determining Party reasonably believes in good faith that such quotations or relevant market data are not readily available or would produce a result that would not satisfy those standards. When considering information described in clause (i), (ii) or (iii) above, the Determining Party may include costs of funding, to the extent costs of funding are not and would not be a component of the other information being utilised. Third parties supplying quotations pursuant to clause (i) above or market data pursuant to clause (ii) above may include, without limitation, dealers in the relevant markets, end-users of the relevant product, information vendors, brokers and other sources of market information.

决定方将按本定义中的标准及程序考虑以上(i)款的报价或以上(ii)款的相关市场数据，除非决定方按诚信原则合理地认为无法获得此类报价或有关市场数据或其产生的结果可能不符合本定义下的标准。决定方在参考以上(i)、(ii)和(iii)款所述的资料时亦可参考资金成本，只要其使用的其他资料没有包括资金成本。根据以上(i)款提供报价或根据以上(ii)款提供市场数据的第三方可包括但不限于相关市场的交易商、相关产品的最终用户、资料销售者、经纪和市场资料的其他来源。

Without duplication of amounts calculated based on information described in clause (i), (ii) or (iii) above, or other relevant information, and when it is commercially reasonable to do so, the Determining Party may in addition consider in calculating a Close-out Amount any loss or cost incurred in connection with its terminating, liquidating or re-establishing any hedge related to a Terminated Transaction or group of Terminated Transactions (or any gain resulting from any of them).

在不重复计算根据以上(i)、(ii)和(iii)款所述的资料或其他有关资料计算出的款项的前提下，并在商业上合理可行时，决定方在计算结算款项时可另外参考就有关一项终止交易或一组终止交易而终止、清算或重建任何抗风险安排所产生的任何亏损或成本(或因此引致的任何收益)。

Commercially reasonable procedures used in determining a Close-out Amount may include the following:—

确定结算款项合理的商业程序可包括：—

(1) application to relevant market data from third parties pursuant to clause (ii) above or information from internal sources pursuant to clause (iii) above of pricing or other valuation models that are, at the time of the determination of the Close-out Amount, used by the Determining Party in the regular course of its business in pricing or valuing transactions between the Determining Party and unrelated third parties that are similar to the Terminated Transaction or group of Terminated Transactions; and

(1) 适用按以上(ii)款由第三方提供的相关市场数据或适用按以上(iii)款来源于内部的信息或其他评估模式，只要这些数据、信息或模式是在决定结算款项时，决定方在日常商业过程中评估与第三方之间的类似于该项或该组终止交易的过程中所使用的模式；及

(2) application of different valuation methods to Terminated Transactions or groups of Terminated Transactions depending on the type, complexity, size or number of the Terminated Transactions or group of Terminated Transactions.

(2) 根据一项终止交易或一组终止交易的类型、复杂性、规模和数量对该项或该组终止交易适用不同的评估办法。

"Confirmation" has the meaning specified in the preamble.

"确认书" 具有前言规定的含义。

"consent" includes a consent, approval, action, authorisation, exemption, notice, filing, registration or exchange control consent.

"同意" 包括同意、批准、行动、授权、豁免、通知、备案、注册或外汇管制同意。

"Contractual Currency" has the meaning specified in Section 8(a).

"合同货币" 具有第8(a)条规定的含义。

"Convention Court" means any court which is bound to apply to the Proceedings either Article 17 of the 1968 Brussels Convention on Jurisdiction and the Enforcement of Judgments in Civil and Commercial Matters or Article 17 of the 1988 Lugano Convention on Jurisdiction and the Enforcement of Judgments in Civil and Commercial Matters.

"公约法院" 指需要在诉讼中适用1968年《关于民商事案件的司法管辖以及承认和执行判决的布鲁塞尔规定》第17条以及1988年《关于民商事案件的司法管辖以及承认和执行判决的卢根诺公约》第17条的任何法院。

"Credit Event Upon Merger" has the meaning specified in Section 5(b).

"因合并造成的信用事件" 具有第5(b)条规定的含义。

"Credit Support Document" means any agreement or instrument that is specified as such in this Agreement.

"信用支持文件" 指本协议规定为信用支持文件的任何协议或文件。

"Credit Support Provider" has the meaning specified in the Schedule.

"信用支持提供者" 具有附件规定的含义。

"Cross-Default" means the event specified in Section 5(a)(vi).

"交叉违约" 指第5(a)(vi)条规定的事件。

"Default Rate" means a rate per annum equal to the cost (without proof or evidence of any actual cost) to the relevant payee (as certified by it) if it were to fund or of funding the relevant amount plus 1% per annum.

"违约利率" 指相等於收款人(经其认证的)获得有关资金的资金成本的年利率(无需对任何实际成本提供证明或证据)加1%。

"Defaulting Party" has the meaning specified in Section 6(a).

"违约方" 具有第6(a)条规定的含义。

"Designated Event" has the meaning specified in Section 5(b)(v).

*"指定事件"*具有第5(b)(v)条规定的含义。

"Determining Party" means the party determining a Close-out Amount.

*"决定方"*指确定结算款项的当事方。

"Early Termination Amount" has the meaning specified in Section 6(e).

*"提前终止款项"*具有第6(e)条规定的含义。

"Early Termination Date" means the date determined in accordance with Section 6(a) or 6(b)(iv).

*"提前终止日"*指按第6(a)条或第6(b)(iv)条决定的日期。

"electronic messages" does not include e-mails but does include documents expressed in markup languages, and ***"electronic messaging system"*** will be construed accordingly.

*"电子信息"*不包括电子邮件，但包括以标记语言表达的文件。*"电子信息系统"*将据此予以解释。

"English law" means the law of England and Wales, and ***"English"*** will be construed accordingly.

*"英国法律"*指英格兰及威尔士的法律。*"英国的"*将据此予以解释。

"Event of Default" has the meaning specified in Section 5(a) and, if applicable, in the Schedule.

*"违约事件"*具有第5(a)条规定的含义及附件(按情况适用)规定的含义。

"Force Majeure Event" has the meaning specified in Section 5(b).

*"不可抗力事件"*具有第5(b)条规定的含义。

"General Business Day" means a day on which commercial banks are open for general business (including dealings in foreign exchange and foreign currency deposits).

*"一般营业日"*指商业银行开门营业(包括外汇交易及外币存款)的日子。

"Illegality" has the meaning specified in Section 5(b).

*"非法"*具有第5(b)条规定的含义。

"Indemnifiable Tax" means any Tax other than a Tax that would not be imposed in respect of a payment under this Agreement but for a present or former connection between the jurisdiction of the government or taxation authority imposing such Tax and the recipient of such payment or a person related to such recipient (including, without limitation, a connection arising from such recipient or related person being or having been a citizen or resident of such jurisdiction, or being or having been organised, present or engaged in a trade or business in such jurisdiction, or having or having had a permanent establishment or fixed place of business in such jurisdiction, but excluding a connection arising solely from such recipient or related person having executed, delivered, performed its obligations or received a payment under, or enforced, this Agreement or a Credit Support Document).

*"可获补偿税项"*指任何税项，不包括本来不会对本协议项下的付款征收，而只是因为征收该税项的政府或税务机关的管辖地与该款项收款人或与该款项收款人有关的个人之间现时或之前有联系(这种联系包括但不限於因该收款人或有关人员为该管辖地的公民或居民，或正在或已在该管辖地组织或从事贸易或其它业务，或在该管辖地有永久机构或固定的营业地而产生的联系，但是这种联系不包括仅因该收款人或有关人员签署、交付本协议或信用支持文件或按本协议或信用支持文件履行义务或收款，或执行本协议或信用支持文件而产生的联系)方才征收的税项。

"law" includes any treaty, law, rule or regulation (as modified, in the case of tax matters, by the practice of any relevant governmental revenue authority), and ***"unlawful"*** will be construed accordingly.

*"法律"*包括任何条约、法律、规则或条例(及经任何有关政府税务机关的惯例所修改的税务事宜)，并且*"非法"*将据此予以解释。

"Local Business Day" means (a) in relation to any obligation under Section 2(a)(i), a General Business Day in the place or places specified in the relevant Confirmation and a day on which a relevant settlement system is open or operating as specified in the relevant Confirmation or, if a place or a settlement system is not so specified, as otherwise agreed by the parties in writing or determined pursuant to provisions contained, or incorporated by reference, in this Agreement, (b) for the purpose of determining when a Waiting Period expires, a General Business Day in the place

"当地营业日"(a)对於第2(a)(i)条项下任何义务，指有关确认书规定的地点的一般营业日并且有关确认书规定的有关结算系统开门营业的日子，或如果没有规定相关地点或结算系统，则双方以其它书面方式同意的或按本协议所载或纳入的规定而决定的地点；(b)当确定等待期何时届满时，指构成或导致非法或不可抗力事件(视情况而定)事件或情况发生地的一般营业日；(c)对於其它任何付款，指有关帐户的所在地的一般营业日，如帐户所在地不同则指付款货币的主要金融中心(如有的话)的一般营业日，或如果该货币没有一个单独获认可的主要金融中心，则指结算系统为

where the event or circumstance that constitutes or gives rise to the Illegality or Force Majeure Event, as the case may be, occurs, (c) in relation to any other payment, a General Business Day in the place where the relevant account is located and, if different, in the principal financial centre, if any, of the currency of such payment and, if that currency does not have a single recognised principal financial centre, a day on which the settlement system necessary to accomplish such payment is open, (d) in relation to any notice or other communication, including notice contemplated under Section 5(a)(i), a General Business Day (or a day that would have been a General Business Day but for the occurrence of an event or circumstance which would, if it occurred with respect to payment, delivery or compliance related to a Transaction, constitute or give rise to an Illegality or a Force Majeure Event) in the place specified in the address for notice provided by the recipient and, in the case of a notice contemplated by Section 2(b), in the place where the relevant new account is to be located and (e) in relation to Section 5(a)(v)(2), a General Business Day in the relevant locations for performance with respect to such Specified Transaction.

果该货币没有一个单独获认可的主要金融中心，则指结算系统为完成该付款而需开门的日子；(d)对於任何通知或其他通讯，包括第5(a)(I)条下的通知，指收款人提供的接收通知地的一般营业日(或若非某一事件或情况的发生而本应为一般营业日的一日，条件是这一事件或情况如发生于某项交易的付款、交付或遵行协议的行为时会构成非法或不可抗力)，如为第2(b)条下的通知则指有关新帐户的所在地的一般营业日；及(e)对於第5(a)(v)(2)条，则指该特定交易的履行地的一般营业日。

"Local Delivery Day" means, for purposes of Sections 5(a)(i) and 5(d), a day on which settlement systems necessary to accomplish the relevant delivery are generally open for business so that the delivery is capable of being accomplished in accordance with customary market practice, in the place specified in the relevant Confirmation or, if not so specified, in a location as determined in accordance with customary market practice for the relevant delivery.

*"当地交付日"*就第5(a)(i)和5(d)条而言，指有关确认书规定地点的完成有关交付所必须的结算系统能够按照市场惯例为完成有关交付而通常开门营业的一日，或如果确认书没有规定地点，则指按有关交付的市场惯例决定的地点。

"Master Agreement" has the meaning specified in the preamble.

*"主协议"*具有前言规定的含义。

"Merger Without Assumption" means the event specified in Section 5(a)(viii).

*"不承担债务的合并"*具有第5(a)(iii)条规定的事件。

"Multiple Transaction Payment Netting" has the meaning specified in Section 2(c).

*"多项交易付款？额结算"*具有第2(c)条规定的含义。

"Non-affected Party" means, so long as there is only one Affected Party, the other party.

*"不受影响方"*若仅有一个受影响方的，指另一方。

"Non-default Rate" means the rate certified by the Non-defaulting Party to be a rate offered to the Non-defaulting Party by a major bank in a relevant interbank market for overnight deposits in the applicable currency, such bank to be selected in good faith by the Non-defaulting Party for the purpose of obtaining a representative rate that will reasonably reflect conditions prevailing at the time in that relevant market.

*"守约利率"*指经守约方认证的在有关银行同业市场上一家主要银行就有关货币隔夜存款给予守约方的利率，该银行由守约方按诚信原则选择以获得可合理反映该市场当时状况的有代表性的利率。

"Non-defaulting Party" has the meaning specified in Section 6(a).

*"守约方"*具有第6(a)条规定的含义。

"Office" means a branch or office of a party, which may be such party's head or home office.

*"办事处"*指一方的分支机构或办事处，有可能是该方的总部或总办事处。

"Other Amounts" has the meaning specified in Section 6(f).

*"其他款项"*具有第6(f)条规定的含义。

"Payee" has the meaning specified in Section 6(f).

*" 收款人"*具有第6(f)条规定的含义。

"Payer" has the meaning specified in Section 6(f).

*" 付款人"*具有第6(f)条规定的含义。

"Potential Event of Default" means any event which, with the giving of notice or the lapse of time or both, would constitute an Event of Default.

"潜在违约事件" 指任何经发送通知或随时间流逝(或两者同时发生)可构成违约事件的任何事件。

"Proceedings" has the meaning specified in Section 13(b).

"诉讼" 具有第13(b)条规定的含义。

"Process Agent" has the meaning specified in the Schedule.

"传票代理人" 具有附件规定的含义。

"rate of exchange" includes, without limitation, any premiums and costs of exchange payable in connection with the purchase of or conversion into the Contractual Currency.

"兑换率" 包括但不限于就购买或兑换合同货币应付的任何溢价或兑换成本。

"Relevant Jurisdiction" means, with respect to a party, the jurisdictions (a) in which the party is incorporated, organised, managed and controlled or considered to have its seat, (b) where an Office through which the party is acting for purposes of this Agreement is located, (c) in which the party executes this Agreement and (d) in relation to any payment, from or through which such payment is made.

"有关管辖区" 指有关一方而言，(a)该方成立、组成、被管理及控制或视作有其席位的管辖区，(b)该方为本协议的目的采取行动的办事处的管辖区，(c)一方签署本协议的管辖区，及(d)若与支付款项有关，则为该等支付款项的管辖区。

"Schedule" has the meaning specified in the preamble.

"附件" 具有前言规定的含义。

"Scheduled Settlement Date" means a date on which a payment or delivery is to be made under Section 2(a)(i) with respect to a Transaction.

"预定结算日" 指有关交易根据第2(a)(i)条应作出付款或交付的日期。

"Specified Entity" has the meaning specified in the Schedule.

"特定机构" 具有附件规定的含义。

"Specified Indebtedness" means, subject to the Schedule, any obligation (whether present or future, contingent or otherwise, as principal or surety or otherwise) in respect of borrowed money.

"特定负债" 除非附件另有规定，指有关借款的任何义务(不论是现有的或将来的、或有的或其他的，作为主债务人或担保人的债务或其他义务)。

"Specified Transaction" means, subject to the Schedule, (a) any transaction (including an agreement with respect to any such transaction) now existing or hereafter entered into between one party to this Agreement (or any Credit Support Provider of such party or any applicable Specified Entity of such party) and the other party to this Agreement (or any Credit Support Provider of such other party or any applicable Specified Entity of such other party) which is not a Transaction under this Agreement but (i) which is a rate swap transaction, swap option, basis swap, forward rate transaction, commodity swap, commodity option, equity or equity index swap, equity or equity index option, bond option, interest rate option, foreign exchange transaction, cap transaction, floor transaction, collar transaction, currency swap transaction, cross-currency rate swap transaction, currency option, credit protection transaction, credit swap, credit default swap, credit default option, total return swap, credit spread transaction, repurchase transaction, reverse repurchase transaction, buy/sell-back transaction, securities lending transaction, weather index transaction or forward purchase or sale of a security, commodity or other financial instrument or interest (including any option with respect to any of these transactions) or (ii) which is a type of transaction that is similar to any transaction referred to in clause (i) above that is currently, or in the future becomes, recurrently entered into in the financial markets (including terms and conditions incorporated by reference in such agreement) and which is a forward, swap, future, option or other derivative on one or more rates, currencies, commodities, equity securities or other equity instruments, debt securities or other debt

"特定交易" 除非附件另有规定，指(a)本协议一方(或该方的任何信用支持提供者或该方的任何适用特定机构)与本协议另一方(或该方的任何信用支持提供者或该方的任何适用特定机构)现在或日後达成的任何交易(包括与任何此等交易有关的协议)，该特定交易不包括本协议项下的交易，但属于：(i)利率掉期交易、掉期期权、利率基础掉期交易、远期利率交易、商品掉期交易、商品期权、股权或股权指数掉期交易，股权或股权指数期权、债券期权、利率期权、外汇交易、上限交易、下限交易、上下限交易、货币掉期交易、交叉货币利率掉期交易、货币期权、信用保护交易、信用掉期、信用违约掉期、信用违约期权、全部利润掉期、信用利差交易、回购交易、逆回购交易，买回/卖回交易，证券出借交易、天气指数交易或证券、商品或其它其他金融工具或利益(包括以上任何交易的期权)；或(ii)任何与(i)款中所列交易类似的，目前或将来在金融市场上重复进行的交易(包括该协议中的条款和条件)，并且该交易是以一种或多种利率、货币、商品、股票或其他股权凭证、债券或其他债权凭证、经济指数或经济风险或价值的测量方法或其他基准作为付款和交易基础的远期、掉期、期货、期权或其他衍生交易，(b)任何该些交易的组合，及(c)任何本协议或有关确认书中规定为特定交易的任何其它交易。

instruments, economic indices or measures of economic risk or value, or other benchmarks against which payments or deliveries are to be made, (b) any combination of these transactions and (c) any other transaction identified as a Specified Transaction in this Agreement or the relevant confirmation.

"Stamp Tax" means any stamp, registration, documentation or similar tax.

"印花税" 指任何印花税、登记税、文件税或类似的税项。

"Stamp Tax Jurisdiction" has the meaning specified in Section 4(e).

"印花税司法管辖区" 具有第4(e)条规定的含义。

"Tax" means any present or future tax, levy, impost, duty, charge, assessment or fee of any nature (including interest, penalties and additions thereto) that is imposed by any government or other taxing authority in respect of any payment under this Agreement other than a stamp, registration, documentation or similar tax.

"税项" 指印花税、登记税、文件税或类似的税项以外的与本协议项下任何付款有关的任何政府或其它税务机关征收的任何性质的现有或将征收的税项、征税、进口税、关税、收费评估或费用(包括其利息、罚款及附加费)。

"Tax Event" has the meaning specified in Section 5(b).

"税务事件" 具有第5(b)条规定的含义。

"Tax Event Upon Merger" has the meaning specified in Section 5(b).

"因合并造成的税务事件" 具有第5(b)条规定的含义。

"Terminated Transactions" means, with respect to any Early Termination Date, (a) if resulting from an Illegality or a Force Majeure Event, all Affected Transactions specified in the notice given pursuant to Section 6(b)(iv), (b) if resulting from any other Termination Event, all Affected Transactions and (c) if resulting from an Event of Default, all Transactions in effect either immediately before the effectiveness of the notice designating that Early Termination Date or, if Automatic Early Termination applies, immediately before that Early Termination Date.

"已终止交易" 对於任何提前终止日而言(a)如因非法或不可抗力事件产生，指根据第6(b)(iv)条作出的通知中规定的所有受影响交易，(b)如因任何其他终止事件产生，指所有受影响的交易及(c)如因违约事件产生，指在载明提前终止日的通知生效前，或如适用自动提前终止指在该提前终止日之前有效的所有交易。

"Termination Currency" means (a) if a Termination Currency is specified in the Schedule and that currency is freely available, that currency, and (b) otherwise, euro if this Agreement is expressed to be governed by English law or United States Dollars if this Agreement is expressed to be governed by the laws of the State of New York.

"终止货币" 如附件中规定终止货币，而该货币可无限制获得，指该货币；(b)否则，如本协议表明是适用英国法律，指欧元，或如本协议表明是适用纽约州法律，则指美元。

"Termination Currency Equivalent" means, in respect of any amount denominated in the Termination Currency, such Termination Currency amount and, in respect of any amount denominated in a currency other than the Termination Currency (the "Other Currency"), the amount in the Termination Currency determined by the party making the relevant determination as being required to purchase such amount of such Other Currency as at the relevant Early Termination Date, or, if the relevant Close-out Amount is determined as of a later date, that later date, with the Termination Currency at the rate equal to the spot exchange rate of the foreign exchange agent (selected as provided below) for the purchase of such Other Currency with the Termination Currency at or about 11:00 a.m. (in the city in which such foreign exchange agent is located) on such date as would be customary for the determination of such a rate for the purchase of such Other Currency for value on the relevant Early Termination Date or that later date. The foreign exchange agent will, if only one party is obliged to make a determination under Section 6(e), be selected in good faith by that party and otherwise will be agreed by the parties.

"终止货币等值额" 对於以终止货币为单位的任何款项，指该终止货币额,对於以终止货币以外货币为单位的任何数额(" 其他货币")，则指作出决定的一方在有关提前终止日，或如果有关结算款项在较後日期才确定，则于该日用以购买该数额的其他货币所需的终止货币，购买时使用的汇率应为(按以下方式选择的)外汇机构的现货兑换率:在该日上午十一时或左右(以该外汇机构所在的城市为准),在有关提前终止日或该较后日期用终止货币购买其他货币时，通常适用的汇率。如果只有一方有义务按第6(e)条决定，该方应以诚信的原则选择外汇机构，如果不只有一方则以各方同意的方式选择。

"Termination Event" means an Illegality, a Force Majeure Event, a Tax Event, a Tax Event Upon Merger or, if specified to be applicable, a Credit Event Upon Merger or an Additional Termination Event.

"终止事件" 指非法、不可抗力事件、税务事件或因合并造成的税务事件，或(如规定适用)因合并造成的信用事件或其他终止事件。

"Termination Rate" means a rate per annum equal to the arithmetic mean of the cost (without proof or evidence of any actual cost) to each party (as certified by such party) if it were to fund or of funding such amounts.

"终止利率" 指相等於各方(经该方认证的)获得有关金额的成本(无需提供任何实际成本的证明或证据)的算术平均值的年利率。

"Threshold Amount" means the amount, if any, specified as such in the Schedule.

"起点金额" 如附件加以规定的话，具有附件规定的含义。

"Transaction" has the meaning specified in the preamble.

" 交易" 具有前言规定的含义。

"Unpaid Amounts" owing to any party means, with respect to an Early Termination Date, the aggregate of (a) in respect of all Terminated Transactions, the amounts that became payable (or that would have become payable but for Section 2(a)(iii) or due but for Section 5(d)) to such party under Section 2(a)(i) or 2(d)(i)(4) on or prior to such Early Termination Date and which remain unpaid as at such Early Termination Date, (b) in respect of each Terminated Transaction, for each obligation under Section 2(a)(i) which was (or would have been but for Section 2(a)(iii) or 5(d)) required to be settled by delivery to such party on or prior to such Early Termination Date and which has not been so settled as at such Early Termination Date, an amount equal to the fair market value of that which was (or would have been) required to be delivered and (c) if the Early Termination Date results from an Event of Default, a Credit Event Upon Merger or an Additional Termination Event in respect of which all outstanding Transactions are Affected Transactions, any Early Termination Amount due prior to such Early Termination Date and which remains unpaid as of such Early Termination Date, in each case together with any amount of interest accrued or other compensation in respect of that obligation or deferred obligation, as the case may be, pursuant to Section 9(h)(ii)(1) or (2), as appropriate. The fair market value of any obligation referred to in clause (b) above will be determined as of the originally scheduled date for delivery, in good faith and using commercially reasonable procedures, by the party obliged to make the determination under Section 6(e) or, if each party is so obliged, it will be the average of the Termination Currency Equivalents of the fair market values so determined by both parties.

"未付款项" 对於提前终止日而言，指欠任何一方的下列各项之和：(a)就所有已终止交易而言，指按第2(a)(i)或2(d)(i)(4)条应在该提前终止日当日或之前支付给该方但在该提前终止日仍未付(或本来应付，但因按第2(a)(iii)条未付或第5(d)款到期未付)的数额，及(b)对於每一笔已终止交易，就第2(a)(i)条之下的每一项需在该终止日或之前向该方交付而未交付(或本应交付但因第2(a)(iii)条或第5(d)条而未交付)的义务而言，指应该或本来应该在原定交付日交付的实物的公平市值，以及(c)如因违约事件、因合并造成的信用事件或其他终止事件导致提前终止日，而使所有未完成交易变成受影响交易，指该提前终止日前到期，而截至该提前终止日仍未清偿的任何提前终止款项。在以上任何一种情况下均包括根据第9(h)(ii)(1)或(2)条(视情况而定)决定的有关该义务或迟延履行的义务(视情况而定)累计的利息或其他补偿。上述(b)款所指的任何义务的公平市值将由根据第6(e)条由有义务作决定的一方按诚信原则并使用合理的商业程序于原定交付日确定，或如各方均有责任，则为各方按上述办法确定的公平市值的平均终止货币等值额。

"Waiting Period" means:—

"等待期" 指：—

(a) in respect of an event or circumstance under Section 5(b)(i), other than in the case of Section 5(b)(i)(2) where the relevant payment, delivery or compliance is actually required on the relevant day (in which case no Waiting Period will apply), a period of three Local Business Days (or days that would have been Local Business Days but for the occurrence of that event or circumstance) following the occurrence of that event or circumstance; and

(a) 除第5(b)(i)(2)条实际上于当日要求有关付款、交付或遵守协议(此时不适用等待期)的情况以外，就第5(b)(i)条下的事件或情况而言，指发生事件或情况之後的三个当地工作日(或若非该事件或情况的发生本应为当地营业日之日)；及

(b) in respect of an event or circumstance under Section 5(b)(ii), other than in the case of Section 5(b)(ii)(2) where the relevant payment, delivery or compliance is actually required on the relevant day (in which case no Waiting Period will apply), a period of eight Local Business Days (or days that would have been Local Business Days but for the occurrence of that event or circumstance) following the occurrence of that event or circumstance.

(b) 除第5(b)(ii)(2)条规定的实际上于当日要求有关付款、交付或遵守规定(此时不适用等待期)的情况以外，就第5(b)(ii)条事件或情况而言，指发生事件或情况之後的八个当地工作日(或若非该事件或情况的发生本应为当地营业日之日)。

IN WITNESS WHEREOF the parties have executed this document on the respective dates specified below with effect from the date specified on the first page of this document.

兹证明双方已於下列日期签署本文件，生效日为本文件首页载明的日期。

____________ (Name of Party)	____________ (Name of Party)	____________ (签署方名称)	____________ (签署方名称)
By: ____________	By: ____________	签名：____________	签名：____________
Name:	Name:	姓名：	姓名：
Title:	Title:	职位：	职位：
Date:	Date:	日期：	日期：

ISDA® International Swaps and Derivatives Association, Inc.	国际掉期及衍生工具协会
SCHEDULE **to the** **2002 Master Agreement**	2002主协议附件
dated as of	_____年_____月_____日
between _______________ and ___________________ ("Party A") ("Party B")	______________________与____________________ ("A方") ("B方")
[established as a [COUNTERPARTY TYPE]] [established as a [COUNTERPARTY TYPE]]	*[成立的[有关方的类型]]* *[成立的[有关方的类型]]*
[with company number [NUMBER]] *[with company number [NUMBER]]*	*[公司号码[号码]]* *[公司号码[号码]]*
[under the laws of [JURISDICTION]] *[under the laws of [JURISDICTION]]*	*[依照[司法管辖区]法律]* *[依照[司法管辖区]法律]*
[acting through its [BRANCH]]# *[acting through its [BRANCH]]*#	*[通过其[办事处]交易]*# *[通过其[办事处]交易]*#
Part 1. **Termination Provisions.**	第一部分 终止条款。
(a) ***"Specified Entity"*** means in relation to Party A for the purpose of:—	(a) *"特定机构"* 就A方而言，为下列条款的目的指：－
Section 5(a)(v), ... Section 5(a)(vi), ... Section 5(a)(vii), ... Section 5(b)(v), ...	第5(a)(v)条，.............................. 第5(a)(vi)条，.............................. 第5(a)(vii)条，.............................. 第5(b)(v)条，..............................
and in relation to Party B for the purpose of:—	就B方而言，为以下条款的目的指：－
Section 5(a)(v), ... Section 5(a)(vi), ... Section 5(a)(vii), ... Section 5(b)(v), ...	第5(a)(v)条，.............................. 第5(a)(vi)条，.............................. 第5(a)(vii)条，.............................. 第5(b)(v)条，..............................
(b) ***"Specified Transaction"*** [will have the meaning specified in Section 14 of this Agreement.][means ....]*	(b) *"特定交易"* [具有本协议第14款规定的含义。][指 ....]*
(c) The ***"Cross-Default"*** provisions of Section 5(a)(vi) [will][will not]* apply to Party A [will][will not]* apply to Party B	(c) 第5(a)(vi)条" *交叉违约*" [将会][不会]*适用于A方 [将会][不会]*适用于B方
[***"Specified Indebtedness"*** [will have the meaning specified in Section 14 of this Agreement.][means ....]*	[*"特定负债"* [具有本协议第14条之含义。][指 ....]*
"Threshold Amount" means ....]**	*"起点金额"* 指 ....]**
(d) The ***"Credit Event Upon Merger"*** provisions of Section	(d) 第5(b)(v)条 *"因合并造成的信用事件"*

# Include if applicable.	# 视情况包括。
* Delete as applicable.	* 视情况删除。
** Include if Cross-Default will apply to either Party A or Party B.	** 如交叉违约适用于A方或B方，应包括。

5(b)(v) [will][will not]* apply to Party A
[will][will not]* apply to Party B

[将会][不会]*适用于A方
[将会][不会]*适用于B方

(e) The ***"Automatic Early Termination"*** provision of Section 6(a) [will][will not]* apply to Party A
[will][will not]* apply to Party B

(e) 第6(a)条"*自动提前终止*"
[将会][不会]*适用于A方
[将会][不会]*适用于B方

(f) ***"Termination Currency"*** [will have the meaning specified in Section 14 of this Agreement.][means ....]*

(f) "*终止货币*"[具有本协议第14条规定的含义。][指 ....]*

(g) ***Additional Termination Event*** [will][will not]* apply. [The following will constitute an Additional Termination Event:—..
....
....
....

For the purpose of the foregoing Termination Event, the Affected Party or Affected Parties will be:—.................
....]***

(g) *其他终止事件*[将会][不会]*适用。[下列事件构成一项其他终止事件：－ ....
....
....
....

为上述终止事件之目的，受影响方或各受影响方指：－........
....]***

Part 2. **Tax Representations.******

第二部分 税务陈述****

(a) ***Payer Representations.*** For the purpose of Section 3(e) of this Agreement[, Party A and Party B do not make any representations.][:—

(a) *付款人陈述*。为本协议第3(e)条的目的[，A方和B方不会*作出任何陈述。][：－

[[(i)] [Party A] [and] [Party B] [each] make[s] the following representation:—

It is not required by any applicable law, as modified by the practice of any relevant governmental revenue authority, of any Relevant Jurisdiction to make any deduction or withholding for or on account of any Tax from any payment (other than interest under Section 9(h) of this Agreement) to be made by it to the other party under this Agreement. In making this representation, it may rely on (i) the accuracy of any representations made by the other party pursuant to Section 3(f) of this Agreement, (ii) the satisfaction of the agreement contained in Section 4(a)(i) or 4(a)(iii) of this Agreement and the accuracy and effectiveness of any document provided by the other party pursuant to Section 4(a)(i) or 4(a)(iii) of this Agreement and (iii) the satisfaction of the agreement of the other party contained in Section 4(d) of this Agreement, except that it will not be a breach of this representation where reliance is placed on clause (ii) above and the other party does not deliver a form or document under Section 4(a)(iii) by reason of material prejudice to its legal or commercial position.]*

[[(i)] [A方][和][B方][各自]作出陈述如下：－

经有关政府财税部门的惯例修改的任何有关管辖地的任何适用的法律均不要求从该方根据本协议向另一方支付的任何款项(本协议第9(h)条下的利息除外)中扣除或预提任何税项。在作出此项陈述时，该方可以依赖：(i)另一方按本协议第3(f)条所作出任何陈述的准确性；(ii)本协议第4(a)(i)条或4(a)(iii)条中所载的约定的履行，以及另一方按本协议第4(a)(i)条或4(a)(iii)条所提供的任何文件的准确性和有效性；和(iii)本协议第4(d)条中所载另一方约定的履行，但是，若该方依赖上述第(ii)款时，另一方为免对其法律或商业地位造成严重损害而没有递交第4(a)(iii)条项下的表格或文件则不构成对本陈述的违反。]*

[[(ii)] [Party A] [and] [Party B] [each] make[s] the following representation[s]:— ....

[[(ii)] [A方][和][B方][各自]作出陈述如下：－ ....
....

* Delete as applicable.
*** Include if Additional Termination Event will apply.
**** N.B.: the following representations may need modification if either party is a Multibranch Party.

* 视情况删除。
*** 如其他终止事件适用的话，应包括。
**** 注意：如任何一方为拥有多个办事处的交易方，下述陈述可能需进行调整。

....
....
....]]*

....
....]]*

(b) ***Payee Representations.*** For the purpose of Section 3(f) of this Agreement[, Party A and Party B do not make any representations.][:—

(b) ***收款人陈述。***为本协议第3(f)条的目的[，A方和B方不会作出任何陈述。][：-

[[(i)] [Party A] [and] [Party B] [each] make[s] the following representation:—

[[(i)] [A方][和][B方][各自]作出陈述如下：-

It is fully eligible for the benefits of the "Business Profits" or "Industrial and Commercial Profits" provision, as the case may be, the "interest" provision or the "Other Income" provision, if any, of the Specified Treaty with respect to any payment described in such provisions and received or to be received by it in connection with this Agreement and no such payment is attributable to a trade or business carried on by it through a permanent establishment in the Specified Jurisdiction.

该方具有完全资格获得适用于本协议项下收到或将收到之款项的特定条约中规定的"商业利润"或"工商业利润"条款(视情况而定)，及"利息"条款或"其他收入"条款(如有的话)所赋予之利益，并且该款项与该方在特定司法管辖区的永久营业地从事的商业或贸易没有任何关联。

"Specified Treaty" means with respect to Party A ....
....

"特定条约"就A方而言，指 ....
....

"Specified Jurisdiction" means with respect to Party A
....

"特定司法管辖区"就A方而言，指 ....
....

"Specified Treaty" means with respect to Party B ....
....

"特定条约"就B方而言，指 ....
....

"Specified Jurisdiction" means with respect to Party B
....]*

"特定司法管辖区"就B方而言，指 ....
....]*

[[(ii)] [Party A] [and] [Party B] [each] make[s] the following representation:—

[[(ii)] [A方][和][B方][各自]作出陈述如下：-

Each payment received or to be received by it in connection with this Agreement will be effectively connected with its conduct of a trade or business in the Specified Jurisdiction.

其就本协议收到或将收到的每一笔款项将会与该方在特定司法管辖区从事的贸易或商业行为具有实际联系。

"Specified Jurisdiction" means with respect to Party A
....

"特定司法管辖区"就A方而言，指 ....
....

"Specified Jurisdiction" means with respect to Party B
....]*

"特定司法管辖区"就B方而言，指 ....
....]*

[[(iii)] [Party A] [and] [Party B] [each] make[s] the following representation:—

[[(iii)] [A方][和][B方][各自]作出陈述如下：-

It is a "U.S. person" (as that term is used in section 1.1441-4(a)(3)(ii) of United States Treasury Regulations) for United States federal income tax purposes.]*

就美国联邦税务目的而言，其为一名"美国人"(如美国财政法规第1.441-4(a)(3)(ii)条中所使用的该词的含义)]*

[[(iv)] [Party A] [and] [Party B] [each] make[s] the following representation:—

[[(iv)] [A方][和][B方][各自]作出陈述如下：-

It is a "non-U.S. branch of a foreign person" (as that term is used in section 1.1441-4(a)(3)(ii) of United

就美国联邦税务目的而言，其为一个"外国人的非美国办事处"(如美国财政法规第1.441-4(a)(3)(ii)条中所使用的该词

* Delete as applicable.

* 视情况删除。

States Treasury Regulations) for United States federal income tax purposes.]*

[[(v)] [Party A] [and] [Party B] [each] make[s] the following representation:—

With respect to payments made to an address outside the United States or made by a transfer of funds to an account outside the United States, it is a "non-U.S. branch of a foreign person" (as that term is used in section 1.1441-4(a)(3)(ii) of United States Treasury Regulations) for United States federal income tax purposes.]*

[[(vi)] [Party A] [and] [Party B] [each] make[s] the following representation:—

It is a "foreign person" (as that term is used in section 1.6041-4(a)(4) of United States Treasury Regulations) for United States federal income tax purposes.]*

[[(vii)] [Party A] [and] [Party B] [each] make[s] the following representation[s]:—

....
....
....]]*

Part 3. **Agreement to Deliver Documents.**

For the purpose of Sections 4(a)(i) and 4(a)(ii) of this Agreement, each party agrees to deliver the following documents, as applicable:—

(a) Tax forms, documents or certificates to be delivered are[: none][:—

Party required to deliver document	Form/Document/ Certificate	Date by which to be delivered
....	....	....
....	....	....
....	....	....
....	....	....
....	....	..........................]*

(b) Other documents to be delivered are[: none][:—

Party required to deliver document	Form/Document/ Certificate	Date by which to be delivered	Covered by Section 3(d) Representation
....	....	....	[Yes][No]
....	....	....	[Yes][No]
....	....	....	[Yes][No]
....	....	....	[Yes][No]
....	....	....	[Yes][No]]*

的含义)]*

[[(v)] [A方][和][B方][各自]作出陈述如下：–

关于向美国以外的地址作出付款或向美国以外的帐户汇入资金事宜，就美国联邦税务目的而言，其为一个" 外国人的非美国办事处" (如美国财政法规第1.441-4(a)(3)(ii)条中使用的该词的含义)]*

[[(vi)] [A方][和][B方][各自]作出陈述如下：–

就美国联邦税务目的而言，其为一个" 外国人" (如美国财政法规第1.6041-4(a)(4)条中使用的该词的含义)]*

[[(vii)] [A方][和][B方][各自]作出陈述如下：–

....
....
....]]*

第三部分 **同意交付文件。**

为第4(a)(i)和第4(a)(ii)条的目的，每一方同意交付下列相关的文件：–

(a) 须交付的税务表、文件或证书为[：无][：–

须交付文件一方	表格/文件/证书	交付的期限
....	....	....
....	....	....
....	....	....
....	....	....
....	....	..........................]*

(b) 其他须交付的文件为[：无][：–

须交付文件的一方	表格/文件/证书	交付的期限	是否为第3(d)条下之陈述所涵盖
....	....	....	[是][否]
....	....	....	[是][否]
....	....	....	[是][否]
....	....	....	[是][否]
....	....	....	[是][否]]*

* Delete as applicable.

* 视情况删除。

Part 4. **Miscellaneous.**

(a) ***Addresses for Notices.*** For the purpose of Section 12(a) of this Agreement:—

Address for notices or communications to Party A:—

Address: ....
Attention: ....
Telex No.: .... Answerback: ....
Facsimile No.: .... Telephone No.: ....
E-mail: ....
Electronic Messaging System Details: ....
Specific Instructions: ....

Address for notices or communications to Party B:—

Address: ....
Attention: ....
Telex No.: .... Answerback: ....
Facsimile No.: .... Telephone No.: ....
E-mail: ....
Electronic Messaging System Details: ....
Specific Instructions: ....

(b) ***Process Agent.*** For the purpose of Section 13(c) of this Agreement:—

Party A appoints as its Process Agent: [not applicable] [..........]*
Party B appoints as its Process Agent: [not applicable] [..........]*

(c) ***Offices.*** The provisions of Section 10(a) [will][will not]* apply to this Agreement.

(d) ***Multibranch Party.*** For the purpose of Section 10(b) of this Agreement:—

Party A [is not a Multibranch Party.][is a Multibranch Party and may enter into a Transaction through any of the following Offices:—

....
....]*

Party B [is not a Multibranch Party.][is a Multibranch Party and may enter into a Transaction through any of the following Offices:—

....
....]*

[(e) ***Calculation Agent.*** The Calculation Agent is , unless otherwise specified in a Confirmation in relation to the relevant Transaction.]**

[(f)] ***Credit Support Document.*** Details of any Credit Support Document:— [none][..........

* Delete as applicable.
** Include if applicable.

第四部分 其他规定。

(a) ***通知地址***。为本协议第12(a)条之目的：－

A方收取通知或通讯的地址为：－

地址：..........
收件人：..........
电传号码：.......... 应答码：..........
传真号码：.......... 电话号码：..........
电子邮件：..........
电子信息系统资料：..........
特殊指示：..........

B方收取通知或通讯的地址为：－

地址：..........
收件人：..........
电传号码：.......... 应答码：..........
传真号码：.......... 电话号码：..........
电子邮件：..........
电子信息系统资料：..........
特殊指示：..........

(b) ***传票代理人***。为本协议第13(c)条之目的：－

A方指定其传票代理人如下：[不适用][..........]*
B方指定其传票代理人如下：[不适用][..........]*

(c) 办事处。第10(a)条的规定将[会][不会]*适用于本协议。

(d) ***拥有多个办事处的交易方***。为本协议10(b)条之目的：－

A方[不是一个拥有多个办事处的交易方。][A方是一个拥有多个办事处的交易方，可以通过以下任何办事处进行交易：－

....
....]*

B方[不是一个拥有多个办事处的交易方。][B方是一个拥有多个办事处的交易方，可以通过以下办事处进行交易：－

....
....]*

[(e) ***计算代理人***。除非有关交易的确认书另有规定，否则计算代理人为 .... 。]**

[(f)] ***信用支持文件***。信用支持文件的详情如下：－[无][..........
....

* 视情况删除。
** 视情况包括。

....
....
....]*

[(g)]***Credit Support Provider.*** Credit Support Provider means in relation to Party A, [none][..............................
....
....]*

Credit Support Provider means in relation to Party B, [none][..
....]*

[(h)]***Governing Law.*** This Agreement will be governed by and construed in accordance with [English law][the laws of the State of New York (without reference to choice of law doctrine)]*.

[(i)] ***Netting of Payments.*** "Multiple Transaction Payment Netting" [will not apply for the purpose of Section 2(c) of this Agreement.][will apply for the purpose of Section 2(c) of this Agreement to [all Transactions][the following Transactions or groups of Transactions:— ....
....]
(in each case starting from [the date of this Agreement][..])]*

[(j)] ***"Affiliate"*** [will have the meaning specified in Section 14 of this Agreement.][means ....
....]*

[(k)]***Absence of Litigation.*** For the purpose of Section 3(c):—

"Specified Entity" means in relation to Party A, ...

"Specified Entity" means in relation to Party B, ...

[(l)] ***No Agency.*** The provisions of Section 3(g) [will][will not]* apply to this Agreement.

[(m)]***Additional Representation*** [will][will not]* apply. [For the purpose of Section 3 of this Agreement, the following will constitute an Additional Representation:—

[[(i)] ***Relationship Between Parties.*** Each party will be deemed to represent to the other party on the date on which it enters into a Transaction that (absent a written agreement between the parties that expressly imposes affirmative obligations to the contrary for that Transaction):—

[(1)] *Non-Reliance.* It is acting for its own account, and it has made its own independent decisions to enter into that Transaction and as to whether that Transaction is appropriate or proper for it based upon its own judgment and upon advice from such advisers as it has deemed necessary. It is not relying on any communication (written or oral) of the other party as investment advice or as a

* Delete as applicable.

....
....]*

[(g)]*信用支持提供者*。就A方而言，信用支持提供者指，[无][....
....
....]*

就B方而言，信用支持提供者指，[无][................................
....
....]*

[(h)]*管辖法律*。本协议将受[英国法律][纽约州法律(不包括法律选择原则)的管辖并按其解释]*。

[(i)] *付款净额结算*。"多项交易付款？额结算"[为本协议第2(c)条的目的不适用。][为本协议第2(c)条的目的适用于[所有交易][下列交易或交易组：－ ....
....]
(每种情况下从[本协议之日期起][..................................])]*

[(j)] *"关联企业"*[具有本协议第14条规定的含义。][指 ....]*

[(k)] *"不存在诉讼"*为第3(c)条的目的：－

*"特定机构"*就A方而言，指 ....

*"特定机构"*就B方而言，指 ....

[(l)] *无代理*。第3(g)条的规定将[会][不会]*适用于本协议。

[(m)]*其他陈述*将[会][不会]*适用。[为本协议第3条的目的，以下将构成其他陈述：－

[[(i)] *各方之间的关系*。一方在每次进行交易当日应被视为向另一方作出如下陈述(各方之间存在明确规定与此相反的义务的书面协议的情况除外)：－

[(1)] *不依赖*。该方代表自己行事，已自行独立决定进行该交易，并自行判断和在认为必要时听取顾问的意见后决定该交易是否恰当适宜。该方并不依赖来自于另一方的任何(书面或口头的)通讯并不以此作为进行该交易的投资意见或建议，该方理解有关交易条款和条件的信息和解释不会被当作进行该交易的投资意见或建议。从另一方收到的任何(书面或口头的)通讯不会被视为对该交易预计效益的担保或保证。

* 视情况删除。

recommendation to enter into that Transaction, it being understood that information and explanations related to the terms and conditions of a Transaction will not be considered investment advice or a recommendation to enter into that Transaction. No communication (written or oral) received from the other party will be deemed to be an assurance or guarantee as to the expected results of that Transaction.

[(2)] *Assessment and Understanding.* It is capable of assessing the merits of and understanding (on its own behalf or through independent professional advice), and understands and accepts, the terms, conditions and risks of that Transaction. It is also capable of assuming, and assumes, the risks of that Transaction.

[(2)] *评估和理解*。该方能够评估该交易的价值并(自己或通过独立的专业意见的帮助)能够理解并且理解和接受该交易的条款、条件和风险。该方能够承担并会承担该交易的风险。

[(3)] *Status of Parties.* The other party is not acting as a fiduciary for or an adviser to it in respect of that Transaction.]]*

[(3)] *地位*。另一方就该交易而言并非该方的受托人或顾问。]]*

[[(n)]***Recording of Conversations.*** Each party (i) consents to the recording of telephone conversations between the trading, marketing and other relevant personnel of the parties in connection with this Agreement or any potential Transaction, (ii) agrees to obtain any necessary consent of, and give any necessary notice of such recording to, its relevant personnel and (iii) agrees, to the extent permitted by applicable law, that recordings may be submitted in evidence in any Proceedings.]**

[[(n)]***谈话录音***。各方(i)同意对交易双方的交易、营销和其他人员进行的有关本协议或任何潜在交易的电话谈话进行录音，(ii)同意从其有关人员就此等录音获取任何必要的同意及签发必要的通知，及(iii)同意在适用法律允许范围内此等录音可在任何诉讼中作为证据提交。]**

Part 5. **Other Provisions.**

第五部分 其它规定。

________________	________________	________________	________________
(Name of Party)	(Name of Party)	(签署方名称)	(签署方名称)
By: ____________	By: ____________	签名：____________	签名：____________
Name:	Name:	姓名：	姓名：
Title:	Title:	职位：	职位：
Date:	Date:	日期：	日期：

* Delete as applicable.
** Include if applicable.

* 视情况删除。
** 视情况包括。

Glossary

A

Absolute viscosity

An observation of liquid's rate of flow under pressure applied to neutralize density's influence. This property, sometimes called dynamic viscosity, converts to kinematical viscosity by division. With density expressed in grams/cm, centistokes are the units of kinematical viscosity, and centipoises the units of absolute viscosity. Centipoises/density = centistokes

Accrual accounting

When swaps are used to hedge specific on-balance-sheet exposures, they are often accounted for on an accrual basis. Under the accrual method, the net payment or receipt in each period is accrued and recorded as an adjustment to income or expense.
See Hedge accounting, Mark-to-market

Accrued interest

Interest earned between the most recent interest payment and the present date but not yet paid to the lender.

Accumulation

1. An addition to a trader's original market position. The first of three distinct phases in a major trend in which investors are buying.
2. A single oil or gas deposit as defined by the trap, charge, and reservoir characteristics of the play.

Accumulation/distribution line

See Chaikin oscillator.

Acidizing

Treatment of oil-bearing limestone or carbonate formations with a solution of hydrochloric acid and other chemicals to increase production. The acid is forced under pressure into the formation where it enlarges the flow channels by dissolving the limestone.

Activity
The level of catalyst's ability to do its work. The scale descends from fresh (full capacity right from the box or rejuvenator) to spent (coated, poisoned, or other wise neutralized.)

Actual peak day
The day during which the greatest gas demand occurs in a one-year period.

Actuals
Refers to actual physical commodities, as distinguished from futures.

Actual specifications
The quality reports on a specific parcel of fuel or feedstock. Such specifications do not constitute guarantees on the oil unless the seller says so. But they give a good description of the product available aboard a vessel or in a storage tank.

Adaptive filter
Smoothing and/or forecasting prices with continuously updated weighting of past prices.

Add-on method
A method of paying interest where the interest is added onto the principal at maturity or interest payment dates.

AFRA
Average Freight Rate Assessments. A monthly estimate of tanker rates issued by London tanker brokers, AFRA, quoted on a Worldscale basis, assists large oil companies' internal accounting, provides a freight element for some netback deals, and serves other purposes somewhat removed from the daily tanker business.

Against actuals
A transaction generally used by two hedgers who want to exchange futures for cash positions. Also referred to as "against actuals" or "versus cash."

Aggregation
The policy under which all futures positions owned or controlled by one trader or a group of traders are combined to determine reportable positions and speculative limits.

Air draft
The distance between the surface of navigable water, such as a channel, and the lowest point on some obstruction above it, a bridge for instance. A ship cannot use a waterway if it needs more vertical clearance than available. This consideration prevents certain tankers from reaching some terminals.

American-style option
An American-style option may be exercised at any time during its lifetime, up to and including the expiration date. *See* European-style option.

Anaume
Candlestick formation. An exceptional exhaustion pattern (meaning "gap filling") composed of five candles. The anaume occurs when the gap is filled in after a market price has changed directions. This pattern coupled with the other patterns indicate a strong potential for a bullish reversal and price advance.

Aniline point
A specification, quoted in degree Fahrenheit in the USA and Centigrade elsewhere, which reports the aromatics content of a hydrocarbon mixture. This quality consideration indicates the susceptibility of a vacuum gasoil to catalytic cracking because paraffins crack well, but aromatics do not. The higher the temperature the better, since higher temperatures mean less aromatics, hence more paraffins.

Annual contract quantity (ACQ)
The amount of gas specified in a buyer's nomination purchase contract for one year. Some rights, such as make-up gas and take-or-pay, may need to be taken into account depending on the amount of gas taken versus the amount contracted for.

Anthracite
The highest rank of coal; used primarily for residential and commercial space heating. It is a hard, brittle, and black lustrous coal, often referred to as hard coal, containing a high percentage of fixed carbon and a low percentage of volatile matter. The moisture content of fresh-mined anthracite generally is less than 15%. The heat content of anthracite ranges from 22 to 28 million Btu per ton on a moist, mineral-matter-free basis. The heat content of anthracite coal consumed in the United States averages 25 million Btu per ton, on the as-received basis (i.e., containing both inherent moisture and mineral matter). Note: Since the 1980's, anthracite refuse or mine waste has been used for steam electric power generation. This fuel typically has a heat content of 15 million Btu per ton or less.

Anthracite briquets
See Coal briquets.

Antiknock index
The average of a motor gasoline's or blending component's RON and MON (RON + MON)/2, sometimes written (R + M)/2.

Annual cap
In a gas buyer's purchase agreement there is often a limit higher than the annual contract quantity (ACQ), above which the seller is not liable to sell. This is the annual cap and is usually stated as a percentage of the ACQ. Also known as maximum annual quantity (MAQ).

API
The American Petroleum Institute, a trade association. Publishes weekly information on US petroleum stock figures, refinery throughput, imports, exports, and stock levels. This information is divided into five geographical areas known as PADDS. The API also established the internationally recognized system for grading crude oils by specific gravity (API gravity).

API degrees (`API)
The units of API's density scale. *See* below.

API gravity
An arbitrary scale expressing the gravity or density of liquid petroleum products, as established by the American Petroleum Institute (API). The measuring scale is calibrated in terms of degrees API. The higher the API gravity, the lighter the compound. Light crude oils generally exceed 38 degrees API and heavy crude oils are commonly labeled as all crude oils with an API gravity of 22 degrees or below. Intermediate crude oils fall in the range of 22 degrees to 38 degrees API gravity.

Apparent consumption (coal)
As used here, a calculated amount equal to primary coal production plus imports of coal and coke, minus exports of coal and coke minus changes in stocks of coal and coke. Notes: 1) For the United States, coal consumption data are reported by major end-use sector and do not have to be calculated; 2) A net withdrawal from stocks increases consumption and a net addition to stocks decreases consumption.

Apparent consumption (natural gas)
As used here, a calculated amount equal to dry natural gas production, plus imports of natural gas, minus exports of natural gas, minus changes in natural gas stocks.

Note: A net withdrawal from stocks increases consumption and a net addition to stocks decreases consumption.

Apparent consumption of refined petroleum products
See Apparent Consumption (Petroleum).

Apparent consumption (petroleum)
As used here, a calculated amount that includes domestic inland consumption, refinery fuel and loss, and international bunker fuels. Also included, where available, are liquefied petroleum gases sold directly from natural gas processing plants for fuel or chemical uses.

Appraisal well
A well drilled as part of an appraisal drilling program which is carried out to determine the physical extent, reserves, and likely production rate of a field.

Aquifer
A water-bearing rock strata. In a water-drive field the aquifer is the water zone of the reservoir underlying the oil zone.

ARA
Amsterdam–Rotterdam–Antwerp area – a port and refining area in the Belgian-Dutch region. A cargo or barge of a refined product traded on a CIF ARA basis means that ports within this area are covered in the cost. A cargo traded on a FOB basis means the oil can come from any of these ports.

AR
American rate. Tanker hire prices according to the American Tanker Rate Schedule. This system applies to voyages that begin and end in US ports. US law (the Jones Act) allows only US flag ships in this domestic service.

Arbitrage
The simultaneous purchase and sale of similar commodities in different markets to take advantage of price discrepancy.

Arbitration
The procedure of settling disputes between members, or between members and customers.

Aromatics
A family of hydrocarbons characterized by a single or multiple ring structure containing unsaturated carbon–carbon bonds. Common aromatics which boil in the gasoline range (benzene, toluene, and xylenes, in particular) have a very high octane rating. Reformers produce high octane blend-stock by making aromatics. The "A" in PONA and N + A stands for aromatics.

Artificial lift
Any system that adds energy to the fluid column in a wellbore with the objective of initiating and improving production from the well. Artificial-lift systems use a range of operating principles, including rod pumping, gas lift, and electrical submersible pumps.

Ash
Carbonaceous residue produced by burning crude oil and petroleum products. The industry tests fuels and other hydrocarbon mixtures in order to determine how much of this combustion by-product will form in ordinary use of its products. Refiners and others also use ash yield to deduce the presence of metallic soaps, abrasive solids, and other ash-causing contaminants in hydrocarbon mixtures.

Asian option
Asian (or average) options have payoffs that depend on an average of prices for the underlying commodity over a period of time, rather than the price of the commodity on a single date. The averaging period may correspond to the entire life of the option, or may be shorter.

Asphalt
A mixture of heavy carbon-based compounds containing a high percentage of multiple-ring aromatics, many of them involving sulfur, nitrogen, and oxygen atoms. Some folks use the word, asphalt, interchangeably with bitumen, the name of its characteristic constituent.

Note: The conversion factor for asphalt is 5.5 barrels per short ton.

See **Asphalt cement**
A derivative, nearly or completely solid at room temperature, of certain crude oils. This black, tarry material usually comes from vacuum residue. It has several industrial applications. Pavers heat it to liquid form and mix in gravel to make road surface materials called blacktop, macadam, tarmac, or "asphalt". Builders use it to make and join bricks, to coat roofs, and to form shingles. It glues together various manufactured goods.

Asphaltenes
Complex molecules which reveal their ring-structures by dissolving in aromatic liquids but not in paraffins. These compounds may influence the burning and blending characteristics of residual oils, if present in sufficient concentrations. They contribute to the high melting temperature and adhesion of bitumen and asphalt cement.

Asphalt (refined)
See Asphalt.

Assay
An elaborate laboratory report describing in detail the quality of grades of crude oil. The data presented includes, among other items, density, sulfur, naphthenicity, pour point, viscosity, distillation, and information on the quality of individual fractions. They tell a refiner what products he can make from a specific crude.

Assign
To make an option seller perform his obligation to assume a short futures position (as a seller of a call option) or a long futures position (as a seller of a put option).

Associated-dissolved natural gas
Natural gas that occurs in crude oil reservoirs either as free gas (associated) or as a gas in solution with crude oil (dissolved gas). *See* Natural gas.

Associated gas
See Associated-dissolved natural gas and Natural gas.

Associated natural gas
See Associated-dissolved natural gas and Natural gas.

Associated person (AP)
An individual who solicits orders, customers, or customer funds (or who supervises persons performing such duties) on behalf of a Futures Commission Merchant, an Introducing Broker, a Commodity Trading Adviser, or a Commodity Pool Operator and who is registered with the Commodity Futures Trading Commission.

ASTM
American Society for Testing and Materials. An organization which determines and publishes consensus standards of suitability and quality for a wide variety of materials including petroleum and refined products. ASTM develops and endorses methods of

testing hydrocarbons properties as well as definitive specifications for such classes of refined product as fuel oils, aviation kerosene, burning kerosene, and motor gasoline.

Atmos
Abbreviation of atmospheric-pressure distillation, as in atmos bottoms and atmos gasoil.

Atmospheric crude oil distillation unit
See Distillation unit (Atmospheric).

Atmospheric distillation
A technique for separating hydrocarbon mixtures which uses distillation apparatus operated at atmospheric pressure. Generally, the industry specifies ambient pressure to distinguish products of crude distillers, atmospheric fractions, from the products of vacuum flashers which, as the name implies distill atmospheric residue in a partial vacuum.

Atmospheric gasoil
The heaviest product boiled by a crude distillation unit operating at atmospheric pressure. This fraction ordinarily sells as distillate fuel oil, either in pure form or blended with cracked stocks. In blends atmospheric gasoil, often abbreviated AGO, usually serves as the premium quality component used to lift lesser streams to the standards of saleable furnace oil or diesel engine fuel. Certain ethylene plants, called heavy oil crackers, can take AGO as feedstock.

Atmospheric residue
The portion of crude oil taken as a bottoms product in a crude distillation unit which operates at atmospheric pressure under several other names apply to this product including atmos (atmospheric) residue, atmos bottoms, atmospheric fuel oil long residue, straight-run heavy fuel oil and topped crude.

At-the-money option

1. At-the-money spot – An option whose strike is the same as the prevailing market price of the underlying rate or price.
2. At-the-money forward – An option whose strike is at the same level as the prevailing market price of the underlying forward contract.

Attenuation
The fractional part of reduced energy or lost power due to smoothing or filtering.

Autoregressive
Using previous data to predict future data.

Availability
A quantity of crude or product a supplier could sell.

Average Option
See Asian option

Average reserve life index
Ratio between the amount of reserves at the end of the year and total production for the year.

Avgas
High octane aviation gasoline used in piston type aircraft engines. Familiar designation of aviation gasoline.

Aviation gasoline blending components
Naphthas that are used for blending or compounding gasoline into finished aviation gasoline (e.g., straight-run gasoline, alkylate, and reformate). Excluded are oxygenates (alcohols, ethers), butane, and pentanes plus.

Aviation gasoline (finished)
A complex mixture of relatively volatile hydrocarbons with or without small quantities of additives, blended to form a fuel suitable for use in aviation reciprocating engines. Fuel specifications are provided in ASTM Specification D 910 and Military Specification MIL-G-5572. Note: Data on blending components are not counted in data on finished aviation gasoline. *See* Jet Fuel; Kerosene-Type Jet Fuel; and Naphtha-Type Jet Fuel.

Average directional movement index (ADX)
Indicator developed by J. Welles Wilder to measure market trend intensity.

Aviation gasoline
High-grade motor fuel blended to meet the requirements of piston-type air plane engines. This specialty product differs in all critical respects from aviation turbine fuel (jet).

Aviation turbine fuel (ATF)
The fuel burned by air planes' jet engines. Civilian aircrafts consumes a kerosene-range product variously known as jet kero, jet A-1, avtur, DERD-2494, and JP1. Warplanes needed special fuels. Two military grades, JP-4 and JP-5 fall within the common notion of AFT.

B

%b
Indicates where the closing price is within Bollinger bands.

Backhaul
A tanker's revenue-producing return voyage. Some ships shuttle between two tankers ports. They travel in one direction as dictated by normal oil flow patterns or refining system's needs. Often, they have no natural employment from when they discharge to their port of origin where another load awaits. They would like to find a cargo to pay their costs on this return trip. Otherwise, they must return in ballast. Charters often relet ships at bargain back haul rates for these voyages. They prefer some income to none.

Back month
Back month contracts are any exchange-traded derivatives contracts apart from the nearest, or front, contract month.

Back-propagation network
A feedforward multilayered neural network that is a commonly used neural network paradigm.

Back-testing
A strategy is tested or optimized on historical data and then the strategy is applied to new data to *See* if the results are consistent.

Backwardation
When the price of nearer (typically prompt or spot) crude, product or another underlying commodity, or instrument trades at a premium to the same commodity or instrument traded further forward. Also known as an inverse. *See* Contango.

Bad oil
Oil not acceptable for delivery to the pipeline purchaser because of too high BS&W; oil requiring additional treating.

Baffles
Plates or obstructions built into a tank or other vessel to change the direction of fluid flow.

Ballast
Water taken aboard a vessel to increase its draft, steady its motion, correct its trim, or otherwise make it more seaworthy when sailing without cargo. The trade uses this word to describe repositioning voyages or empty backhauls forced on ship. Hence, phrases appear like "ballasting Trans-Atlantic"

Bar chart
A chart that graphs the high, low, and settlement prices for a specific trading session over a given period of time.

Barge lots
Quantities of petroleum product accommodated in the sizes of barges in common use in a particular area. This term usually applies to small (less than cargo-size) volumes of product intended for regional distribution. On the US Gulf Coast, for instance, petroleum products barges typically range from 10,000 to 50,000 barrels. On the Rhine, barges typically carry lots as large as 1000 tons.

Barrel
A unit of volume equal to 42 US. gallons.

Barrels of oil equivalent (BOE)
Gas volume that is expressed in terms of its energy equivalent in barrels of oil.
6000 cubic feet of gas equals 1 barrel of oil equivalent (BOE); or
42 US. gallons of oil at 40 degrees Fahrenheit.

Barrels per calendar day
The amount of input that a distillation facility can process under usual operating conditions. The amount is expressed in terms of capacity during a 24-hour period and reduces the maximum processing capability of all units at the facility under continuous operation (*see* Barrels per Stream Day) to account for the following limitations that may delay, interrupt, or slow down production:

1. the capability of downstream processing units to absorb the output of crude oil processing facilities of a given refinery. No reduction is necessary for intermediate streams that are distributed to other than downstream facilities as part of refinery's normal operation;
2. the types and grades of inputs to be processed;
3. the types and grades of products expected to be manufactured;
4. the environmental constraints associated with refinery operations;
5. the reduction of capacity for scheduled downtime due to such conditions as routine inspection, maintenance, repairs, and turnaround; and
6. the reduction of capacity for unscheduled downtime due to such conditions as mechanical problems, repairs, and slowdowns.

Barrels per stream day
The maximum number of barrels of input that a distillation facility can process within a 24-hour period when running at full capacity under optimal crude and product slate conditions with no allowance for downtime.

Barrier option
Barrier options are exotic options which either come to life (are knocked-in) or are extinguished (knocked-out) under conditions stipulated in the option contract. The conditions are usually defined in terms of a price level (barrier, knock-out, or knock-in price) that may be reached at any time during the lifetime of the option.

Baseload
The minimum amount of electric power delivered or required over a given period of time at a steady rate.

Base stock
A hydrocarbon mixture which makes up much of the volume of a gasoline blend. Usually such stocks have properties not too far removed from finished fuel because the minor components have to bring the entire blend within accepted limits of gasoline quality. Base stocks in today's US motor gasoline include cat gasoline, reformate, and alkylate.

Basis
The difference between spot (cash) prices and the futures contract price. Unless otherwise specified, the price of the nearby futures contract month is generally used to calculate the basis.

Basis points
The measure of yields on bonds and notes; one basis point equals 0.01% of yield.

Basis risk
Basis risk is the risk that the value of a futures contract (or an over-the-counter hedge) will not move in line with that of the underlying exposure. Alternatively, it is the risk that the cash-futures spread will widen or narrow between the times at which a hedge position is implemented and liquidated.

There are various types of basis risk. For example, a heating oil wholesaler which sells its product in Baltimore will be exposed to basis risk if it hedges using New York Harbor heating oil futures contracts listed by NYMEX. This is a "locational" basis risk. Other forms of basis risk include "product" basis, arising from mismatches in type or quality of hedge and underlying (e.g., hedging jet fuel with heating oil); and "time" or "calendar" basis (e.g., hedging an exposure to physical prices in December with a January futures contract).

Basis swap
Basis swaps are used to hedge exposure to basis risk, such as locational risk or time exposure risk. For example, a natural gas basis swap could be used to hedge a locational price risk: the seller receives from the buyer a NYMEX Division settlement value (usually the average of the last three days' closing prices) plus a negotiated fixed basis, and pays the buyer the published index value of gas sold at a specified location.

Basket trades
Large transactions made up of a number of different stocks.

Batch
A definite amount of oil, mud, chemicals, cement, or other material in a treatment or operation.

Battery (tank battery)
The production handling equipment on the lease.

bbl
One barrel of oil; 1 barrel = 35 Imperial gallons (approx.), or 159 liters (approx.); 7.5 barrels = 1 ton (approx.); 6.29 barrels = 1 cubic meter.

bcf
Billion cubic feet; 1 bcf = 0.83 million tons of oil equivalent.

bcm
Billion cubic meters (1 cubic meter = 35.31 cubic feet).

bbl/D
The abbreviation for barrels per day. Other related abbreviations are: BPD for barrels per day; BOPD for barrels of oil per day; BWPD for barrels of water per day; BLPD for barrels of liquid per day.

Beam
The breadth of a ship at its widest point.

Beam well
A well whose fluid is being lifted by rods and pump actuated by a beam pump rig unit.

Bear
Someone who thinks market prices will decline.

Bear market (Bear/Bearish)
A market in which prices are declining. A market participant who believes prices will move lower is called a "bear." A news item is considered bearish if it is expected to result in lower prices.

Bear spread
In most commodities and financial instruments, the term refers to selling the nearby contract month, and buying the deferred contract, to profit from a change in the price relationship.

Benzene
The simplest aromatic. This unsaturated six-carbon ring forms the basis of a whole class of compounds. The coal processing business first produced benzene in commercial quantities. This source still provides some of the material on the market. But refinery and petrochemical plant reformers, toluene hydrodealkylators, and steam crackers now make most of the supply. The products of benzene range from egg cartons to pesticides to nylon stockings.

Benchmark crude
Synonymous with reference crude or marker crude. A crude oil whose price is used as a reference against which other crudes are priced. Because of their liquidity, the NYMEX light sweet crude oil and IPE Brent crude oil futures contracts are used as global benchmarks. Dubai crude is widely used as a benchmark for Middle Eastern crudes, especially for sale to Asian markets.

Beta
A regression of the estimated coefficient that belongs to a particular variable.

Beta (coefficient)
A measure of the market/nondiversifiable risk associated with any given security in the market. A ratio of an individual's stock historical returns to the historical returns of the stock market. If a stock increased in value by 12% while the market increased by 10%, the stock's beta would be 1.2.

Bias
The difference between the expected value of an estimator and the actual value to be estimated.

Bid
An expression indicating a desire to buy a commodity at a given price, opposite of offer.

Bid and Ask
Highest price and lowest price that an investor will pay for a tradable.

Bilateral energy trading
Trading whereby two parties (for example a generator and a supplier) enter into a contract to deliver electricity at an agreed time in the future.

Bilateral netting
An agreement between two counterparties to offset the value of all in-the-money contracts with all out-of-the-money contracts, resulting in a single net exposure amount owed by one counterparty to the other.

Bill of lading
Documentation associated with a specific cargo of oil and is signed by the captain of the ship and the contract supplier.

Bimodal distribution
In which observations are displayed as having two distinct peaks.

Binomial model
Any model that incorporates a binomial tree, also called a binomial lattice. A binomial model describes the evolution of a random variable over a series of time steps, assigning given probabilities to a rise or fall in the variable. After the initial rise or fall, the next two branches will each have two possible outcomes and so the process will continue, building a "tree" over time. The process is usually specified such that an upward movement followed by a downward movement results in the same price, so that the branches recombine. Binomial trees are of interest because they can be used to deal with American-style features; the early exercise condition can be tested at each point in the tree.

Biodiesel
A renewable fuel synthesized from soybeans, other oil crops, or animal tallow that can substitute for petroleum diesel fuel.

Biofuels
Liquid fuels and blending components produced from biomass (plant) feedstocks, used primarily for transportation.

Biogas
A medium Btu gas containing methane and carbon dioxide, produced from the anaerobic decomposition of organic material in a landfill. Also called biomass gas.

Biogenic
Produced by the actions of living organisms.

Biomass
Nonfossil material of biological origin constituting a renewable energy resource. Included in Wood and Waste.

Biomass gas
See Biogas.

Biosphere
The portion of the Earth and its atmosphere that can support life. The part of the global carbon cycle that includes living organisms and biogenic organic matter.

Bit
The cutting or boring element used in drilling oil and gas wells.

Bitumen
Mineral pitch rich in asphaltenes and other complex, high-molecular-weight molecules. These mixtures of heavy hydrocarbons and resins form the base of, and impart adhesive, semi-solid consistency to asphalt cement and tar.

Bituminous briquets
See Coal briquets.

Bituminous coal
A dense coal, usually black, sometimes dark brown, often with well-defined bands of bright and dull material, used primarily as fuel in steam-electric power generation, with substantial quantities also used for heat and power applications in manufacturing and to make coke. Bituminous coal is the most abundant coal in active US mining regions. Its moisture content usually is less than 20%. The heat content of bituminous coal ranges from 21 to 30 million Btu per ton on a moist, mineral-matter-free basis. The heat content of bituminous coal consumed in the United States averages 24 million Btu per ton, on the as-received basis (i.e., containing both inherent moisture and mineral matter).

Black box
A proprietary, computerized trading system whose rules are not disclosed or readily accessible.

Black liquor
A byproduct of the paper production process that can be used as a source of energy.

Black–Scholes option pricing model
An option-pricing model initially derived by Fischer Black and Myron Scholes in 1973 for securities options and later refined by Black in 1976 for options on futures.

Blender
Someone or some organization which combines various components to produce motor gasoline. The term may accurately apply to refiners for they blend motor fuel from blendstock they produce or purchase. In many cases, however, the word designates gasoline makers who do not refine any crude oil and distinguishes them from the "refiners" who do.

Blendstock
A component combined with other materials to produce a finished petroleum product. The term applies most frequently to motor gasoline ingredients.

Block
An acreage sub-division measuring approximately 10 × 20 kms, forming part of a quadrant. For example, Block 9/13 is the 13th block in Quadrant 9.

Block trades
Large transactions of a particular stock sold as a unit.

Blow-down
Condensate and gas is produced simultaneously from the outset of production.

Blow-off top
A steep and rapid increase in price followed by a steep and rapid drop in price.

Blow-out preventers (BOPs)
Are high-pressure wellhead valves, designed to shut off the uncontrolled flow of hydrocarbons.

Board of trade
See Contract Market.

Board of trade clearing corporation
An independent corporation that settles all trades made at the Chicago Board of Trade acting as a guarantor for all trades cleared by it, reconciles all clearing member firm accounts each day to ensure that all gains have been credited and all losses have been collected, and sets and adjusts clearing member firm margins for changing market conditions. Also referred to as clearing corporation. An agency or separate corporation of a

futures exchange that is responsible for settling trading accounts, clearing trades, collecting and maintaining margin monies, regulating delivery, and reporting trading data. Clearinghouses act as third parties to all futures and options contracts acting as a buyer to every clearing member seller and a seller to every clearing member buyer.

Boe
Barrel of Oil Equivalent. It is used as a standard unit measure for oil and natural gas. The latter is converted from standard cubic meters into barrels of oil equivalent using a coefficient equal to 0.0061 in the case of gas produced abroad and 0.0063 in the case of gas produced in Italy due to their different calorific values.

Boiler
A device for generating steam for power, processing, or heating purposes; or for producing hot water for heating purposes or hot water supply. Heat from an external combustion source is transmitted to a fluid contained within the tubes in the boiler shell. This fluid is delivered to an end-use at a desired pressure, temperature, and quality.

Boilerhouse
To make up or fake a report without actually doing the work.

Boiling range
The temperature spread between the points where a material starts and finishes evaporating. This term has an abstract usage- naphtha-range, for example. It also has a specific one, such as "naphtha with a 140–350 °F range."

Boolean
Describes a variable that may have one of only two possible values: true or false. After George Boole, English logician, credited with the invention of "Boolean logic."

Bottoms
Unvaporized material drawn from the lowest point of a fractionation column.

Breakaway gap
When a tradable exits a trading range by trading at price levels that leaves a price area where no trading occurs on a bar chart. Typically, these gaps appear at the completion of important chart formations.

Breakout
The point when the market price moves out of the trend channel.

Brent blend crude oil
UK Brent Blend is a blend of crude oil from various fields in the East Shetland Basin. The crude is landed at the Sullom Voe terminal and is used as a benchmark for the pricing of much of the world's crude oil production.

British thermal unit (Btu)
See Btu (British Thermal Unit).

Broker
A company or individual that executes futures and options orders on behalf of financial and commercial institutions and/or the general public.

Broker-dealer
A firm that handles transactions for its customers and also purchases securities for its own account, selling them to customers.

Brokerage fee
A fee charged by a broker for executing a transaction.

Brokerage house
An individual or organization that solicits or accepts orders to buy or sell futures contracts or options on futures and accepts money or other assets from customers to support such orders. Also referred to as "commission house" or "wire house."

Broker's deck
Orders physically held by the floor broker in the trading pit.

Bromine number
A measure of the olefins content of a hydrocarbon mixture. In the petroleum intermediates trade, it serves primarily to indicate the presence of cracked stock in a cargo or stream. California air pollution laws also make it an important specification for motor gasoline and blendstocks offered in Los Angeles. As a rule-of-thumb, a mixture's bromine number equals roughly twice its olefin content.

Btu (British Thermal Unit)
A standard unit for measuring the quantity of heat energy equal to the quantity of heat needed to raise the temperature of 1 pound of water by 1 degree Fahrenheit at or near 39.2 degrees Fahrenheit. The Btu is a convenient measure by which to compare the energy content of various fuels. *See* Heat Content of a Quantity of Fuel, Gross and Heat Content of a Quantity of Fuel, Net.

BTX
An abbreviation for benzene, toluene, and xylene.

BTX extraction
A solvent recovery process for capturing benzene, toluene, and xylenes from refinery and petrochemical plant process streams (reformate and pyrolysis gasoline).

Bucketing
Directly or indirectly taking the opposite side of a customer's order into the broker's own account or into an account in which the broker has an interest, without open and competitive execution of the order on an exchange.

Bull
Someone who thinks market prices will rise.

Bull market (bull/bullish)
A market in which prices are rising. A market participant who believes prices will move higher is called a "bull." A news item is considered bullish if it is expected to result in higher prices.

Bull spread
In most commodities and financial instruments, the term refers to buying the nearby month, and selling the deferred month, to profit from the change in the price relationship.

Bunker C
A residual fuel used as ship's fuel, usually has a high sulfur content and high viscosity.

Bunker fuels
Fuel supplied to ships and aircraft, both domestic and foreign, consisting primarily of residual and distillate fuel oil for ships and kerosene-type jet fuel for aircraft. The term "international bunker fuels" is used to denote the consumption of fuel for international transport activities. Notes: 1) For the purposes of greenhouse gas (GHG) emissions inventories, data on emissions from combustion of international bunker fuels are subtracted from national emissions totals. However, because it was often difficult to separate out international bunker fuels, this adjustment was not made in estimating the carbon dioxide emissions that appear here. 2) Historically, bunker fuels have meant only ship fuel. *See* Vessel bunkering.

Bunkers
See Bunker fuels.

Burning kerosene
Kerosene intended for use as domestic stove lamp fuel.

Butadiene
A four-carbon olefin. More precisely, a di-olefin because the molecule has two double bonds. Synthetic rubber production consumes much of the butadiene supply. Smaller amounts find an outlet in high-strength resins manufacturing.

Butane
A normally gaseous straight-chain or branched-chain hydrocarbon (C_4H_{10}). It is extracted from natural gas or refinery gas streams. It includes isobutane and normal butane and conforms to ASTM Specification D 1835 and Gas Processors Association Specifications for commercial butane.

Butterfly spread
The placing of two interdelivery spreads in opposite directions with the center delivery month common to both spreads.

Butylene
An olefinic hydrocarbon (C_4H_8) recovered from refinery processes.

Buy and hold
The acquisition of a tradable for the long term rather than quick turnover.

Buy/sell
A swap in which, for accounting purposes or other reasons, company A sells a parcel to company B while B sells a second parcel to A. Each party buys one and sells another.

Buying hedge
Buying futures contracts to protect against a possible price increase of cash commodities that will be purchased in the future. At the time the cash commodities are bought, the open futures position is closed by selling an equal number and type of futures contracts as those that were initially purchased.

C

C + F
Cost and freight. The price includes the cost of the cargo and the freight/vessel hiring costs but not the insurance.

Calendar spread
The purchase of one delivery month of a given futures contract and simultaneous sale of another delivery month of the same commodity on the same exchange. The purchase of either a call or put option and the simultaneous sale of the same type of option with typically the same strike price but with a different expiration month.

Call option
A contract that gives the buyer of the option the right but not the obligation to take delivery of the underlying security at a specific price within a certain time.

Calmar ratio
Takes the average rate of return for the last 36 months and divides it by the maximum drawdown for the same period. It is usually calculated on a monthly basis. A negative

value for the Calmar ratio means that the system or trader had a negative performance over the last three years.

Canceling order
An order that deletes a customer's previous order.

Candlestick charts
A charting method, originally from Japan, in which the high and low are plotted as a single line and are referred to as shadows. The price range between the open and the close is plotted as a narrow rectangle and is referred to as the body. If the close is above the open, the body is white. If the close is below the open, the body is black.

CAP
A supply contract between a buyer and seller, whereby the buyer is assured that he or she will not have to pay more than a given maximum price. This type of contract is analogous to a call option.

Capital gains distribution
A distribution to investment company shareholders from net long-term capital gains realized by a regulated investment company on the sale of portfolio securities.

Capital losses
Losses resulting from selling at a loss.

Carbon budget
The balance of the exchanges (incomes) and losses) of carbon between carbon sinks (e.g., atmosphere and biosphere) in the carbon cycle. *See* Carbon cycle and Carbon sink.

Carbon cycle
All carbon sinks and exchanges of carbon from one sink to another by various chemical, physical, geological, and biological processes. *See* Carbon Sink and Carbon Budget.

Carbon dioxide (CO_2)
A colorless, odorless, non-poisonous gas that is a normal part of Earth's atmosphere. Carbon dioxide is a product of fossil-fuel combustion as well as other processes. It is considered a greenhouse gas as it traps heat (infrared energy) radiated by the Earth into the atmosphere and thereby contributes to the potential for global warming. The global warming potential (GWP) of other greenhouse gases is measured in relation to that of carbon dioxide, which by international scientific convention is assigned a value of one (1). *See* Global Warming Potential (GWP) and Greenhouse Gases.

Carbon dioxide equivalent
The amount of carbon dioxide by weight emitted into the atmosphere that would produce the same estimated radiative forcing as a given weight of another radiatively active gas. Carbon dioxide equivalents are computed by multiplying the weight of the gas being measured (for example, methane) by its estimated global warming potential (which is 21 for methane). "Carbon equivalent units" are defined as carbon dioxide equivalents multiplied by the carbon content of carbon dioxide (i.e., 12/44).

Carbon intensity
The amount of carbon by weight emitted per unit of energy consumed. A common measure of carbon intensity is weight of carbon per British thermal unit (Btu) of energy. When there is only one fossil fuel under consideration, the carbon intensity and the emissions coefficient are identical. When there are several fuels, carbon intensity is based on their combined emissions coefficients weighted by their energy consumption levels. *See* Emissions coefficient and carbon output rate.

Carbon output rate
The amount of carbon by weight per kiloWatthour of electricity produced.

Carbon residue
The solid, impure carbon deposits (coke) left behind by burned hydrocarbon fuels. The industry uses two tests, Conradson carbon (Con Carbon) and Ramsbottom carbon to measure oils' tendency to form such solids.

Carbon sequestration
The fixation of atmospheric carbon dioxide in a carbon sink through biological or physical processes.

Carbon sink
A reservoir that absorbs or takes up released carbon from another part of the carbon cycle. The four sinks, which are regions of the Earth within which carbon behaves in a systematic manner, are the atmosphere, terrestrial biosphere (usually including freshwater systems), oceans, and sediments (including fossil fuels).

Carrying broker
A member of a futures exchange, usually a clearinghouse member, through which another firm, broker or customer chooses to clear all or some trades.

Carrying charge
For physical commodities such as grains and metals, the cost of storage space, insurance, and finance charges incurred by holding a physical commodity. In interest rate futures markets, it refers to the differential between the yield on a cash instrument and the cost of funds necessary to buy the instrument. Also referred to as cost of carry or carry.

Carryover
Grain and oilseed commodities not consumed during the marketing year and remaining in storage at year's end. These stocks are "carried over" into the next marketing year and added to the stocks produced during that crop year.

Cash commodity
An actual physical commodity someone is buying or selling, for example, soybeans, corn, gold, silver, Treasury bonds, and others. Also referred to as actuals.

Cash contract
A sales agreement for either immediate or future delivery of the actual product.

Cash market
A place where people buy and sell the actual commodities, that is., grain elevator, bank, etc. Spot usually refers to a cash market price for a physical commodity that is available for immediate delivery. A forward contract is a cash contract in which a seller agrees to deliver a specific cash commodity to a buyer sometime in the future. Forward contracts, in contrast to futures contracts, are privately negotiated and are not standardized. *See* also Forward (cash) contract and spot.

Cash settlement
Transactions generally involving index-based futures contracts that are settled in cash based on the actual value of the index on the last trading day, in contrast to those that specify the delivery of a commodity or financial instrument.

Catalytic cracker
These refinery units, also widely known as cat crackers and FCC's (for fluid catalytic crackers) or FCCU's, convert heavy distillate, most commonly vacuum gasoil, to lighter

fractions. Refiners use them, basically, to break molecules, which boil in the heavy distillate range to shorter, more volatile hydrocarbon chains suitable for making motor gasoline.

Catalytic cracking
The refining process of breaking down the larger, heavier, and more complex hydrocarbon molecules into simpler and lighter molecules. Catalytic cracking is accomplished by the use of a catalytic agent and is an effective process for increasing the yield of gasoline from crude oil. Catalytic cracking processes fresh feeds and recycled feeds.

Catalytic reforming
A refining process using controlled heat and pressure with catalysts to rearrange certain hydrocarbon molecules, thereby converting paraffinic and naphthenic type hydrocarbons (e.g., low-octane gasoline boiling range fractions) into petrochemical feedstocks and higher octane stocks suitable for blending into finished gasoline.

Catfeed
The charge fed to a catalytic cracker. Common usage generally restricts this term to describing vacuum gasoils.

Cat gasoline
The motor fuel-blending component produced by catalytic cracking units.

Cat naphtha
See Cat gasoline. Some refiners could, if their markets made it desirable, hydrotreat cat gasoline to make a naphtha suitable for some use other than motor fuel blending, such as steam cracker feedstock.

CBOT
Chicago Board of Trade.

Centigrade degrees (C)
Also known as Celsius degrees. A temperature scale according to which water boils at 100 and freezes at 0. Centigrade, or Celsius, degrees convert to Fahrenheit degrees by the following formula: $(C \times 1.8) + 32 = F$.

Centistoke
The unit, commonly abbreviated cSt, of kinematic viscosity which reports a liquid's resistance to flow in terms of its measured viscosity divided by its density.

Central limit theorem
From statistics, the theorem that the distribution of sample means taken from a large population approaches a normal, Gaussian, curve.

Certificate of Deposit (CD)
A time deposit with a specific maturity evidenced by a certificate.

Cetane
A paraffinic hydrocarbon used as an additive in diesel fuel.

Cetane index (CI)
An estimated diesel fuel performance rating which relies on samples' API gravity and mid-point

$CI = -420.34 + 0.016G2 + 0192G \log M + 65.01 (LOG M)2 - 0.0001809M2$

where G = API gravity and M = mid-point in F.

Cetane number
A performance indicator for diesel fuel analogous to the octane rating applied to gasolines. The more paraffinic the gasoil, the higher its cetane number.

Cetan rating
See Cetane number.

CFD
Contract for differences. A type of crude oil swap.

Chaikin oscillator
An oscillator created by subtracting a 10-day EMA from a three-day EMA of the accumulation/distribution line.

Chains
This term has a chemical and a commercial usage in the oil business. It describes the strands of carbon atoms (carbon chains) fundamental to hydrocarbon molecules. It also serves as a designation for the strings of transactions assembled to settle a period's business in unregulated paper commodities like Russian gasoil.

Channel
In charting, a price channel contains prices throughout a trend. There are three basic ways to draw channels: parallel, rounded, and channels that connect lows (bear trend) or highs (bull trend).

Charter party
A document in which a ship owner and a charterer state their agreement to terms for carriage of cargo.

Charterer
The party who contracts for use of a ship. He can do so for a voyage, a spot charter, or a period, a time-charter.

Charting
The use of charts to analyze market behavior and anticipate future price movements. Those who use charting as a trading method plot such factors as high, low, and settlement prices; average price movements; volume; and open interest. Two basic price charts are bar charts and point- and-figure charts. Anticipating future price movement using historical prices, trading volume, open interest and other trading data to study price patterns. *See* also Technical analysis.

Charts
A display or picture of a security that plots price and/or volume (the number of shares sold). The chart is the foundation of technical analysis, and over the years, many different types of charts have been developed.

Cheap
Colloquialism implying that a commodity is underpriced.

Cheapest to deliver
A method to determine which particular cash debt instrument is most profitable to deliver against a futures contract.

Chemical carrier
See Parcel tanker.

Christmas tree spread
The simultaneous purchase and writing of options with either a different strike price or expiration date or combination of the two.

C.I.F. (Cost, Insurance, and Freight)
A sales transaction in which the seller pays for the transportation and insurance of the goods up to the port of destination specified by the buyer.

Circuit
A conductor or a system of conductors through which electric current flows.

Circuit breaker
A system of trading halts and price limits on equities and derivatives markets designed to provide a cooling-off period during large, intraday market declines.

Classifier systems
In artificial intelligence, these systems perform a type of machine learning that generates rules from examples.

Clean
Unleaded, when used to describe motor gasoline or blendstock.

Clear
The process by which a clearinghouse maintains records of all trades and settles margin flow on a daily mark-to-market basis for its clearing member.

Clearing corporation
An independent corporation that settles all trades made at the Chicago Board of Trade acting as a guarantor for all trades cleared by it, reconciles all clearing member firm accounts each day to ensure that all gains have been credited and all losses have been collected, and sets and adjusts clearing member firm margins for changing market conditions.

Clearing margin
Financial safeguards to ensure that clearing members (usually companies or corporations) perform on their customers' open futures and options contracts. Clearing margins are distinct from customer margins that individual buyers and sellers of futures and options contracts are required to deposit with brokers. *See* Customer margin. Within the futures industry, financial guarantees required of both buyers and sellers of futures contracts and sellers of options contracts to ensure fulfilling of contract obligations. FCMs are responsible for overseeing customer margin accounts. Margins are determined on the basis of market risk and contract value. Also referred to as performance-bond margin.

Clearing member
A member of an exchange clearinghouse. Memberships in clearing organizations are usually held by companies. Clearing members are responsible for the financial commitments of customers that clear through their firm.

Clearinghouse
An agency or separate corporation of a futures exchange that is responsible for settling trading accounts, clearing trades, collecting and maintaining margin monies, regulating delivery, and reporting trading data. Clearinghouses act as third parties to all futures and options contracts acting as a buyer to every clearing member seller and a seller to every clearing member buyer.

Climate
The average course or condition of the weather over a period of years as exhibited by temperature, humidity, wind velocity, and precipitation.

Climate change
A term used to refer to all forms of climatic inconsistency, but especially to significant change from one prevailing climatic condition to another. In some cases, "climate change" has been used synonymously with the term "global warming"; scientists, however, tend to use the term in a wider sense inclusive of natural changes in climate, including climatic cooling.

Clone fund
A smaller version of a retail mutual fund, it is offered as a subaccount in a variable annuity. The daily price of a clone fund is different among variable annuities that carry it because each clone fund starts on a different date and with a base price of $10.

Closed-end funds
A mutual fund that does not sell unlimited shares; one with a specific number of outstanding shares.

Closed trades
Positions that have been either liquidated or offset.

Closing price
The last price paid for a commodity on any trading day. The exchange clearinghouse determines a firm's net gains or losses, margin requirements, and the next day's price limits, based on each futures and options contract settlement price. If there is a closing range of prices, the settlement price is determined by averaging those prices. Also referred to as settlement price.

Closing range
A range of prices at which buy and sell transactions took place during the market close.

Cloud point
The temperature where wax crystals begin to appear in a cooled hydrocarbon mixture. This quality consideration, usually applied to gasoil, indicates how cold the air must become to make a stream form solids, which block filters halting fuel delivery. Cloud point of gasoil resembles freezing point of kerosene.

Clustering
Locating the presence of groups of vectors that are similar in some fashion.

CME
The Chicago Mercantile Exchange.

CNR
Charterer not revealed

COA
Contract of affreightment. An arrangement between a ship owner and a charterer for the carriage of a certain amount of specified grade or grades of cargo on named routes over a period of time. Owners may use any suitable ships at their disposable to meet the contract's requirements.

Coal
A readily combustible black or brownish-black rock whose composition, including inherent moisture, consists of more than 50% by weight and more than 70% by volume of carbonaceous material. It is formed from plant remains that have been compacted, hardened, chemically altered, and metamorphosed by heat and pressure over geologic time. *See* Coal rank.

Coalbed
A bed or stratum of coal. Also called a coal seam.

Coalbed methane
Methane produced from coalbeds in the same way that natural gas is produced from other strata. *See* Methane.

Coal briquets
Anthracite, bituminous, and lignite briquets are secondary solid fuels manufactured from coal by a process in which the coal is partly dried, warmed to expel excess moisture, and then compressed into briquets, usually without the use of a binding substance.

Coal coke
See Coke (Coal).

Coal production
The sum of sales, mine consumption, issues to miners, and issues to coke, briquetting, and other ancillary plants at mines. Production data include quantities extracted from surface and underground mines, and normally exclude wastes removed at mines or associated preparation plants.

Coal rank
The classification of coals according to their degree of progressive alteration from lignite to anthracite. In the United States, the standard ranks of coal include lignite, subbituminous coal, bituminous coal, and anthracite and are based on fixed carbon, volatile matter, heating value, and agglomerating (or caking) properties.

Coal stocks
Coal quantities that are held in storage for future use and disposition. Note: When coal data are collected for a particular reporting period (month, quarter, or year), coal stocks are commonly measured as of the last day of this period.

Coefficient
A constant used to multiply another quantity or series; as in $3x$ and ax, 3 and a are *coefficients* of x.

Coefficient of determination
R-squared. The proportion of the variation in the data explained by the model.

Cogeneration
The production of electrical energy and another form of useful energy (such as heat or steam) through the sequential use of energy.

Cogenerator
A generating facility that produces electricity and another form of useful thermal energy (such as heat or steam) used for industrial, commercial, heating, or cooling purposes. *See* Electric utility and Nonutility power producer.

Coiled
Tankers fitted with tubes that carry hot water or steam through viscous cargoes, such as heavy fuel oil and certain crudes, to keep them fluid.

Coincidence
In Gann theory, a projected reversal point.

Coke
Solid, almost hydrogen-free carbon made on purpose in fuel oil destruction units called cokers or inescapably in other processing hardware. Coke forms on the catalyst in cat crackers and in the furnaces of ethylene plants. The coke manufactured intentionally may go to the graphite industry if it meets certain quality requirements. Otherwise it sells as solid fuel. The incidental accretions require removal to keep process units efficient.

Coke oven gas
The gaseous portion of volatile substances driven off in the coking process after other coal chemicals are removed.

Coke (Petroleum)
A residue high in carbon content and low in hydrogen that is the final product of thermal decomposition in the condensation process in cracking. This product is reported

as marketable coke or catalyst coke. The conversion is 5 barrels (of 42 U.S. gallons each) per short ton. Coke from petroleum has a heating value of 6.024 million Btu per barrel.

Coke plant
A plant where coal is carbonized in slot or beehive ovens for the manufacture of coke.

Coker
A thermal processing unit which cracks heavy refinery streams, such as vacuum still bottoms, into light products while reducing much of that feedstock to solid carbon. The liquids yielded by these units, often called coker naphtha and coker gasoil, usually pass through upgrading equipment on the way to finished fuels production.

Coking coal
Bituminous coal suitable for making coke. *See* Coke (coal).

Cold blender
See blender. European producers of motor gasoline who have no distillation or other refining equipment go by this name. They make their product by mixing purchased "cold" components. This term has the advantage over the simple "blender" used in the United States of emphatically distinguishing a certain group of low-capital motor fuel makers from the refinery-based gasoline producers who also, of course, blend streams to obtain their finished products.

Cold filter plugging point
A measure of diesel fuel's suitability for use in cold weather. Usually called by its initials, CFPP, this specification reports the temperature where clotted wax stops fuel from passing through a test filter. CFFP goes beyond cloud point, which indicates where the cause of problems appears. It tells the fuel temperature where real trouble, like a stalled truck, happens.

Colinear
See Multicolinearity.

Colonial grade
Light petroleum product, which conforms to one of the specifications of Colonial Pipeline Company.

Colonial pipeline
The on-land pipeline system connecting US Gulf Coast refineries to Southeast and Atlantic Coast markets. The main artery runs from Deer Park, Texas, to Linden, NJ. It has the effective capability to carry roughly 2.1 million barrels per day of clean products, including gasoline, home heating oils, diesel fuels and kerosene. The system serves more than 280 petroleum-marketing terminals in thirteen states. Specifications required to move motor gasoline and No. 2 oil through the Colonial pipeline have become the quality standard for cargoes of these products imported on the US East Coast. Transporting a gallon of gasoline from Houston, Texas, to the New York harbor area via the Colonial pipeline costs about 2.3 cents. Moving product through roughly 1550 miles of pipeline typically takes three to four weeks.

COLLAR (Often structured as a Zero-cost collar)
A supply contract between a buyer and a seller of a commodity, whereby the buyer is assured that he will not have to pay more than some maximum price, and whereby the seller is assured of receiving some minimum price. Frequently, this takes the form of an options collar, involving the simultaneous purchase of an out-of-the-money call and sale of an out-of-the-money put.

Combination carriers
Vessels fitted to transport more than one type of cargo. The petroleum industry uses a good-sized fleet of OBO's, ships, which transport dry cargo or oil.

Combined cycle
An electric generating technology in which electricity is produced from otherwise lost waste heat exiting from one or more gas (combustion) turbines. The exiting heat is routed to a conventional boiler or to a heat recovery steam generator for utilization by a steam turbine in the production of electricity. Such designs increase the efficiency of the electric generating unit.

Combined cycle unit
An electric generating unit that consists of one or more combustion turbines and one or more boilers with a portion of the required energy input to the boiler(s) provided by the exhaust gas of the combustion turbine(s).

Combined forecast
The weighted average of two or more forecasts.

Combined pumped-storage electric power plant
A pumped-storage hydroelectric power plant that uses both pumped water and natural stream flow to produce electricity. *See* Pumped-storage hydroelectric power plant and Pure pumped-storage hydroelectric power plant.

Combustion
Chemical oxidation accompanied by the generation of light and heat.

Commercial field
An oil and/or gas field judged to be capable of producing enough net income to make it worth developing.

Commission
A fee charged by a broker to a customer for executing a transaction.

Commission fee
A fee charged by a broker for executing a transaction. Also referred to as brokerage fee.

Commission house
An individual or organization that solicits or accepts orders to buy or sell futures contracts or options on futures and accepts money or other assets from customers to support such orders. Also referred to as "wire house." Also see Futures commission merchant.

Commodity
An article of commerce or a product that can be used for commerce. In a narrow sense, products traded on an authorized commodity exchange. The types of commodities include agricultural products, metals, petroleum, foreign currencies, and financial instruments and index, to name a few.

Commodity Exchange Act (CEA)
The federal act that provides for federal regulation of futures trading.

Commodity future
A futures contract on a commodity. Unlike financial futures, the prices of commodity futures are determined by supply and demand as well as the cost-of-carry of the underlying. Commodity futures can, therefore, either be in contango (where futures prices are higher than spot prices) or backwardation (where futures are lower than spot).

Commodity swap
Commodity swaps enable both producers and consumers to hedge commodity prices. The consumer is usually a fixed payer and the producer a floating payer: if the floating-rate price of the commodity is higher than the fixed price, the difference is paid by the floating payer, and vice versa. Usually only the payment streams, not the principal, are exchanged, although physical delivery is becoming increasingly common. Swaps are sometimes done to hedge risks that can not readily be hedged with futures contracts. This could be a geographical or quality basis risk, or it could arise from the maturity of a transaction.

Commodity Futures Trading Commission (CFTC)
A commission established in 1974 that oversees the commodity exchanges in the US.

Comparative relative strength
Compares the price movement of a stock with that of its competitors, industry group or the entire market. This is distinct from J. Welles Wilder's Relative Strength Index, which compares current price movement to previous price movement of the same instrument.

Comparitor
A device of some kind that compares two inputs.

Compatibility
The suitability of two or more residues for blending. Some stocks – certain visbroken residues and hydrotreated bottoms, for instance – do not combine well enough to yield stable fuel oils.

Component
One part of a blend. The word most commonly names streams combined to make motor gasoline. In that usage, it serves as short version of "mogas component." Though not used casually, "gasoil component," "heavy fuel oil component" and similar designations make perfect sense.

Completion
Installation of permanent equipment for the production of oil or gas. If a well is equipped to produce only oil or gas from one zone or reservoir, the definition of a well (classified as an oil well or gas well) and the definition of a completion are identical. However, if a well is equipped to produce oil and/or gas separately from more than one reservoir, a well is not synonymous with a completion. *See* Well.

Compounding
The payment, through interest, based on the sum of the original principal amount and its accrued interest.

Condensate
Natural gas liquids heavier than butane. The term condensates commonly covers two quite different kinds of streams: natural gasolines and heavy condensates. Natural gasolines come from LPG or LNG plants. They have properties similar to naphthas. Heavy condensates resemble very light crude oils. Sometimes called field condensates, they come from gas/oil separation plants which process the raw stream from a gas field. Since they come as a by-product of gas production, much as associated gas comes as a by-product of crude production, associated crude suits them as a description.

Confidence factor
A measure of the degree of likelihood that a rule is correct, which may reflect the percentage of times that it has proven to be correct in the past or just a subjective measure of our confidence in its degree of reliability.

Confidence level
The degree of assurance that a specified failure rate is not exceeded.

Confirmation
Indication that at least two indices, in the case of Dow theory the industrials and the transportation, corroborate a market trend or a turning point.

Confirmation statement
A statement sent by a futures commission merchant to a customer when a futures or options position has been initiated. The statement shows the price and the number of contracts bought or sold. Sometimes combined with a purchase and sale statement.

Congestion area or pattern
A series of trading days in which there is no visible progress in price.

Consumer Price Index (CPI)
A major inflation measure computed by the US Department of Commerce. It measures the change in prices of a fixed market basket of some 385 goods and services in the previous month.

Consumption
See Energy consumption.

Contango
A futures market in which prices in succeeding delivery months are progressively higher. The opposite of Backwardation.

Contingent premium option
An option for which the purchaser pays no premium unless the option is exercised. As a rule of thumb, the premium eventually paid is equal to the premium payable on a normal option, divided by the option delta. Hence the price increases dramatically for out-of-the-money options.

Contingent swap
A swap which is only activated when rates reach a certain level or a specific event occurs. For example, drop-lock swaps only activate if rates or prices drop to a certain level or if a specified level over a benchmark is achieved.

Continuation chart
A chart in which the price scale for the data for the end of a given contract and the data for the beginning of the next contract are merged in order to ease the transition of one contract to the next.

Continuous-type deposit
A hydrocarbon accumulation that is pervasive throughout a large area, that is not significantly affected by hydrodynamic influences, and for which the standard methodology for assessment of sizes and numbers of discrete accumulations is not appropriate.

Contract
An agreement as in options in which rights are exchanged by law. Correlation coefficient – When two random variables X and Y tend to vary together. The measurement is given by the ratio of the covariance of X and Y to the square root of the product of the variance of X and the variance of Y.

Contract deal
See Term deal.

Contracts for differences (CFDs)
Long-term UK electricity swaps agreed bilaterally, generally between generators and electricity supply companies, and referenced to prices in the Electricity Pool for England

and Wales. The UK government announced in late 1998 that it planned to replace the Pool system with a three-tier market. A short-dated swap agreement used to minimize the basis risk between the daily published Platt's quote for dated or physical Brent in a specific time window in the future and the forward price quote for a specific month (15-day market). Settlement of CFDs is based upon the published price difference at a designated time.

Contract grades
The standard grades of commodities or instruments listed in the rules of the exchanges that must be met when delivering cash commodities against futures contracts. Grades are often accompanied by a schedule of discounts and premiums allowable for delivery of commodities of lesser or greater quality than the standard called for by the exchange.

Contract market
A board of trade designated by the CFTC to trade futures or options contracts on a particular commodity. Commonly used to mean any exchange on which futures are traded. Also referred to as an Exchange.

Contract month
The month in which delivery is to be made in accordance with the terms of the futures contract. Also referred to as Delivery month.

Controlled account
An arrangement by which the holder of the account gives written power of attorney to another person, often his broker, to make trading decisions. Also known as a discretionary or managed account.

Conventional accumulation
A discrete deposit, usually bounded by a downdip water contact, from which oil, gas, or NGL can be extracted using traditional development practices, including production at the surface from a well as a consequence of natural pressure within the subsurface reservoir, artificial lifting of oil from the reservoir to the surface where applicable, and the maintenance of reservoir pressure by means of water or gas injection.

Conventional gasoline
Finished motor gasoline not included in the oxygenated or reformulated gasoline categories. Note: This category excludes reformulated gasoline blendstock for oxygenate blending (RBOB) as well as other blendstock. *See* Motor gasoline (Finished).

Conventional mill (Uranium)
A facility engineered and built principally for processing of uraniferous ore materials mined from the earth and the recovery, by chemical treatment in the mill's circuits, of uranium and/or other valued coproduct components from the processed one.

Conventional thermal electricity generation
Electricity generated by an electric power plant using coal, petroleum, or gas as its source of energy.

Convergence
A term referring to cash and futures prices tending to come together (i.e., the basis approaches zero) as the futures contract nears expiration.

Conversion
Cracking molecules which boil above the threshold temperature into smaller ones which boil below it. Traditionally, the term applied to catalytic crackers. They convert oil which boils above 430 °F to hydrocarbons which boil below that point. In other words, they convert gasoil to naphtha. The recent popularity of residue crackers has established another conversion standard around 720 °F. This point marks the elevation of fuel oil to

light products. Loosely, the term refers to any processing step which breaks molecules into pieces which boil at lower temperatures.

Conversion arbitrage
Traders buy and sell two different securities (or synthetic securities), forcing equivalent prices for equivalent securities.

Cost, Insurance, and Freight
See C.I.F. (Cost, Insurance, and Freight).

Cost of carry (or Carry)
For physical commodities such as grains and metals, the cost of storage space, insurance, and finance charges incurred by holding a physical commodity. In interest rate futures markets, it refers to the differential between the yield on a cash instrument and the cost of funds necessary to buy the instrument.

Correction
Any price reaction within the market leading to an adjustment by as much as one-third to two-thirds of the previous gain.

Correction wave
A wave or cycle of waves moving against the current impulse trend's direction.

Correlation coefficient
Degree to which two series of numbers plot as a straight line. A correlation coefficient of 1 (or −1) indicates that the two series of numbers plot exactly along a straight line. A correlation coefficient of zero indicates that there is no straight-line relationship between the two series of numbers. As applied to two portfolios, a high correlation coefficient for the relative returns indicates that the portfolio values have moved in tandem and a low correlation coefficient means the opposite. When the correlation coefficient is high, one portfolio could have been used as a surrogate or a hedge for the other.

Cost basis
The cost of a given share or group of stock shares.

Covariance
Multiplies the deviation of each variable from its mean, adds those products, and then divides by the number of observations.

Cover
Purchasing back a contract sold earlier.

Covered option
A covered call option is one where the writer owns the underlying asset on which the option is written. Generally, a covered call would only be written if the writer believed volatility to be overpriced in the market; the lower the volatility, the less premium the writer gains in return for giving up their upside in the underlying. A covered put option is one where the writer sells the option while holding cash. This technique is used to increase income by receiving option premium. If the market goes down and the option is exercised, the cash can be used to buy the underlying to cover. Covered put writing is often used as a way of target buying: if an investor has a target price at which he wants to buy, he can set the strike price of the option at that level and receive option premium to increase the yield of the asset. Investors also sell covered puts if markets have fallen rapidly but seem to have bottomed, because of the high volatility typically received in the option.

Covered write
Writing a call against a long position in the underlying stock. By receiving a premium, the writer intends to realize additional return on the underlying common stock or gain

some element of protection (limited to the amount of the premium less transaction costs) from a decline in the value of that underlying stock.

COW
Crude oil wash. A cleaning technique used by some ships. They spray a few tons of crude around their tanks to rinse off the remains of previous cargoes. This method cannot make a dirty vessel clean. But it can do enough good to prevent excessive darkening of not particularly color-sensitive cargo.

Crack spreads
The spread between crude oil and its products: heating oil and unleaded gasoline plays a major role in the trading process.

Cracked
Broken by a thermal or catalytic process. This term frequently describes an oil product which contains cracked components made by such a process.

Cracked component
An ingredient in a hydrocarbon blend produced by a cracking process. The opposite of a virgin or straight-run component. Blends containing any cracked components do not qualify as straight-run. The presence of cracked components makes refinery streams unsuited for certain feedstock uses. The issue arises most frequently regarding heavy fuel oils. Companies buying such streams to produce catfeed want a virgin material containing no cracked components.

Cracked cutters
Cycle oils used to reduce the sulfur content or, especially, the viscosity of fuel oil.

Cracked fuel
Fuel oil containing molecules broken in a cracking unit. The term most frequently applies to residue. It distinguishes streams unsuitable for upgrading from straight-run material of interest as feedstock.

Cracked gas
See Unsaturated gases.

Cracked naphtha
General term for any naphtha-range fraction produced by a molecule breaking process. The category includes cat gasoline from a catalytic cracker, visbroken naphtha from a visbreaker, and coker naphtha from a coking unit. In ordinary usage, this term signifies streams with a high olefin content. That custom discourages its application to hydrocrackate and pyrolysis gasoline, known, respectively, for their naphthenes and aromatics concentrations.

Cracked stock
See Cracked component. Cracking units produce cracked stocks such as cycle oils and cat naphthas used for blending finished products.

Cracker
A processing unit which breaks molecular bonds, usually to produce lighter hydrocarbons with lower boiling points. Commercial crackers (cracking units) include cat crackers, hydrocrackers, thermal crackers, visbreakers, and stream crackers.

Cracking
The refining process of breaking down the larger, heavier, and more complex hydrocarbon molecules into simpler and lighter molecules. *See* Catalytic cracking and Thermal cracking.

Credit
Terms of payment, that is, 5, 10 days.

Credit spread
The difference in value of two options, where the value of the one sold exceeds the value of the one purchased.

Cross correlations
The extent to which the revenue streams of individual traders within a single enterprise tend to exhibit similar patterns over time.

Crop (marketing) year
The time span from harvest to harvest for agricultural commodities. The crop marketing year varies slightly with each agricultural (ag) commodity, but it tends to begin at harvest and end before the next year's harvest, for example, the marketing year for soybeans begins September 1 and ends August 31. The futures contract month of November represents the first major new-crop marketing month, and the contract month of July represents the last major old-crop marketing month for soybeans.

Crop reports
Reports compiled by the US Department of Agriculture on various agricultural commodities that are released throughout the year. Information in the reports includes estimates on planted acreage, yield, and expected production, as well as comparison of production from previous years.

Cross-hedging
Hedging a cash commodity using a different but related futures contract when there is no futures contract for the cash commodity being hedged and the cash and futures markets follow similar price trends (e.g., using soybean meal futures to hedge fish meal).

Crude oil
A full-ranging hydrocarbon mixture produced from a reservoir after any associated gas has been removed. Among the most commonly traded crudes are the North Sea's Brent Blend, the US's West Texas Intermediate (WTI) and Dubai.

1. Small amounts of hydrocarbons that exist in gaseous phase in natural underground reservoirs but are liquid at atmospheric pressure after being recovered from oil well (casinghead) gas in lease separators and are subsequently commingled with the crude stream without being separately measured. Lease condensate recovered as a liquid from natural gas wells in lease or field separation facilities and later mixed into the crude stream is also included;
2. Small amounts of nonhydrocarbons produced with the oil, such as sulfur and various metals;
3. Drip gases, and liquid hydrocarbons produced from tar sands, Gilsonite, and oil shale.

Liquids produced at natural gas processing plants are excluded. Crude oil is refined to produce a wide array of petroleum products, including heating oils; gasoline, diesel, and jet fuels; lubricants; asphalt; ethane, propane, and butane; and many other products used for their energy or chemical content.

Crude oil (including lease condensate)
See Crude oil.

Crude oil landed cost
The dollar-per-barrel price of crude oil at the port of discharge. Included are the charges associated with the purchase, transporting, and insuring of a cargo from the purchase point to the port of discharge. Not included are charges incurred at the discharge port (e.g., import tariffs or fees, wharfage charges, and demurrage charges).

Crude oil less lease condensate
A mixture of hydrocarbons that exists in liquid phase in natural underground reservoirs and remains liquid at atmospheric pressure after passing through surface separating facilities. Such hydrocarbons as lease condensate and natural gasoline recovered as liquids from natural gas wells in lease or field separation facilities and later mixed into the crude stream are excluded. Depending upon the characteristics of the crude stream, crude oil may also include:

1. Small amounts of hydrocarbons that exist in gaseous phase in natural underground reservoirs but are liquid at atmospheric pressure after being recovered from oil well (casinghead) gas in lease separators and are subsequently commingled with the crude stream without being separately measured;
2. Small amounts of nonhydrocarbons produced with the oil, such as sulfur and various metals.

Crude oil production
The volume of crude oil produced from oil reservoirs during given periods of time. The amount of such production for a given period is measured as volumes delivered from lease storage tanks (i.e., the point of custody transfer) to pipelines, trucks, or other media for transport to refineries or terminals with, adjustments for (1) net differences between opening and closing lease inventories, and (2) basic sediment and water.

CST
Abbreviation of centistoke.

Cubic foot (cf), natural gas
The amount of natural gas contained at standard temperature and pressure (60 degrees Fahrenheit and 14.73 pounds standard per square inch) in a cube whose edges are one foot long.

Current ratio
The current assets of a company divided by its current liabilities. Balance-sheet strength indication.

Customer margin
Within the futures industry, financial guarantees required of both buyers and sellers of futures contracts and sellers of options contracts to ensure fulfilling of contract obligations. FCMs are responsible for overseeing customer margin accounts. Margins are determined on the basis of market risk and contract value. Also referred to as performance-bond margin. Financial safeguards to ensure that clearing members (usually companies or corporations) perform on their customers' open futures and options contracts. Clearing margins are distinct from customer margins that individual buyers and sellers of futures and options contracts are required to deposit with brokers.

Customer segregated funds
See Segregated account.

Cut
To divide a hydrocarbon mixture into fractions by distillation. Also a name for the fractions obtained, as in kerosene cut or naphtha cut.

Cutter (cutter stock)
A refinery stream used to thin a fuel oil or gasoil. Viscosity reduction and sulfur level adjustment provide most of the requirement for the cutter.

Cycle oil
Cat cracking unit produced in the fuel oil or gasoil boiling range. The term light cycle oil generally describes products of this kind suitable for blending into diesel or home

heating oil. Heavy cycle oil, accordingly, refers to the cat cracked material that boils at temperatures in the fuel oil range.

Cycling
The practice of producing natural gas for the extraction of natural gas liquids, returning the dry residue to the producing reservoir to maintain reservoir pressure and increase the ultimate recovery of natural gas liquids.

Cycling plants
See Natural gas processing plants.

D

%D
A stochastic indicator that has had its values smoothed a second time, usually with a three-period moving average.

Daily range
The difference between the high and low price during one trading day.

Daily trading limit
The maximum price range set by the exchange cash day for a contract.

Day order
An order that if not executed expires automatically at the end of the trading session on the day it was entered.

Day traders
Speculators who take positions in futures or options contracts and liquidate them prior to the close of the same trading day.

Dead cat bounce
A rebound in a market that sees prices recover and come back up somewhat.

Deadweight tonnage (DWT)
The standard measure of ships' carrying capacity. The trade usually abbreviates this term to speak simply of tankers "deadweight." This specification reports total weight, usually in long tons, of fresh water, stores, bunkers, and cargo a vessel can carry. For oil tankers, cargo averages 95 to 96% of the total.

Debit spread
The difference in value of two options, where the value of the long position exceeds the value of the short position.

Deep-in-the-money
A deep-in-the-money call option has the strike price of the option well below the current price of the underlying instrument. A deep-in-the-money put option has the strike price of the option well above the current price of the underlying instrument.

Deep waters
Waters deeper than 200 meters.

Default
The failure to perform on a futures contract as required by exchange rules, such as a failure to meet a margin call or to make or take delivery.

Deferred (delivery) month
The more distant month(s) in which futures trading is taking place, as distinguished from the nearby (delivery) month.

Degrees API Gravity = (141.5/Specific Gravity at 60 Deg. F) Ð131.5.

Delay
The amount of time that elapses between a change in an input event and the resultant change in a related output event or time series.

Delayed coking
A process by which heavier crude oil fractions can be thermally decomposed under conditions of elevated temperature and pressure to produce a mixture of lighter oils and petroleum coke.

Deliverable grades
The standard grades of commodities or instruments listed in the rules of the exchanges that must be met when delivering cash commodities against futures contracts. Grades are often accompanied by a schedule of discounts and premiums allowable for delivery of commodities of lesser or greater quality than the standard called for by the exchange. Also referred to as contract grades.

Delivery
The transfer of the cash commodity from the seller of a futures contract to the buyer of a futures contract. Each futures exchange has specific procedures for delivery of a cash commodity. Some futures contracts, such as stock index contracts, are cash settled.

Delivery day
The third day in the delivery process at the Chicago Board of Trade, when the buyer's clearing firm presents the delivery notice with a certified check for the amount due at the office of the seller's clearing firm.

Delivery month
A specific month in which delivery may take place under the terms of a futures contract. Also referred to as contract month.

Delivery points
The locations and facilities designated by a futures exchange where stocks of a commodity may be delivered in fulfillment of a futures contract, under procedures established by the exchange.

Delivery
The transfer of the cash commodity from the seller of a futures contract to the buyer of a futures contract. Each futures exchange has specific procedures for delivery of a cash commodity. Some futures contracts, such as stock index contracts, are cash settled.

Delta
The amount by which the price of an option changes for every dollar move in the underlying instrument.

Delta-hedged
An options strategy that protects an option against small price changes in the option's underlying instrument. These hedges are constructed by taking a position in the underlying instrument that is equal in magnitude but opposite in sign (+/−) to the option's delta.

Delta neutral
This is an "options/options" or "options/underlying instrument" position constructed so that it is relatively insensitive to the price movement of the underlying instruments. This is arranged by selecting a calculated ratio of offsetting short and long positions.

Delta position
A measure of option price vs the underlying futures contract or stock price.

Demand
See Energy demand.

Demand (electric)
See Electricity demand.

Demand index
An index that shows the buying and selling power of markets and stocks from mathematical calculations of volume and price ratios.

Demonstrated reserves
See Energy reserves.

Demurrage
The cost of delaying a ship. Busy channels, occupied berths, commercial considerations, lack of shore tankage, pumping limitations, and a host of other eventualities related to how or where a charterer uses a vessel can prevent it from loading or unloading promptly. When they do, the ship's owner charges for a waiting time.

Density
A description of oil by some measurement of its volume to weight ratio. The industry usually relies on two expressions of oil's volume–weight relationship-specific gravity and API degrees. The larger a specific gravity number and the smaller an API number, the denser the oil.

Density function
For any measure *m*, a function that gives rise to *m* when integrated with respect to some other specified measure. A probability density function is a function whose integral over any set gives the probability that a random variable has values in this set.

Dependence
A relationship between two different experimental results in which the first result does not directly influence the chances of the second result occurring, but instead, the two results are indirectly related because they are subject to influences from a common outside factor.

Derivative
A financial instrument, traded on or off an exchange, the price of which is directly dependent upon the value of one or more underlying securities, equity indices, debt instruments, commodities, other derivative instruments, or any agreed upon pricing index or arrangement. Derivatives involve the trading of rights or obligations based on the underlying product but do not directly transfer property. They are used to hedge risk or to exchange a floating rate of return for a fixed rate of return.

Development well
A well drilled within the proved area of an oil or gas reservoir to the depth of a stratigraphic horizon known to be productive.

Diesel index
A measure of the ignition quality of a diesel fuel calculated from a formula involving the gravity of the fuel and its aniline point.

Differentials
Price differences between classes, grades, and delivery locations of various stocks of the same commodity.

Diffusion index
An index that measures the percentage of individual series that are positive compared with the aggregate group that is, the percentage of S&P groups that are above their 30-week moving average.

Direct current
An electric current that flows in a constant direction. The magnitude of the current does not vary or has a slight variation.

Directional Movement Index (DMI)
Developed by J. Welles Wilder, DMI measures market trend.

Discount

1. The amount a price would be reduced to purchase a commodity of lesser grade;
2. sometimes used to refer to the price differences between futures of different delivery months, as in the phrase "July is trading at a discount to May," indicating that the price of the July future is lower than that of May;
3. applied to cash grain prices that are below the futures price.

Distillate fuel oil
A general classification for one of the petroleum fractions produced in conventional distillation operations. It includes diesel fuels and fuel oils. Products known as No. 1, No. 2, and No. 4 diesel fuel are used in on-highway diesel engines, such as those in trucks and automobiles, as well as off-highway engines, such as those in railroad locomotives and agricultural machinery. Products known as No. 1, No. 2, and No. 4 fuel oils are used primarily for space heating and electric power generation.

1. No. 1 Distillate: A light petroleum distillate that can be used as either a diesel fuel (*see* No. 1 Diesel Fuel) or a fuel oil (*see* No. 1 Fuel Oil).
   a. No. 1 Diesel Fuel: A light distillate fuel oil that has distillation temperatures of 550°Fahrenheit at the 90-% recovery point and meets the specifications defined in ASTM Specification D 975. It is used in high-speed diesel engines, such as those in city buses and similar vehicles.
   b. No. 1 Fuel Oil: A light distillate fuel oil that has distillation temperatures of 400° Fahrenheit at the 10-% recovery point and 550° Fahrenheit at the 90-% recovery point and meets the specifications defined in ASTM Specification D 396. It is used primarily as fuel for portable outdoor stoves and portable outdoor heaters.
2. No. 2 Distillate: A petroleum distillate that can be used either as a diesel fuel (*see* No. 2 Diesel Fuel) or a fuel oil (*see* No. 2 Fuel Oil).
   a. No. 2 Diesel Fuel: A fuel that has distillation temperatures of 500° Fahrenheit at the 10-% recovery point and 640° Fahrenheit at the 90-% recovery point and meets the specifications defined in ASTM Specification D 975. It is used in high-speed diesel engines, such as those in railroad locomotives, trucks, and automobiles.
      i. Low Sulfur No.2 Diesel Fuel: No. 2 diesel fuel that has a sulfur level no higher than 0.05% by weight. It is used primarily in motor vehicle diesel engines for on-highway use.
      ii. High Sulfur No. 2 Diesel Fuel: No. 2 diesel fuel that has a sulfur level above 0.05 % by weight.
   b. No. 2 Fuel Oil (Heating Oil): A distillate fuel oil that has distillation temperatures of 400° Fahrenheit at the 10-% recovery point and 640° Fahrenheit at the 90-% recovery point and meets the specifications defined in ASTM Specification D 396. It is used in atomizing-type burners for domestic heating or for moderate capacity commercial/industrial burner units.

3. No. 4 Fuel: A distillate fuel oil made by blending distillate fuel oil and residual fuel oil stocks. It conforms to ASTM Specification D 396 or Federal Specification VV-F-815C and is used extensively in industrial plants and in commercial burner installations that are not equipped with preheating facilities. It also includes No. 4 diesel fuel used for low- and medium-speed diesel engines and conforms to ASTM Specification D 975.
   a. No. 4 Diesel Fuel: *See* No. 4 Fuel.
   b. No. 4 Fuel Oil: *See* No. 4 Fuel.

Distillation curve
The boiling temperature distribution of a material's component molecules. Tests report this characteristic as temperature at which various percentages of a sample have boiled or as the percentages which have boiled at various temperatures.

Distillation unit (atmospheric)
The primary distillation unit that processes crude oil (including mixtures of other hydrocarbons) at approximately atmospheric conditions. It includes a pipe still for vaporizing the crude oil and a fractionation tower for separating the vaporized hydrocarbon components in the crude oil into fractions with different boiling ranges. This is done by continuously vaporizing and condensing the components to separate higher boiling point material. The selected boiling ranges are set by the processing scheme, the properties of the crude oil, and the product specifications.

Distiller
See Distillation unit. A term most often used as shorthand for "crude oil distillation unit."

Distribution
Any set of related values described by an average (that is, mean), which identifies its midpoint, a measure of spread (that is, standard distribution) and a measure of its shape (that is, skew or kurtosis).

Distribution system
The portion of an electric system that is dedicated to delivering electric energy to an end user.

Distributors
Inland wholesalers.

Divergence
When two or more averages or indices fail to show confirming trends.

Dividend
Stockholder payment of a share of a company's profits.

Doji
A session in which the open and close are the same (or almost the same). Different varieties of doji lines (such as a gravestone or long-legged doji) depend on where the opening and close are in relation to the entire range. Doji lines are among the most important individual candlestick lines. They are also components of important candlestick patterns.

Double bottom (top)
The price action of a security or market average where it has declined (advanced) two times to the same approximate level, indicating the existence of a support (resistance) level and a possibility that the downward (upward) trend has ended.

Double-smoothed
A price series that has been smoothed by a mathematical technique such as a moving average. This first series of smoothed price data is then smoothed a second time.

Double top

See Double bottom. A price pattern seen on a chart. The pattern occurs when prices rise to a resistance level on significant volume, retreat to a support level, and subsequently return to the resistance level on decreased volume. Prices then decline and break through the support level, marking the beginning of a new downtrend in the price of the stock.

Downstream

A relative term, which indicates greater removal from origins than some point of reference. For example, a petrochemical plant which cracks naphtha lies downstream from a refinery. Money made by marketing products constitutes downstream profits compared to earnings on crude sales. The opposite of upstream.

DPK

Dual-purpose kerosene. Product suitable for use as burning kerosene and aviation turbine fuel.

Draft

The distance between a ship's keel and waterline. The lowest part of a vessel lies this far below the surface of the water. Every ship's draft changes with the amount of cargo aboard it, its trim and the temperature and salt content of the water in which it floats. A ship reaches its deepest draft when fully laden in warm fresh water. The shipping industry calls that distance "tropical fresh" or "TF" draft. "Fresh" (F),"tropical" (T), "summer" (s), and "winter" (W) report increasingly shallow drafts for a vessel; reflecting denser and denser water.

Drawdown

The reduction in account equity as a result of a trade or series of trades.

Dry gas

See Dry natural gas.

Dry hole

An exploratory or development well found to be incapable of producing either oil or gas in sufficient quantities to justify completion as an oil or gas well.

Dry natural gas

Natural gas which remains after: 1) the liquefiable hydrocarbon portion has been removed from the gas stream (i.e., gas after lease, field, and/or plant separation); and 2) any volumes of nonhydrocarbon gases have been removed where they occur in sufficient quantity to render the gas unmarketable.

Note: Dry natural gas is also known as consumer-grade natural gas. The parameters for measurement are cubic feet at 60° Fahrenheit and 14.73 pounds per square inch absolute. *See* Natural gas.

Dry natural gas production

The process of producing consumer-grade natural gas. Natural gas withdrawn from reservoirs is reduced by volumes used at the production (lease) site and by processing losses. Volumes used at the production site include (1) the volume returned to reservoirs in cycling, repressuring of oil reservoirs, and conservation operations; and (2) gas vented and flared. Processing losses include (1) nonhydrocarbon gases (e.g., water vapor, carbon dioxide, helium, hydrogen sulfide, and nitrogen) removed from the gas stream; and (2) gas converted to liquid form, such as lease condensate and plant liquids. Volumes of dry gas withdrawn from gas storage reservoirs are not considered part of production. Dry natural gas production equals marketed production less extraction loss.

Dry production

See Dry natural gas production.

Dual fired unit
A generating unit that can produce electricity using two or more input fuels. In some of these units, only the primary fuel can be used continuously; the alternate fuel(s) can be used only as a start-up fuel or in emergencies.

Dual trading
Dual trading occurs when (1) a floor broker executes customer orders and, on the same day, trades for his own account or an account in which he has an interest; or (2) a Futures commission merchant carries customer accounts and also trades, or permits its employees to trade, in accounts in which it has a proprietary interest, also on the same day.

Durbin–Watson statistic
The probability that first order correlation exists. With a range between zero and 4, the closer to 2.0, the lower the probability is.

E

E-4
C.I.S. high sulfur straight-run feedstock. Formerly called F-10.

Electric plant (physical)
See Electric power plant.

Electric power
The rate at which electric energy is transferred. Electric power is measured by capacity and is commonly expressed in megawatts (mW).

Electric power plant
A facility containing prime movers, electric generators, and auxiliary equipment for converting mechanical, chemical, and/or fission energy into electric energy.

Electric system
Physically connected generation, transmission, and distribution facilities operated as an integrated unit under one central management, or operating supervision.

Electric utility
A corporation, person, agency, authority, or other legal entity or instrumentality that owns and/or operates facilities for the generation, transmission, distribution, or sale of electric energy for use primarily by the public. Utilities provide electricity within a designated franchised service area and file forms listed in the Code of Federal Regulations, Title 18, Part 141. Note: Facilities that qualify as cogenerators or small power producers under the Public Utility Regulatory Policies Act (PURPA) are not considered electric utilities. *See* Nonutility power producer.

Electrical generating capacity
See Generator capacity.

Electricity
A form of energy characterized by the presence and motion of elementary charged particles generated by friction, induction, or chemical change.

Electricity capacity
The maximum load of electric power, commonly expressed in megawatts (mW), by which generators, turbines, transformers, transmission circuits, stations, or systems are rated.

Electricity demand
The rate at which energy is delivered to loads and scheduling points by generation, transmission, and distribution facilities.

Electricity generation
The process of producing electric energy or the amount of electric energy produced by transforming other forms of energy, commonly expressed in kilowatthours (kWh) or megawatthours (mWh).

Electricity generation, gross
See Gross generation.

Electricity generation, net
See Net generation.

Electricity installed capacity
See Generator nameplate capacity (installed).

Electronic communications network
Independent execution systems set up by brokerage firms, matching new retail limit orders with compatible orders already in the system.

Electronic order
An order placed electronically (without the use of a broker) either via the Internet or an electronic trading system.

Electronic trading systems
Systems that allow participating exchanges to list their products for trading after the close of the exchange's open outcry trading hours (i.e., Chicago Board of Trade's Project A, Chicago Mercantile Exchange's GLOBEX and New York Mercantile Exchange's ACCESS.)

Elliott wave theory
A pattern-recognition technique published by Ralph Nelson Elliott in 1939, which holds that the stock market follows a rhythm or pattern of five waves up and three waves down to form a complete cycle of eight waves. The three waves down are referred to as a "correction" of the preceding five waves up.

EMA
See Exponential moving average.

Emissions
Anthropogenic releases of gases to the atmosphere. In the context of global climate change, they consist of radiatively important greenhouse gases (e.g., the release of carbon dioxide during fuel combustion). *See* Greenhouse gases.

Emissions coefficient
A unique value for scaling emissions to activity data in terms of a standard rate of emissions per unit of activity (e.g., pounds of carbon dioxide emitted per British thermal unit (Btu) of fossil fuel consumed.)

Energy
The capacity for doing work as measured by the capability of doing work (potential energy) or the conversion of this capability to motion (kinetic energy). Energy has several forms, some of which are easily convertible and can be changed to another form useful for work. Most of the worlds convertible energy comes from fossil fuels that are burned to produce heat that is then used as a transfer medium to mechanical or other means in order to accomplish tasks. Electrical energy is usually measured in kiloWatthours, while heat energy is usually measured in British thermal units.

Energy consumption
The use of energy as a source of heat or power or as a raw material input to a manufacturing process.

Energy demand
The requirement for energy as an input to provide products and/or services.

Energy loss (power)
See Power loss.

Energy production
See production terms associated with specific energy types.

Energy reserves
Estimated quantities of energy sources that are demonstrated to exist with reasonable certainty on the basis of geologic and engineering data (proved reserves) or that can reasonably be expected to exist on the basis of geologic evidence that supports projections from proved reserves (probable/indicated reserves). Knowledge of the location, quantity, and grade of probable/indicated reserves is generally incomplete or much less certain that it is for proved energy reserves.

Note: This term is equivalent to "Demonstrated Reserves" as defined in the resource/reserve classification contained in the US Geological Survey Circular 831, 1980. Demonstrated reserves include measured and indicated reserves but exclude inferred reserves.

Energy source
Any substance or natural phenomenon that can be consumed or transformed to supply heat or power. Included are petroleum, coal, natural gas, nuclear, wood and waste, electricity, wind, sunlight, geothermal, and water movement.

Energy supply
Energy made available for future disposition. Supply can be considered and measured from the point of view of the energy provider or the receiver.

Engulfing pattern
In candlestick terminology, a multiple candlestick line pattern; a major reversal signal with two opposing-color real bodies making up the pattern. (Also referred to as *tsutsumi.*)

Enhanced recovery
Techniques used to increase or stretch over time the production of wells.

Envelope
Lines surrounding an index or indicator that is, trading bands.

Entry
The point at which a trader gets into a position in the market.

Equilibrium market
A price region that represents a balance between demand and supply.

Equilibrium price
The market price at which the quantity supplied of a commodity equals the quantity demanded.

Equity
The value of a futures trading account if all open positions were offset at the current market price.

Equity holders
Companies entitled to some portion of an oil field's production due to their investment in its development. *See* Producers.

ETBE
See Ethyl Tertiary Butyl Ether (ETBE).

Ethane
A normally gaseous straight-chain hydro-carbon, (C2H6). It is a colorless, paraffinic gas that boils at a temperature of −127.48° Fahrenheit. It is extracted from natural gas and refinery gas streams.

Ether
A generic term applied to a group of organic chemical compounds composed of carbon, hydrogen, and oxygen, characterized by an oxygen atom attached to two carbon atoms (e.g., methyl tertiary butyl ether).

Ethylene
An olefinic hydrocarbon recovered from refinery processes or petrochemical processes. Ethylene is used as a petrochemical feedstock for numerous chemical applications and the production of consumer goods.

Evening star pattern
The bearish counterpart of the morning star pattern; a top reversal, it should be acted on if it arises after an uptrend.

Exchange
See Contract market.

Exchange for physicals
A transaction generally used by two hedgers who want to exchange futures for cash positions. Also referred to as "against actuals" or "versus cash."

Exchange-traded funds
Collections of stocks that are bought and sold as a package on an exchange, principally the American Stock Exchange (AMEX), but also the New York Stock Exchange (NYSE) and the Chicago Board Options Exchange (CBOE).

Exercise
The process by which the holder of an option makes or receives delivery of futures contracts of the underlying futures market.

Exercise price
The price at which the futures contract underlying a call or put option can be purchased (if a call) or sold (if a put). Also referred to as strike price.

Exit
The point at which a trader closes out of a trade.

Expiration
The last day on which an option can be traded.

Expiration date
Options on futures generally expire on a specific date during the month preceding the futures contract delivery month. For example, an option on a March futures contract expires in February but is referred to as a March option because its exercise would result in a March futures contract position.

Exploration
Oil and natural gas exploration that includes land surveys, geological and geophysical studies, seismic data gathering and analysis, and well drilling.

Exploratory well
A hole drilled: a) to find and produce oil or gas in an area previously considered unproductive; b) to find a new reservoir in a field previously found to be producing oil or gas from another reservoir; or c) to extend the limit of a known oil or gas reservoir.

Exponential moving average
The EMA for day D is calculated as: where PR is the price on day D and a (alpha) is a smoothing constant . Alpha may be estimated as $2/(n+1)$, where n is the simple moving average length.

Exponential smoothing
A mathematical-statistical method of forecasting that assumes future price action is a weighted average of past periods; a mathematic series in which greater weight is given to more recent price action.

Exports (US)
Shipments of goods from within the 50 States and the District of Columbia to US possessions and territories or to foreign countries *See* United States (U.S.).

Extreme
The highest or lowest price during any time period, a price extreme; in the CBOT Market Profile, the highest/lowest prices the market tests during a trading day.

Extraction loss
The reduction in volume of natural gas due to the removal of natural gas liquid constituents, such as ethane, propane, and butane, at natural gas processing plants.

Extrinsic value
The amount of money option buyer are willing to pay for an option in the anticipation that, over time, a change in the underlying futures price will cause the option to increase in value. In general, an option premium is the sum of time value and intrinsic value. Any amount by which an option premium exceeds the option's intrinsic value can be considered time value. Also referred to as time value.

F

Failure swings
The inability of price to reaffirm a new high in an uptrend or a new low in a downtrend.

Failure
In Elliott wave theory, a five-wave pattern of movement in which the fifth impulse wave fails to move above the end of the third, or in which the fifth wave does not contain the five subwaves.

Fair values
The theoretical prices generated by an option pricing model (i.e., the Black–Scholes option pricing model).

F.A.S. Value (Free Alongside Ship Value)
The value of a commodity at the port of exportation, generally including the purchase price, plus all charges incurred in placing the commodity alongside the carrier at the port of exportation in the country of exportation.

FAS 133
FAS 133, the standard for financial reporting of derivatives and hedging transactions, was adopted in 1998 by the Financial Accounting Standards Board to resolve inconsistent

previous reporting standards and practices. It went into effect at most US companies at the beginning of 2001.

Fast Fourier transform
A method by which to decompose data into a sum of sinusoids of varying cycle length, with each cycle being a fraction of a common fundamental cycle length.

Fast market
A declaration that market conditions in the futures pit are so disorderly temporarily to the extent that floor brokers are not held responsible for the execution of orders.

FCCC
See Framework Convention on Climate Change (FCCC).

Federal deposit insurance corporation
A self-sustaining, independent executive agency established to insure deposits of all US banks entitled to federal deposit insurance, as stated by the Federal Reserve Act.

Federal funds rate
The rate of interest charged for the use of federal funds.

Federal reserve bank
The governing central bank of the United States.

Feedstock
Material used in a processing plant.

Fibonacci ratio
The ratio between any two successive numbers in the Fibonacci sequence, known as phi (f). The ratio of any number to the next higher number is approximately 0.618 (known as the Golden Mean or Golden Ratio), and to the lower number approximately 1.618 (the inverse of the Golden Mean), after the first four numbers of the series. The three important ratios the series provides are 0.618, 1.0 and 1.618.

Fibonacci sequence
The sequence of numbers (0, 1, 2, 3, 5, 8, 13, 21, 34, 55, 89, 144, 233 …), discovered by the Italian mathematician Leonardo de Pisa in the thirteenth century and the mathematical basis of the Elliott wave theory, where the first two terms of the sequence are 0 and 1 and each successive number in the sequence is the sum of the previous two numbers. Technically, it is a sequence and not a series.

Field
An individual producing unit consisting of a single pool or multiple pools of hydrocarbons grouped on, or related to, a single structural or stratigraphic feature

Field separation facility
A surface installation designed to recover lease condensate from a produced natural gas stream usually originating from more than one lease and managed by the operator of one or more these leases.

Fill
An executed order; sometimes the term refers to the price at which an order is executed.

Fill order
An order that must be filled immediately (or canceled).

Fill or kill
A customer order that is a price limit order that must be filled immediately or canceled.

Filter point
The time at which a portfolio insurance program makes an adjusting trade.

Flash point
The lowest temperature under very specific conditions at which a combustible liquid will give off sufficient vapor to form a flammable mixture with air in a standardized vessel. Assesses the volatility of the product.

Flared
Gas disposed of by burning in flares usually at the production sites or at gas processing plants.

Flared natural gas
See Flared.

Float
The number of shares currently available for trading.

Floor Broker (FB)
An individual who executes orders for the purchase or sale of any commodity futures or options contract on any contract market for any other person.

Floor Trader (FT)
An individual who executes trades for the purchase or sale of any commodity futures or options contract on any contract market for such individual's own account.

Fluid coking
A thermal cracking process utilizing the fluidized-solids technique to remove carbon (coke) for continuous conversion of heavy, low-grade, oils into lighter products.

Flyers
Speculative or high-risk trades.

F.O.B. (Free On Board)
A sales transaction in which the seller makes the product available for pick up at a specified port or terminal at a specified price and the buyer pays for the subsequent transportation and insurance.

FOD
Fuel Oil Domestique

Forecast origin
The most recent historical period for which data is used to build a forecasting model. The next time period is the first forecast period.

Foreign exchange market
An over-the-counter market where buyers and sellers conduct foreign exchange business by telephone and other means of communication. Also referred to as a forex market.

Forex market
An over-the-counter market where buyers and sellers conduct foreign exchange business by telephone and other means of communication. Also referred to as foreign exchange market.

FORTIES
The first substantial oil field in the British sector of the North Sea.

Forward (cash) contract
A cash contract in which a seller agrees to deliver a specific cash commodity to a buyer sometime in the future. Forward contracts, in contrast to futures contracts, are privately negotiated and are not standardized.

Forward-Rate Agreements (FRAs)
Cash payments are made daily as the spot rate varies above or below an agreed-upon forward rate and can be hedged with Eurodollar futures.

Fossil fuel
An energy source formed in the Earth's crust from decayed organic material. The common fossil fuels are petroleum, coal, and natural gas.

Fossil fueled steam-electric power plant
An electricity generation plant in which the prime mover is a turbine rotated by high-pressure steam produced in a boiler by heat from burning fossil fuels.

Fossil-fuel electric generation
Electric generation in which the prime mover is a turbine rotated by high-pressure steam produced in a boiler by heat from burning fossil fuels.

Fractionation
The process by which saturated hydrocarbons are removed from natural gas and separated into distinct products, or "fractions," such as propane, butane, and ethane.

Free On Board
See F.O.B. (Free On Board).

Frequency
The number of complete cycles observed per time period (i.e., cycles per year).

Frequency component
That part of a time series that may be represented as a cycle.

Frequency distribution
A chart showing the number of times (or "frequency") an event occurs for each possible value of the event. The vertical or y-axis of the chart is the frequency axis and the horizontal or x-axis shows the different values the variable being measured can take.

Frequency domain
Variation in a time series is accounted for by cyclical components at different frequencies.

Frequency response
The transfer of the frequency of the underlying data, usually prices, to the frequency of its moving average.

Front-loaded
Commission and fees taken out of investment capital before the money is put to work.

Front month
The first expiration month in a series of months.

Front-running
The practice of trading ahead of large orders to take advantage of favorable price movement. Brokers are prohibited from this practice.

Fuel
Any material substance that can be consumed to supply heat or power. Included are petroleum, coal, and natural gas (the fossil fuels), and other consumable materials, such as uranium, biomass, and hydrogen. *See* Energy Source.

Fuel ethanol
An anhydrous, denatured aliphatic alcohol (C_2H_5OH) intended for motor gasoline blending. *See* Oxygenates.

Fuelwood
See Wood energy.

Full carrying charge market
A futures market where the price difference between delivery months reflects the total costs of interest, insurance, and storage

Full membership (CBOT)
A Chicago Board of Trade membership that allows an individual to trade all futures and options contracts listed by the exchange.

Fundamental analysis
The analytical method by which only the sales, earnings, and the value of a given tradable's assets may be considered.

Fundamentals
The theory that holds that stock market activity may be predicted by looking at the relative data and statistics of a stock as well as the management of the company in question and its earnings.

Future volatility
A prediction of what volatility may be like in the future.

Futures Commission Merchant (FCM)
An individual or organization that solicits or accepts orders to buy or sell futures contracts or options on futures and accepts money or other assets from customers to support such orders. Also referred to as "commission house" or "wire house."

Futures contract
A legally binding agreement, made on the trading floor of a futures exchange, to buy or sell a commodity or financial instrument sometime in the future. Futures contracts are standardized according to the quality, quantity, and delivery time and location for each commodity. The only variable is price, which is discovered on an exchange trading floor.

Futures Exchange
A central marketplace with established rules and regulations where buyers and sellers meet to trade futures and options on futures contracts.

Futures market
A trade center for quoting prices on contracts for the delivery of a specified quantity of a commodity at a specified time and place in the future.

G

Gamma
The degree by which the delta changes with respect to changes in the underlying instrument's price.

Gann Theory
Various analytical techniques developed by legendary trader W.D. Gann.

Gap
A day in which the daily range is completely above or below the previous day's daily range.

Gas condensate well
A gas well that produces from a gas reservoir containing considerable quantities of liquid hydrocarbons in the pentane and heavier range generally described as "condensate." *See* Lease condensate.

Gas (electric)
A fuel burned under boilers and by internal combustion engines for electric generation. These include natural gas, manufactured gas, and waste gas.

Gas oil
European and Asian designation for No. 2 heating oil and No. 2 diesel fuel.

Gasoline
See Motor gasoline (finished).

Gasoline blending
See Motor gasoline blending.
Gasoline grades: The classification of gasoline by octane ratings. Each type of gasoline (conventional, oxygenated, and reformulated) is classified by three grades – Regular, Midgrade, and Premium.

Note: Gasoline sales are reported by grade in accordance with their classification at the time of sale. In general, automotive octane requirements are lower at high altitudes. Therefore, in some areas of the United States, such as the Rocky Mountain States, the octane ratings for the gasoline grades may be 2 or more octane points lower.

1. Regular Gasoline: Gasoline having an antiknock index, that is, octane rating, greater than or equal to 85 and less than 88. Note: Octane requirements may vary by altitude.
2. Midgrade Gasoline: Gasoline having an antiknock index, that is, octane rating, greater than or equal to 88 and less than or equal to 90. Note: Octane requirements may vary by altitude.
3. Premium Gasoline: Gasoline having an antiknock index, that is, octane rating, greater than 90. Note: Octane requirements may vary by altitude.

Gas to Liquids (GTLs)
A process that combines the carbon and hydrogen elements in natural gas molecules to make synthetic liquid petroleum products, such as diesel fuel.

Gas-turbine electric power plant
A plant in which the prime mover is a gas turbine. A gas turbine typically consists of an axial-flow air compressor and one or more combustion chambers where liquid or gaseous fuel is burned. The hot gases expand to drive the generator and then are used to run the compressor.

Gas well
A well completed for the production of natural gas from one or more gas zones or reservoirs. (Wells producing both crude oil and natural gas are classified as oil wells.)

Generating facility
An existing or planned location or site at which electricity is or will be produced.

Generating unit
Any combination of physically connected generator(s), reactor(s), boiler(s), combustion turbine(s), or other prime mover(s) operated together to produce electric power.

Generation (electricity)
See Electricity generation.

Generator
A machine that converts mechanical energy into electrical energy.

Generator capacity
The maximum output, commonly expressed in megawatts (mW), that generating equipment can supply to system load, adjusted for ambient conditions.

Generator nameplate capacity (installed)
The maximum rated output of a generator, prime mover, or other electric power production equipment under specific conditions designated by the manufacturer. Installed generator nameplate capacity is commonly expressed in megawatts (mW) and is usually indicated on a nameplate physically attached to the generator.

Giga
One billion (109).

Gigawatt (gW)
One billion (109) Watts. *See* Watt.

Gigawatthour (GWh)
One billion (109) Watthours. *See* Watthour.

Give-up
When a broker executes an order for another broker's client and the two brokers split the commission; the client pays nothing extra.

Global climate change
See Climate change.

Global warming
An increase in the near surface temperature of the Earth. Global warming has occurred in the distant past as the result of natural influences, but the term is today most often used to refer to the warming some scientists predict will occur as a result of increased anthropogenic emissions of greenhouse gases. *See* Climate change.

Global Warming Potential (GWP)
An index used to compare the relative radiative forcing of different gases without directly calculating the changes in atmospheric concentrations. GWPs are calculated as the ratio of the radiative forcing that would result from the emission of one kilogram of a greenhouse gas to that from the emission of one kilogram of carbon dioxide over a fixed period of time, such as 100 years.

Golden mean or Golden ratio
The ratio of any two consecutive numbers in the Fibonacci sequence, known as phi and equal to 0.618; a proportion that is an important phenomenon in music, art, architecture, and biology.

Golden section
Any length divided so that the ratio of the smaller to the larger part is equivalent to the ratio between the larger part and the whole and is always 0.618.

Grain terminal
Large grain elevator facility with the capacity to ship grain by rail and/or barge to domestic or foreign markets.

Grantor
A person who sells an option and assumes the obligation to sell (in the case of a call) or buy (in the case of a put) the underlying futures contract at the exercise price. Also referred to as an Option seller or Writer.

Greeks
Jargon; a loose term encapsulating the set of risk variables used by options traders.

Greenhouse gases
Those gases, such as water vapor, carbon dioxide, nitrous oxide, methane, hydrofluorocarbons (HFCs), perfluorocarbons (PFCs), and sulfur hexafluoride, that are transparent to solar (short-wave) radiation but opaque to long-wave (infrared) radiation, thus preventing long-wave radiant energy from leaving Earth's atmosphere. The net effect is a trapping of absorbed radiation and a tendency to warm the planet's surface.

Grid
The layout of an electrical distribution system.

Gross Domestic Product
Value of all goods and services produced domestically.

Gross electricity generation
See Gross generation.

Gross generation
The total amount of electric energy produced by generating units and measured at the generating terminal in kiloWatthours (kWh) or megaWatthours (mWh).

Gross input to atmospheric crude oil distillation units
Total input to atmospheric crude oil distillation units. Includes all crude oil, lease condensate, natural gas plant liquids, unfinished oils, liquefied refinery gases, slop oils, and other liquid hydrocarbons produced from tar sands, Gilsonite, and oil shale. *See* Distillation unit (atmospheric).

Gross processing margin
The difference between the cost of soybeans and the combined sales income of the processed soybean oil and meal.

Gross production, natural gas
See Gross Withdrawals, Natural Gas.

Gross withdrawals, natural gas
Full well-stream volume of produced natural gas, including all natural gas plant liquids and all nonhydrocarbon gases, but excluding lease condensate.

GW
See Gigawatt.

GWh
See Gigawatthour.

H

Harami
In candlestick terminology, a small real body contained within a relatively long real body.

Head and shoulders
When the middle price peak of a given tradable is higher than those around it.

Heat content of a quantity of fuel, gross
The total amount of heat released when a fuel is burned. Coal, crude oil, and natural gas all include chemical compounds of carbon and hydrogen. When those fuels are burned, the carbon and hydrogen combine with oxygen in the air to produce carbon dioxide and

water. Some of the energy released in burning goes into transforming the water into steam and is usually lost. The amount of heat spent in transforming the water into steam is counted as part of gross heat content but is not counted as part of net heat content. Gross heat content is also referred to as the higher heating value. Btu conversion factors typically used by the Energy Information Administration represent gross heat content.

Heat content of a quantity of fuel, net
The amount of usable heat energy released when a fuel is burned under conditions similar to those in which it is normally used. Net heat content is also referred to as the lower heating value. Btu conversion factors typically used by the Energy Information Administration represent gross heat content.

Heating value
See Heat content of a quantity of fuel, Gross and heat content of a quantity of fuel, net.

Heavy crude oil
Has API gravity lower than 28 degrees. The lower the API gravity, the heavier the oil.

Heavy gas oils
Petroleum distillates with an approximate boiling range from 651° Fahrenheit to 1000° Fahrenheit.

Hedge fund
A mutual fund involving speculative investing in futures, swaps, and options.

Hedger
An individual or company owning or planning to own a cash commodity corn, soybeans, wheat, US Treasury bonds, notes, bills etc. and concerned that the cost of the commodity may change before either buying or selling it in the cash market. A hedger achieves protection against changing cash prices by purchasing (selling)futures contracts of the same or similar commodity and later offsetting that position by selling (purchasing) futures contracts of the same quantity and type as the initial transaction.

Hedging

1. The practice of offsetting the price risk inherent in any cash market position by taking an equal but opposite position in the futures market. Hedgers use the futures markets to protect their business from adverse price changes. Selling (Short) Hedge – Selling futures contracts to protect against possible declining prices of commodities that will be sold in the future. At the time the cash commodities are sold, the open futures position is closed by purchasing an equal number and type of futures contracts as those that were initially sold. Purchasing (Long) Hedge – Buy futures contracts to protect against a possible price increase of cash commodities that will be purchased in the future. At the time the cash commodities are bought, the open futures position is closed by selling an equal number and type of futures contracts as those that were initially purchased. Also referred to as a buying hedge.
2. In everyday speech, hedging is a gardening term which describes tending a row of bushes or trees that divides one garden or field from another.

High
The highest price of the day for a particular futures contract.

High sulfur no. 2 diesel fuel
No. 2 diesel fuel that has a sulfur level above 0.05% by weight.

High-temperature collector
See Solar thermal collector, High-temperature.

High-ticking
To pay the offered price.

Historic volatility
How much contract price has fluctuated over a period of time in the past; usually calculated by taking a standard deviation of price changes over a time period.

Historical data
A series of past daily, weekly, or monthly market prices (open, high, low, close, volume, open interest).

Horizontal spread
The purchase of either a call or put option and the simultaneous sale of the same type of option with typically the same strike price but with a different expiration month. Also referred to as a calendar spread.

Hydrocarbon
An organic chemical compound of hydrogen and carbon in either gaseous, liquid, or solid phase. The molecular structure of hydrocarbon compounds varies from the simplest (e.g., methane, a constituent of natural gas) to the very heavy and very complex.

Hydroelectric power
The production of electricity from the kinetic energy of falling water.

Hydroelectric power generation
Electricity ge-nerated by an electric power plant whose turbines are driven by falling water. It includes electric utility and industrial generation of hydroelectricity, unless otherwise specified. Generation is reported on a net basis, that is, on the amount of electric energy generated after the electric energy consumed by station auxiliaries and the losses in the transformers that are considered integral parts of the station are deducted.

Hydroelectric power plant
A plant in which the turbine generators are driven by falling water.

Hydroelectric pumped storage
Hydroelectricity that is generated during peak loads by using water previously pumped into an elevated storage reservoir during off-peak periods when excess generating capacity is available to do so. When additional generating capacity is needed, the water can be released from the reservoir through a conduit to turbine generators located in a power plant at a lower level.

Hydrogen
A colorless, odorless, highly flammable gaseous element. It is the lightest of all gases and the most abundant element in the universe, occurring chiefly in combination with oxygen in water and also in acids, bases, alcohols, petroleum, and other hydrocarbons.

I

IEA
A Paris-based organization of leading oil-consuming nations mainly in the West, which co-ordinates its members' energy policies. It also compiles energy statistics including forward supply/demand projections for countries both within and outside its membership.

Implied Alpha
The excess return expected from a stock to justify its current weighing in the portfolio.

Implied volatility
The volatility computed using the actual market prices of an option contract and one of a number of pricing models. For example, if the market price of an option rises without a change in the price of the underlying stock or future, implied volatility will have risen.

Improved recovery
Extraction of crude oil or natural gas by any method other than those that rely primarily on natural reservoir pressure, gas lift, or a system of pumps.

Impulse
A sharply defined change in a series of input data being studied, such as market prices or volume.

In-the-money
A call option whose strike price is lower than the stock or future's price, or a put option whose strike price is higher than the underlying stock or future's price. For example, when a commodity price is $500, a call option with a strike price of $400 is considered in-the-money.

Income dividends
Payments to mutual fund shareholders consisting of dividends, interest and short-term capital gains earned on the fund's portfolio securities after deduction of operating expenses.

Independent introducing broker
A firm or individual that solicits and accepts commodity futures orders from customers but does not accept money, securities or property from the customer. Unlike a Guaranteed introducing broker, an Independent introducing broker is subject to minimum capital requirements and can introduce accounts to any registered Futures Commission Merchant.

Independent power producer
A corporation, person, agency, authority, or other legal entity or instrumentality which is a wholesale electricity producer that operates within the franchized service territory of a host electric utility and is usually authorized to sell at market-based rates. Unlike traditional electric utilities, independent power producers do not possess transmission facilities, unless authorized by law, nor do they sell electricity in the retail market. Independent power producers are considered to be nonutility power producers. *See* Electric utility and Nonutility power producer.

International Energy Agency (IEA)
A Paris-based organization of leading oil-consuming nations mainly in the West, which co-ordinates its members' energy policies. It also compiles energy statistics including forward supply/demand projections for countries both within and outside its membership.

International Petroleum Exchange(IPE)
London oil exchange which has futures and options contracts in Brent Blend crude oil and gas oil, and a futures contract in UK natural gas. The IPE and the New York Mercantile Exchange announced merger discussions in November 1998.

Interruptible Service
Gas or electricity sales that are subject to interruption for a specified number of days or hours during times of peak demand or in the event of system emergencies. In exchange for interruptibility, buyers pay lower prices. *See* Firm service, Nonfirm service.

IPE
www.theipe.com. The International Petroleum Exchange, second largest oil futures exchange in the world. Owned by the Intercontinental Exchange.

ISDA Master Agreement
The International Swaps and Derivatives Association (ISDA) over-the-counter derivatives master agreement was drawn up by the New York-based trade association in 1987 and revised in 1992. www.isda.org. The agreement is commonly used for contracts in various energy derivatives markets, especially the US gas market.

Initial margin
The amount a futures market participant must deposit into his margin account at the time he places an order to buy or sell a futures contract. Also referred to as original margin.

Inside day
A day in which the daily price range is completely within the previous day's daily price range.

Intercommodity spread
The purchase of a given delivery month of one futures market and the simultaneous sale of the same delivery month of a different, but related, futures market.

Interdelivery spread
The purchase of one delivery month of a given futures contract and simultaneous sale of another delivery month of the same commodity on the same exchange. Also referred to as an intramarket or calendar spread.

Intermarket spread
The sale of a given delivery month of a futures contract on one exchange and the simultaneous purchase of the same delivery month and futures contract on another exchange.

International bunker fuels
See Bunker fuels.

Intrinsic value
The portion of an option's premium that is represented when the cash market price is greater than the exercise price; a known constant equal to the difference between the strike price and underlying market price.

Introducing broker (IB)
A person or organization that solicits or accepts orders to buy or sell futures contracts or commodity options but does not accept money or other assets from customers to support such orders.

Inverted market
A futures market in which the relationship between two delivery months of the same commodity is abnormal.

J

Jet Fuel
A refined petroleum product used in jet aircraft engines. It includes kerosene-type jet fuel and naphtha-type jet fuel.

Joule
The meter-kilogram-second unit of work or energy, equal to the work done by a force of one newton when its point of application moves through a distance of one meter in the direction of the force; equivalent to 107 ergs and one Watt-second.

K

Kagi
One of three types of Japanese candlestick charts that does not have time on the horizontal axis.

Kerogen
The solid, bituminous mineraloid substance in oil shales which yields oil when the shales undergo destructive distillation.

Kerosene
A light petroleum distillate that is used in space heaters, cook stoves, and water heaters and is suitable for use as a light source when burned in wick-fed lamps. Kerosene has a maximum distillation temperature of 400° Fahrenheit at the 10% recovery point, a final boiling point of 572° Fahrenheit, and a minimum flash point of 100° Fahrenheit. Included are No. 1-K and No. 2-K, the two grades recognized by ASTM Specification D 3699 as well as all other grades of kerosene called range or stove oil, which have properties similar to those of No. 1 fuel oil. *See* Kerosene-type jet fuel.

Kerosene-type jet fuel
A kerosene-based product having a maximum distillation temperature of 400° Fahrenheit at the 10% recovery point and a final maximum boiling point of 572° Fahrenheit and meeting ASTM Specification D 1655 and Military Specifications MIL-T-5624P and MIL-T-8133D (Grades JP-5 and JP-8). It is used for commercial and military turbojet and turboprop aircraft engines.

KiloWatt (kW)
One thousand (103) Watts. *See* Watt.

KiloWatthour (kWh)
One thousand (103) Watthours. *See* Watthour.

kW
See KiloWatt (kW).

kWh
See KiloWatthour (kWh).

Kyoto Protocol
The result of negotiations at the third Conference of the Parties (COP-3) in Kyoto, Japan, in December 1997. The Kyoto Protocol sets binding greenhouse gas emissions targets for countries that sign and ratify the agreement. The gases covered under the Protocol include carbon dioxide, methane, nitrous oxide, hydrofluorocarbons (HFCs), perfluorocarbons (PFCs), and sulfur hexafluoride.

L

Landed cost (crude oil)
See Crude oil landed cost.

Last trading day
The last day on which trading may occur in a given futures or option.

Lead
The number of data points that a filter, much as a moving average, precedes the input price data.

Leading indicators
Market indicators that signal the state of the economy for the coming months. Some of the leading indicators include average manufacturing workweek, initial claims for unemployment insurance, orders for consumer goods and material, percentage of companies reporting slower deliveries, change in manufacturers' unfilled orders for durable goods, plant and equipment orders, new building permits, index of consumer expectations, change in material prices, prices of stocks and change in money supply.

Lease condensate
A mixture consisting primarily of pentanes and heavier hydrocarbons, which is recovered as a liquid from natural gas in lease separation facilities. This category excludes natural gas plant liquids, such as butane and propane, which are recovered at downstream natural gas processing plants or facilities.

Lease separation facility (lease separator)
A facility installed at the surface for the purpose of (a) separating gases from produced crude oil and water at the temperature and pressure conditions set by the separator and/or (b) separating gases from that portion of the produced natural gas stream that liquefies at the temperature and pressure conditions set by the separator.

Least Squares Method
A technique of fitting a curve close to some given points that minimizes the sum of the squares of the deviations of the given points from the curve.

Leg
One side of a spread.

Leg out
In rolling forward in futures, a method that would result in liquidating a position.

Leverage
The ability to control large dollar amounts of a commodity with a comparatively small amount of capital.

Lifting
Tankers and barges loading petroleum at a terminal or transfer point.

Light crude oil
Has an API gravity higher than 33 degrees. The higher the API gravity, the lighter the crude oil.

Light gas oils
Light petroleum distillates heavier than naphtha, with an approximate boiling range of 401° Fahrenheit to 650° Fahrenheit.

Light products, light ends
The group of petroleum products with lower boiling temperatures including gasolines and distillate fuels.

Lignite
The lowest rank of coal, often referred to as brown coal, used almost exclusively as fuel for steam-electric power generation. It is brownish-black and has a high inherent moisture content, sometimes as high as 45%. The heat content of lignite ranges from 9 to 17 million Btu per ton on a moist, mineral-matter-free basis. The heat content of lignite consumed in the United States averages 13 million Btu per ton, on the as-received basis (i.e., containing both inherent moisture and mineral matter).

Lignite briquets
See Coal briquets.

Limit
See Position limit, Price limit, and Variable limit.

Limit move
A change in price that exceeds the limits set by the exchange on which the contract is traded.

Limit order
An order to buy or sell when a price is fixed.

Limit up, limit down
Commodity exchange restrictions on the maximum upward or downward movements permitted in the price for a commodity during any trading session day.

Limits
The maximum number of speculative futures contracts one can hold as determined by the Commodity Futures Trading Commission and/or the exchange upon which the contract is traded. Also referred to as trading limit. The maximum advance or decline from the previous day's settlement permitted for a contract in one trading session by the rules of the exchange. According to the Chicago Board of Trade rules, an expanded allowable price range set during volatile markets.

Linkage
The ability to buy (sell) contracts on one exchange and later sell (buy) them on another exchange.

Liquefied Natural Gas (LNG)
Natural gas (primarily methane) that has been liquefied by reducing its temperature to −260° Fahrenheit at atmospheric pressure. (The volume of the LNG is 1/600 that of the gas in its vapor state.)

Liquefied Petroleum Gases (LPG)
A group of hydrogen-based gases derived from crude oil refining or natural gas fractionation. They include ethane, ethylene, propane, propylene, normal butane, butylene, isobutane, and isobutylene. For convenience of transportation, these gases are liquefied through pressurization.

Liquefied Refinery Gases (LRG)
Liquefied petroleum gases fractionated from refinery or still gases. Through compression and/or refrigeration, they are retained in the liquid state. The reported categories are ethane/ethylene, propane/propylene, normal butane/butylene, and isobutane. Excludes still gas used for chemical or rubber manufacture, which is reported as petrochemical feedstock, and also excludes liquefied petroleum gases intended for blending into gasoline, which are reported as gasoline blending components.

Liquid
A characteristic of a security or commodity market with enough units outstanding to allow large transactions without a substantial change in price. Institutional investors are inclined to seek out liquid investments so that their trading activity will not influence the market price.

Liquid collector
A medium-temperature solar thermal collector, employed predominately in water heating, which uses pumped liquid as the heat transfer mechanism. *See* Solar thermal collector, Medium-temperature.

Liquidate
Selling (or purchasing) futures contracts of the same delivery month purchased (or sold) during an earlier transaction or making (or taking) delivery of the cash commodity represented by the futures contract. Taking a second futures or options position opposite to the initial or opening position. Also referred to as Offset.

Liquidity (Liquid market)
A characteristic of a security or commodity market with enough units outstanding to allow large transactions without a substantial change in price.

LNG
See Liquefied Natural Gas (LNG).

Load (Electric)
The amount of electric power delivered or required at any specific point or points on an electric system. The requirement originates at the energy-consuming equipment of the consumers.

Local
The trader in a pit of a commodity exchange who buys and sells for his or her account.

Long
Establishing ownership of the responsibilities of a buyer of a tradable; holding securities in anticipation of a price increase in that security.

Long hedge
Buying futures contracts to protect against a possible price increase of cash commodities that will be purchased in the future. At the time the cash commodities are bought, the open futures position is closed by selling an equal number and type of futures contracts as those that were initially purchased. Also referred to as a buying hedge.

Low
The lowest price of the day for a particular futures contract.

Low sulfur no. 2 diesel fuel
No. 2 diesel fuel that has a sulfur level no higher than 0.05% by weight. It is used primarily in motor vehicle diesel engines for on-highway use.

Low-temperature collector
See Solar thermal collector, Low-temperature.

Low-ticking
To sell at the bid price.

LPG
See Liquefied Petroleum Gases.

LRG
See Liquefied Refinery Gases.

Lubricants
Substances used to reduce friction between bearing surfaces, or incorporated into other materials used as processing aids in the manufacture of other products, or used as carriers of other materials. Petroleum lubricants may be produced either from distillates or residues. Lubricants include all grades of lubricating oils, from spindle oil to cylinder oil to those used in greases.

M

MACD
See Moving Average Convergence/Divergence.

Maintenance
A set minimum margin (per outstanding futures contract) that a customer must maintain in his margin account.

Maintenance margin
A set minimum margin (per outstanding futures contract) that a customer must maintain in his margin account to retain the futures position. *See* also Margin.

Major auction
The overall trend of the market such as might be observed on a bar chart.

Manufactured gas
A gas obtained by destructive distillation of coal, or by thermal decomposition of oil, or by the reaction of steam passing through a bed of heated coal or coke. Examples are coal gases, coke oven gases, producer gas, blast furnace gas, blue (water) gas, and carbureted water gas.

Margin
An amount of money deposited by both buyers and sellers of futures contracts and by sellers of options contracts to ensure performance of the terms of the contract (the making or taking delivery of the commodity or the cancellation of the position by a subsequent offsetting trade). Margin in commodities is not a down payment, as in securities, but rather a performance bond. *See also* Initial margin, Maintenance margin, and variation margin.

Margin call
A call from a clearinghouse to a clearing member, or from a brokerage firm to a customer, to bring margin deposits up to a required minimum level.

Marked to market
At the end of each business day the open positions carried in an account held at a brokerage firm are credited or debited funds based on the settlement price of the open positions that day.

Market-based pricing
Prices of electric power or other forms of energy determined in an open market system of supply and demand under which prices are set solely by agreements as to what buyers will pay and sellers will accept. Such prices could recover less or more than full costs, depending upon what the buyer and seller. *See* as their relevant opportunities and risks.

Market breadth
The shares of a particular stock traded during a specific period. Usually refers to the overall strength and trading volume of the market.

Market if touched
Resting order with the floor broker that becomes a market order to be executed if the trigger price is traded.

Market maker
A broker or bank continually prepared to make a two-way price to purchase or sell for a futures, options, or swaps contract.

Market on close
An order specification that requires the broker to get the best price available on the close of trading.

Market order
Instructions to the broker to immediately sell to the best available bid or to buy from the best available offer.

Market risk
The uncertainty of returns attributable to fluctuation of the entire market.

Market sentiment
Crowd psychology, typically a measurement of bullish or bearish attitudes among investors and traders.

Market timing
Using analytical tools to devise entry and exit methods.

Market value
Company value determined by investors, obtained by multiplying the current price of company stock by the common shares outstanding.

Marketed production, natural gas
Gross withdrawals of natural gas from reservoirs less gas used for reinjection into reservoirs for repressuring, gas that is vented and flared, and nonhydrocarbon gases removed in treating or processing operations.

Marking-to-Market
To debit or credit on a daily basis a margin account based on the close of that day's trading session. In this way, buyers and sellers are protected against the possibility of contract default.

Mean
When the sum of the values is divided by the number of observation, that is, Mean of Platts Singapore (MOPS) where traders take the High value and Low value to create the MOPS reference price which most Over The Counter Swaps derivatives and physical oil markets are priced against.

Mean P/L
The average profitability of a trader's account, as measured over a given period.

Mean reverting
The term adopted in academic literature for one possible state of a price series: that state when price is oscillating randomly about some (unknown) mean value. That is, it is not trending.

Measured recoverable reserves, coal
See Proved (measured) reserves, Coal and proved recoverable reserves, coal.

Measured reserves
See Proved energy reserves.

Median line
The line that is drawn from an extreme that bisects a line drawn through the next corrective phase after the pivot point. *See* Andrews method.

MegaWatt (mW)
One million (106) Watts of electricity. *See* Watt.

MegaWatthour (mWh)
One million (106) Watthours. *See* Watthour.

MEM
See Maximum Entropy Method.

Methane (CH_4)
A hydrocarbon gas that is the principal constituent of natural gas. Methane has a 100-year Global Warming Potential of 21.

Methanol
A light alcohol that can be used for motor gasoline blending. *See* Oxygenates.

Methyl Tertiary Butyl Ether (MTBE)
A colorless, flammable, liquid oxygenated hydrocarbon containing 18.15% oxygen. *See* Oxygenates.

Metric ton
A unit of weight equal to 2204.6 pounds.

Midgrade gasoline
Gasoline having an antiknock index, that is, octane rating, greater than or equal to 88 and less than or equal to 90.

Note: Octane requirements may vary by altitude. *See* Gasoline grades.

Midgrade unleaded
Unleaded gasoline with a 89 R + M/2 octane rating.

Million Btu
One million (106) British thermal units (Btu). *See* British Thermal Unit (Btu).

Minimum price fluctuation
The smallest allowable increment of price movement for a futures contract.

Momentum
A time series representing change of today's price from some fixed number of days back in history.

Momentum indicator
A market indicator utilizing price and volume statistics for predicting the strength or weakness of a current market and any overbought or oversold conditions, and to note turning points within the market.

Morning star
A bottom reversal pattern, according to Steve Nison a signal that the bulls have seized control.

Motor gasoline blending
Mechanical mixing of motor gasoline blending components, and oxygenates when required, to produce finished motor gasoline. Finished motor gasoline may be further mixed with other motor gasoline blending components or oxygenates, resulting in increased volumes of finished motor gasoline and/or changes in the formulation of finished motor gasoline (e.g., conventional motor gasoline mixed with MTBE to produce oxygenated motor gasoline).

Motor gasoline blending components
Naphthas (e.g., straight-run gasoline, alkylate, reformate, benzene, toluene, xylene) used for blending or compounding into finished motor gasoline. These components include reformulated gasoline blendstock for oxygenate blending (RBOB) but exclude oxygenates (alcohols, ethers), butane, and pentanes plus.

Note: Oxygenates are reported as individual components and are included in the total for other hydrocarbons, hydrogen, and oxygenates.

Motor gasoline, conventional
See Conventional gasoline.

Motor gasoline (finished)
A complex mixture of relatively volatile hydrocarbons with or without small quantities of additives, blended to form a fuel suitable for use in spark-ignition engines. Motor gasoline, as defined in ASTM Specification D 4814 or Federal Specification VV-G-1690C, is characterized as having a boiling range of 122° to 158° Fahrenheit at the 10% recovery point to 365° to 374° Fahrenheit at the 90% recovery point. "Motor Gasoline" includes conventional gasoline; all types of oxygenated gasoline, including gasohol; and reformulated gasoline, but excludes aviation gasoline.

Note: Volumetric data on blending components, such as oxygenates, are not counted in data on finished motor gasoline until the blending components are blended into the gasoline.

1. Conventional gasoline: Finished motor gasoline not included in the oxygenated or reformulated gasoline categories. Note: This category excludes reformulated gasoline blendstock for oxygenate blending (RBOB) as well as other blendstock.
2. Oxygenated gasoline: Finished motor gasoline, other than reformulated gasoline, having an oxygen content of 2.7% or higher by weight and required by the US Environmental Protection Agency (EPA) to be sold in areas designated by EPA as carbon monoxide (CO) nonattainment areas. *See* Nonattainment area. Note: Oxygenated gasoline excludes oxygenated fuels program reformulated gasoline (OPRG) and reformulated gasoline blendstock for oxygenate blending (RBOB). Data on gasohol that has at least 2.7% oxygen, by weight, and is intended for sale inside CO nonattainment areas are included in data on oxygenated gasoline. Other data on gasohol are included in data on conventional gasoline.
3. Reformulated gasoline: Finished motor gasoline formulated for use in motor vehicles, the composition and properties of which meet the requirements of the reformulated gasoline regulations promulgated by the US Environmental Protection Agency under Section 211(k) of the Clean Air Act. Note: This category includes oxygenated fuels program reformulated gasoline (OPRG) but excludes reformulated gasoline blendstock for oxygenate blending (RBOB).

Motor gasoline grades
See Gasoline grades.

Motor gasoline, oxygenated
See Oxygenated gasoline.

Motor gasoline, reformulated
See Reformulated gasoline.

Moving average
A mathematical procedure to smooth or eliminate the fluctuations in data and to assist in determining when to buy and sell. Moving averages emphasize the direction of a trend, confirm trend reversals and smooth out price and volume fluctuations or "noise" that can confuse interpretation of the market; the sum of a value plus a selected number of previous values divided by the total number of values.

Moving-average charts
A statistical price analysis method of recognizing different price trends. A moving average is calculated by adding the prices for a predetermined number of days and then dividing by the number of days.

Moving average crossovers
The point where the various moving average lines intersect each other or the price line on a moving average price bar chart. Technicians use crossovers to signal price-based buy and sell opportunities.

Moving average model
A time series equation representing an observed value at time t as a linear combination of present and past random shocks et (forecast errors).

Moving Average Convergence/Divergence (MACD)
The crossing of two exponentially smoothed moving averages that are plotted above and below a zero line. The crossover, movement through the zero line, and divergences generate buy and sell signals.

MTBE
See Methyl Tertiary Butyl Ether.

mW
See MegaWatt (mW).

mWh
See MegaWatthour (mWh).

N

Naked option
See Uncovered option.

Naked put
The writer of a put option contract who is not short the underlying security.

Naphtha
A generic term applied to a petroleum fraction with an approximate boiling range between 122° and 400° Fahrenheit.

Naphthas
Refined or partly refined light distillates with an approximate boiling point range of 27° to 221° Centigrade. Blended further or mixed with other materials, they make high-grade motor gasoline or jet fuel. Also used as solvents, petrochemical feedstocks, or as raw materials for the production of town gas.

Naphtha-type jet fuel
A fuel in the heavy naphtha boiling range having an average gravity of 52.8° API, 20 to 90% distillation temperatures of 290° to 470° Fahrenheit, and meeting Military Specification MIL-T-5624L (Grade JP-4). It is used primarily for military turbojet and turboprop air-craft engines because it has a lower freeze point than other aviation fuels and meets engine requirements at high altitudes and speeds.

Naphthenic naphtha
Usually favored as reformer feedstock.

Narrow range day
A trading day with a smaller price range relative to the previous day's price range.

National Futures Association (NFA)
An industrywide, industry-supported, self-regulatory organization for futures and options markets. The primary responsibilities of the NFA are to enforce ethical standards and customer protection riles, screen futures professional for membership, audit and monitor professionals for financial and general compliance rules and provide for arbitration of futures-related disputes.

Natural gas
A gaseous mixture of hydrocarbon compounds, the primary one being methane.

Note: The Energy Information Administration measures wet natural gas and its two sources of production, associated-dissolved natural gas and nonassociated natural gas, and dry natural gas, which is produced from wet natural gas.

1. Wet natural gas: A mixture of hydrocarbon compounds and small quantities of various nonhydrocarbons existing in the gaseous phase or in solution with crude oil in porous rock formations at reservoir conditions. The principal hydrocarbons normally contained in the mixture are methane, ethane, propane, butane, and pentane. Typical nonhydrocarbon gases that may be present in reservoir natural gas are water vapor, carbon dioxide, hydrogen sulfide, nitrogen, and trace amounts of helium. Under reservoir conditions, natural gas and its associated liquefiable portions occur either in a single gaseous phase in the reservoir or in solution with crude oil and are not distinguishable at the time as separate substances. Note: The Securities and Exchange Commission and the Financial Accounting Standards Board refer to this product as natural gas. *See* Natural gas.
   a. Associated-dissolved natural gas: Natural gas that occurs in crude oil reservoirs either as free gas (associated) or as a gas in solution with crude oil (dissolved gas).
   b. Nonassociated natural gas: Natural gas that is not in contact with significant quantities of crude oil in the reservoir.
2. Dry natural gas: Natural gas which remains after: (1) the liquefiable hydrocarbon portion has been removed from the gas stream (i.e., gas after lease, field, and/or plant separation); and (2) any volumes of nonhydrocarbon gases have been removed where they occur in sufficient quantity to render the gas unmarketable. Note: Dry natural gas is also known as consumer-grade natural gas. The parameters for measurement are cubic feet at 60° Fahrenheit and 14.73 pounds per square inch absolute. *See* Natural gas.

Natural gas, "dry"
See Dry natural gas.

Natural gas, dry production
See Dry natural gas.

Natural gas dry production
Gross withdrawals of natural gas from reservoirs less gas used for reinjection into reservoirs for repressuring, gas that is flared or vented, gas lost in transmission, and shrinkage. Derived by subtracting shrinkage or extraction loss from marketed production. It represents the amount of natural gas that can be marketed and consumed as a gas.

Natural gas gross production
See Gross withdrawals, Natural gas.

Natural gas gross withdrawals
See Gross withdrawals, Natural gas.

Natural gas hydrates
Solid, crystalline, wax-like substances composed of water, methane, and usually a small amount of other gases, with the gases being trapped in the interstices of a water-ice lattice. They form beneath permafrost and on the ocean floor under conditions of moderately high pressure and at temperatures near the freezing point of water.

Natural Gas Liquids (NGL)
A general term for all liquid products separated from natural gas in gas processing or cycling plants. They include natural gas plant liquids and lease condensate.

Natural gas marketed production
See Marketed production, natural gas.

Natural gasoline
A term used in the gas processing industry to refer to a mixture of liquid hydrocarbons (mostly pentanes and heavier hydrocarbons) extracted from natural gas. It includes isopentane.

Natural gas, pipeline quality
See Pipeline quality natural gas.

Natural Gas Plant Liquids (NGPL)
Those hydrocarbons in natural gas that are separated as liquids at downstream natural gas processing plants or at fractionating and cycling plants. Data on lease condensate are excluded. Products obtained include liquefied petroleum gases and pentanes plus.

Natural gas processing plants
Facilities designed to recover natural gas liquids from a stream of natural gas that may or may not have passed through lease separators and/or field separation facilities. These facilities also control the quality of natural gas to be marketed. Cycling plants are classified as natural gas processing plants.

Natural gas production
See Dry natural gas production.

Natural gas storage
Use of a depleted formation (or well) near a market to store gas bought in from another field or location.

Natural gas, wet
See Wet natural gas.

Nearby (delivery) month
The futures contract month closest to expiration. Also referred to as spot month.

Near-month contract/Far-month contract
Contract whose expiration is near/far.

Near-the-money
An option with a strike price close to the current price of the underlying tradable.

Neckline
A trendline drawn along the support or resistance points of various reversal and consolidation pattern (i.e., head and shoulder, double and triple top/bottom formations).

Negative amortization
This means that a payment of the stated size is insufficient to repay even the interest on the debt, meaning the total debt actually increases each month instead of falling.

Negative divergence
When two or more averages, indices, or indicators fail to show confirming trends.

Negative yield curve
A chart in which the yield level is plotted on the vertical axis and the term to maturity of debt instruments of similar creditworthiness is plotted on the horizontal axis. The yield curve is positive when long-term rates are higher than short-term rates. However, yield curve is negative or inverted.

NETA
New Electricity Trading Arrangements in England and Wales.

Net asset value
The total market value of all securities contained in a mutual fund; also known as price per share.

Net electricity consumption
Consumption of electricity computed as generation, plus imports, minus exports, minus transmission and distribution losses.

Net electricity generation
See Net generation.

Net electric power generation
See Net generation.

Net generation
The amount of gross generation less the electrical energy consumed at the generating station(s) for station service or auxiliaries.

Note: Electricity required for pumping at pumped-storage plants is regarded as electricity for station service and is deducted from gross generation.

Net heat content of a quantity of fuel
See Heat content of a quantity of fuel, net.

Net performance
An increase or decrease in net asset value exclusive of additions, withdrawals, and redemptions.

Network code
A code containing norms and regulations for access to, management and operation of natural gas pipelines.

NGL
See Natural Gas Liquids.

NGPL
See Natural Gas Plant Liquids.

Nitrogen oxides (NO_x)
Compounds of nitrogen and oxygen produced by the combustion of fossil fuels.

Nitrous oxide (N_2O)
A colorless gas, naturally occurring in the atmosphere. Nitrous oxide has a 100-year Global Warming Potential of 310.

No. 1 Diesel fuel
A light distillate fuel oil that has distillation temperatures of 550° Fahrenheit at the 90% recovery point and meets the specifications defined in ASTM Specification D 975. It is

Nuclear reactor
An apparatus in which a nuclear fission chain reaction can be initiated, controlled, and sustained at a specific rate. A reactor includes fuel (fissionable material), moderating material to control the rate of fission, a heavy-walled pressure vessel to house reactor components, shielding to protect personnel, a system to conduct heat away from the reactor, and instrumentation for monitoring and controlling the reactor's systems.

Null hypothesis
The hypothesis that there is no validity to the specific claim that two variations (treatments) of the same thing can be distinguished by a specific procedure.

NYMEX
New York Mercantile Exchange (www.nymex.com) the world's largest energy futures exchange.

O

OBV
See On-Balance Volume.

Octane
A flammable liquid hydrocarbon found in petroleum. Used as a standard to measure the antiknock properties of motor fuel.

Octane rating
A number used to indicate gasoline's antiknock performance in motor vehicle engines. The two recognized laboratory engine test methods for determining the antiknock rating, that is, octane rating, of gasolines are the Research method and the Motor method. In the United States, to provide a single number as guidance to the consumer, the antiknock index (R + M)/2, which is the average of the Research and Motor octane numbers, was developed.

Odd lot
An order to buy/sell fewer than 100 shares of stock.

OECD
See Organization for Economic Cooperation and Development (OECD).

OECD Europe
See Organization for Economic Cooperation and Development, Europe (OECD Europe).

Off farm
The amount of stocks held by nonproducers including supplies held at mills, elevators, terminals, and processors.

Off peak
Period of relatively low system demand. These periods often occur in daily, weekly, and seasonal patterns.

Offer
An expression indicating one's desire to sell a commodity at a given price; opposite of bid.

Offset
Taking a second futures or options position opposite to the initial or opening position. Selling (or purchasing) futures contracts of the same delivery month purchased (or sold)

during an earlier transaction or making (or taking) delivery of the cash commodity represented by the futures contract.

Offshore/Onshore
The term offshore indicates a portion of open sea and, by induction, the activities carried out in such area, while onshore refers to land operations.

Ohm
The unit of measurement of electrical resistance. The resistance of a circuit in which a potential difference of 1 volt produces a current of 1 ampere.

Oil
See Crude oil.

Oil reservoir
An underground pool of liquid consisting of hydrocarbons, sulfur, oxygen, and nitrogen trapped within a geological formation and protected from evaporation by the overlying mineral strata.

Oil shale
A sedimentary rock containing kerogen, a solid organic material.

Oil well
A well completed for the production of crude oil from one or more oil zones or reservoirs. Wells producing both crude oil and natural gas are classified as oil wells.

Oil well (Casinghead) gas
Associated and dissolved gas produced along with crude oil from oil completions.

Olefins
A group of petrochemicals characterized by their straight or branched structure. Includes ethylene, the largest volume petrochemical, and propylene and butadiene.

Omnibus account
An account carried by one Futures Commission Merchant (FCM) with another FCM in which the transactions of two or more persons are combined and carried in the name of the originating FCM rather than of the individual customers; the opposite of Fully Disclosed.

On farm
The amount of stocks held by producers.

On-balance volume
Plotted as a line representing the cumulative total of volume. The volume from a day's trading with a higher close when compared with the previous day is assigned a positive value, while volume on a lower close from the previous day is assigned a negative value. Traders look for a confirmation of a trend in OBV with the market or a divergence between the two as an indication of a potential reversal.

OPEC
Organization of Petroleum Exporting Countries, emerged as the major petroleum pricing power in 1973, when the ownership of oil production in the Middle East transferred from the operating companies to the governments of the producing countries or to their national oil companies. Members are Algeria, Ecuador, Gabon, Indonesia, Iran, Iraq, Kuwait, Libya, Nigeria, Qatar, Saudi Arabia, the United Arab Emirates, and Venezuela. (www.opec.org)

OPEC
Organization of Petroleum Exporting Countries

Open
The period at the beginning of the trading session officially designated by the exchange during which all transactions are considered made "at the open."

Open interest
The total number of futures or options contracts of a given commodity that have not yet been offset by an opposite futures or option transaction nor fulfilled by delivery of the commodity or option exercise. Each open transaction has a buyer and a seller, but for calculation of open interest, only one side of the contract is counted.

Open market operation
The buying and selling of government securities Treasury bills, notes, and bonds by the Federal Reserve.

Open outcry
Method of public auction for making verbal bids and offers in the trading pits or rings of futures exchanges.

Open trade equity
The unrealized gain or loss on open positions.

Opening call
A period at the opening of a futures market in which the price for each contract is established by outcry.

Opening range
The range of prices that occur during the first 30 seconds to five minutes of trading, depending on the preference of the individual analyst.

Operable unit (electric)
A unit available to provide electric power to the grid.

Opportunity costs
Income foregone by the commitment of resources to another use.

Option
A contract that provides the right but not the obligation to buy or sell a specified amount of a security within a specified time period.

Option buyer
The purchaser of either a call or put option. Option buyers receive the right, but not the obligation, to assume a futures position. Also referred to as the holder.

Option contract
A contract which gives the buyer the right, but not the obligation, to buy or sell a specified quantity of a commodity or a futures contract at a specific price within a specified period of time. The seller of the option has the obligation to sell the commodity or futures contract or buy it from the option buyer at the exercise price if the option is exercised. *See* also Call option and Put option.

Option premium
The price of an option and the sum of money that the option buyer pays and the option seller receives for the rights granted by the option.

Option seller
The person who sells an option in return for a premium and is obligated to perform when the holder exercises his right under the option contract. Also referred to as the writer. Also *See* Grantor.

Option spread
The simultaneous purchase and sale of one or more options contracts, futures, and/or cash positions.

Option writer
The person who sells an option in return for a premium and is obligated to perform when the holder exercises his right under the option contract. Also referred to as the Option Seller.

Optional cash purchase
Buying additional shares made through the dividend reinvestment account.

Organization for Economic Cooperation and Development (OECD)
Current members are Australia, Austria, Belgium, Canada, Czech Republic, Denmark Finland, France, Germany, Greece, Hungary, Iceland, Ireland, Italy, Japan, Luxembourg, Mexico, Netherlands, New Zealand, Norway, Poland, Portugal, Slovakia, South Korea (usually listed here as Korea, South), Spain, Sweden, Switzerland, Turkey, United Kingdom, and United States. Note: Data for Guam, the former Hawaiian Trade Zone, Puerto Rico, and the US Virgin Islands (usually listed here as Virgin Islands, US) are included in the OECD-related data reported here.

Organization for Economic Cooperation and Development, Europe (OECD Europe)
Includes Austria, Belgium, Czech Republic, Denmark, Finland, France, Germany, Greece, Hungary, Iceland, Ireland, Italy, Luxembourg, Netherlands, Norway, Poland, Portugal, Slovakia, Spain, Sweden, Switzerland, Turkey, and United Kingdom.

Organization of Petroleum Exporting Countries (OPEC)
Current members are Algeria, Indonesia, Iran, Iraq, Kuwait, Libya, Nigeria, Qatar, Saudi Arabia, the United Arab Emirates, and Venezuela. (Ecuador withdrew from OPEC on December 31, 1992 and Gabon withdrew on December 31, 1994.)

Original margin
The amount a futures market participant must deposit into his margin account at the time he places an order to buy or sell a futures contract. Also referred to as initial margin.

Order
The number of days of past price history used to predict the following day's price.

Oscillator
Technical indicator used to identify overbought and oversold price regions. An indicator that detrends data, such as price.

Out-of-sample
An item within the range of a sample that does not conform to the mean of the sample.

Out-of-the-money
A call option whose exercise price is above the current market price of the underlying security or futures contract. For example, if a commodity price is $500, then a call option purchased for a strike price of $550 is considered out-of-the-money.

Out-turn
Quantity of oil unloaded from vessel at discharge point.

Out trade
A mismatched trade between two traders in the pit, and which is settled the next day.

Outside reversal month
A month in which the recent monthly trading range exceeds the previous month's range and closes opposite (reverses) the previous month's close.

Oxidize
To chemically transform a substance by combining it with oxygen.

Oxygenate
Oxygen-containing blend stocks favored for their octane and their clean burning quality. Includes MTBE and ethanol.

Oxygenated gasoline
Finished motor gasoline, other than reformulated gasoline, having an oxygen content of 2.7% or higher by weight and required by the US Environmental Protection Agency (EPA) to be sold in areas designated by EPA as carbon monoxide (CO) nonattainment areas. *See* Nonattainment area.

Note: Oxygenated gasoline excludes oxygenated fuels program reformulated gasoline (OPRG) and reformulated gasoline blendstock for oxygenate blending (RBOB). Data on gasohol that has at least 2.7% oxygen, by weight, and is intended for sale inside CO nonattainment areas are included in data on oxygenated gasoline. Other data on gasohol are included in data on conventional gasoline. *See* Motor gasoline (Finished).

Oxygenates
Substances which, when added to gasoline, increase the amount of oxygen in that gasoline blend. Ethanol, Methyl Tertiary Butyl Ether (MTBE), Ethyl Tertiary Butyl Ether (ETBE), and methanol are common oxygenates.

Overbought
Market prices that have risen too steeply and too fast.

Overbought/oversold indicator
An indicator that attempts to define when prices have moved too far and too fast in either direction and thus are vulnerable to a reaction. (Relative Strength Index).

Oversold
Market prices that have declined too steeply and too fast.

Over-the-Counter market (OTC)
The largest derivatives market in Energy, is in the Over-the-Counter market, the majority of these contracts are traded bilaterally between companies. Also the majority of trades are conducted under a bilateral ISDA Master Agreement (www.isda.org). These OTC Trades, as they are known, can be cleared via the New York Mercantile Exchange (www.nymex.com) and the Intercontinental Exchange (www.theice.com).

P

PADD (Petroleum Allocation for Defense District)
A group of five geographic areas in the United States used in reference to petroleum distribution.

Paper market
A market for contracts where delivery is settled in cash, rather than by delivery of the physical product on which the contract is based.

Paraffin (oil)
A light-colored, wax-free oil obtained by pressing paraffin distillate.

Paraffin (wax)
The wax removed from paraffin distillates by chilling and pressing. When separating from solutions, it is a colorless, more or less translucent, crystalline mass, without odor

and taste, slightly greasy to touch, and consisting of a mixture of solid hydrocarbons in which the paraffin series predominates.

Paraffin base stock
The crude oils that come out of the ground are put into three categories.Ê The Naphthenic and paraffin crudes are used to produce engine oils.Ê Paraffin oils have a naturally higher viscosity index and produce the best engine oils.

Paraffinic
A high paraffins content.

Paraffinic naphtha
Usually favored quality of naphtha for ethylene plant feedstock.

Parameter
A variable, set of data, or rule that establishes a precise format for a model.

Path-dependent option
A path-dependent option has a payout dependent on the price history of the underlying over all or part of the life of the option. The commonest form of option in over-the-counter energy risk management (the Asian option) is a path-dependent option, as are lookback and barrier options.

Peaking generation
Electric generating equipment normally operated to serve loads only during annual peak loads or during system emergencies. Often combustion turbines.

Peak load
The maximum load during a specified period of time.

Pennants
A short compact wedge accompanied by receding volume.

Pentanes plus
A mixture of hydrocarbons, mostly pentanes and heavier, extracted from natural gas. Includes isopentane, natural gasoline, and plant condensate.

Percentile
A value on a scale of one hundred that indicates the % of a distribution that is equal to or below it.

Performance bond margin
The amount of money deposited by both buyer and seller of a futures contract or an options seller to ensure performance of the term of the contract. Margin in commodities is not a payment of equity or down payment on the commodity itself, but rather it is a security deposit. Within the futures industry, financial guarantees required of both buyers and sellers of futures contracts and sellers of options contracts to ensure fulfilling of contract obligations. FCMs are responsible for overseeing customer margin accounts. Margins are determined on the basis of market risk and contract value. Financial safeguards to ensure that clearing members (usually companies or corporations) perform on their customers' open futures and options contracts. Clearing margins are distinct from customer margins that individual buyers and sellers of futures and options contracts are required to deposit with brokers.

Petrochemical feedstock
Feedstock derived from petroleum, used principally for the manufacture of chemicals, synthetic rubber, and a variety of plastics. The categories reported are naphthas (endpoint less than 401° Fahrenheit) and other oils (endpoint equal to or greater than 401° Fahrenheit).

Petrochemicals
Chemicals derived from petroleum; feedstocks for the manufacture of plastics and synthetic rubber. Petrochemicals include benzene, toluene, xylene, styrene, and methanol.

Petroleum
A broadly defined class of liquid hydrocarbon mixtures. Included are crude oil, lease condensate, unfinished oils, refined products obtained from the processing of crude oil, and natural gas plant liquids. Note: Volumes of finished petroleum products include nonhydrocarbon compounds, such as additives and detergents, after they have been blended into the products.

Petroleum coke
See Coke (petroleum).

Petroleum consumption
See Apparent consumption (petroleum).

Petroleum jelly
A semi-solid oily product produced from dewaxing lubricating oil basestocks.

Petroleum products
Products obtained from the processing of crude oil (including lease condensate), natural gas, and other hydrocarbon compounds. Petroleum products include unfinished oils, liquefied petroleum gases, pentanes plus, aviation gasoline, motor gasoline, naphtha-type jet fuel, kerosene-type jet fuel, kerosene, distillate fuel oil, residual fuel oil, petrochemical feedstocks, special naphthas, lubricants, waxes, petroleum coke, asphalt, road oil, still gas, and other miscellaneous products.

Petroleum stocks
Primary stocks of crude oil and petroleum products held in storage at (or in) leases, refineries, natural gas processing plants, pipelines, tankfarms, and bulk terminals that can store at least 50,000 barrels of petroleum products or that can receive petroleum products by tanker, barge, or pipeline. Crude oil that is in-transit by water from Alaska or that is stored on Federal leases or in the Strategic Petroleum Reserve is included. Primary stocks exclude stocks of foreign origin that are held in bonded warehouse storage.

Pipeline quality natural gas
A mixture of hydrocarbon compounds existing in the gaseous phase with sufficient energy content, generally above 900 B t u, and a small enough share of impurities for transport through commercial gas pipelines and sale to end-users.

Pit
The area on the trading floor where futures and options on futures contracts are bought and sold. Pits are usually raised octagonal platforms with steps descending on the inside that permit buyers and sellers of contracts to *See* each other.

Pivot point
In market activity, a price reversal point.

Plant condensate
One of the natural gas liquids, mostly pentanes and heavier hydrocarbons, recovered and separated as liquids at gas inlet separators or scrubbers in natural gas processing plants. Does not include lease condensate.

Plant (electric)
A facility at which are located prime movers, electric generators, and auxiliary equipment for converting mechanical chemical, and/or nuclear energy into electric energy. A plant may contain more than one type of prime mover.

Point and figure chart
A price-only chart that plots up prices as Xs and down prices as Os. The minimum price recorded is called the box size. Typically, a three-box reversal indicates a change in the direction of prices.

Position
A market commitment. A buyer of a futures contract is said to have a long position and, conversely, a seller of futures contracts is said to have a short position.

Position limit
The maximum number of speculative futures contracts one can hold as determined by the Commodity Futures Trading Commission and/or the exchange upon which the contract is traded. Also referred to as trading limit.

Position trader
An approach to trading in which the trader either buys or sells contracts and holds them for an extended period of time.

Possible reserves
Amounts of hydrocarbons that have a lower degree of certainty than probable reserves and are estimated with lower certainty, for which it is not possible to foresee production.

Posted price
A statement of the price requested by a seller of crude oil or products. The "list price."

Pour point
Lowest temperature which oil will readily flow without disturbance when chilled.

Power (electric)
See Electric power.

Power loss
The difference between electricity input and output as a result of an energy transfer between two points.

Prearranged trading
Trading between brokers in accordance with an expressed or implied agreement or understanding. Prearranged trading is a violation of the Commodity Exchange Act.

Premium
Refers to (1) the amount a price would be increased to purchase a better quality commodity; (2) a futures delivery month selling at a higher price than another; (3) cash prices that are above the futures price; (4) the price paid by the buyer of an option; or (5) the price received by the seller of an option.

Premium gasoline
Gasoline having an antiknock index, that is, octane rating, greater than 90. Note: Octane requirements may vary by altitude. *See* Gasoline grades.

Price discovery
The generation of information about "future" cash market prices through the futures markets.

Price limit
The maximum advance or decline from the previous day's settlement permitted for a contract in one trading session by the rules of the exchange. According to the Chicago Board of Trade rules, an expanded allowable price range set during volatile markets.

Price limit order
A customer order that specifies the price at which a trade can be executed.

Processing gain
See Refinery processing gain (petroleum).

Processing loss
See Refinery processing loss (petroleum).

Processing plant (natural gas)
See Natural gas processing plant.

Production
See production terms associated with specific energy types.

Production sharing agreement
Contract in use in African, Middle Eastern, Far Eastern, and Latin American countries, regulating relationships between State and oil companies with regards to the exploration and production of hydrocarbons. The mining concession is assigned to the national oil company jointly with the foreign oil company who has exclusive right to perform exploration, development, and production activities and can enter agreements with other local or international entities. In this type of contract the national oil company assigns to the international contractor the task of performing exploration and production with the contractor's equipment and financial resources. Exploration risks are borne by the contractor and production is divided into two portions: "cost oil" is used to recover costs borne by the contractor, "profit oil" is divided between contractor and national company according to variable schemes and represents the profit deriving from exploration and production. Further terms and conditions may vary from one country to the other.

Profit taking
Selling tradables that have appreciated since initial purchase in order to take advantage of the appreciation.

Program trading
Trades based on signals from computer programs, usually entered directly from the trader's computer to the market's computer system.

Propane
A normally gaseous straight-chain hydro-carbon, (C_3H_8). It is a colorless paraffinic gas that boils at a temperature of $-43.67°$ Fahrenheit. It is extracted from natural gas or refinery gas streams. It includes all products covered by Gas Processors Association Specifications for commercial propane and HD-5 propane and ASTM Specification D 1835.

Propylene
An olefinic hydrocarbon (C_3H_6) recovered from refinery and petrochemical processes.

Proved energy reserves
Estimated quantities of energy sources that analysis of geologic and engineering data demonstrates with reasonable certainty are recoverable under existing economic and operating conditions. The location, quantity, and grade of the energy source are usually considered to be well established in such reserves. Note: This term is equivalent to "Measured Reserves" as defined in the resource/reserve classification contained in the US Geological Survey Circular 831, 1980. Measured and indicated reserves, when combined, constitute demonstrated reserves. *See* also Energy reserves.

Proved (measured) reserves, coal
Reserves or resources for which tonnage is computed from dimensions revealed in outcrops, trenches, workings, and drill holes and for which the grade is computed from the results of detailed sampling. The sites for inspection, sampling, and measurement are spaced so closely and the geologic character is so well defined that size, shape, and

mineral content are well established. The computed tonnage and grade are judged to be accurate within limits that are stated, and no such limit is judged to be different from the computed tonnage or grade by more than 20%. *See* Proved energy reserves.

Proved recoverable reserves, coal
Defined by the World Energy Council as the tonnage within the Proved amount in place that can be recovered (extracted from the earth in raw form) under present and expected local economic conditions with existing available technology. It approximates the US term Proved (measured) reserves, coal. *See* Proved (measured) reserves, coal.

Proved reserves, crude oil
The estimated quantities of all liquids defined as crude oil that geological and engineering data demonstrate with reasonable certainty to be recoverable in future years from known reservoirs under existing economic and operating conditions.

Proved reserves, natural gas
The estimated quantities of natural gas that analysis of geological and engineering data demonstrates with reasonable certainty to be recoverable in future years from known oil and gas reservoirs under existing economic and operating conditions.

Purchase and sell statement
A statement sent by a commission house to a customer when his futures or options on futures position has changed, showing the number of contracts bought or sold, the prices at which the contracts were bought or sold, the gross profit or loss, the commission charges, and the net profit or loss on the transaction.

Purchasing hedge or long hedge
Buying futures contracts to protect against a possible price increase of cash commodities that will be purchased in the future. At the time the cash commodities are bought, the open futures position is closed by selling an equal number and type of futures contracts as those that were initially purchased. Also referred to as a buying hedge. The practice of offsetting the price risk inherent in any cash market position by taking an equal but opposite position in the futures market. Hedgers use the futures markets to protect their business from adverse price changes.

Put option
A contract to sell a specified amount of a stock or commodity at an agreed time at the stated exercise price.

Pyramid
To increase holdings that an investor has by using the most buying power available in a margin account with paper and real profits.

Q

Quadrillion Btu
One quadrillion (1015) British thermal units (Btu). *See* British thermal unit (Btu).

Quarterly net profit margin
(%) Net operating earnings after taxes for the latest quarter divided by revenues for the quarter.

Quotation
The actual price or the bid or ask price of either cash commodities or futures or options contracts at a particular time.

R

R-squared
The percentage of variation in the dependent variable that is explained by the regression equation. A relative measure of fit.

Rack pricing
Selling to petroleum jobbers or other resellers FOB at the refinery, with the customer picking up transportation charges. The price of petroleum products at the refinery loading rack; cash and carry at the refinery's loading dock.

Radiative forcing
A change in average net radiation at the top of the troposphere (known as the tropopause) because of a change in either incoming solar or exiting infrared radiation. A positive radiative forcing tends on average to warm the Earth's surface; a negative radiative forcing on average tends to cool the Earth's surface. Greenhouse gases, when emitted into the atmosphere, trap infrared energy radiated from the Earth's surface and therefore tend to produce positive radiative forcing. *See* Greenhouse gases.

Radiatively active gases
Gases that absorb incoming solar radiation or outgoing infrared radiation, affecting the vertical temperature profile of the atmosphere. *See* Radiative forcing.

Rally tops
A price level that concludes a short-term rally in an ongoing trend. A bull market will be made up of a series of rally tops.

Random shock
The unexplained component of an equation that models a time series (*See* Forecast errors).

Random walk
A theory that says there is no sequential correlation between prices from one day to the next, that prices will act unpredictably as they seek a level in response to supply and demand.

Range
The difference between the high and low price during a given period.

Range extension
In the CBOT market profile, a price movement beyond the range set by the initial auction.

Rate of change
In which today's closing price is divided by the closing price n days ago. Multiply by 100. Subtract 100 from this value. ((C today/Cn) × 100) – 100.

Ratio
The relation that one quantity bears to another of the same kind, with respect to magnitude or numerical value.

RBAR-squared
The R-squared value adjusted for the number of degrees of freedom.

Reaction
A short-term decline in price.

Realized/Unrealized P/L
The difference between trading revenues that are generated on positions that have been offset and closed, versus those associated with the marking of open positions to current market prices.

Rebate
A rebate is paid to the holder of a derivative such as a barrier option if the instrument is knocked out or is never activated.

Red
This is exchange notation for contracts trading beyond the next 12 months. For example, in February of 1999, red December refers to December 2000.

Reciprocal of European terms
One method of quoting exchange rates, which measured the US dollar value of one foreign currency unit, that is, US dollars per foreign units. *See* European Terms.

Reciprocity
This term refers to the new obligations introduced by the European Directive on natural gas. At the international level, the concept of reciprocity entails the adoption of measures on the part of any country regarding foreign operators to be reciprocated by analogous measures in the home country of the foreign operator to which such measures apply. According to Legislative Decree 164/00 Italian companies are allowed to sell natural gas to eligible customers from other EU member countries only if such customers are defined eligible in Italy too. This constraint is applied reciprocally to companies from other European countries or companies located in Italy but controlled by companies from other European countries.

Recoverable coal
See Proved recoverable reserves, coal and Proved (measured) reserves, coal.

Recoverable reserves of coal
See Proved recoverable reserves, coal and Proved (measured) reserves, coal.

Rectangle
A trading area bounded by horizontal, or near horizontal, lines. It can either be a reversal or continuation pattern, depending on the breakout.

Recursive
A process that is repetitive and usually dependent upon the results of the previous repetition.

Reference price
In an energy derivatives contract, the settlement price of the contract based on a particular location or particular blend of the commodity.

Refiner acquisition cost of crude oil
The cost of crude oil, including transportation and other fees, paid by the refiner. The composite cost is the weighted average of domestic and imported crude oil costs. *See* US Refiner acquisition cost of imported crude oil. Note: The refiner acquisition cost does not include the cost of crude oil purchased for the Strategic Petroleum Reserve (SPR).

Refinery fuel
Crude oil and petroleum products consumed at the refinery for all purposes.

Refinery gain (petroleum)
See Refinery losses and gains.

Refinery gas
See Still gas (refinery gas).

Refinery input (petroleum)
The raw materials and intermediate materials processed at refineries to produce finished petroleum products. They include crude oil, products of natural gas processing plants, unfinished oils, other hydrocarbons and alcohol, motor gasoline and aviation blending components, and finished petroleum products.

Refinery loss (petroleum)
See Refinery losses and gains (petroleum).

Refinery losses and gains (petroleum)
Refinery processing gains and refinery processing losses that take place during the refining process itself. Excludes losses that do not take place during the refining process, for example, spills, fire losses, and contamination during blending, transportation, or storage.

Refinery output (petroleum)
The total amount of petroleum products produced at a refinery. Includes petroleum consumed by the refinery.

Refinery (petroleum)
An installation that manufactures finished petroleum products from crude oil, unfinished oils, natural gas plant liquids, other hydrocarbons, and alcohol.

Refinery processing gain (petroleum)
The amount by which the total volume of refinery output is greater than the total volume of refinery input for a given period of time. The processing gain arises when crude oil and other hydrocarbons are processed into petroleum products that are, on average, less dense than the input.

Refinery processing loss (petroleum)
The amount by which the total volume of refinery output is less than the total volume of refinery input for a given period of time. The processing loss arises when crude oil and other hydrocarbons are processed into petroleum products that are, on average, more dense than the input.

Reformate
A high-aromatics, high-octane product made in a reformer and used to blend motor gasoline or aviation gasoline.

Reforming, catalytic
See Catalytic reforming.

Reformulated gasoline
Finished motor gasoline formulated for use in motor vehicles, the composition and properties of which meet requirements of the reformulated gasoline regulations promulgated by the US Environmental Protection Agency under Section 211(k) of the Clean Air Act. Note: This category includes oxygenated fuels program reformulated gasoline (OPRG) but excludes reformulated gasoline blendstock for oxygenate blending (RBOB).
See Motor gasoline (finished).

Regression (simple)
A mathematical way of stating the statistical linear relationship between one independent and one dependent variable.

Regular gasoline
Gasoline having an antiknock index, that is, octane rating, greater than or equal to 85 and less than 88. Note: Octane requirements may vary by altitude. *See* Gasoline grades.

Regulations (CFTC)
The regulations adopted and enforced by the CFTC in order to administer the Commodity Exchange Act.

Reinjected (natural gas)
The forcing of gas under pressure into an oil reservoir in an attempt to increase recovery.

Relative return standard deviation
Measures the amount of variability of the relative return. A large relative return standard deviation indicates that the relative return experienced during the holding period fluctuated dramatically and, if the holding period was different, a significantly different relative return would have been achieved. A small relative return standard deviation indicates the opposite.

Relative strength index
An indicator invented by J. Welles Wilder and used to ascertain overbought/oversold and divergent situations.

Renewable energy resources
Energy resources that are naturally replenishing but flow-limited. They are virtually inexhaustible in duration but limited in the amount of energy that is available per unit of time. Renewable energy resources include: biomass, hydro, geothermal, solar, wind, ocean thermal, wave action, and tidal action.

Renko
A kind of candlestick chart that does not take time into account for constructing the chart.

Reparations
The term is used in conjunction with the CFTC's customer claims procedure to recover civil damages.

Reportable positions
The number of open contracts specified by the CFTC when a firm or individual must begin reporting total positions by delivery month to the authorized exchange and/or the CFTC.

Repressuring
The injection of a pressurized fluid (such as air, gas, or water) into oil or gas reservoir formations to effect greater ultimate recovery.

Representativeness
Behavioral finance. Judgment by stereotype.

Repurchase agreements or Repo
An agreement between a seller and a buyer, usually in US government securities, in which the seller agrees to buy back the security at a later date.

Reserve requirements
The minimum amount of cash and liquid assets as a percentage of demand deposits and time deposits that member banks of the Federal Reserve are required to maintain.

Reservoir
A porous and permeable underground formation containing an individual and separate natural accumulation of producible hydrocarbons (crude oil and/or natural gas) which is confined by impermeable rock or water barriers and is characterized by a single natural pressure system.

Residual fuel oil
A general classification for the heavier oils, known as No. 5 and No. 6 fuel oils, that remain after the distillate fuel oils and lighter hydrocarbons are distilled away in refinery

operations. It conforms to ASTM Specifications D 396 and D 975 and Federal Specification VV-F-815C. No. 5, a residual fuel oil of medium viscosity, is also known as Navy Special and is defined in Military Specification MIL-F-859E, including Amendment 2 (NATO Symbol F-770). It is used in steam-powered vessels in government service and inshore power plants. No. 6 fuel oil includes Bunker C fuel oil and is used for the production of electric power, space heating, vessel bunkering, and various industrial purposes.

Residual value
The standard deviation of the unexplained portion of the monthly return.

Residuum
Residue from crude oil after distilling off all but the heaviest components, with a boiling range greater than 1,000° Fahrenheit.

Resistance
A price level at which rising prices have stopped rising and either moved sideways or reversed direction; usually Seen as a price chart pattern.

Resistance line
On a chart, a line drawn indicating the price level at which rising prices have stopped rising and have moved sideways or reversed direction.

Resting order
An order placed with a condition or qualifier but not yet executed.

Resumption
The reopening the following day of specific futures and options markets that also trade during the evening session at the Chicago Board of Trade.

Retracement
A price movement in the opposite direction of the previous trend.

Reverse exponential moving average
An exponential moving average computed working backward through the time series, rather than forward, as is the case with a standard EMA. A REMA is used so the target would reflect only future price behavior, not past action that would induce spurious correlation.

Reversal gap
A chart formation where the low of the last day is completely above the previous day's range with the close above midrange and above the open.

Risk (implied)
In which the formula produces the percentage overbought/oversold for a contract using the price, a moving average and the option's implied volatility.

Risk management
Control and limitation of the risks faced by an organization due to its exposure to changes in financial market variables, such as foreign exchange and interest rates, equity and commodity prices or counterparty creditworthiness. This may be because of the financial impact of an adverse move in the market variable (market risk), because the organization is ill-prepared to respond to such a move (operational risk), because a counterparty defaults (credit risk) or because a specific contract is not enforceable (legal risk). Market risks are usually managed by hedging with financial instruments, although a firm may also reduce risk by adjusting its business practices (*see* Natural hedge). While financial derivatives lend themselves to this purpose, risk can also be reduced through judicious use of the underlying assets, for example, by diversifying portfolios.

Risk measurement
Assessment of a firm's exposure to risk.

Roll
Substituting a far option for a near option on the same underlying instrument at the same strike price; also to roll forward or roll over.

Roll-over risk
The risk that a derivative hedge position will be at a loss at expiry, necessitating a cash payment when the expiring hedge is replaced with a new one. The cash cost can be significant, as in the case of the New York arm of German industrial conglomerate Metallgesellschaft in 1993. Metallgesellschaft's hedging policy relied on repeatedly rolling over short-term crude oil contracts, but roll-over losses grew so large that the company suffered a severe liquidity crisis, driving it close to collapse.

Round turn
A completed futures transaction involving both a purchase and a liquidating sale, or a sale followed by a covering purchase.

Runners
Messengers who rush orders received by phone clerks to brokers for execution in the pit.

Running market
A market wherein prices are changing rapidly in one direction with very few or no price changes in the opposite direction.

S

Scallop
Chart formation in which the price dips momentarily, forming a cup, before resuming its upward course.

Scalp
In commodities, purchasing and selling in equal amounts so there is no net position at the end of the trading day; a speculative attempt to make a quick profit by buying at the initial offering price in the hope the issue will increase and can be sold.

Scalper
A trader who trades for small, short-term profits during the course of a trading session, rarely carrying a position overnight.

Seasonal trend
A consistent but short-lived rise or drop in market activity that occurs due to predictable changes in climate or calendar.

Seasonality
All energy futures markets are affected to some extent by an annual seasonal cycle or "seasonality." This seasonal cycle or pattern refers to the tendency of market prices to move in a given direction at certain times of the year.

Seasonal supplies
Supplies of gas used for winter demand. This often includes gas from storage systems.

Securitization
The packaging of assets (normally debt of some description) into securities. These securities may be higher-yielding and more freely tradable than the unpackaged assets.

Securitizing production revenues has become increasingly popular with commodity producers over the last few years. Electric utilities have also started securitizing their retail revenue.

Segregated account
A special account used to hold and separate customers' assets from those of the broker or firm.

Selling hedge or Short hedge
Selling futures contracts to protect against possible declining prices of commodities that will be sold in the future. At the time the cash commodities are sold, the open futures position is closed by purchasing an equal number and type of futures contracts as those that were initially sold. The practice of offsetting the price risk inherent in any cash market position by taking an equal but opposite position in the futures market. Hedgers use the futures markets to protect their business from adverse price changes.

Selling short
Selling a security and then borrowing the security for delivery with the intent of replacing the security at a lower price. In futures trading, selling short is to assume the responsibility of the seller vs. the buyer in the establishment of the futures contract between parties.

Settle
The last price paid for a commodity on any trading day. The exchange clearinghouse determines a firm's net gains or losses, margin requirements, and the next day's price limits, based on each futures and options contract settlement price. If there is a closing range of prices, the settlement price is determined by averaging those prices. Also referred to as settlement price or closing price.

Settlement
The price at which all outstanding positions in a stock or commodity are marked to market. Typically, the closing price.

Settlement price
The last price paid for a commodity on any trading day. The exchange clearinghouse determines a firm's net gains or losses, margin requirements, and the next day's price limits, based on each futures and options contract settlement price. If there is a closing range of prices, the settlement price is determined by averaging those prices. Also referred to as settle or closing price.

Settlement risk
Settlement risk is the risk that arises when payments are not exchanged simultaneously. The simplest case is when a bank makes a payment to a counterparty but will not be recompensed until some time later; the risk is that the counterparty may default before making the counter-payment. Settlement risk is most pronounced in the foreign exchange markets, where payments in different currencies take place during normal business hours in their respective countries and can therefore be made up to 18 hours apart, and where the volume of payments makes it impossible to monitor receipts except on a delayed basis.

Shaved candlestick
In candlestick charting, when the shadows of a candle which mark the area between the real body and the extremes and give the appearance of being wicks are absent.

Ship-or-pay
Clause included in natural gas transportation contracts according to which the customer for whom the transportation is carried out is bound to pay for the transportation of the gas also in case the gas is not transported.

Short (noun)
One who has sold futures contracts or plans to purchase a cash commodity. (verb) Selling futures contracts or initiating a cash forward contract sale without offsetting a particular market position.

Short hedge
Selling futures contracts to protect against possible declining prices of commodities that will be sold in the future. At the time the cash commodities are sold, the open futures position is closed by purchasing an equal number and type of futures contracts as those that were initially sold.

Short interest
Shares that have been sold short but not yet repurchased.

Short interest ratio
A ratio that indicates the number of trading days required to repurchase all of the shares that have been sold short. A short interest ratio of 2.50 would tell us that based on the current volume of trading, it will take two and a half days' volume to cover all shorts.

Short ton (coal)
A unit of weight equal to 2000 pounds.

Signal
In the context of stock or commodity time series historical data, this is usually daily or weekly prices.

Signal line
In artificial intelligence, a numeric variable that is prevalued in the knowledge base. In moving average jargon, the first moving average is smoothed by a second moving average. The second moving average is the signal line.

Simex now called SGX
Singapore Monetary Exchange now called Singapore Exchange (SGX)

Simple moving average
The arithmetic mean or average of a series of prices over a period of time. The longer the period of time studied (that is, the larger the denominator of the average), the less impact an individual data point has on the average.

Shrinkage (natural gas)
The volume of natural gas that is transformed into liquid products during processing, primarily at natural gas processing plants.

Skew
A descriptive measure of lopsidedness in a distribution.

Slippage
The difference between estimated transaction costs and actual transaction costs.

Sleeving
A transaction whereby a counterparty, which does not have credit with another counterparty, asks a third party that has credit with both parties to be a middle person to facilitate a trade. This practice achieved some notoriety in 1998 when it emerged that the collapsed US power marketer Power Company of America had been regularly sleeving forward electricity deals.

Sludge
A dense, slushy, liquid-to semifluid-product that accumulates as an end result of an industrial or technological process designed to purify a substance. Industrial sludges are

produced from the processing of energy-related raw materials, chemical products, water, mined ores, sewage, and other natural and man-made products. Sludges can also form from natural processes, such as the runoff produced by rainfall, and accumulate on the bottom of bogs, streams, lakes, and tidelands.

SMA
See Simple Moving Average.

Small Order Execution System (SOES)
Computerized system developed by Nasdaq for immediate electronic execution of up to 1000 shares of stock.

Small Power Producer (SPP)
Under the Public Utility Regulatory Policies Act (PURPA), a small power production facility (or small power producer) generates electricity using renewable energy (wood, waste, conventional hydroelectric, wind, solar, and geothermal) as a primary energy source. Fossil fuels can be used, but renewable resources must provide at least 75% of the total energy input. *See* Nonutility power producer.

Smoothing
Simply, a mathematical technique that removes excess data variability while maintaining a correct appraisal of the underlying trend.

SO_2
See Sulfur dioxide.

SO_2 allowance trading
Allowance trading is the centerpiece of the Washington, DC-based Environmental Protection Agency's (EPA) Acid Rain Program. The EPA is a US Governmental agency. Allowances are the currency with which compliance with SO_2 emission requirements is achieved. They authorize a unit within a utility or industrial source to emit one US ton of SO_2 during a given year or any year thereafter. Utilities that can use high sulpfur coal, which commands a lower price per British thermal unit (Btu) than low sulfur coals, can buy an SO_2 allowance and bundle it with a high sulfur coal purchase to produce more energy.

Solution, gas in
Natural energy derived from the expansion of natural gas in solution in oil.

Sour/Sweet crude
Definitions which describes the degree of a given crude's sulfur content. Sour refers to high sulfur and sweet to low sulfur.

Spark-spread/spark arb(itrage)
The difference between the price of electricity sold by a generator and the price of the fuel used to generate it, adjusted for equivalent units. The spark spread can be expressed in $/mWh or $/mmBm (or other applicable units). To express in $/mWh, the spread is calculated by multiplying the price of gas, for example (in $/mmmBtu), by the heat rate (in Btu/kWh), dividing by 1000, and then subtracting the electricity price (in $/mWh).

Special naphthas
All finished products within the naphtha range that are used as paint thinners, cleaners, or solvents. These products are refined to a specified flash point. Special naphthas include all commercial hexane and cleaning solvents conforming to ASTM Specifications D 1836 and D 484, respectively. Naphthas to be blended or marketed as motor gasoline or aviation gasoline, or that are to be used as petrochemical and synthetic natural gas (SNG) feedstocks are excluded.

Specialist
A trader on the market floor assigned to fill bids/orders in a specific stock out of his/her own account when the order has no competing bid/order to ensure a fair and orderly market.

Specific gravity
In the case of liquids, the ratio between the weight of equal volumes of water and another substance measured at standard temperature, where the weight of the water is assigned the value 1.

Speculator
A market participant who tries to profit from buying and selling futures and options contracts by anticipating future price movements. Speculators assume market price risk and add liquidity and capital to the futures markets.

Spike
A sharp rise in price in a single day or two; may be as great as 15–30%, indicating the time for an immediate sale.

Spot
Usually refers to a cash market price for a physical commodity that is available for immediate delivery.

Spot-market price
See Spot price.

Spot month
In trading, the current contract month. Also known as the front month.
Also *See* Nearby delivery month.

Spot price
The price for a one-time open market transaction for immediate delivery of a specific quantity of product at a specific location where the commodity is purchased "on the spot" at current market rates.

Spot prices
Same as cash price, the price at which a commodity is selling at a particular time and place.

SPR
See Strategic Petroleum Reserve (SPR).

Spread
A trade in which two related contracts/stocks/bonds/options are traded to exploit the relative differences in price change between the two.

Spreading
The simultaneous buying and selling of two related markets in the expectation that a profit will be made when the position is offset. Examples includebuying one futures contract and selling another futures contract of the same commodity but different delivery month; buying and selling the same delivery month of the same commodity on different futures exchanges; buying a given delivery month of one futures market and selling the same delivery month of a different, but related, futures market.

Spread option
An option written on the differential between the prices of two commodities. Spread options may be based on the price differences between prices of the same commodity at two different locations (location spreads); prices of the same commodity at two different

points in time (calendar spreads); prices of inputs to, and outputs from, a production process (processing spreads); and prices of different grades of the same commodity (quality spreads). The New York Mercantile Exchange offers the only exchange-traded options on energy spreads: the heating oil/crude oil and gasoline/crude oil crack spread options.

Spread rolls
Using a spread order to bridge the closing of one position and the establishment of a new one.

Standard deviation
The positive square root of the expected value of the square of the difference between a random variable and its mean. A measure of the fluctuation in a stock's monthly return over the preceding year.

Steam cracker (ethylene plant)
A petrochemical plant that produces olefins, particularly ethylene, and, in some cases, aromatics.

Steam-electric power plant (conventional)
A plant in which the prime mover is a steam turbine. The steam used to drive the turbine is produced in a boiler where fossil fuels are burned.

Step function
A function defined on an interval so that the interval can be partitioned into a finite number of subintervals on each of which the function is a constant. Also known as a simple function.

Stepwise regression
A mathematical technique to choose the independent variables that best describe the behavior of the dependent, in order of improving description.

Still gas (refinery gas)
Any form or mixture of gases produced in refineries by distillation, cracking, reforming, and other processes. The principal constituents are methane, ethane, ethylene, normal butane, butylene, propane, and propylene. Still gas is primarily used as a refinery fuel and as a petrochemical feedstock.

Stochastic
Literally means random.

Stochastic oscillator
An overbought/oversold indicator that compares today's price to a preset window of high and low prices. These data are then transformed into a range between zero and 100 and then smoothed.

Stock change
The difference between stocks at the beginning of the reporting period and stocks at the end of the reporting period.

Stock index futures
A futures contract traded that uses a market index as the underlying instrument. Typically, the value of the contract is $500 times the underlying index. The delivery mechanism is usually cash settlement.

Stocks
Inventories of fuel stored for future use. *See* Coal stocks and Petroleum stocks.

Stop and Reverse (SAR)
A stop that, when hit, is a signal to reverse the current trading position, that is, from long to short. Also known as reversal stop.

Stop-limit order
A variation of a stop order in which a trade must be executed at the exact price or better. If the order cannot be executed, it is held until the stated price or better is reached again.

Stop loss
The risk management technique in which the trade is liquidated to halt any further decline in value.

Stop order
An order to buy or sell when the market reaches a specified point. A stop order to buy becomes a market order when the futures contract trades (or is bid) at or above the stop price. A stop order to sell becomes a market order when the futures contract trades (or is offered) at or below the stop price.

Stop-running
After a trend, the market will enter into a trading range and have a tendency to trade to levels where stop-loss orders have been placed.

Stops
Buy stops are orders that are placed at a predetermined price over the current price of the market. The order becomes a "buy at the market" order if the market is at or above to the price of the stop order. Sell stops are orders that are placed with a predetermined price below the current price. Sell-stop orders become "Sell at the market" orders if the market trades at or below the price of the stop order.

Straddle
The purchase or sale of an equivalent number of puts and calls on an underlying stock with the same exercise price and expiration date.

Straight-run
Material which has come straight from an atmospheric distillation unit and has not been cracked or reformed, and which is usually used as a feedstock or as a utility fuel.

Strange attractor
A balance point between a set of conflicting forces.

Strangle
The purchase or sale of an equivalent number of puts and calls on an underlying stock with the same expiration date but a different exercise price. Usually, the put has a low strike price and the call has a higher strike price.

Strategic Petroleum Reserve (SPR)
Petroleum stocks maintained by the US Federal government for use during periods of major supply interruption.

Strategic storage
Volumes required for covering lack or reduction of supplies from extra-European sources or crises in the natural gas system.

Strike price
The price per unit at which the holder of an option may receive or deliver the underlying unit; also known as the exercise price.

Strips
An option strategy in which an investor buys one call and two puts on the same underlying security with the same exercise price and expiration date.

Struck
The price at which an exercised option delivers the underlying securities.

Sulfur dioxide (SO_2)
A toxic, irritating, colorless gas soluble in water, alcohol, and ether. Used as a chemical intermediate, in paper pulping and ore refining, and as a solvent.

Supply
See Energy supply.

Supply, Law of
The relationship between product supply and its price.

Support
The place on a chart where the buying of futures contracts is sufficient to halt a price decline.

Support
A historical price level at which falling prices have stopped falling and either moved sideways or reversed direction; usually seen as a price chart pattern.

Support line
On a chart, a line drawn indicating the price level at which falling prices have stopped falling and have moved sideways or reversed direction.

Surface mine (coal)
A coal-producing mine that is usually within a few hundred feet of the surface. Earth and rock above or around the coal (overburden) is removed to expose the coalbed, which is then mined with surface excavation equipment such as draglines, power shovels, bulldozers, loaders, and augers. It may also be known as an area, contour, open-pit, strip, or auger mine.

Suspension
The end of the evening session for specific futures and options markets traded at the Chicago Board of Trade.

Swap
An agreement whereby a floating price is exchanged for a fixed price over a specified period. It is an off-balance-sheet financial arrangement, which involves no transfer of physical energy; both parties settle their contractual obligations by means of a transfer of cash. The agreement defines the volume, duration and fixed reference price. Differences are settled in cash for specific periods – monthly, quarterly or six-monthly. Swaps are also known as contracts for differences and as fixed-for-floating contracts. (*See* ISDA.)

Swaption
An option to purchase (call option) or sell (put option) a swap at some future date.

Sweet crude
Crude oil containing a relatively low percentage by weight of sulfur, typically less than 1%.

Swing
Variations in gas demand.

Swing factor
In gas purchasing agreements the swing factor is a measure of the flexibility to vary nominations and is expressed as a ratio of peak to average supplies.

Swing option
The right to take more or less of a specified commodity. The opportunity to swing up is effectively a call option on the commodity specified in the contract, and the opportunity to swing down is a put option on the commodity, subject to obligations to take certain quantities over the entire life of the contract. Swing options are most commonly used in the gas market.

Swing producer
A company or country which changes its crude oil output to meet fluctuations in market demand. Saudi Arabia is seen as the world's major swing producer as it deliberately limits its crude oil production in an attempt to keep supply and demand roughly in balance.

Synergistic market analysis
Also known as synergistic analysis . An analytical method that merges technical and fundamental analysis with an emphasis on intermarket analysis.

Synthetic Natural Gas (SNG)
A manufactured product chemically similar in most respects to natural gas, resulting from the conversion or reforming of petroleum hydrocarbons or from coal gasification. It may easily be substituted for, or interchanged with, pipeline quality natural gas.

Synthetic securities
Security created by buying and writing a combination of options that imitate the risk and profit profile of a security.

System (electric)
See Electric system.

SWU
See Separative units.

T

T-Statistics
The probability distribution used to test the hypothesis that a random sample of n observations comes from a normal population with a given mean.

T-test
A statistical test of significance for a distribution that changes its shape as N gets smaller; based on a variable t equal to the difference between the mean of the sample and the mean of the population divided by a result obtained by dividing the standard deviation of the sample by the square root of the number of individuals in the sample.

Take-or-pay
In a buyer's contract take-or-pay is the obligation to pay for a specified amount of gas whether this amount is taken or not. Depending on the contract terms under-takes or over-takes may be taken as make-up or carry forward into the next contract period. When it is credited into another contract period this is called make-up gas.

Tall oil
The oily mixture of rosin acids, fatty acids, and other materials obtained by acid treatment of the alkaline liquors from the digesting (pulping) of pine wood.

Tangibles
Cash equivalents of the futures contracts.

Tanker and barge
Vessels that transport crude oil or petroleum products.

Tar sands
Naturally occurring bitumen-impregnated sands that yield mixtures of liquid hydrocarbon and that require further processing other than mechanical blending before becoming finished petroleum products.

Tax-deferred
In which an investment allows an investor to postpone paying taxes on money put into the investment until the investor literally takes possession of the money invested.

Technical analysis
Technical analysis is based on the presumption that price takes into consideration all factors that could influence the price of the commodity. It is therefore broader than fundamental analysis, which looks at supply and demand. Past price movements can be analyzed for indication of future commodity price movements.

Technical rally
A short rise in commodity futures prices within a general declining trend. Such a rally may result from bargain hunting by market participants or because technical analysts have noticed a particular support level at which the commodity price is expected to increase.

Technical sign
A significant short-term trend identified through technical analysis of a commodities' price movement.

Term structure
Also known as yield curve. The slope of the term structure is the yield on long-term government bonds minus the yield on short-term instruments such as Treasury bills.

Therm
One hundred thousand (105) British thermal units.

Thermal cracking
A refining process in which heat and pressure are used to break down, rearrange, or combine hydrocarbon molecules. Thermal cracking includes gas oil visbreaking, fluid coking, delayed coking, and other thermal cracking processes (e.g., flexicoking).

Theta
The measurement of the time decay of a position.

Third party access to natural gas networks
Legislative Decree 164/00, introducing the European Union Directive on natural gas into Italian legislation, decreed that companies active in natural gas transmission and dispatching are to allow access to their network to third parties requesting such access, provided that they have sufficient capacity for it and that linking works are technically feasible, based on criteria published by the Authority on Electricity and Gas. The Authority is also responsible for defining tariffs for transmission and dispatching services, obligations of operators and criteria ensuring access to all network users at equal conditions, impartiality and neutrality.

Thrust
A comparison between the price difference of successively lower pivot bottoms or higher pivot tops. For example, a reduction in the difference between pivot bottoms shows loss of momentum; an increase in the difference shows increased momentum.

Tick
The minimum fluctuation of a tradable. For example, bonds trade in thirty-seconds (32), while most stocks trade in eighths.

Tick indicator
The number of stocks whose last trade was an uptick or a downtick.

Time and sales ticker
Part of the Chicago Board of Trade Market Profile. system consisting of an on-line graphic service that transmits price and time information throughout the day.

Time domain
Variation of a time series is accounted for by an autocorrelation function and other time series.

Time limit order
A customer order that designates the time during which it can be executed.

Time series
A collection of observations made sequentially in time and indexed by time.

Time-stamped
Part of the order-routing process, in which the time of day is stamped on an order. An order is time-stamped when it is (1) received on the trading floor, and (2) completed.

Time value
The amount of money options buyers are willing to pay for an option in anticipation that over time a change in the underlying futures price will cause the option to increase in value. In general, an option premium is the sum of time value and intrinsic value. Any amount by which an option premium exceeds the option's intrinsic value can be considered time value. Also referred to as Extrinsic value.

Topping process
A basic refining process. It is simply a distillation process in which the crude petroleum is heated in a heater then run through a fractionating tower in which different fractions are separated and drawn off at different levels at varying controlled temperatures.

TPO
Time–Price Opportunity; a price that occurs during designated half-hour periods of trading; a price-time relationship developed for the Chicago Board of Trade's Market Profile and Liquidity Data Bank reports.

Tradable
Trading instrument.

Trade facilitation
Liquidity.

Trade balance
The difference between a nation's imports and exports of merchandise.

Trading bands
Lines plotted in and around the price structure to form an envelope, answering whether prices are high or low on a relative basis and forewarning whether to buy or sell by using indicators to confirm price action.

Trading limit
The maximum number of speculative futures contracts one can hold as determined by the Commodity Futures Trading Commission and/or the exchange upon which the contract is traded. Also referred to as position limit.

Trading range
The difference between the high and low prices traded during a period of time; in commodities, the high/low price limit established by the exchange for a specific commodity for any one day's trading.

Trailing stop
A stop-loss order that follows the prevailing price trend.

Transfer agent
Financial institution that manages ownership records of company stock.

Transfer function
The mathematical relationship between the output of a control system and its input for a linear system, it is the Laplace transform of the output divided by the Laplace transform of the input under conditions of zero initial energy.

Transfer response
Refers to the shape of the wave coming out of a filter in comparison to the shape going into it.

Transmission
The movement or transfer of electric energy over an interconnected group of lines and associated equipment between points of supply and points at which it is transformed for delivery to consumers, or is delivered to other electric systems. Transmission is considered to end when the energy is transformed for distribution to the consumer.

Transmission and distribution loss
Electric energy lost due to the transmission and distribution of electricity. Much of the loss is thermal in nature. *See* Power Loss.

Transmission system (electric)
An interconnected group of electric transmission lines and associated equipment for moving or transferring electric energy in bulk between points of supply and points at which it is transformed for delivery over the distribution system lines to consumers, or is delivered to other electric systems.

Trap
The occurrence of those structures, pinch-outs, permeability changes, and similar features necessary for the entrapment of oil and (or) gas in at least one accumulation of the minimum size. Included in this attribute are existence of seals sufficient for entrapping hydrocarbons and capable of holding oil and gas accumulations during appropriate ranges of geologic time.

Treasury bill
A Treasury bill is a short-term US government obligation with an original maturity of one year or less. Unlike a bond or note, a bill does not pay a semi-annual, fixed rate coupon. A bill is typically issued at a price below its par value and is therefore a discounted instrument. The level of the discount depends on the level of prevailing interest rates. In general, the higher short-term interest rates are, the greater the discount. The return to an investor in bills is simply the difference between the issue price and par value.

Trend
The general drift, tendency, or bent of a set of statistical data as related to time.

Trend channel
A parallel probable price range centered about the most likely price line. Historically, this term has been used to denote the area between the base trendline and the reaction trendline defined by price moves against the prevailing trend.

Trend day
A day in which the price of a futures contract moves consistently away from the opening range and does not return to the opening range prior to the close.

Trend-following
Moving in the direction of the prevailing price movement.

Trending market
Price moves in a single direction, generally closing at an extreme for the day.

Trendless
Price movement that vacillates to the degree that a clear trend cannot be identified.

Trendline
A line drawn that connects either a series of highs or lows in a trend. The trendline can represent either support as in an uptrend line or resistance as in a downtrend line. Consolidations are marked by horizontal trendlines.

Triangle
A pattern that exhibits a series of narrower price fluctuations over time; top and bottom boundaries need not be of equal length.

Trigger condition
The payout of path-dependent options such as barrier options and digital options depends on a specified market variable satisfying a specific trigger condition. The most common condition is that the spot rate (or price) of the underlying must trade through a specified level before the option becomes active (or inactive), but many other types of condition are possible.

True range
The largest of the following: Today's high minus today's low, today's high minus yesterday's close, today's low minus yesterday's close.

Turbine
A machine for generating rotary mechanical power from the energy of a stream of fluid (such as water, steam, or hot gas). Turbines convert the kinetic energy of fluids to mechanical energy through the principles of impulse and reaction, or a mixture of the two.

Turning point
The approximate time at which there is a change in trend.

Tweezers bottoms and tops
Candlestick formations. Both candles must have identical highs and lows. Significant when found at contract highs or lows, and can indicate a breakout.

U

Uncovered option
The buy or sale of an option without a position in the underlying futures contract; also known as a naked option.

Underlying futures contract
The specific futures contract that the option conveys the right to buy (in case of a call) or sell (in the case of a put).

Underlying instrument
A trading instrument subject to purchase upon exercise.

Underlying security
In options, the futures contract subject to purchase/sale upon exercise of the option.

Upside/Downside risk
A short forward position taken without an offsetting long physical position in the underlying commodity is said to have upside risk. This means that the trader is speculating that the price of the commodity will decline. A long forward position taken without an offsetting short physical position in the underlying commodity is said to have downside risk. It means that the trader is speculating that the price of the commodity will increase.

Upstream/Downstream
The term upstream refers to all hydrocarbon exploration and production activities. The term downstream includes all activities inherent to the oil sector that are downstream of exploration and production activities.

Underlying futures contract
The specific futures contract that is bought or sold by exercising an option.

Utility
See Electric utility.

V

Value at risk (VaR)
The value-at-risk (VaR) of a portfolio is the worst loss expected to be suffered over a given period of time with a given probability. The time period is known as the holding period and the probability is known as the confidence interval. Value-at-risk is not an estimate of the worst possible loss, but the largest likely loss. For example, a firm might estimate its VaR over ten days to be $100 million with a confidence interval of 95%. This would mean there is a one-in-twenty (5%) chance of a loss larger than $100 million in the next 10 days. In order to calculate VAR, a firm must model both the way the relevant market factors will change over the holding period and the way (if any) in which these changes are correlated between market factors. It must then evaluate the potential effects of these changes on its portfolio at the desired level of consolidation (by asset class, group or business line, for example).

Variation margin
During periods of great market volatility or in the case of high-risk accounts, additional margin deposited by a clearing member firm to an exchange.

Vega
The amount by which the price of an option changes when the volatility changes.

Vented
Gas released into the air on the production site or at processing plants.

Vented, Flared (natural gas)
Gas that is disposed of by releasing (venting) or burning (flaring).

Vented Natural Gas
See Vented.

Versus cash
A transaction generally used by two hedgers who want to exchange futures for cash positions. Also referred to as "against actuals" or "exchange for physicals."

Vessel
A ship used to transport crude oil, petroleum products, or natural gas products. Vessel categories are as follows: Ultra Large Crude Carrier (ULCC), Very Large Crude Carrier (VLCC), Other Tanker, and Specialty Ship (LPG/LNG). *See* Tanker and Barge.

Visbreaking
A thermal cracking process in which heavy atmospheric or vacuum-still bottoms are cracked at moderate temperatures to increase production of distillate products and reduce viscosity of the distillation residues.

Viscosity
One of the physical properties of a liquid, namely its ability to flow. It is expressed inversely, that is the less viscous the fluid the greater its mobility. The viscosity of oil in a reservoir affects the rate and amount of recovery. While viscosity is related to specific gravity, it is also affected by the amount of gas in solution in the oil. Greater recoveries can be obtained where the solution gas is not allowed to escape prior to the time the oil is removed from the reservoir.

Volatile matter (coal)
Those products, exclusive of moisture, given off by a material as gas or vapor. Volatile matter is determined by heating the coal to 950° Centigrade under carefully controlled conditions and measuring the weight loss, excluding weight of moisture driven off at 105° Centigrade.

Volatility
A measure of the variability of a market factor, most often the price of the underlying instrument. Volatility is defined mathematically as the annualized standard deviation of the natural log of the ratio of two successive prices; the actual volatility realized over a period of time (the historic or historical volatility) can be calculated from recorded data.

Volatility is one of the variables which must be specified in the Black–Scholes model of option pricing: a vanilla or non-exotic option will cost more when volatility is high than when it is low. However, volatility is the only one of these variables whose value must be estimated. The estimate used (known as the implied volatility) can be derived from the prices of options in the market and the known input variables. However, the Black–Scholes model also assumes that volatility is constant, which is not true. New techniques have been developed to cope with volatility's variability, including mean-reverting models (such as Garch) and stochastic volatility models.

Volatility skew
The difference in implied volatility between out-of-the-money puts and calls. The origins of the volatility skew are not always clear, but factors may include reluctance to write calls rather than puts, sentiment about market direction, and supply and demand.

Volatility smile
If the implied volatility of an option is plotted against its strike on a graph, the chart is typically shaped like a smile (less frequently a frown). This curve is known as the volatility smile. It may reflect the fact that out-of-the-money events are more common than geometric Brownian motion would predict. This leads to extra value for out-of-the-money options.

Volatility trading
Trading, usually through the options markets, based on the belief that implied volatility will not match the volatility actually realized over a given period, or that the difference

in implied volatility between different options will alter over a given period. Options are used because of their sensitivity to volatility.

Volume
The number of purchases and sales of futures contracts made during a specified period of time, often the total transactions for one trading day.

W

W formation
A double-bottom formation.

Warehouse receipt
Document guaranteeing the existence and availability of a given quantity and quality of a commodity in storage; commonly used as the instrument of transfer of ownership in both cash and futures transactions.

Warrant
A company-issued certificate that represents an option to buy stock shares at a given time.

Waste
Municipal solid waste, landfill gas, methane, digester gas, liquid acetonitrile waste, tall oil, waste alcohol, medical waste, paper pellets, sludge waste, solid byproducts, tires, agricultural byproducts, closed loop biomass, fish oil, and straw.

Waste energy
Municipal solid waste, landfill gas, methane, digester gas, liquid acetonitrile waste, tall oil, waste alcohol, medical waste, paper pellets, sludge waste, solid byproducts, tires, agricultural byproducts, closed loop biomass, fish oil, and straw used as fuel.

Watt (W)
The unit of electrical power equal to one ampere under a pressure of one volt. A Watt is equal to 1/746 horsepower.

Watthour (Wh)
The electrical energy unit of measure equal to one Watt of power supplied to, or taken from, an electric circuit steadily for one hour.

Wave
In Elliott wave theory, a sustained move by a market's price in one direction as determined by the reversal points that initiated and terminated it.

Wave cycle
An impulse wave followed by a correction wave, the impulse wave being made up of five smaller, numbered waves of alternating direction designated 1, 2, 3, 4, and 5, and the correction wave being composed of three smaller alternating waves designated a, b, and c.

Waxes
Solid or semi-solid materials derived from petroleum distillates or residues by such treatments as chilling, precipitating with a solvent, or de-oiling. Waxes are light-colored, more-or-less translucent crystalline masses, slightly greasy to the touch, consisting of a mixture of solid hydrocarbons in which the paraffin series predominates. Included are all marketable waxes, whether crude scale or fully refined. The three grades included are microcrystalline, crystallinefully refined, and crystalline-other. Waxes are used primarily as industrial coatings for surface protection.

Weather derivatives
Forward instruments used to hedge against or speculate on weather. Virtually all of the instruments are based on degree-days, though precipitation swaps and sunshine options are among other possible instruments.

West Texas Intermediate (WTI)
US crude oil used as a benchmark for pricing much of the world's crude oil production.

Wedge
A pattern in which two converging lines connect a group of price peaks and troughs.

Weighted Moving Average (WMA)
A moving average that puts more weight on recent prices. A three-day weighted moving average would add a multiple of 1 to the first date, 2 to the second date and 3 to the third date.

Well
A hole drilled in the Earth for the purpose of (1) finding or producing crude oil or natural gas; or (2) producing services related to the production of crude oil or natural gas. *See* also Completion, Development Well, Dry Hole, Exploratory Well, Gas Well, and Oil Well.

Wellhead
The top of, or a structure built over, a well.

Wet natural gas
A mixture of hydrocarbon compounds and small quantities of various nonhydrocarbons existing in the gaseous phase or in solution with crude oil in porous rock formations at reservoir conditions. The principal hydrocarbons normally contained in the mixture are methane, ethane, propane, butane, and pentane. Typical nonhydrocarbon gases that may be present in reservoir natural gas are water vapor, carbon dioxide, hydrogen sulfide, nitrogen, and trace amounts of helium. Under reservoir conditions, natural gas and its associated liquefiable portions occur either in a single gaseous phase in the reservoir or in solution with crude oil and are not distinguishable at the time as separate substances. Note: The Securities and Exchange Commission and the Financial Accounting Standards Board refer to this product as natural gas.

Whiplash
Alternating buy and sell signals that result in losses.

Whipsaw
Losing money on both sides of a price swing.

Williams' %R
Overbought and oversold indicator that is used to determine market entry and exit points.

Wind energy
The kinetic energy of wind converted into mechanical energy by wind turbines (i.e., blades rotating from the hub) that drive generators to produce electricity.

Window
Set period of time such as a lookback period for market indicator in question.

Writer
The person who sells an option in return for a premium and is obligated to perform when the holder exercises his right under the option contract. Also referred to as the option seller.

WTI
West Texas Intermediate. The WTI spot price of crude is reported from Cushing, Oklahoma.

Y

Yield
A measure of the annual return on an investment.

Yield curve
A chart in which the yield level is plotted on the vertical axis and the term to maturity of debt instruments of similar creditworthiness is plotted on the horizontal axis. The yield curve is positive when long-term rates are higher than short-term rates. However, yield curve is negative or inverted.

Z

Zeta
The percentage change in an options price per 1% change in implied volatility.

Zero-cost option
An option strategy, under which one option is purchased by simultaneously selling another option of equal value.

Index